Introduction to

The Life of D. L. Moody

By John R. Rice

D. L.Moody died in the last days of the 19th century. Dr. R. A. Torrey was probably his closest associate and friend. Torrey was the first superintendent of the Moody Bible Institute and set up a curriculum for that Bible Institute which has been a pattern for others like it.

When Moody died, Torrey soon took worldwide lead in great citywide campaigns in Australia, England and America. In 1923 Dr. Torrey was asked to speak at a great memorial service on "Why God Used D. L. Moody," a remarkable address about that amazing man, probably the greatest man of his generation.

Dr. Torrey said:

> Eighty-six years ago (February 5, 1837), there was born of poor parents in a humble farmhouse in Northfield, Massachusetts, a little baby who was to become the greatest man, as I believe, of his generation or of his century—Dwight L. Moody. After our great generals, great statesmen, great scientists and great men of letters have passed away and been forgotten, and their work and its helpful influence has come to an end, the work of D. L. Moody will go on and its saving influence continue and increase, bringing blessing not only to every state in the Union but to every nation on earth. Yes, it will continue throughout the ages of eternity.
>
> My subject is "Why God Used D. L. Moody," and I can think of no subject upon which I would rather speak. I shall not seek to glorify Mr. Moody, but the God who by His grace, His entirely unmerited favor, used him so mightily, and the Christ who saved him by His atoning death and resurrection life, and the Holy Spirit who lived in him and wrought through him and who alone made him the mighty power that he was to this world. Furthermore: I hope to make it clear that the God who used D. L. Moody in his day is just as ready to use you and me in this day if we, on our part, do

what D. L. Moody did, which was what made it possible for God to so abundantly use him.

The whole secret of why D. L. Moody was such a mightily used man you will find in Psalm 62:11: "God hath spoken once; twice have I heard this; that power belongeth unto God." I am glad it does. I am glad that power did not belong to D. L. Moody; I am glad that it did not belong to Charles G. Finney; I am glad that it did not belong to Martin Luther; I am glad that it did not belong to any other Christian man whom God has greatly used in this world's history. Power belongs to God. If D. L. Moody had any power, and he had great power, he got it from God.

But God does not give His power arbitrarily. It is true that He gives it to whomsoever He will, but He wills to give it on certain conditions, which are clearly revealed in His Word; and D. L. Moody met those conditions and God made him the most wonderful preacher of his generation; yes, I think the most wonderful man of his generation.

But how was it that D. L. Moody had that power of God so wonderfully manifested in his life? Pondering this question it seemed to me that there were seven things in the life of D. L. Moody that accounted for God's using him so largely as He did.

Dr. Torrey named these seven characteristics of Mr. Moody:

1. "He was a fully surrendered man."
2. "Mr. Moody was in the deepest and most meaning sense a man of prayer."
3. "He was a deep and practical student of the Word of God."
4. "He was a humble man."
5. "His entire freedom from the love of money."
6. "His consuming passion for the salvation of the lost."
7. "He had a very definite enduement with power from on high, a very clear and definite baptism with the Holy Ghost."

1837  1899

The Autobiography of DWIGHT L. MOODY

SOME day you will read in the papers that D. L. Moody, of East Northfield, is dead. Don't you believe a word of it! At that moment I shall be more alive than I am now, I shall have gone up higher, that is all; out of this old clay tenement into a house that is immortal—a body that death cannot touch; that sin cannot taint; a body fashioned like unto His glorious body.

I was born of the flesh in 1837. I was born of the Spirit in 1856. That which is born of the flesh may die. That which is born of the Spirit will live forever.

D. L. Moody

The Life of... Dwight L. Moody

By His Son
William R. Moody

The Official Authorized Edition

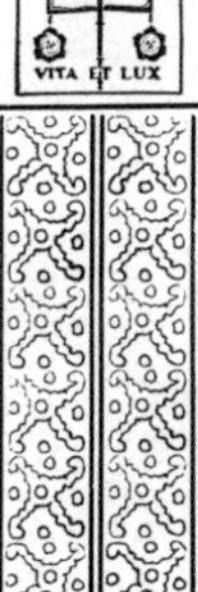

Illustrated with more than One Hundred Reproductions from Original Photographs, many of which being the Exclusive Property of the Family, were reserved solely for this volume

Sword of the Lord Publishers
Murfreesboro, Tennessee 37130

ISBN 0-87398-508-7

Printed in U. S. A.

Introduction

THE preparation of my Father's biography has been undertaken as a sacred trust. Early in the spring of 1894 he was asked by an old friend for permission to issue a biography with his approval. This my Father declined to do, and, on that occasion, expressed the wish that I should assume the task when his life-work was ended. In reply to my objection that such an undertaking demanded a literary experience that I did not possess, he said: "I don't care anything about that. What I want is that you should correct inaccuracies and misstatements that it would be difficult to straighten out during my life. You are the one to do this. All my friends will unite on you and give you their assistance. There are many who think they know me better than any one else, and would feel themselves best able to interpret my life. If you do not do this work there will be many inaccurate and conflicting 'Lives.'"

Whatever diffidence I have felt in executing this trust, it has been undertaken as a filial duty and esteemed to be a great privilege. It would have been my choice to have had more leisure for accomplishing the work, but the announcement of unauthorized biographies has necessitated the immediate publication of the present volume. Otherwise the desire of my Father would have been thwarted. At a later date it is intended that a more studied interpretation of his life should be prepared to meet the expressed desire for a fuller account of his career.

Introduction

I would gratefully acknowledge the kindness of many friends who have contributed important data and incidents. Special acknowledgment is also due to Rev. John Bancroft Devins, of "The New York Observer," whose valuable assistance has greatly facilitated the early completion of the work.

Father lived solely for the glory of God and for the spread of the Gospel of Jesus Christ. It is the earnest prayer of his family that in this record of his career his life's purpose may be conserved.

WILLIAM R. MOODY.

EAST NORTHFIELD, MASS., April 10, 1900.

Table of Contents

CHAPTER VII

CITY MISSIONARY WORK

CHAPTER VIII

THE CIVIL WAR AND THE CHRISTIAN COMMISSION

CHAPTER IX

SUNDAY-SCHOOL CONVENTION WORK

CHAPTER X

EARLY EVANGELISTIC EFFORTS

CHAPTER XI

CHRISTIAN ASSOCIATION WORK

CHAPTER XII

YOUNG MEN'S CHRISTIAN ASSOCIATION CONVENTIONS

CHAPTER XIII

FIRST VISIT TO GREAT BRITAIN

CHAPTER XIV

INFLUENCE OF HENRY MOOREHOUSE

CHAPTER XV

THE CHICAGO FIRE AND ITS RESULTS

CHAPTER XVI

FIRST EXTENDED MISSION IN GREAT BRITAIN

CHAPTER XVII

BIRTH OF THE "MOODY AND SANKEY HYMN-BOOK"

CHAPTER XVIII

THE AWAKENING IN EDINBURGH

CHAPTER XXV

CHICAGO AND BOSTON

CHAPTER XXVI

SECOND EXTENDED MISSION IN GREAT BRITAIN

CHAPTER XXVII

LATER MISSIONS IN AMERICAN CITIES

CHAPTER XXVIII

NORTHFIELD SEMINARY

CHAPTER XXIX

MOUNT HERMON SCHOOLS

CHAPTER XXX

THE BIBLE INSTITUTE FOR HOME AND FOREIGN MISSIONS

CHAPTER XXXI

AMONG COLLEGE STUDENTS

CHAPTER XXXVII

THE USE OF THE PRESS

CHAPTER XXXVIII

PREPARING SERMONS

CHAPTER XXXIX

ASKING AND ANSWERING QUESTIONS

CHAPTER XL

LATER EXPERIENCES WITH THE YOUNG MEN'S CHRISTIAN ASSOCIATIONS

CHAPTER XLI

THE INQUIRY-ROOM

CHAPTER XLII

HIS BELIEF AND PRACTICE

List of Illustrations

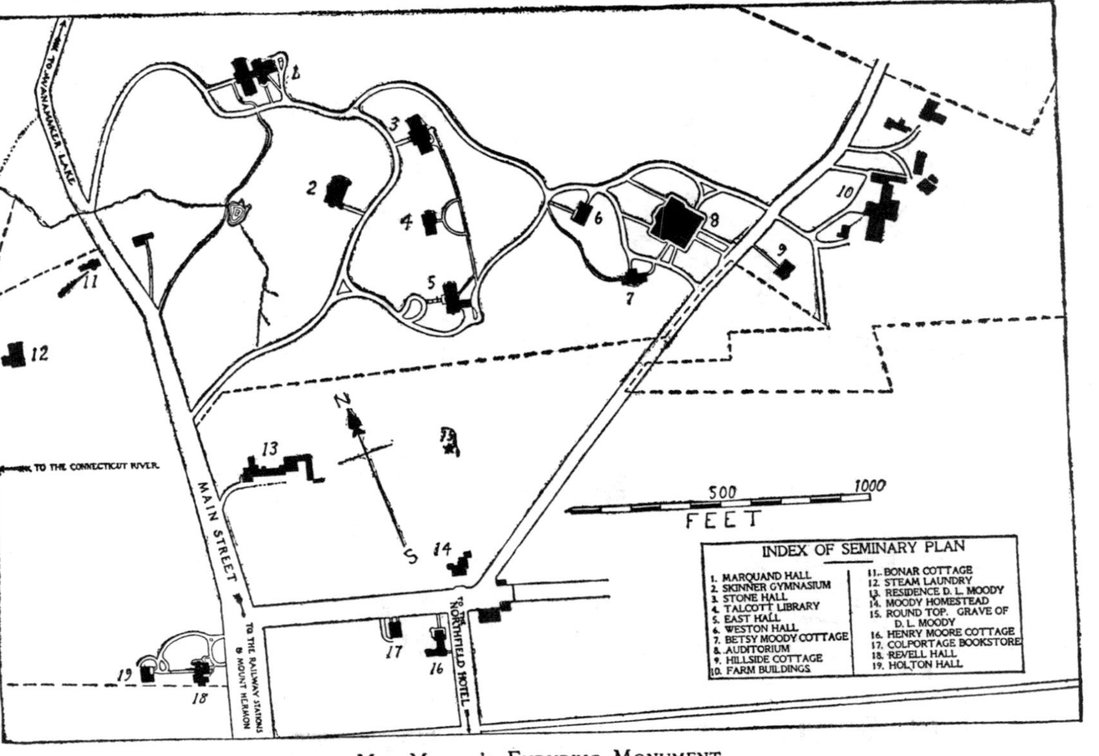
TO WANAMAKER LAKE
TO THE CONNECTICUT RIVER
MAIN STREET
TO THE RAILWAY STATIONS & MOUNT HERMON
TO THE NORTHFIELD HOTEL
N
S
500
1000
FEET
INDEX OF SEMINARY PLAN
1. MARQUAND HALL
2. SKINNER GYMNASIUM
3. STONE HALL
4. TALCOTT LIBRARY
5. EAST HALL
6. WESTON HALL
7. BETSY MOODY COTTAGE
8. AUDITORIUM
9. HILLSIDE COTTAGE
10. FARM BUILDINGS
11. BONAR COTTAGE
12. STEAM LAUNDRY
13. RESIDENCE D. L. MOODY
14. MOODY HOMESTEAD
15. ROUND TOP. GRAVE OF D. L. MOODY
16. HENRY MOORE COTTAGE
17. COLPORTAGE BOOKSTORE
18. REVELL HALL
19. HOLTON HALL

MR. MOODY'S ENDURING MONUMENT.

The Northfield Seminary.

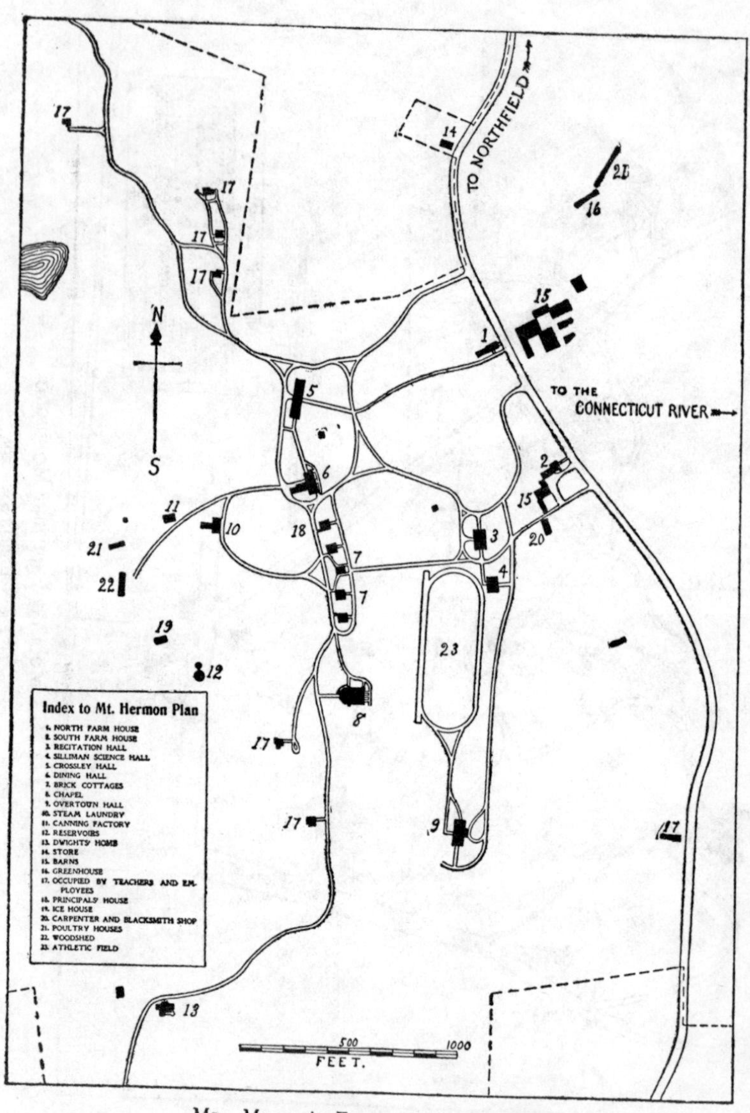

MR. MOODY'S ENDURING MONUMENT.

The Mount Hermon Schools.

D. L. Moody's Grandmother.

From a portrait taken in 1856.

D. L. Moody's Mother.

From a portrait taken in 1856.

THE HOME OF ISAIAH MOODY, GRANDFATHER OF D. L. MOODY.

BIRTHPLACE OF D. L. MOODY.—OCCUPIED BY HIS MOTHER UNTIL HER DEATH IN HER NINETY-FIRST YEAR (1896).

The Life of Dwight L. Moody

CHAPTER I

Early Life

"NEVER mind the ancestry! A man I once heard of was ambitious to trace his family to the Mayflower, and he stumbled over a horse-thief. Never mind a man's ancestry!"

In this democratic spirit Mr. Moody disposed of the history of past generations, taking no credit to himself for their achievements, and feeling in no way responsible for their failings. It is nevertheless of interest that for two hundred years his ancestors lived their quiet lives in the seclusion of their farm-homes in the Connecticut Valley. Beyond the limits of local politics they do not seem to have figured much in public affairs. Among the number there were a few professional men, and in the early struggles for independence, representatives of the Moody and Holton families were among those who counted their lives not too dear a price for those rich privileges of religious and national liberty which they sought to insure to their posterity. But for the most part their careers were bounded by a limited horizon, and they served their day and generation in the simple station to which they were called.

As pioneers they were successful, and the same traits of character which distinguished his ancestors in this respect found expression, under different conditions and in a more remarkable degree, in their descendant. Mr. Moody inherited from that hardy stock an iron constitution capable of great physical endurance and a capacity for hard, continuous work. He early developed those distinguishing traits of his New England forefathers: a strong love of liberty, loyalty to conviction, courage in the face of obstacles, and sound judgment in organization; and these constituted his most valuable legacy from his seven generations of Puritan ancestors.

The earliest records of the Moody family in America date from the landing of John Moody in 1633. Settling first in Roxbury, he moved later to the Connecticut Valley, where he became one of the original proprietors of Hartford; from here he moved to Hadley, Mass. At the beginning of the nineteenth century Isaiah Moody and his sons were settled in Northfield; and the eldest of these boys was Edwin, the father of Dwight L. Moody.

Here for years they followed the family trade of masonry, which, in those early days, included the making and burning of bricks as well as the laying of foundations and the building of houses and chimneys. To the conscientious performance of their work many an old farmhouse in and about Northfield still bears silent witness. A member of Mr. Moody's family was introduced a few years ago to a centenarian of Warwick, a neighboring village. The visitor was presented as a son of D. L. Moody, but the old farmer found a far stronger recommendation in the fact that the young man's great-grandfather and grandfather had, three-quarters of a century before, laid the foundation and built the chimney of the house they were in; and, with a slight touch of jealous pride for the former generation, he declared that "the work was well done and had stood the test of time."

From his mother's family, too, Mr. Moody received a goodly heritage of Puritan pluck, the Holtons antedating the Moodys in America by three years. They landed in 1630, and were among the first settlers of Northfield, where for more than two hundred years they have been residents. They cherish a natural pride in the fact that, from the date of the original grant from the British Crown, no deed of transfer of the old Holton homestead has ever been recorded. This farm, beautiful in its situation, lies on the west bank of the Connecticut River, a mile or two from Northfield Street, adjoining the commanding site, purchased by Mr. Moody, upon which is built the well-known Mount Hermon School. Some idea of the hardships through which the Moody and Holton families passed, in common with their neighbors, is preserved in the early records of the towns of Hadley and Northfield. In the local cemetery, near the Mount Hermon School, lie the remains of many of the Holton family, whose names for more than seven generations are recorded on the old headstones.

Betsy Holton and Edwin Moody were married on January 3, 1828. It had been arranged that the ceremony should take place on New Year's day, but the Connecticut River had little regard for the lovers, and unexpectedly rose above its banks after a sudden thaw. Although the young people's homes were but four miles apart, in those days before bridges spanned the river the swollen stream was an insurmountable obstacle even to so resolute a character as Edwin Moody, and only by making a detour of many miles was the marriage celebrated without a still longer postponement. The bride was twenty-three years old and her husband twenty-eight when they left the old Holton homestead that January evening to make a new home in Northfield.

It was a true love match between the reckless, dashing, and open-handed young man and his pretty wife, and for twelve and a half years they enjoyed their happiness. God blessed their union with seven children during this time, and by the skill and industry of his trade the father provided amply for his family support.

Dwight Lyman, the sixth child, was born February 5, 1837. The old family record adds the name of Ryther, but this was early discarded. In those days it was customary for one who was complimented by the bestowal of his name upon a child to present a sheep to the baby in recognition of the honor his babyhood was innocently conferring. The feelings of the fond parents were wounded by the omission, in Dwight's case, of the customary gift, and "Ryther" does not seem to appear again after its entry on the record of the births in the large family Bible.

It was foreign to the disposition of Edwin Moody to give much thought to the future, and so it is not strange that he made little or no provision for the contingency of his sudden death. When, therefore, he was stricken down without a moment's warning at the early age of forty-one, the widow was left with practically no means of support. The homestead itself was encumbered with a mortgage, and but for the merciful provision of the law securing dower rights, the widow would have been left without even a shelter for the family. The creditors took everything which they could secure, to the very kindling wood in the shed, and left the widow with her seven children in the utmost straits. It was at this time that one of Mrs. Moody's brothers ministered most opportunely and generously to the needs of the family. The supply of firewood had been completely exhausted, and the children had been told that they must stay in bed till school-time to keep warm. It was then that "Uncle Cyrus" Holton came to the rescue with a load of wood, and, good Samaritan that he was, sawed and split it for immediate use.

"I remember," said Mr. Moody in later years, "just as vividly as if it were yesterday, how I heard the sound of chips flying, and I knew some one was chopping wood in our wood-shed, and that we should soon have a fire. I shall never forget Uncle Cyrus coming with what seemed to me the biggest pile of wood I ever saw in my life." It was such remembrances as these that always made his heart vibrate with peculiar sympathy for those who were in want.

A less determined and courageous heart than the resolute widow's would have been overcome by the dark prospect for the future, but that true soul had inherited the sturdy strength and undaunted courage which had distinguished her early ancestors as pioneers in the new world, and with a strong faith in God she faced the conflict with poverty.

Some of her neighbors urged her to break up the little home and place the children in families where they might be cared for by strangers. Even those from whom more practical help might have been expected strongly advised this course, and because their advice was not accepted seemed to feel that they were absolved from any further duty. The birth of twins after her husband died added greatly to the cares and difficulties of her position, and during the long summer that followed there were many times when it seemed that the burden was too great for human endurance. It was during these days that Mrs. Moody's brother aided her, and at this time, too, the old minister of the Unitarian Church, the Rev. Mr. Everett, interested himself in the family's behalf.

Shortly after the father's death this good man visited the destitute family and helped them both by counsel and material assistance. The older children were all enrolled in the Sunday-school of the church, and from the hands of this minister the entire family received the ordinance of baptism " in the name of the Father and of the Son and of the Holy Ghost." No sooner had the attendance of the Moody children been secured than they were commissioned to bring in other scholars. In a sense, therefore, Mr. Moody's Sunday-school mission work began at an earlier date than is commonly supposed, for as a child he and his brother George frequently acted as aggressive home missionaries in securing recruits for the village Sunday-school.

With the sole care of so large a family the religious instruction in the home was not so thoroughly doctrinal as in some households of to-day, but the mother instructed her children in the true religion of the heart that seeks first God and His righteousness, and though Dwight at seventeen, as a member of a young men's Bible class in Boston, was bewildered by the request to turn to a simple Scriptural reference, it is doubtful if any of his amused companions were more thoroughly established in " pure religion and undefiled before God and the Father " than he. Certainly none was purer and more innocent in heart than the keen, awkward country boy.

It was not till after he left home that his actual personal conversion occurred, but it was to a tender conscience and an open heart that the gospel invitation was given, and a soul already trained to love and honor God readily accepted His offer of salvation. The Christian training of his mother and the faithfulness of her good pastor were a sacred remembrance in all his after experiences, and he ever spoke appreciatively of the debt he owed to the ministry of Mr. Everett.

" Trust in God " was the brief creed of his mother's simple Christian faith, and early in life the children learned to love that God and pray to Him who is the strength of the fatherless and the widow. Many evidences of the thoroughness with which this lesson was taught to Dwight and his brothers are found in their early experiences.

One night in the late fall Dwight's older brother, a boy of twelve, and himself, then only eight years of age, started to a neighboring farm about four miles away, where they had secured employment in the cutting of broom corn. Boylike, they had not started on their journey until the evening had set in, and long before they reached the old ferry across the Connecticut River it had become very dark.

Hand in hand they crossed the meadow to the landing, and then shouted over the river for the ferryman to bring his skiff. Soon they could hear voices and see a lantern approaching from the opposite bank. Then a voice shouted across the flood that one man would cross the river with the boat, while the other would remain where he was with the lantern to direct their course. In the intense darkness they soon lost sight of the approaching boat, and for a long time they could hear nothing of the ferryman, who had been carried far down the stream by the swift current. After some suspense they heard the boat approaching along the bank of the river, and finally the boatman reached them. When they had taken their places and were pushing out from the bank, the boys found that the old man was intoxicated and in no condition to row them safely across the river. Dwight held tightly to his brother, who, seeing that they were being carried far away from the lantern on the opposite bank, urged to be allowed to take the oars and help. But the old man in his maudlin condition stubbornly refused, and as the current bore them swiftly down the stream they became more and more alarmed. Then Dwight, taking his brother's hand, tried to encourage him by assuring him that God would care for them and guard them even in their present peril. Many a child in similar circumstances would have thought only of human expedients, but at that early age he had been taught an implicit trust in God as the true resource in time of danger.

Mrs. Moody was tender-hearted, and the children early learned the privilege of giving from their scanty store. The hungry were never turned away from her door, and on one occasion when the provision for the evening meal was very meagre it was put to the vote of the little ones whether they should give of their small supply to a poor beggar who appealed for aid. The children begged that he should be aided and offered to have their own slices cut thinner.

It was also one of the irrevocable laws of her home that no fault-finding or complaining of neighbors or friends would be tolerated. The mother thus implanted in the children a spirit of independence as well as charity; and even those whose neglect was most inexcusable never heard directly or indirectly one word of complaint from the little family in their want and adversity. Dwight Moody was not the only Yankee boy who could look back on that combination of charity for others with inflexible independence for one's self that has made the New England character what it is. His very limitations taught the poor boy of that day the "sharpness" and "contrivance" that grow into what we call executive ability, just as the almost

Spartan simplicity of diet and training developed in a good constitution the wonderful powers of endurance that have marked many New Englanders.

While the mother was truly kind and loving she was withal a strict disciplinarian. Order was enforced by rules, with old-fashioned whippings as a penalty. These events were more or less frequent in the case of Dwight, who was the leader in all kinds of boyish mischief. In later years he described these punishments and his futile attempts to escape them:

"Mother would send me out for a stick, and I thought I could fool her and get a dead one. But she would snap the stick and then tell me to get another. She was rarely in a hurry, and certainly never when she was whipping me. Once I told her that the whipping did not hurt at all. I never had occasion to tell her so again, for she put it on so it did hurt."

To these whippings Mr. Moody always referred with great approval, but with delightful inconsistency never adopted the same measures in the government of his own family. In his home grace was the ruling principle and not law, and the sorest punishment of a child was the sense that the father's loving heart had been grieved by waywardness or folly.

Among the principles which this Puritan mother taught her children to observe was the inviolable sanctity of a promise. In later years it was characteristic of Mr. Moody that he hated to commit himself absolutely by promises, and doubtless that aversion was in part the outgrowth of the stern but wholesome teachings of his youth. If the children tried to avoid an obligation the question they had to meet was not, "*Can* you?" but, "Did you *say* you would?" If a promise had been made, it must be kept. Once when Dwight went to his older brother to be released from an agreement to work for a neighbor for his board during the winter, while he was also attending school, the case was carried to their mother. Dwight's cause of complaint was that for nineteen consecutive meals his only food had been cornmeal and milk. When his mother found that he had had enough to eat, such as it was, Dwight was sent back to keep his agreement.

But with all the strictness of her discipline the mother was tenderly wise, in a manner not so common at that day as now, when the needs of the child are so carefully studied. Knowing the dangers that awaited her children in the outside world, she determined to guard them as long as she could. To do this it was necessary to make home attractive, and this she proved herself able to do far better than many who have had more means with which to secure the luxuries of life. She discouraged her children from going to the neighbors to find their recreation, but always welcomed their friends to the hospitality of their own little home. They were spirited children and given to wild romps, but she would sit quietly at her mending, though the very roof seemed threatened by the boisterous games of her own and her neighbors' boys and girls.

The advent of a Sabbath's rest, beginning with sundown on Saturday and ending at the same time Sunday evening, must have been to her a most welcome respite. Church attendance was not a debatable question in the family, but was as inevitable as a law of nature. The boys used to go barefoot, carrying their shoes and stockings in their hands, and putting them on when they came in sight of the church. The elder boys, who were out at work during the week, came home on Saturday night to attend church with their brothers and sisters. They carried luncheon and stayed all day, hearing the two sermons and attending the Sunday-school which came in between; and then all would troop home again for supper, the older ones returning later to their work, while the younger children, as the sunset announced the end of the day of rest, would release their long pent-up spirits in wild romps and shouts. In spite of the poverty which parted them during the week, the mother thus preserved the home-life on the one day in seven.

In later years Mr. Moody looked back with gratitude to this strict requirement of church attendance. Those hours in the village church, tedious as they were, listening as he must to sermons which he could not understand, he came to look upon as a blessing because they fixed upon him the habit of attending God's house.

"I remember blaming my mother for sending me to church on the Sabbath," he once said. "On one occasion the preacher had to send some one into the gallery to wake me up. I thought it was hard to have to work in the field all the week, and then be obliged to go to church and hear a sermon I didn't understand. I thought I wouldn't go to church any more when I got away from home; but I had got so in the habit of going that I couldn't stay away. After one or two Sabbaths, back again to the house of God I went. There I first found Christ, and I have often said since: 'Mother, I thank you for making me go to the house of God when I didn't want to go.'"

Sunday evenings, after supper, the mother would gather the children about her before the old-fashioned fireplace, in winter, or under one of the great sugar-maple trees in the front yard, if it were summer, and read to them out of the books which they brought home from the Sunday-school library. Three books constituted the home library: a large family Bible, in which were written the family records; a catechism, and a book of devotions, comprising contemplations and written prayers. From the latter a portion was read each morning, and also a prayer before the family entered upon the work of the day.

Mr. Moody could never speak of those early days of want and adversity without the most tender references to that brave mother whose self-sacrifice and devotion had sacredly guarded the home intrusted to her care. When, at the age of ninety, her life-voyage ended, she entered the Haven of Rest, her children, her children's children, and an entire community rose up to call her blessed. And well she deserved the praise they gave her, for she had wisely and discreetly discharged the duties God had placed upon her, and entering the presence of her Master, could render a faithful account of the stewardship of motherhood. To rule a household of seven sturdy boys and two girls, the eldest twelve years old, required no ordinary tact and sound judgment, but so discreet was this loyal mother that to the very end she made "home" the most loved place on earth to her family, and so trained her children as to make them a blessing to society.

"For nearly fifty years I have been coming back to Northfield," said Mr. Moody long after that little circle had been broken up, "and I have always been glad to get back. When I get within fifty miles of home I grow restless and walk up and down the car. It seems as if the train will never get to Northfield. When I come back after dark I always look to see the light in mother's window."

CHAPTER II

Leaving Home

IT was an early characteristic of Moody that his determination to accomplish his purpose was not easily thwarted. On one occasion he wished to visit his grandmother Holton, who lived about four miles away. The little man was scarce five years of age, and so long a journey seemed even greater than many times that distance to an older child. Some one had given him five cents, but this was only half the required amount for a child's stage-fare for this distance. Nothing daunted, however, little Dwight stopped the passing stage and, having stated his case to the driver, asked if he would accept the five cents for his fare. The stage was already full inside, but the stage driver consented to take him as baggage, and for five cents placed him on top of the coach within the rack that guarded the trunks. He reached his grandmother's, the only other home in the world where the Moody children were assured of a welcome, and after spending a day at the old farm was urged by his relatives to make an early start for home, as it was supposed that he intended to walk back to Northfield. The little fellow had made up his mind, however, that the stage coach was far preferable to a long tramp, and had already made his plans for riding home. Going out into the fields, he picked a bouquet of wild flowers, and another of caraway, and once more hailed the coach, proffering his flowers for his return journey. We can imagine the surprise of his mother at seeing Dwight returning in triumph perched upon the stage box.

It was this spirit which made him a leader among the boys in his native town, and the wild escapades into which he led his companions were the source of amusing reminiscences in later years. "Squire" Alexander, from the fact that his was the nearest residence to the old red schoolhouse of that district, was most frequently the victim of these pranks. Stories are told of how Dwight and his companions would appropriate the Squire's old "pung" to coast down the steep hill below his house, the recklessness of the venture only adding the greater zest to its enjoyment. On another occasion he led his followers to the cattle sheds of the Squire, where they quietly climbed up on the empty rafters, and then of a sudden raised the most awful whoops and yells, at the same time jumping about on the loose planks. The effect of this tumult upon a lot of young steers may be better imagined than described, and the rush of the animals through the barnyard fences gave the youngsters occupation suited exactly to their tastes. Of course, no one knew who was to blame for the stampede, for, before the Squire could reach the barn, there were no boys in sight, and in the "round up" of the cattle young Dwight was the most indignant at the inexcusable vandalism of the act.

The "Closing Exercises" in the district school was an event of great local importance to the younger element, and Dwight was not the boy to let pass such an opportunity for some unusual excitement. On one such occasion he was to give as a recitation Mark Antony's oration over Julius Cæsar, and to add, as was supposed, to the dramatic effect introduced a small box to represent the coffin of the illustrious dead. The teacher's desk served as a bier upon which this rested, and as the eloquence of the orator found added expression in extravagant gestures the lid of the box was knocked off, and out jumped a very frightened old tom-cat. The scene which followed had just the effect "Mark Antony" seemed to have aimed at, for though the stones of Rome did not rise, every animate being in the room did.

Even simpler tricks delighted him. Once when asked to hand a jug of cider to a farmer in his wagon, Dwight, who was then working on the farm, intending, indeed, to go home in that very wagon, waited only till the jug was at the farmer's lips to startle the horses so that their sudden jump unseated the driver, who fell back into the bottom of the wagon, unable to rise and equally unwilling to relinquish the jug, which would have drenched him had he taken it from his lips.

Dwight's busy hand and brain were always occupied, and he wanted to see others busy too. In those younger days he seemed to love the excitement of a crowd, and once when an unusually uneventful winter had dragged by he decided that "something must be done." This he arranged without conference with any one, not daring to trust his closest friend. Writing out an announcement for a temperance meeting to be addressed by an out-of-town lecturer, he posted it on the district schoolhouse door. On the evening announced there was quite a gathering in the schoolhouse, which was warmed and lighted for the occasion, but no lecturer put in an appearance, and Dwight, with the others, scolded the practical joker, whom no one could discover.

For such mischief he frequently received a double chastisement, first at the hands of the school teacher and afterward from his mother; for, according to the strange reasoning of that day, it was thought that if the boy was so naughty in school as to be punished, the same offence called loudly upon the mother also not to "spare the rod and spoil the child." But evidently Dwight thought the fun was worth the whipping, for his love of practical jokes never grew less. It should be said, however, that when the joke was at his own expense he enjoyed it just as much. For, as he expressed it, "No man has a right to play a joke unless he's willing to take one."

A new teacher came at last to the little school, and another order of things appeared. To begin with, she opened the exercises with prayer, which greatly impressed the boys, and when later she announced that she proposed to rule the school without the old-fashioned whippings, their astonishment was increased. It was not long before young Dwight had broken a rule, and with the summons to "remain after school," he expected the customary punishment and immediately assumed the attitude of injured innocence. To his surprise, when they were alone, the teacher began to talk kindly to him and to tell him how sorry she was to have him disobey. This treatment was worse than the rattan cane, and Dwight did not like it. After telling him how it grieved her to find that he could not be trusted, the teacher said:

"I have made up my mind that if I cannot rule the school by love, I will give it up. I will have no punishment. If you love me, try to keep the rules and help me in the school."

This was too much for Dwight, and where law had failed grace had a complete victory.

"You will never have any more trouble with me," he answered, capitulating, "and I will *whack* the first boy that makes you any trouble!" And "whack" him he did the very next day, to the surprise of his companions and to the consternation of the teacher.

"Swapping" is a Yankee weakness, and in common with other boys Dwight was keen on a bargain. Sentiment in those youthful days was less pronounced than the love of a trade, for he bought off with a broken slate pencil the affections of a rival suitor for a little companion. But it was more especially to shrewdness in horse-trading that Dwight aspired, and at the earliest opportunity he earned his title for it. The older brother, George, who had fathered the younger children and conducted the farm, was away from home one day, when a party of gypsies came along. As usual, they had a number of horses to trade, and Dwight, who was only ten years old at the time, was alive to business.

The farm-horse in the possession of the family at this time was old and lazy enough, and Dwight reasoned that in an exchange he couldn't get a worse animal, so he challenged the gypsies to a trade. Before any of the family knew it he had made what actually proved to be a good bargain, though the new horse was a lank, raw-boned animal with a docked tail. The consciousness of his success filled him with pride. On the first occasion after the new horse had been duly tested, Dwight harnessed him into a wagon, and taking an empty barrel for a seat, started to mill for the weekly supply of meal. The new horse seemed to rise to the occasion. He started briskly down the hill and all too swiftly around the corner, leaving the barrel and its occupant by the roadside.

When Dwight grew older he found employment, like his brothers, in neighboring towns. His first experience was never forgotten, and the homesickness that came with the first separation from his family left a lasting impression.

"There were nine of us children," he said in describing this, "and my widowed mother had very great difficulty in keeping the wolf from the door. My next older brother had found a place for me to work during the winter months in a neighboring village about thirteen miles away, and early one November morning we started out together on our dismal journey. Do you know, November has been a dreary month to me ever since? As we passed over the river and up the opposite side of the valley we turned to look back for a last view of home. It was to be my last for weeks, for months, perhaps forever, and my heart well-nigh broke at the thought. That was the longest journey I ever took, for thirteen miles was more to me at ten than the world's circumference has ever been since.

"When at last we arrived in the town I had hard work to keep back my tears, and my brother had to do his best to cheer me. Suddenly he pointed to some one and said:

"'There's a man that'll give you a cent; he gives one to every new boy that comes to town.' He was a feeble, old, white-haired man, and I was so afraid that he would pass me by that I planted myself directly in his path. As he came up to us my brother spoke to him, and he stopped and looked at me. 'Why, I have never seen you before. You must be a new boy,' he said. He asked me about my home, and then, laying his trembling hand upon my head, he told

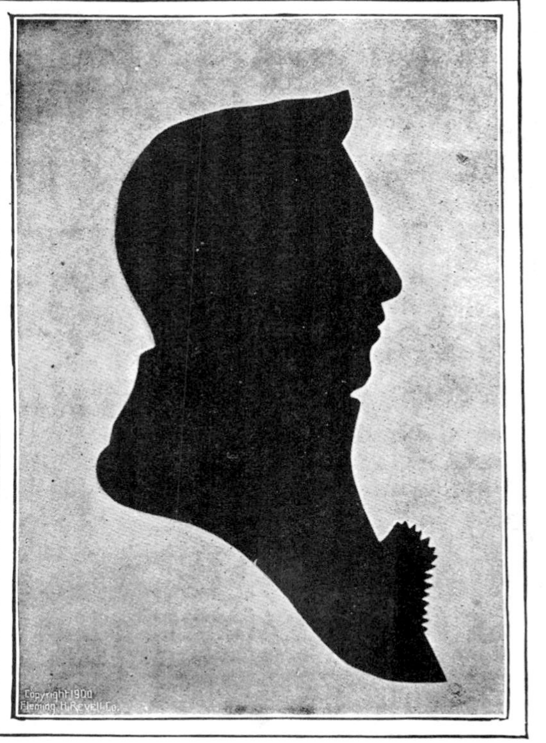

D. L. MOODY'S FATHER.

Silhouette portrait taken about 1835 (only portrait in existence).

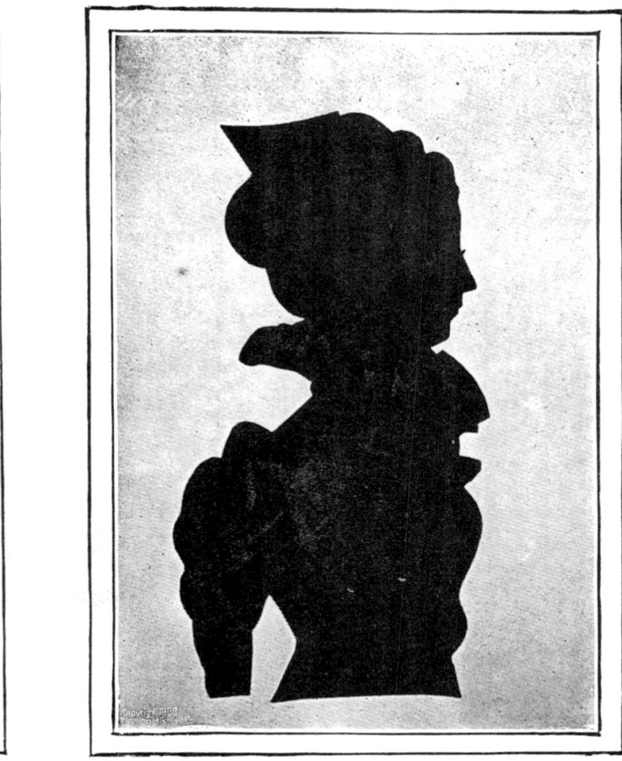

D. L. MOODY'S MOTHER.

Silhouette portrait taken about the time of her marriage to Edwin Moody.

Dwight L. Moody at the Time of Leaving Home for Boston.

me that, although I had no earthly father, my Heavenly Father loved me, and then he gave me a bright new cent. I do not remember what became of that cent, but that old man's blessing has followed me for over fifty years, and to my dying day I shall feel the kindly pressure of that hand upon my head. A loving deed costs very little, but done in the name of Christ it will be eternal."

A few years later he tried to get employment in Clinton, Mass., and found an engagement in a printing establishment. His first task was to address by hand, from the mailing list, the wrappers of a local paper. To the country lad who knew nothing of crowded streets or houses containing several tenements the half-numbers of some of the addresses had no meaning, and such a street address he set down to the next number beyond. This naturally caused confusion, and when the mistake was traced to young Moody he was discharged. Again he went home, and for a time worked on the neighboring farms. But his ambition had been roused, and he realized the greater possibilities and opportunities of a larger sphere. While cutting and hauling logs on the mountain side with his brother Edwin one day in the early spring of 1854, he exclaimed, in his characteristically abrupt manner:

"I'm tired of this! I'm not going to stay around here any longer. I'm going to the city."

The family had been strongly opposed to his going to Boston, as no one believed that he had any special qualification for a successful career in the city. The cities, they understood, were full of young men looking for positions, while at Northfield he was at least assured of steady work on the farms. But young Moody had made up his mind that the one thing for him to do was to go to Boston and, in spite of all obstacles, make a career for himself.

Saying good-bye to his mother and the rest of the family, he started from home without any very definite plans as to how he should get to Boston, but determined to go even if he had to walk every step of the hundred miles. Half-way between his home and the depot he met his older brother George, who inquired where he was going.

Dwight said he was on his way to Boston to make his living in whatever business he found he was best suited for. Seeing that it was useless to try to discourage him, his brother gave him five dollars, which was just enough to carry him to the city, where he arrived with nothing to live on while he was looking for work.

For several days young Moody experienced the same bitter disappointment that so many other young men have known in like circumstances. Although he had two uncles in the retail boot and shoe business in the city, they made no offer to give him work. When asked by these uncles how he thought he could get a start, Dwight replied that he wanted to work, and he " guessed " he could find a position. It is quite possible that a consciousness of his awkwardness may have given the country boy that appearance of a false independence which prejudiced his relatives against him.

Long afterward, when preaching in Boston, he described with deep feeling those days of suffering. " I remember how I walked up and down the streets trying to find a situation," he said, " and I recollect how, when they answered me roughly, their treatment would chill my soul. But when some one would say: '*I* feel for you; I would like to help you, but I can't; but you'll be all right soon!' I went away happy and light-hearted. That man's sympathy did me good.

" It seemed as if there was room for every one else in the world, but none for me. For about two days I had the feeling that no one wanted me. I never have had it since, and I never want it again. It is an awful feeling. It seems to me that must have been the feeling of the Son of God when He was down here. They did not want Him. He had come to save men, and they did not want to be saved. He had come to lift men up, and they did not want to be lifted up. There was no room for Him in this world, and there is no room for Him yet.

" I went to the post-office two or three times a day to see if there was a letter for me. I knew there was not, as there was but one mail a day from Northfield. I had no employment and was very homesick, and so I went constantly to the post-office, thinking perhaps that when the mail had come in my letter had been mislaid. At last, however, I got a letter. It was from my youngest sister—the first letter she ever wrote me. I opened it with a light heart, thinking there was some good news from home, but the burden of the whole letter was that she had heard there were pickpockets in Boston, and warned me to beware of them. I thought that I had better get some money in hand first, and then I might look out for pickpockets!"

At the end of a week he was utterly discouraged. There seemed nothing for him in Boston, and he announced his purpose of trying what he could do in New York.

At first his attitude toward his uncles had been the independent one of waiting for them to offer him work, and when advised to ask them for employment himself he said: "They know I am looking for work and they may help me or not as they please." But at length his pride gave way under the dreadful sense of being adrift in a world that seemed to care nothing for him. Learning of his changed state of mind, one of his uncles ventured to offer him a little advice, telling him that his self-will was greatly in his way, that modesty was sometimes as needful as courage, and suggesting that his uncle Samuel Holton would no doubt be glad to do something for him if he would show himself a little more willing to be governed by people who were older and wiser than himself. Dwight demurred, saying his uncle Samuel knew perfectly well what he wanted. But the uncle insisted, so that at last the boy asked for a place in the shoe shop.

"Dwight, I am afraid if you come in here you will want to run the store yourself," said Mr. Holton. "Now, my men here want to do their work as I want it done. If you want to come in here and do the best you can and do it right, and if you'll be willing to ask whenever you don't know, and if you promise to go to church and Sunday-school, and if you will not go anywhere that you wouldn't want your mother to know about, we'll see how we can get along. You can have till Monday to think it over."

"I don't want till Monday," was the prompt response. "I'll promise now."

Young Moody had little acquaintance with city ways and city manners, but it soon became evident that he was by natural wit and brightness one of the best of salesmen. With his keen perception and irrepressible energy he made an unusual success of the work.

He was not satisfied with the ordinary methods of the salesman, and, like the merchants of old, he cried his wares before the door, and actually went out into the street to persuade uninterested passers that they wanted to buy. Nothing delighted him so much as a success of this kind, and that he had many is not surprising.

His new occupation, far from lessening his love of practical joking, seemed to make it keener. Always on the lookout for some one whom he could tease, he found a tempting victim in a cobbler who worked in the store. One day in his absence young Moody, with a sharp knife, made a clean slit in the leather seat of the cobbler's box. Then taking a pan of water, he set it under the box so that the cobbler's weight would bring the seat in contact with the water, which, of course, would rise through the cut. Having set his trap, the joker awaited the result. Presently the cobbler came in and sat down. The effect may be imagined. The victim took his seat only to jump up hurriedly, but as soon as the leather was relieved of his weight the hole closed, and after wiping the seat dry he again seated himself to begin his work. It was not till the third or fourth time that he discovered the trouble, and Moody had to make a hurried escape.

This was the nonsense of a lively boy of seventeen, but from that harmless love of fooling the happy geniality of the mature man was to result. This sense of humor, this healthy appreciation of the ridiculous, is the very salt of a great temperament. Such a man, however intense, can never be a fanatic, and the people—the men in the street—feel this instantly.

CHAPTER III

Conversion

IN accordance with the agreement by which he entered his uncle's employment, Moody became a regular attendant of the Mount Vernon Congregational Church, of which the well-known Dr. Edward N. Kirk was the pastor. He was also enrolled as a member of the Sunday-school, where he was assigned to a young men's Bible class conducted by Mr. Edward Kimball.

The Bible was not a familiar book to the new student, for in his home, though he had always lived in a truly Christian atmosphere, there was only one copy of God's Word, and that a ponderous family Bible, too sacred for the inquisitiveness of the little children, and too uninviting in its massive appearance for the older ones. So when some reference was made to a chapter in the Gospel of John, the young man began to search the Old Testament industriously, and but for the kindness of the teacher, who quickly perceived the difficulty and offered him his Bible, the boy's embarrassment would have been painful.

By giving close attention, however, he soon began to take that deep interest in Bible study which, increasing with his years, soon developed into a reverential love. Many years later, wishing to give a token of special value to his first grandchild, he sent a beautiful copy of the Bible with this inscription:

"The Bible for the last forty years has been the dearest thing on earth to me, and now I give a copy as my first gift to my first grandchild, Irene Moody, with a prayer that it may be her companion through life and guide her to those mansions that Christ has gone to prepare for those who love and serve Him on earth. D. L. Moody."

Realizing his disadvantage in not having a greater familiarity with the Bible text, he seldom took an active part in the class at first. But at times his interest would betray him, and he would ask a question that showed his clear grasp of the subject. On one occasion the teacher was depicting Moses as a man of great natural ability, self-control, and statesmanlike foresight and wisdom. There was just one word in the young clerk's mind that was sufficiently comprehensive for such a character, and with a naive earnestness he exclaimed:

" Say, Mr. Kimball, that man Moses must have been *smart*." In that one word " smart " was included the New England lad's conception of all that was comprehended by native ability and intellectual endowment without the sense of a discreditable shrewdness.

There is a vast difference between what may be termed a religious man and an earnest Christian; just such a difference, in fact, as distinguished Saul of Tarsus and the Apostle Paul. In the former the life is regulated to a degree by external authority—" thou shalt " and " thou shalt not "; in the latter a new bias is given to the life itself, bringing it into harmony with God's will, and the precepts of the external law are merged in the greater law of love to God and man. The former is cold, cheerless, and intolerant, only too often unavailing in severe temptation, and frequently expressing itself in formalism and pharisaism. The latter is a vital force making the soul stronger through temptation, and by unselfish service to others radiating love and joy throughout society.

By his early training Mr. Moody was religious, but he had never experienced the regenerating work of God's Spirit by a definite acceptance of Christ. In theory he knew that giving way to a violent temper was wrong, but in his self-will he found it hard to yield to restraint. " It was not more ethics he needed, but greater dynamics." But in the Mount Vernon Sunday-school his Bible-class teacher had been gradually leading the young man to a fuller knowledge of God's plan of salvation, until it needed only an additional personal interview to bring him to that decision of the will which should determine whether he would accept or reject God's provision for overcoming sin and entering into harmony with Himself. The opportunity for this interview was not a chance event, but one carefully and prayerfully sought by Mr. Kimball, who thus relates the story of Dwight L. Moody's conversion:

"I determined to speak to him about Christ and about his soul, and started down to Holton's shoe store. When I was nearly there I began to wonder whether I ought to go in just then during business hours. I thought that possibly my call might embarrass the boy, and that when I went away the other clerks would ask who I was, and taunt him with my efforts in trying to make him a good boy. In the meantime I had passed the store, and, discovering this, I determined to make a dash for it and have it over at once. I found Moody in the back part of the building wrapping up shoes. I went up to him at once, and putting my hand on his shoulder, I made what I afterwards felt was a very weak plea for Christ. I don't know just what words I used, nor could Mr. Moody tell. I simply told him of Christ's love for him and the love Christ wanted in return. That was all there was. It seemed the young man was just ready for the light that then broke upon him, and there, in the back of that store in Boston, he gave himself and his life to Christ."

From the moment that Moody accepted Christ his whole life changed. The merely passive religious life that suffered the restrictions of the moral law suddenly became a life of joyful service. Whereas church attendance had been observed simply because it was a duty, from this time forth for nearly fifty years he found his greatest joy in the service of his God.

"Before my conversion," as he himself used to express it, "I worked towards the Cross, but since then I have worked from the Cross; then I worked to be saved, now I work because I am saved."

Forty years afterward, preaching in Boston, he thus described the effect of his conversion upon his life:

"I can almost throw a stone from Tremont Temple to the spot where I found God over forty years ago. I wish I could do something to lead some of you young men to that same God. He has been a million times better to me than I have been to Him.

"I remember the morning on which I came out of my room after I had first trusted Christ. I thought the old sun shone a good deal brighter than it ever had before—I thought that it was just smiling upon me; and as I walked out upon Boston Common and heard the birds singing in the trees I thought they were all singing a song to me. Do you know, I fell in love with the birds. I had never cared for them before. It seemed to me that I was in love with all creation. I had not a bitter feeling against any man, and I was ready to take all men to my heart. If a man has not the love of God shed abroad in his heart, he has never been regenerated. If you hear a person get up in the prayer-meeting and he begins to find fault with everybody, you may doubt whether his is a genuine conversion; it may be counterfeit. It has not the right ring, because the impulse of a converted soul is to love, and not to be getting up and complaining of every one else and finding fault."

Bread cast upon the waters returns again, and the Bible-class teacher received a blessing in his own household, seventeen years later, in the conversion of his own son. Mr. Kimball's eldest son was visiting an uncle in Worcester, Mass., while Mr. Moody was conducting a mission in that city. After one of the services young Kimball introduced himself to Mr. Moody as the son of his old Bible-class teacher.

"What! are you the son of Mr. Edward Kimball, of Boston? What is your name?"

"Henry."

"I am glad to see you. Henry, are you a Christian?"

"No, sir, I do not think I am."

"How old are you?"

"I am seventeen."

"Henry, when I was just seventeen, and you were a little baby in the crib, your father came to me and put his hand on my shoulder and asked me to be a Christian, and he was the only man that ever came to me and talked to me, because he loved my soul; and now I want you, my boy, to be a Christian. Henry, don't you want to be a Christian?"

"Yes, sir; I think I do," said the boy.

They sat down together, and Mr. Moody opened his Bible, the boy listening attentively to the words that impressed him more and more, till at length they brought him to where their speaker had been himself led so long ago.

After his conversion young Moody was no less energetic and ambitious in the interests of the Kingdom of God than he had been in business. His vigorous and irrepressible spirit was looked upon with misgivings by some of the elder members of the church. In the first glad joy of his Christian experience he longed for some channel into which he might direct his energies and share in the forwarding of the Kingdom. It was, perhaps, a mistake that the young convert was not set to work and directed how to serve the cause most efficiently, in his own particular way. But the conservative deacons could not know that the zeal so unnecessarily directed toward them could have been turned with practical results in other directions, undreamed of by them, and their attitude was one of a somewhat natural repression.

In May, 1855, young Moody presented himself for membership in the Mount Vernon Church, from the records of which the following minute is taken:

"No. 1,079. Dwight L. Moody. Boards, 43 Court Street. Has been baptized. First awakened on the 16th of May. Became anxious about himself. Saw himself a sinner, and sin now seems hateful and holiness desirable. Thinks he has repented; has purposed to give up sin; feels dependent upon Christ for forgiveness. Loves the Scriptures. Prays. Desires to be useful. Religiously educated. Been in the city a year. From Northfield, this State. Is not ashamed to be known as a Christian. Eighteen years old."

At this examination, however, it was felt that the applicant was not sufficiently instructed in Christian doctrine to be taken into membership. In answer to the question: "What has Christ done for you, and for us all, that especially entitles Him to our love and obedience?" Young Moody replied: "I think He has done a great deal for us all, but I don't know of anything He has done in particular."

Nothing, therefore, was elicited at this examination that was in those days considered satisfactory evidence of conversion. Under the circumstances the committee deferred recommending him for admission to the church, but three of their number were appointed to take care of his case, and to explain to him more perfectly the way of God.

The action of the examining committee in refusing admission to young Moody on this occasion has been criticised by others, but the wisdom of the decision was always felt by Mr. Moody himself, who in later years laid great emphasis upon a young convert's being ready to give a reason for the hope that was in him. Upon his second examination he was recommended for membership, and the following minute was recorded:

"No. 1,131. March 12, 1856. Mr. Moody thinks he has made some progress since he was here before—at least in knowledge. Has maintained his habits of prayer and reading the Bible. Believes God will hear his prayers, and reads the Bible. Is fully determined to adhere to the cause of Christ always. Feels that it would be very bad if he should join the church and then turn. Must repent and ask forgiveness, for Christ's sake. Will never give up his hope, or love Christ less, whether admitted to the church or not. His prevailing intention is to give up his will to God."

" In a few days Moody was among the inquirers after the way of life," writes Dr. Kirk with reference to Moody's conversion. " He soon avowed himself as a candidate for church membership; he displayed nothing but his earnestness and want of acquaintance with the Scriptural views of Christian character and life; or, more probably, his case was an instance showing that we, his examiners, were too far bound by routine and wanting in sympathy with Him who was then laying the foundation of the temple of God in that human soul. We could not conscientiously propose him to the church. Disappointed, but not discouraged, he awaited through one or two terms. At last we saw some faint evidences of conversion which justified us in recommending him to the church."

At first Mr. Moody questioned the result his new life would have upon his business prospects. From the very beginning he had entered upon his duties with characteristic energy, and in three months' time he had sold more goods than any one of his fellow-clerks. He had thought that truthfulness might be a hindrance to his success. But he soon found that Christian principles were an aid rather than an obstacle in a successful business career. Customers, finding that they could implicitly rely on his word, preferred to deal with him, and his popularity with them steadily increased.

Thus for two years he continued to work in Boston, when he began to feel that greater opportunities might await him in a larger sphere. His position in his uncle's store seemed to offer little promise for the future; for, with extremely conservative methods, his uncle did not feel the same enthusiasm that fired the young man. Just at that time Chicago, the new city of the Western prairies, was attracting the young men of the Eastern States. Moody, with others, felt the attraction of its appeal, and without telling any one of his purpose, he decided to cast in his lot with the new West.

CHAPTER IV

In Business in Chicago

"I HAVE always been a man of impulse," Mr. Moody once said to the writer. "Almost everything I ever did in my life that was a success was done on the impulse, and I suppose when I get ready to die I will be up and off." In seeking his fortune in the West he displayed this characteristic impulsiveness.

For some months he had fretted under the conservative methods of the business house in which he was engaged, and had longed to enter a larger sphere of activity, and when a crisis finally came in his relations with his employer, and there seemed little opportunity for advancement, he decided to go to Chicago.

Fearing that this change would not be approved by his family, he thought it wise not to consult with them on the subject, and their first news of it was in a letter written from the Western city a thousand miles away. For all these years the mother had striven to keep her little family near her, as if, with that unreasoning conceit of mothers which makes their love unique because it is a law unto itself, she could have guarded her sons from all evil and watched over them with the same solicitude as in babyhood. That thousand miles to Chicago seemed a cruel distance to her, and it was a long time before her heart became reconciled. During the succeeding years she followed her son's course with her prayers, and when the neighbors noted how, on winter evenings, "Widow Moody's" light burned late, they knew she was praying for her son far away.

Young Moody arrived in Chicago in the early autumn of 1856. At first he encountered the same difficulty in securing employment which had so tried his fortitude two years before in Boston. In two days, however, he secured a position that promised greater opportunities than the one he left, and from the very first his energy and keen business judgment were rewarded by a steady increase in responsibility and income.

The same earnest Christian spirit that had shown itself in Boston dominated his life in Chicago, and on his arrival, as his letters prove, he promptly associated himself with Christian people. Writing to his mother under date of September 25, 1856, he says:

"I reached this far-famed city of the West one week ago to-night. . . . I went into a prayer-meeting last night, and as soon as I made myself known, I had friends enough. After meeting they came to me and seemed to be as glad to see me as if I were their earthly brother. God is the same here as He was in Boston, and in Him I can find peace."

Having placed his letter from the Mount Vernon Church with the Plymouth Church, of which Rev. J. E. Roy, D.D., was then pastor, Moody began to cast about for some definite Christian service. Remembering, it may be, his success in childhood as a recruiting agent for the Sunday-school at Northfield, he conceived the idea that he had a special talent for this work, and at once hired a pew, which he undertook to fill every Sunday. He would hail young men on the street corners, or visit their boarding-houses, or even call them out of saloons to share his pew. Whether the novelty of the invitation or the irresistible earnestness and cordiality of the young man induced a large number to attend, the object was at any rate attained, and before long he was renting four pews, which he filled every Sunday with his strangely assorted guests.

The great religious revival that swept over the country in 1856 had reached to Chicago, and young Moody heartily enjoyed the opportunities and blessings it brought. Writing to his mother under date of January 6, 1857, he expressed great delight in the interest that was awakened, introducing the phrases current at the time.

"I have nothing to write that will interest you unless it is that there is a great revival of religion in this city," he says. "I go to meeting every night. Oh, how I do enjoy it! It seems as if God was here Himself. Oh, mother, pray for us. Pray that this work may go on until every knee is bowed. I wish there could be a revival in Northfield, that many might be brought into the fold of Christ. Oh, mother, keep the family away from the Spiritualists' meetings, for I am afraid they may be led astray.

"How did you spend New Year and Christmas? Oh, mother, I pray that this year may be the happiest of your life. It has commenced well with me; hope it will continue. Uncle Calvin urged me to come down and see him Christmas or New Year, but could not leave business. Now, mother, please excuse this short letter and write soon."

To this letter there is an amusing postscript indicating how readily this young man, under twenty years of age, had acquired the spirit of the place.

"Mother, you said in your letter that you were glad to hear that I was getting such good pay. I think you did not understand me, for I did not say I got that amount, but that I could make it soon. If I should build me a house out here that would cost me one hundred dollars, I could rent it for seventy-five dollars a year. That is making money; that is, if I was able to do it, you know."

Soon after his entering Wiswall's boot and shoe house a jobbing department was added to the business, which gave his ability still greater opportunities to display itself. He would carefully watch the depots and hotel registers for possible customers from neighboring towns, and took pride in making better and larger sales than his fellow-clerks. It was his ambition at this time to be worth $100,000—a fortune in those days. His early training had inured him to hardship and had taught him the strictest economy, so that he seemed in a fair way to reach his goal in a reasonably short time.

His success as a salesman in the city store so commended him to his employer that he was soon sent out to represent the firm as a commercial traveller. In this capacity he had many exciting experiences. On one occasion, in order to reach a newly settled frontier town, Mr. Moody had to hire a pair of livery horses to make the trip. All went well until, in driving down a steep hill, the hold-back straps were found to be too loose, allowing the wheels of the carriage to strike the horses' heels. The team immediately became unmanageable and bolted. So long as the driver could keep them in the road all was well. But when at last they dashed out of the roadway into a tract that had been recently cleared of heavy timber, it required unusual nerve power and physical strength to guide them safely. In telling the story years afterward, Mr. Moody used to say that it was the most exciting ride he ever had.

"Standing up in the buggy with my hat gone and my hair on end, I was just able to dodge the huge stumps and get my team back into the road, where at last a steep hill damped the ardor of the horses."

To the duties of a commercial traveller there was added in those days the work of a collector. When the rumor was circulated that any firm was likely to fail, each creditor immediately sent his representative to collect as quickly as possible the amount that was due him. An assignment, in which all creditors share equally, is a practice of later date. On one such occasion Moody was sent to a neighboring town late on Saturday afternoon to collect a debt from a shoe dealer whose credit was under suspicion. There was one other firm to which this country merchant was deeply indebted, and Moody discovered their representative on the train. Now it was against Moody's principles to travel on Sunday, and he had planned to spend Sunday somewhere en route, and start on again early Monday morning. The other collector was not hampered by any such scruples, and intended to arrive Sunday and secure his claim early on Monday morning. Where a principle was involved Moody would never hesitate, but his business pride made it hard for him to see his competitor win so easily, and he determined to do what he could to gain an even chance. In those early days of railway travel "through service" was not common, "changes" being frequent. At one of these changes Moody got his companion to take a walk with him, and succeeded in holding his attention in conversation until he lost his train, with the result that the claims were entered on equal terms on the same day.

In a letter home, written at this time, he said:

"I suppose you would like to know how I am doing. Well, I am doing first-rate. Shall be on there in the summer, if not before. I came very near going last week. A man offered to pay my way if I would go with him to buy some goods, but Mr. Wiswall was so driven for help that he could not spare me. I should like to come back to the Bay State once more. Things don't look out here as they do in Boston. A good many of the stores are kept open on the Sabbath-day. It is a great holiday out here."

In another letter he writes:

"I have made thirty dollars a week ever since I came out here. . . . Don't let Uncle Samuel get hold of it, but as it has turned out, I have done the very best thing in coming. My expenses are high, but I can make more money than in Boston. I will send you a bill of fare of the house where I board, and then you can judge whether I shall starve or not."

"I can make more money here in a week than I could in Boston in a month," he writes to his brother George at this time, "but that is not all. I find the better I live the more enjoyment I have, and the more I think of God and His love the less I think of the world's troubles. George, don't let anything keep you from the full enjoyment of God's love. I think we have things sometimes come upon us to try our faith, and God likes to see us cling on. As the Psalmist says in one place, God likes to chastise them whom He

MOODY'S BODY GUARD.

The crude material from which he evolved his first Sunday-school class in Chicago.

WILL IT PAY?

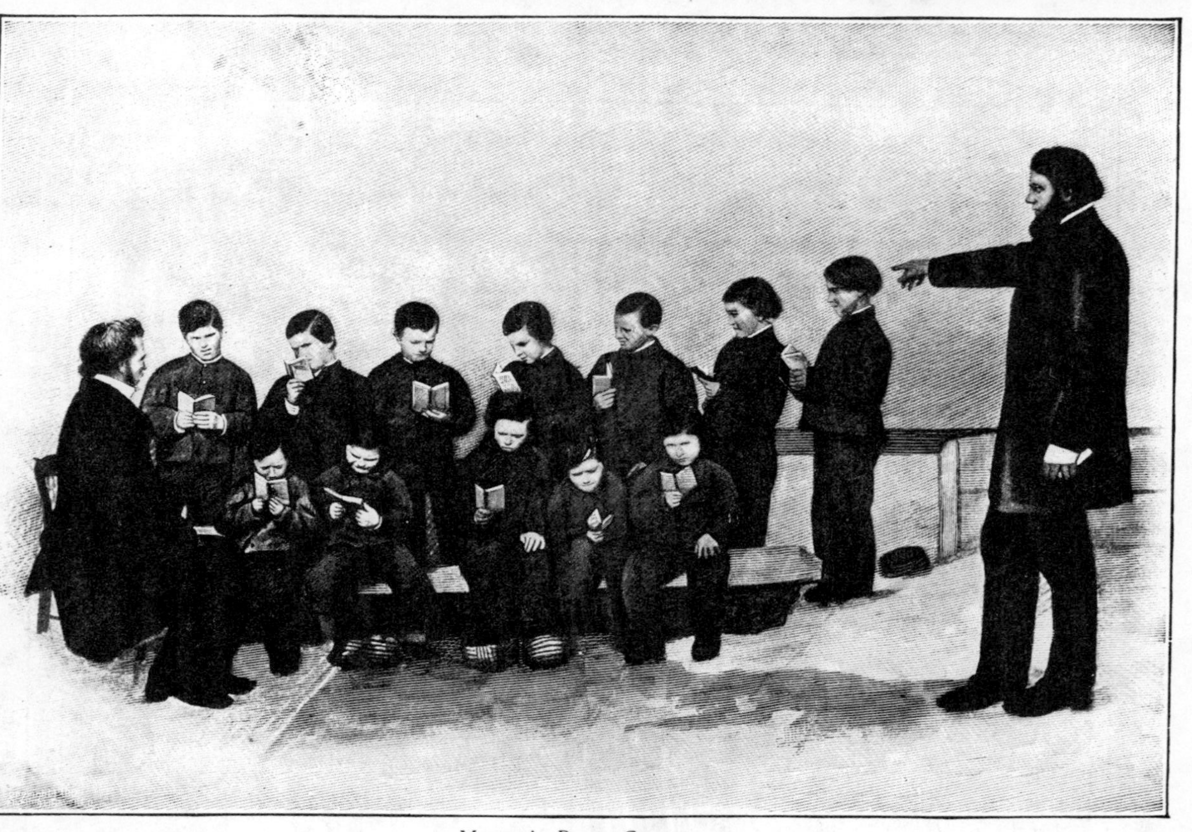

MOODY'S BODY GUARD.

D. L. Moody's first Sunday-school class in Chicago.

loves. So let us pray for each other. I have brought you before God in my prayers, and I hope you have done the same for me."

The many temptations of city life appealed strongly to the ambitious young man, but realizing them fully, he was always on his guard. The following letter, written to his mother in the spring of 1858, illustrates how keenly he felt his situation at that time:

"I have a good position, and I mean to work my cards to make it better. I have been very successful so far, and if nothing happens I shall do well. Luther (his brother) thought it was very foolish in my leaving Wiswall's, but I have got a situation that is worth five of that. If I have my health and my God is with me, I shall succeed better here in Chicago than I ever thought. Mother, I hope you will not forget to pray for your son here in the West, surrounded by temptations on all sides. I never worked in a place since my conversion where there were so many young men as here. I hope you will plead with God that I may live a consistent Christian before them. I am in hope to live so before them that I may succeed in winning their souls to Christ. Pray for me, dear mother."

Mention should be made of the good influence of Moody's landlady, "Mother Phillips," as she was commonly called. Her hearty sympathy was a help that he always deeply appreciated. The friendships he formed in her house at this time with other young men, who, like himself, were just beginning their careers in the Western metropolis, lasted to the end of his life. Among the number were men whose names have since become prominent, not only as foremost citizens of Chicago, but as some of the successful men of the country, including Edward Isham, Norman Williams, Levi Z. Leiter, Gen. George V. Smith, Gen. John L. Thompson, Benjamin B. Page, and William H. Seward. In speaking of his early friend, Mr. Isham said recently:

"Moody was an exceedingly earnest, active, and forceful man, strenuous in all his activities; but he was at the same time a broad-minded, generous-hearted, affectionate man, dear to all who knew him. He was the same in early days as later, and every one of the circle remained fond of him to the very end, no matter how much he differed from him in opinion."

As an illustration of the way in which Mr. Moody continually had the spiritual welfare of his friends on his mind, one of them recently related the following incident:

"The last time I saw him was at the funeral of a common friend. After the services he went back to his hotel and wrote a four-page letter to me with sentences heavily underscored, following his usual line of thought. The letter was one of his efforts to pluck me out of the burning in which I suppose he considered me a brand."

CHAPTER V

First Attempts at Christian Work

ALTHOUGH Moody's Sunday mornings were occupied in securing young men to share his pews at Plymouth Church, his Sunday afternoons and evenings were free. His indomitable energy seemed to need no " day of rest," and a good night's sleep was always sufficient to recuperate the utmost drain upon his strength. Even in later days he was wont to associate rest, not with inactivity, which he considered most wearisome, but with some change of occupation. " How I do pity people who hang about these summer resorts doing nothing! My! it would send me crazy!" he would often exclaim.

He soon solved the problem of occupying his leisure hours on Sunday afternoon by taking up Sunday-school work. Shortly after arriving in Chicago he discovered a little mission Sunday-school on North Wells Street, where he applied for a class. The supply of teachers at that time was in excess of scholars, and the applicant was told that the sixteen teachers were found amply sufficient to instruct twelve children, but that they would welcome his services if he could provide his own class. This was exactly to young Moody's taste, and on the following Sunday he arrived at the school leading a procession of eighteen little " hoodlums " that he had gathered. This success made his special calling clear to him, and he continued to gather new scholars for others to teach, feeling that he was not sufficiently gifted for that work himself.

Through his persistent efforts the Wells Street Sunday-school grew to larger proportions, until its accommodations were well taxed. The experience he gained here in building up the attendance of a Sabbath-school, and in its organization and administration, proved most valuable.

At this time he made the acquaintance of the one who, four years later, became his wife, Emma C. Revell, at this time a girl of fifteen, and a teacher in the school.

Feeling that his success in the Wells Street Mission pointed to greater undertakings, Mr. Moody, in the fall of 1858, determined to begin another mission school on a larger scale in another part of the city. The same success attended these efforts, and it was soon found that a large hall would be necessary to accommodate the attendance. Such a place was secured in the North Market Hall, a public hall over one of the large city markets of Chicago. Here, in company with his friends, Mr. Moody began the Sunday-school work which developed later into the Illinois Street Church, afterwards the Chicago Avenue Church, in which he held membership during the later years of his life.

From a description of the building given by Mr. John T. Dale, an early teacher in the school, it was neither attractive in appearance nor clean. "It was a large, dingy, dilapidated-looking brick building on the outside, while the inside was a great grimy hall with blackened walls and ceiling, and as bare and uninviting as can be imagined. But it was soon crowded to the doors with classes of boys and girls of a type entirely new to me; largely the gamins of the streets, bold, restless, inquisitive youngsters, whose wardrobe was often limited to trousers, shirt, and suspenders—even these in a very advanced stage of decay. The scholars were bubbling over with mischief and exuberance of vitality and sorely tried the patience of the teachers; but the singing was a vent for their spirits, and such singing I had never heard before. The boys who sold papers in the street had an indescribable lung power, and the rest seemed not far behind. There must have been five or six hundred scholars, and it was no easy task to govern such a boisterous crowd, but the teachers seemed to interest their classes, and the exercises passed off with great enthusiasm.

"At the close of the school Mr. Moody took his place at the door and seemed to know personally every boy and girl; he shook hands and had a smile and a cheery word for each. They crowded about him tumultuously, and his arm must have ached many a time after those meetings. It was easy to see the hold he had on those young lives, and why they were drawn to that place week after week. The institution was a veritable hive of activity—meetings almost every evening, with occasional picnics and sociables, and services on the Sabbath that occupied most of the day."

In this "North Market Hall School," as it came to be generally called, Mr. Moody filled a variety of offices from that of janitor to superintendent. "Sunday was a busy day for me then," he would say in relating the story of the work. "During the week I would be out of town as a commercial traveller selling boots and shoes, but I would always manage to be back by Saturday night. Often it was late when I got to my room, but I would have to be up by six o'clock to get the hall ready for Sunday-school. Every Saturday night a German society held a dance there, and I had to roll out beer kegs, sweep up sawdust, clean up generally, and arrange the chairs. This I did not think it right to hire done on Sunday, so sometimes with the assistance of a scholar, and often without any, I would do it myself.

"This usually took most of the morning, and when it was done I would have to drum up the scholars and new boys and girls. By the time two o'clock came we would have the hall full, and then I had to keep order while the speaker for the day led the exercises. We had to keep things going to keep up the children's interest. When school was over I visited absent scholars and found out why they were not at Sunday-school, called on the sick, and invited the parents to attend the evening gospel service. By the time I had made my rounds the hour had come for the evening meeting, where I presided, and following that we had an after-meeting. By the time I was through the day

I was tired out. I didn't know much at that time, for after going from early morning till late at night with only a few crackers and some cheese, I was faint and fatigued. Sometimes after such a day's work I thought I sinned in going to sleep over my prayers, when really I was a fool for neglecting the dictates of common sense. God is not a hard taskmaster, and in later years I have learned that to do your best work you cannot afford to neglect the common laws of health."

It was not Mr. Moody's plan to act as superintendent of the school. He wisely associated with himself John V. Farwell, at that time the largest dry-goods merchant in the city; Isaac H. Burch, president of one of the banks, and others. These gentlemen assisted him, and in turn superintended the school, contributing largely to the success which followed. At no time in his life was Mr. Moody willing to submit to traditional methods if they did not appear to him to be as effective as others of a modern or even an original kind. He was fond of quoting an old Scotch saying: "They say! What do they say? Let them say!" This spirit manifested itself in the North Market School, where "the order of exercises" was never determined by any prearranged programme. Mr. Moody or some other helper would read a passage of Scripture, sing a hymn, tell an anecdote—anything to fill up the time.

The plan by which the unsuccessful teachers were dropped was as novel as it was effective. The rule of the school was that transfers of membership from one class to another could always be made by simply notifying the superintendent of the desired change, which inevitably resulted in the survival of the fittest among the teachers, as the effect of the children's liberty of choice. By degrees the school increased to fifteen hundred; and as new teachers enlisted, order and method grew rapidly. It was before the day of International Lessons, however, and scholars and teachers had but one text-book, the Bible, and denominational lines were not recognized.

Mr. Moody's devices for running the school were eminently successful. He issued stock certificates on the "North Market Sabbath-school Association; capital, $10,000; 40,000 shares at twenty-five cents each." These certified the purchase of shares "for the erection of a new building." "For dividends apply at the school each Sabbath at nine P.M."

Grace was the general rule of the school, but even here the exception proved the rule, and stern law on a few occasions vested in Mr. Moody the duties of sergeant-at-arms. On one such occasion a certain young "bully" seemed more than usually ill-behaved. He was a ringleader among the worst element in the town, and his persistent and malicious attempts to make disturbance caused great annoyance. In response to repeated warnings he only assumed a more threatening attitude and mocked at every effort to induce him to behave. It was against the rules to turn a scholar out, so that, grace having failed, Mr. Moody saw that recourse to law was inevitable, and said to Mr. Farwell:

"If that boy disturbs his class to-day, and you see me go for him and take him to the anteroom, ask the school to rise and sing a very loud hymn until I return."

The programme was executed as arranged. Mr. Moody seized the boy, hurried him into the anteroom before he realized what was happening, and locked the door. He gave the boy such a whipping as he himself had received in early life, and presently returned with face flushed, but with an expression of victory. The boy was converted soon afterwards, and years later acknowledged to a friend that he was still enjoying the benefits of that gospel exercise.

The school grew steadily till it was among the largest in Chicago. President Lincoln's visit to the school when on his way to Washington to enter on his first term of office was a memorable occasion. His popularity in Chicago assured him of a demonstrative welcome, and when, a few months later, the war broke out, the North Market Sunday-school contributed over fifty soldiers in answer to the President's first call for troops. Nor did the influences of this mission school and its consecrated leader become dissipated by time or distance. Not only in the army but wherever members of this school were to be found the impress received was most manifest. An interesting incident is given by the Rev. John Vetter, who says:

"In the autumn of 1863, as a home missionary, I was on a tour in northern Michigan. Arriving at the county seat of M—— County, I inquired about the gospel needs of the place. There was no meeting-house, no preaching. On inquiring about Sunday-school, the man, with some hesitation, as though not quite certain, said: 'Well, yes, a Sunday-school was started last Sunday by a little girl.' I quickly went to her father's house. Mary was all animation telling me about Mr. Moody and the Sunday-school in North Market Hall. Mr. Moody's photograph was hanging on the wall, and another of sixteen street boys with their street names, only one of which I now recall—'Butcher Bill.' I must say that I was taken a little by surprise. I had not heard of D. L. Moody at that time. But her face was all aglow as she spoke of the Sunday-school in Chicago to which she had belonged, and from which she was now so far away. Evidently she had caught Mr. Moody's enthusiasm. Captain Richardson had arrived here with his family but two weeks before, and now a Sunday-school is started by this girl in her teens. Since their arrival here a little child had died in the neighborhood. They were about to bury it without funeral exercises; but Mary proposed to read some Scripture, sing, and pray, which she did to the satisfaction of all. Richardson bought a pony for his daughter, so she was enabled to go to the next town, five miles distant, and organize another Sunday-school, where preaching was established soon after, with a revival following that swept the place. An account of this experience appeared in one of the religious papers at the time.

"During the following summer, having occasion to be in Chicago, a friend asked if I would not like to go to Mr. Moody's Sunday-school in North Market Hall. Having met Mary Richardson, an interest had been awakened to see the man she had described so glowingly.

On being introduced, he at once asked: 'Are you not the man whose account of Mary's work in Michigan I saw in the papers last year? Now, I want you to tell this Sunday-school all about what she is doing. Right over there (pointing toward the northwest corner of the hall) is her Sunday-school class, and there is where she was converted.'"

The Sunday-school of six hundred and its corps of teachers was an enlivening scene. It was a veritable beehive.

Although it had begun with children, the work extended to the parents, and from the mission school of "hoodlums" in North Market Hall a work developed that began to demand more time and effort than the young commercial traveller could give and still continue his business. Gospel meetings were conducted during the week in a room formerly used for a saloon, but which had been made over into a mission hall, and here Dwight L. Moody received the practice and training in preaching that were of such incalculable value in later years.

And it seems that he needed this training, for he attained his powers of extempore speaking only gradually. It is of interest in this connection to know that when he first rose to speak in prayer-meeting one of the deacons assured him that he would, in his opinion, serve God best by keeping still!

Another critic, who commended his zeal in filling the pews he had hired in Plymouth Church, suggested that he should realize the limitations of his vocation and not attempt to speak in public.

"You make too many mistakes in grammar," he complained.

"I know I make mistakes," was the reply, "and I lack a great many things, but I'm doing the best I can with what I've got."

He paused and looked at the man searchingly, adding with his own irresistible manner:

"Look here, friend, you've got grammar enough—what are you doing with it for the Master?"

CHAPTER VI

Giving up Business

"THE greatest struggle I ever had in my life was when I gave up business," Mr. Moody often said. The steadily increasing duties in his pioneer religious work had not prevented his success in business, and though manager of the largest Sunday-school in the country, he could hold this position without detriment to the interests of his employer. In 1858 he entered the establishment of C. N. Henderson, a wholesale boot and shoe dealer, where he worked on commission. This gave him greater freedom to use a part of his time in Christian work without encroaching upon his employer's rights. His warm esteem for his employer, whose friendship he thoroughly appreciated, is shown in the following extract from a letter to his mother, written January 2, 1859:

"On my return from the country last week I found my hopes all vanished. The one to whom I had looked for advice and counsel, who had proved to be more than a friend to me, was dead. That man was my employer, Mr. Henderson. I shall miss him very much. He was the truest friend I have met since I left home. He seemed to take as much interest in my welfare as he would in the welfare of his own son."

That this feeling was fully reciprocated is indicated by the fact that a year later Mrs. Henderson insisted on Moody's settling up her husband's business. A young man of twenty-three years, he shrank from the responsibility of handling an estate worth $150,000. "But I feel greatly honored," he wrote his mother, "for they had a great many friends who are good business men. I never have been put in so responsible a position in my life, and my prayer is that I will do myself credit. Do not say anything about this, will you? I am in hopes that you will not forget to pray for me, for I am nothing without the same God who has been with me since I started out in life."

About this time he was actively connected with a Congregational church on the North Side. The meetings were too slow for Moody, and he went to some good brother and asked him if, at the next meeting, he would not get up and be the first to speak. He said he would. Mr. Moody then went to others, and engaged three to be the second speaker and three others to be third. When the first man had spoken the others followed, several rising at once. This unusual sight inspired the meeting with the enthusiasm of a revival, and was really the beginning of a great quickening of spiritual interest in the church.

In 1860 he was working for Buel, Hill & Granger, and had saved $7,000 towards the $100,000 which had been his early ambition. In one single year he made, by special commissions, in addition to his regular salary, over $5,000, an unusually large sum for a young man under twenty-four.

It was a time of great excitement in the nation. Abraham Lincoln had been nominated and elected President, and, like the young men who were his associates, Mr. Moody was immersed in business and politics, and keenly alive to all the events of the hour. He had an experience at this time, however, that entirely transformed his career and led him to devote himself exclusively to Christian work. All ambitions for wealth were sacrificed, but not until the struggle had lasted three long months. Finally what he felt to be the call of God was triumphant, and he surrendered his own plans for his Father's.

How he came to give up business altogether may best be told in his own words:

"I had never lost sight of Jesus Christ since the first time I met

Him in the store in Boston, but for years I really believed that I could not work for God. No one had ever asked me to do anything.

"When I went to Chicago I hired four pews in a church, and used to go out on the street and pick up young men and fill these pews. I never spoke to the young men about their souls; that was the work of the elders, I thought. After working for some time like that, I started a mission Sunday-school. I thought numbers were everything, and so I worked for numbers. When the attendance ran below one thousand it troubled me, and when it ran to twelve or fifteen hundred I was elated. Still none were converted; there was no harvest.

"Then God opened my eyes.

"There was a class of young ladies in the school who were, without exception, the most frivolous set of girls I ever met. One Sunday the teacher was ill, and I took that class. They laughed in my face, and I felt like opening the door and telling them all to go out and never come back.

"That week the teacher of the class came into the store where I worked. He was pale and looked very ill.

"'What is the trouble?' I asked.

"'I have had another hemorrhage from the lungs. The doctor says I cannot live on Lake Michigan, so I am going back to New York State. I suppose I am going to die.'

"He seemed greatly troubled, and when I asked the reason he replied:

"'Well, I have never led any of my class to Christ. I really believe I have done the girls more harm than good.'

"I had never heard any one talk like that before, and it set me thinking.

"After a while I said: 'Suppose you go and tell them how you feel. I will go with you in a carriage, if you want to go.'

"He consented, and we started out together. It was one of the best journeys I ever had on earth. We went to the house of one of the girls, called for her, and the teacher talked to her about her soul. There was no laughing then. Tears stood in her eyes before long. After he had explained the way of life, he suggested that we have a word of prayer. He asked me to pray. True, I had never done such a thing in my life as to pray God to convert a young lady there and then. But we prayed, and God answered our prayer.

"We went to other houses. He would go upstairs and be all out of breath, and he would tell the girls what he had come for. It wasn't long before they broke down and sought for salvation.

"When his strength gave out I took him back to his lodgings. The next day we went out again. At the end of ten days he came to the store with his face literally shining.

"'Mr. Moody,' he said, 'the last one of my class has yielded herself to Christ.'

"I tell you we had a time of rejoicing.

"He had to leave the next night, so I called his class together that night for a prayer-meeting, and there God kindled a fire in my soul that has never gone out. The height of my ambition had been to be a successful merchant, and if I had known that meeting was going to take that ambition out of me, I might not have gone. But how many times I have thanked God since for that meeting!

"The dying teacher sat in the midst of his class, and talked with them, and read the fourteenth chapter of John. We tried to sing 'Blest be the tie that binds,' after which we knelt to pray. I was just rising from my knees when one of the class began to pray for her dying teacher. Another prayed, and another, and before we rose the whole class had prayed. As I went out I said to myself:

"'Oh, God, let me die rather than lose the blessing I have received to-night!'

"The next evening I went to the depot to say good-bye to that teacher. Just before the train started, one of the class came, and before long, without any prearrangement, they were all there. What a meeting that was! We tried to sing, but we broke down. The last we saw of that teacher, he was standing on the platform of the rear car, his finger pointing upward, telling that class to meet him in Heaven."

Having the sum saved during his business career, Mr. Moody decided to live on this as long as it lasted. If at the end of this time the Lord continued to reward his labor, thus indicating that it was the right course to continue, he believed that the means for it would be provided.

He began to economize at once in every possible manner, leaving his comfortable boarding-place with its congenial associates and sleeping in the prayer-meeting room of the Young Men's Christian Association. He took his meals in cheap restaurants, and lived in a way that would have killed a man of ordinary constitution. He would often say in later years, speaking of those days, " I was an older man before thirty than I have ever been since. A man's health is too precious to be as carelessly neglected as was mine."

He now had time to conduct his Sunday-school work more systematically and visit his scholars in their homes. This was an adventurous proceeding, for in some of the Roman Catholic families he was anything but a welcome caller. But he persisted fearlessly in the work, and won many a family that at first received his invitations to North Market Hall or his mission hall with the bitterest contempt.

In his Christian work, as formerly in business, Moody had little regard for strict conventionalities that did not appeal to his very practical judgment as useful or effective, and many a strange position did he find himself in when he undertook to secure his object without consideration of what was the regular but less immediate method. Often he would hail children on the street, inviting them to his Sunday-school, and would ask an introduction to their parents to secure their consent to the children becoming members.

One Sunday afternoon he met a little girl, of whom he inquired where she attended Sunday-school. As she was not a regular attendant anywhere, Moody asked to be introduced to her mother, to secure permission for the family to attend his school. The child had reasons for not wanting to have Mr. Moody find her home, as she knew who he was. Asking him to wait on the corner for her till she had done the errand on which she had been sent, she disappeared, not to return.

For three hours he waited on the street corner for the little truant before he gave her up at last. Some days later he saw the girl again, and the recognition was mutual. Without waiting to explain why she had deserted him on the former occasion the child turned and fled. At this time the city's system of drainage had just been changed, necessitating the elevation by several feet of the streets in a large portion of the city. In some cases the property owners had not only elevated their houses, but had built new sidewalks on a level with the raised street. In this transition period from low to high grade these innovations had been frequent but irregular, and the connections between old sidewalk levels and new ones were made by a few raised steps. Up and down these sidewalks the girl ran, while close behind her followed the determined Sunday-school teacher. Finally she darted into a saloon, and through the barroom into a little room, and finally upstairs, where he found her hiding under a bed. Having persuaded the child to come out, he was duly introduced to the mother, explained the purpose of his call, and the children were secured for the North Market Hall.

The sad story of the family was afterward confided to Mr. Moody, when he learned that the mother was a widow who had only recently lost her husband. He had come to Chicago to make his fortune, and having failed to secure employment at his trade as a carpenter, had finally opened a saloon. Soon after he had died, leaving this saloon as the only means of support to his widow and children, who had never become reconciled to the business and felt ashamed of this way of gaining a livelihood. This explained the child's unwillingness to have Mr. Moody know where she lived. In time the widow and her children were led into the way of a better life, the saloon was closed, and years afterward Mr. Moody met, in a Western city, the little girl who had given him that wild chase, a woman now, the wife of an earnest Christian, and herself devoted to church work.

A source of very great annoyance to Mr. Moody in his pioneer Sunday-school work at this time was the frequent disturbances which came from the lower class of the Roman Catholic element. Many of the boys would try to interfere with the meetings—broken windows and such disturbances being not the least troublesome expression of their disapproval. At last he felt that extreme measures must be taken, and he called on Bishop Duggan, who was prelate of that diocese. It was not an easy matter to gain access to so high a church dignitary, and a maid who answered his call at the door was not ready to promise him the audience he requested. Bishop Duggan, he was told, was busy and could not be seen, but young Moody had taken the precaution to step over the threshold and was not so easily thwarted. "Well, never mind," he said, "I will remain until he is at leisure," and without waiting for further invitation quietly passed into the hallway.

The maid was not at all sure that the bishop would care to be interviewed by the self-constituted missionary, but it was useless to attempt to dissuade him. He had come to see the bishop, and would wait if necessary for the remainder of the day or until the bishop could find it convenient to give him a hearing. When at length the bishop appeared in the hall, the young man very briefly related his mission, and said that he was engaged in a work for children in a part of the city that was being neglected by everybody else. It was therefore a pity, he said, that he should not be allowed to continue the work unmolested, and he requested the bishop to give orders to the parish priests to prevent all future interferences.

Bishop Duggan refused to believe that any of his people were to blame for the disturbances, to which Moody answered that his only reason for believing that the boys were Roman Catholics was their own statement to that effect. Bishop Duggan then replied that they

MR. MOODY AT 25: CITY MISSIONARY IN CHICAGO.

MR. MOODY AT 27: SUNDAY-SCHOOL WORKER.

Mr. and Mrs. D. L. Moody in 1864 and in 1869.

represented the worst element in the church and that he had no control over them.

"Your zeal and devotion are most commendable in behalf of these people, however," he added, "and all you need to make you a great power for good is to come within the fold of the only true church."

"But," replied the young missionary, "whatever advantage that would give me among your people would be offset by the fact that I could no longer work among the Protestants."

"Why, certainly you could still work among the Protestants," was the reply.

"But surely you would not let me pray with a Protestant if I became a Roman Catholic."

"Yes," replied the Bishop, "you could pray with Protestants as much as ever."

"Well, I didn't know that," said the young man. "Would you, Bishop, pray with a Protestant?"

"Yes," said Bishop Duggan, "I would."

"Well, then," replied Mr. Moody, "I wish that you would pray for me now, that I may be led aright in this matter," and forthwith knelt where they had been standing in the hall. The Bishop and Mr. Moody both prayed.

The result of that short conference was a cessation of all further annoyance from the Roman Catholic element in the city, and a lifelong friendship between the two men.

But his efforts were not always attended with such immediate success. A man does not gain the strength to conquer others in a series of rapid victories alone, and often the result of his most earnest work was apparently little or nothing.

On his way home from meeting one night Mr. Moody saw a man leaning against a lamp-post. Stepping up to him and placing his hands on his shoulders, he said:

"Are you a Christian?"

The man flew into a rage, doubled up his fists, and it seemed for a moment as if the missionary might be pitched into the gutter.

"I'm very sorry if I have offended you," said Mr. Moody.

"Mind your own business!" roared the man.

"That is my business," the other replied quietly, and went on his way.

About three months later, on a bitter cold morning at daybreak, some one knocked at Mr. Moody's door.

"Who's there?" he asked.

A strange voice answered, and he said, "What do you want?"

"I want to become a Christian," was the reply.

Mr. Moody opened the door, and, to his astonishment, there was the man who had cursed him for talking to him as he leaned against the lamp-post.

"I'm very sorry," said the man. "I haven't had any peace since that night. Your words have haunted and troubled me. I couldn't sleep last night, and I thought I would come and get you to pray for me." That man accepted Christ, and the moment he had done so asked:

"What can I do for Him?"

He taught in the Sabbath-school until the war broke out, when he enlisted, and was one of the first to be shot down, but not before he had given his testimony for God.

CHAPTER VII

City Missionary Work

THE compiler of a city directory is not expected to act as an historian, but the variety of occupations there accredited to Mr. Moody between 1858 and 1869 is not without significance. He had arrived in Chicago too late in 1856 for his name to appear in the directory of the succeeding year, and the first record is found in 1858, when he was in the employ of Mr. Wiswall. This item reads: "Moody, Dwight L., clerk, boards 255 Wabash Avenue." A year later it is "Salesman, C. H. Henderson & Co., boards 81 Michigan Avenue," and in 1860, Mr. Henderson having died, he is entered as "Salesman, Buel, Hill & Granger, boards 81 Michigan Avenue." From this time on the agent recorded him first as a "librarian" in the Young Men's Christian Association, then as a "city missionary," and in 1865 he is entered as a "Pastor of Illinois Street Church." In 1867 his occupation is designated as "president Young Men's Christian Association," and the last entry, in 1872, is as "superintendent" of the North Side Tabernacle.

Mr. Moody was always a law unto himself, and the independent and unusual way in which he entered Christian work made it difficult for the directory agent to place him exactly, so, for want of a better title, he was "librarian," "city missionary," or "pastor," as the case might be. The truth of the matter was that Mr. Moody had laid up sufficient money to support himself for some time, and entered Christian work without a salary, turning his back upon an income of over five thousand dollars a year, at the age of twenty-four. During the first year he received about three hundred dollars from friends who had become interested in his work, and by strict economy he hoped to make his savings last some years. Beyond that he planned for nothing, for he felt confident that since the Lord had called him to the work He would support him in it: if such support should fail, moreover, he could go back to selling shoes—had not St. Paul made tents while he preached the Gospel?

And so he began his work, with no Board at his back, no society to guarantee his salary: his dependence was on God.

Beginning his mission work with children, he had gradually, as has been described, gained access to their homes, and unconsciously entered regular evangelistic work before he knew it. It would be difficult to state exactly when he began that special service in which later he became so widely known, as it was rather a developed gift than an ability suddenly displayed.

To aid him in his visiting, Mr. Moody bought a little Indian pony, known as his "missionary horse." The pony was of course a source of special enjoyment to the children, and, by giving rides to the younger ones, was made to contribute to the popularity of "Moody's Sunday-school," as the North Market Hall School had now come to be called.

It was not an uncommon sight to see him on one of his missionary trips with one or two children behind him on the horse, a little one in his arms, and more crowding about seeking the "next turn." Many stories are told of that wonderful pony, among others how Moody, riding at full speed, seized a rather boisterous, mischievous boy who had been throwing stones at him, and lifting him up by the coat collar, placed him across his saddle and carried him two or three blocks, securing thereby his lasting respect.

In those days young Moody did not always receive the sympathy and respect which came to him only as the reward of years of trial in many critical experiences. Writing of those early days, his friend and most intimate associate in evangelistic work, Major D. W. Whittle, thus describes him:

"It must have been in the spring of 1859 that, as I was passing up Clark Street in Chicago, some one on the sidewalk said, 'There goes "Crazy Moody."' I turned, looked down the street, and saw a young man of about twenty-one, short and stocky in figure, weighing about one hundred and fifty pounds. He was riding a small pony, his trousers in his bootlegs, a cap on his head, and as I watched him he reined up to the sidewalk in front of the Methodist Block, at the corner of Clark and Washington streets. I was two years younger than Mr. Moody, and had been in Chicago since April 1, 1857. We were both from the Connecticut Valley in Massachusetts, but had known nothing of each other in the East. I had been interested to some degree in the revival meetings of 1857 and 1858, and had heard how Moody was visiting houses, building up a mission school, talking to people on the streets, and doing all sorts of eccentric things. The newspapers were full of jokes about him, and he was called by the reporters 'Brother Moody.' Like many others, I had the impression that he was crazy. How little I thought as I looked at him that day that my life would be influenced by him and his wonderful career!

"It was during his last summer, as we were talking of the death of Norman Williams, whose funeral he had recently attended, that we spoke of those early days when he had first known Mr. Williams. At that time his ambition had been to become one of the successful merchants of the city; he had devoted himself with great energy to go ahead of all the band of young men with whom he was associated, to sell more goods than any of them. 'There was only one of them but what I felt I could equal, and that was Marshall Field,' he used to say."

It was just at this time that he won the heart of the one who two years later became his wife. It is not permitted the writer to offer to one still living the credit that her heroism, faith, and affectionate devotion deserve, but it may be simply stated that in Emma C. Revell Dwight L. Moody found his greatest human resource. To her wise counsel he gave more heed than to that of any other, and he never failed to express to those nearest him the inestimable debt he owed to "the best wife God ever gave to a man."

It was when he had renounced worldly ambitions and, contrary to the advice of all his friends, had launched out into what was considered a wild undertaking, that she, a girl of only seventeen, promised to cast in her lot with his—a promise fulfilled two years later by their marriage in 1862. Her educational advantages had been greater than his, and she became his most able assistant in every undertaking. No trial was so severe, no burden so heavy, that he could not find in her one whose fellowship afforded the warmest sympathy and whose faith and self-sacrifice could be counted on. In many ways she served to balance his impetuous nature, and he would often acknowledge the helpful service her judgment had been and regret on occasion that he had acted without first consulting her.

Although Mr. Moody now gave a great deal of time to evangelistic meetings, sometimes speaking himself, but more often securing other speakers, he did not neglect the recruiting of students for his Sunday-school, and to keep the interest from flagging he had recourse to every device for sustaining its popularity. He used to make much of picnics, entering into the spirit of them with as great zest as the youngest child. He was not only an unusually strong man, but also a very fast runner. At one of these picnics he picked up a barrel nearly filled with apples, and holding it so that the apples would spill out, he ran ahead, followed by the boys, who gathered up the fruit as it dropped.

Among the premiums for good conduct and regular attendance, one summer season, thirteen boys were promised a new suit each at Christmas if they would attend regularly until that time. Their descriptive names were indicative of their social status, which may be judged from the following list: Red Eye, Smikes, Madden the Butcher, Jackey Candles, Giberick, Billy Blucannon, Darby the Cobbler, Butcher Lilray, Greenhorn, Indian, Black Stove Pipe, Old Man, and Rag-Breeches Cadet. All but one fulfilled the conditions, and

Mr. Moody had them photographed " before " and " after " the donning of the suits, the pictures entitled, " Does it Pay? " and " It Does Pay! " This uniformed group became known as " Moody's bodyguard."

Thirteen years later one of Mr. Moody's friends called at a railway ticket-office. The agent, after looking at him curiously for a moment, asked him to step inside, and said:

" You do not seem to know me."

" No, I have not that pleasure."

" You know Mr. Moody's ' bodyguard '? "

" Yes, I have a picture of them at home."

" Well," said the agent, " when you go home take a square look at the ugliest of the lot, and you will see your humble servant, now a church member and heir to Mr. Moody in that work."

As the success of his evangelistic efforts began to be noticed Mr. Moody was addressed by friends in other cities soliciting his aid in behalf of wild or dissipated young men who had wandered to Chicago. Letters were received from all parts of the country in which parents, brothers, sisters, and friends pleaded with him to look up some wanderer and do what he could to save him, and no such appeal was made in vain. A friend, in describing this personal feature of Mr. Moody's work at this time, says:

" At one of these Sabbath evening services I saw one of the most distinguished lawyers of Illinois, from the heart of the State, sitting by the side of his son, who had been snatched as a brand from the burning by the earnest appeals and prayers of Moody. The lawyer had written to Moody to save his son if he could. Words cannot tell of the work accomplished in those days, nor describe the intense earnestness of the audiences nor the enthusiastic singing of the old evangelical hymns and the Sabbath-school tunes. If ever the Lord was praised from full hearts, it was at these meetings."

It was natural that a man so practical as Mr. Moody should have had a strong desire to see definite results. There were times when he became depressed if he failed to see immediate conversions, but he had lessons to learn here as in other matters. In a characteristic story he describes how he learned to put away doubt and discouragement.

"One Sunday," he says, "I had preached and there did not seem to be any result. On the Monday I was very much cast down. I was sitting in my study, brooding over my want of success, when a young man who conducted a Bible class of one hundred adults in my Sabbath-school called upon me. As he came in I could see he was away up on the mountain top, while I was down in the valley. Said he:

"'What kind of a day did you have yesterday?'

"'Very poor; I had no success, and I feel quite cast down. How did you get on?'

"'Oh, grandly! I never had a better day.'

"'What was your subject?'

"'I had the life and character of Noah. Did you ever preach on Noah? Did you ever study up his life?'

"'Well, no. I don't know that I ever made it a special duty. I thought I knew pretty well all there was in the Bible about him: you know it is all contained in a few verses.'

"'If you never studied it before you had better do it now,' said he. 'It will do you good. Noah was a wonderful character.'

"When the young man went away I got out my Bible and some other books and read ail I could find about Noah. I had not been reading long before the thought came stealing over me: 'Here is a man who toiled on for a hundred and twenty years and never had a single convert outside his own family. Yet he did not get discouraged.'

"I closed my Bible; the cloud had gone; I started out to a noon prayer-meeting. I had not been there long when a man got up and said he had come from a little town in Illinois. On the day before he had admitted a hundred young converts to church membership. As he was speaking I said to myself: 'I wonder what Noah would have given if he could have heard that! He never had any such results from *his* labors.'

"Then in a little while a man who sat right behind me stood up and said: 'I wish you would pray for me; I would like to become a Christian.' Thought I to myself: 'I wonder what Noah would have given if he had heard that! He never heard a single soul asking God for mercy, yet he did not get discouraged.'

"I have never hung my harp on the willows since that day. Let us ask God to take away the clouds and unbelief; let us get out of Doubting Castle; let us move forward courageously in the name of our God and expect to see results."

It is of these early days that Dr. H. C. Mabie writes: "I first met Mr. Moody in the fall of 1863, in Chicago. I had come into the city from my Illinois home on a farm, to enter the old University of Chicago as a student. I was then sixteen years old. Having been introduced to Mr. B. F. Jacobs, of Chicago, and Mr. J. R. Osgood, of Indianapolis, even then famous Sunday-school men and deeply interested in boys and young men, I was by them taken down to the Methodist Church Block to visit, for my first time, the daily noon prayer-meeting of the Young Men's Christian Association. This had become a famous meeting. It was conducted mostly by young laymen, the first meeting of its sort I had ever attended.

"As we passed in there was a stocky, bustling, Simon Peter sort of a man standing at the door and shaking hands with all who entered. He spoke an earnest word to each. At the close of the meeting this same man remained to speak and pray with an inquirer or two who had shown signs of interest during the meeting. This honest man was Mr. Moody, and it made an impression upon me for life. I had never before seen a layman so making it his business to press men into the Kingdom as he seemed to be doing. I had learned to expect that of ministers, but I had never seen a layman so dead in earnest; but I liked it. The entire uncommonness of the thing impressed me, and created in me a yearning to learn the divine art if it were possible.

It soon grew to be a mighty desire in me, and it was not many months until, in the summer vacation, I found myself in the midst of a great revival in my native town, some two hundred of the young people being gathered in. I was for three months immersed in the flood of this blessing. This was several years before I had any definite purpose formed to enter the ministry; indeed, I was never conscious of a formal resolution on that subject until I found myself, through the pressure exercised by others, ordained. I was simply set on fire by the contagion of such earnest lives as I had seen living before me in that circle of Chicago laymen of whom Mr. Moody was the leader, and others like Messrs. Jacobs, Bliss, Rockwell, and Cole were foremost. Having gotten a taste of their joy in soul-winning, I never lost it. It was they who made me feel the responsibility of the ordinary and every-day member of the church for the conversion of sinners as I had never before felt it.

"The Moody of later years, in his great evangelistic triumphs, was simply the Moody of that early time expanded, enlarged, manifolded by the thousand and one auxiliaries and coadjutors which, by his matchless magnetism, he ever continued to gather about him. He had the greatest power to set others to work, and thus multiply himself, of any man I ever knew.

"When, fourteen years later, as a young pastor in Boston, I was again brought into contact with him in his great tabernacle meetings in 1874, I once more came under his spell. It was but to find myself a willing learner at his feet in numberless services and inquiry meetings. His own force of will, greatly enlarged by his contact with eminent British workers, keyed to the high purpose of saving men, made us all feel we were enabled to do anything we ought to do so long as we were under his command. Hence, as we would obey his summons to go down into the lower Tremont Temple to deal with inquirers, or to the market men's meeting in Faneuil Hall, or to the shoe dealers' meeting on High Street, or where not, we confidently went, feeling we could not wholly fail because he sent us."

CHAPTER VIII

The Civil War and the Christian Commission

"I AM going to join the Christian Association to-morrow night," Mr. Moody had written to his brother under date of April 19, 1854, immediately after leaving home for Boston. "Then I shall have a place to go to when I want to go away anywhere, and I can have all the books I want to read free and only have to pay one dollar a year. They have a large room, and the smart men of Boston lecture to them for nothing, and they get up a question box." These attractions and benefits of the Young Men's Christian Association were keenly appreciated by young Moody from the first. On his arrival in Chicago he joined the Association, which had recently been organized in that city as one of the results of the revival movement, and took an active interest in the noonday prayer-meetings conducted under its auspices.

After giving up business he devoted much of his time to Association work, with which he was closely identified at the beginning of the Civil War.

In the days that followed the firing on Fort Sumter, Chicago, like all the other cities in the Union, felt the greatest excitement. Camp Douglas was formed near the southern limits of the city, and there recruits were massed and instructed. Among these new soldiers were a large number of "Moody's boys" of the North Market Hall. A company was also raised among his friends and former associates in business, and on all sides he was urged to enter the service of his country.

The cause of the Union appealed to him most strongly, for by all the traditions of his home and his New England training he was an ardent abolitionist. During his stay in Boston he listened frequently to the eloquence of such orators as William Lloyd Garrison, Wendell Phillips, and Elijah P. Lovejoy.

His uncle's boot and shoe store on Court Street was opposite the court-house, and there he joined in the mob that attempted the liberation of Anthony Burns, a fugitive slave. On this occasion the hot-headed youth of Boston were dispersed by the soldiers' musketry, but the event left an impression even greater than the eloquence of Faneuil Hall. Later, when an employee at Wiswall's boot and shoe store, the clerks from neighboring houses, who met frequently with Mr. Moody and his fellow-salesmen, constituted themselves into a lyceum, where the points of political difference between the North and South were warmly discussed by representatives of both sides.

In spite of all this he could not conscientiously enlist. "There has never been a time in my life when I felt that I could take a gun and shoot down a fellow-being. In this respect I am a Quaker," was his explanation. At the same time he was alive to the opportunity for doing good offered by the military camps, and at once assisted in forming an Army and Navy Committee of the Young Men's Christian Association, consisting of J. V. Farwell, B. F. Jacobs, and himself. Later this work was affiliated with the Northwestern Branch of the Christian Commission.

The first Christian work undertaken by the commission consisted of services held among the soldiers that passed through Chicago. On the forming of Camp Douglas a work was organized which resulted in the erection of a small temporary chapel, in which over fifteen hundred meetings were held. Edgar W. Hawley, who was among Mr. Moody's oldest associates in Christian work in Chicago, thus describes the beginning of this work:

"At one time there were about twelve thousand men there. Regiments were coming in and others going to the front all the time. The

Young Men's Christian Association had a chapel for the use of the men, where frequent meetings were held. The Western Branch of the Christian Commission included among its members J. V. Farwell, B. F. Jacobs, Mr. Moody, and several others. We issued an 'Army Hymn Book' with an American flag on the front page, and it was distributed freely among the soldiers. We visited the tents and barracks and found the men playing cards, and proposed to exchange our hymn-books for the cards. The soldiers agreed quickly enough; indeed, so numerous were these exchanges that several of the Young Men's Christian Association rooms were full of playing-cards which the men had surrendered. This camp was finally struck, the men having all gone to the war. General Grant had captured Fort Donelson and taken ten thousand Confederate prisoners, of whom about nine thousand were sent to Chicago and placed in Camp Douglas with a regiment of our men as guards. It was a period of popular apprehension, and the people of the city were very nervous. A week afterward, at the close of a Union prayer-meeting, Moody said to me:

"'Hawley, let us go down and hold a meeting there in the chapel with the prisoners.' It was about five miles down to the camp, and as we got near the entrance Moody said:

"'Hawley, here is a ministerial pass; take it.'

"'But how will you get in past the guard?'

"'In some way!' was the confident reply. The guard passed me right in, but Moody was halted by fixed bayonets.

"'Stand back!' came the stern order.

"'I am Moody, the president of the Young Men's Christian Association,' he explained to the soldier.

"'I don't care who you are; you can't get in here!' At that moment a captain who was passing stepped up and recognized the evangelist. To him Moody appealed.

"'Let me in,' he urged, 'for the work's sake.' The officer turned to the guard.

"'Let one of your men take Mr. Moody to headquarters; I will be responsible.' We marched in, Moody under military guard. On the matter being explained at headquarters the officer in charge said:

"'Well, seeing you are here and considering your object, you may stay, but don't repeat it. If you are not out of here by eight P.M. you go into the guard-house for the night.' We went to the chapel, arranged things, and invited the men. It was soon packed full. Turning to me with a twinkle in his eye, Moody said:

"'Now, Hawley, you preach.' I remonstrated and said I wasn't a minister.

"'But you came in on a ministerial pass and I didn't,' he persisted. So I quietly acquiesced, and we had an interesting service. Mr. Moody took charge, and it seemed as though the Spirit of the Lord came down upon these men with great power. They came forward to the altar—twenty, thirty, forty at a time. We closed the meeting and began inquiry work. Moody had the platform, and God used him wonderfully. The whole audience melted, and we saw strong men in tears. 'God is here!' Moody whispered to me.

"We looked at our watches. It was but a few seconds of eight, and we had to run to get out of camp, having no notion of passing a night in the guard-house. These meetings we kept up two or three weeks, and many were converted. We formed a Young Men's Christian Association branch at the camp, and there were many kind expressions of gratitude even from the higher officers, who were greatly pleased with the work."

In a letter to his mother, at this time, Moody wrote:

"I am now at work among the soldiers a good deal. I had a good time in Kentucky. The boys wanted to have me become their chaplain, but my friends would not let me go, so I shall remain in the city. . . . I would like to see you all and talk with you about my Saviour, who seems so near to me. Oh, what would life be without Christ! I sometimes get to looking down on this world of sin, but when I look to Jesus it makes me look up."

By gospel services, prayer-meetings, song services, distribution of

Bibles, books, and tracts, and by personal visitation, he tried to win the soldiers to Christ. He organized the Christians into "Bands of Brothers," who were to carry "the Banner of Christ" with them, and be loyal to one another and to their Divine Captain. The experiences gathered from this work constituted most efficient training for his later career as an evangelist. His sermons show many an evidence of the Christian Commission work in the numerous illustrations drawn from his interviews with the soldiers. Even camp phraseology left a permanent influence upon his vocabulary, and in organizing large conventions or conducting evangelistic campaigns he would call upon some worker to "reinforce" another, and would urge his associates to "press the fight all along the line."

The peculia urroundings and impressive conditions under which the work was conducted made it necessary to urge his hearers to accept immediate salvation, and this was ever afterwards a conspicuous feature of his manner of address. With wounded men, hovering between life and death, or with men on the march, resting in some place which they would have to leave the next day, it was, at least as far as he was concerned, the alternative of "now or never"; as he would not allow himself or them to be satisfied with "never," he bent his whole energies to "now."

He was on the ground ministering to the wounded after the battles of Pittsburg Landing, Shiloh, and Murfreesboro'; he was with the army at Chattanooga, and among the first to enter Richmond.

It was after one of these battles that the following incident occurred, which Mr. Moody himself frequently related:

"We were taking a large number of wounded men down the Tennessee River after the battle of Pittsburg Landing. A number of young men of the Christian Commission were with me, and I told them that we must not let a man die on the boat that night without telling him of Christ and Heaven.

"You know the cry of a wounded man is 'Water! water!' As we passed along from one to another giving them water, we tried to tell them of the water of life, of which if they would drink they would never die. I came to one man who had about as fine a face as I ever saw. I spoke to him, but he did not answer. I went to the doctor and said:

"'Doctor, do you think that man will recover?'

"'No, he lost so much blood before we got to him on the field that he fainted while we were amputating his leg. He will never recover.'

"I said: 'I can't find out his name, and it seems a pity to let him die without knowing who he is. Don't you think we can bring him to?'

"'You may give him a little brandy and water,' said the doctor; 'that will revive him if anything will.'

"I sat down beside him and gave him brandy and water every now and then. While I was waiting I said to a man near by:

"'Do you know this man?'

"'Oh, yes, that is my chum.'

"'Has he a father and mother living?'

"'He has a widowed mother.'

"'Has he any brothers or sisters?'

"'Two sisters; but he is the only son.'

"'What is his name?'

"'William Clark.'

"I said to myself that I could not let him die without getting a message for that mother. Presently he opened his eyes, and I said:

"'William, do you know where you are?'

"He looked around a little dazed, and then said: 'Oh, yes! I am on my way home to mother.'

"'Yes, you are on your way home,' I said; 'but the doctor says you won't reach your earthly home. I thought I'd like to ask you if you had any message for your mother.'

"His face lighted up with an unearthly glow as he said: 'Oh, yes, tell my mother that I died trusting in Jesus!'

"It was one of the sweetest messages I ever heard in my life!"

Certificate of Membership.

Office Young Men's Christian Association,

Chicago, Jany 26 1869

In hoc signo vinces.

THIS CERTIFIES That Henry A. Lyon is duly elected an Active Member of the CHICAGO YOUNG MEN'S CHRISTIAN ASSOCIATION from Jany 26 1869 to Jany 26 1870.

D. L. Moody President.

[illegible] Secretary

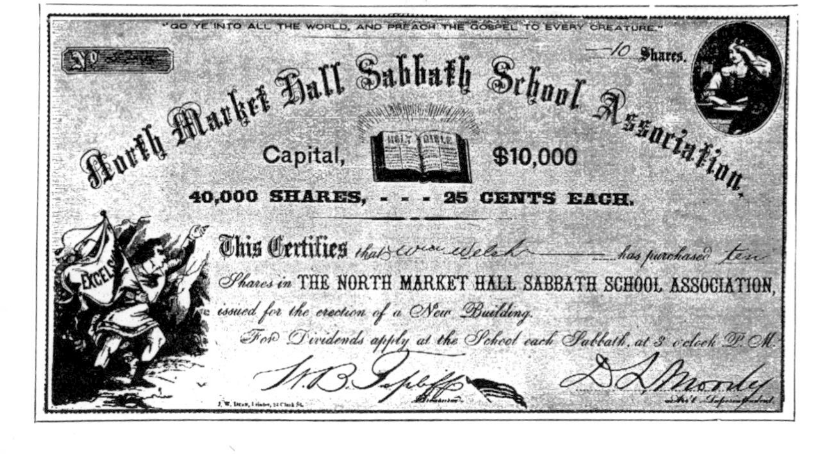

"GO YE INTO ALL THE WORLD, AND PREACH THE GOSPEL TO EVERY CREATURE."

No.

10 Shares.

North Market Hall Sabbath School Association.

Capital, $10,000

40,000 SHARES, - - - 25 CENTS EACH.

This Certifies that Wm Welch has purchased ten Shares in THE NORTH MARKET HALL SABBATH SCHOOL ASSOCIATION, issued for the erection of a New Building.

For Dividends apply at the School each Sabbath, at 3 o'clock P.M.

W. B. [illegible] Treasurer

D. L. Moody Ass't Superintendent

D. L. Moody During Early Years in Chicago.

On returning to Chicago Mr. Moody at once looked up the widowed mother and two sisters and delivered the message from the dying soldier. As he was leaving the house one of the sisters, only a child at the time, came to him and gave him the small savings of her sister and herself with the request that he purchase a Bible to give to some soldier. When he went back to the front Mr. Moody related this incident, asking who wanted that Bible, and there were a number of petitions for it.

Soon after God called the children to join their brother, but not till their childish ministry had been used as a blessing to many a soldier.

Another war incident that Mr. Moody frequently repeated occurred after the battle of Murfreesboro'. "I was stationed in the hospital," he said. "For two nights I had been unable to get rest, and being really worn out, on the third night I had lain down to sleep. About midnight I was called to see a wounded soldier who was very low. At first I tried to put the messenger off, but he told me that if I waited till morning it might be too late. So I went to the ward where I had been directed, and found the man who had sent for me. I shall never forget his face as I saw it that night in the dim, uncertain candle-light. I asked what I could do for him, and he said that he wanted me to 'help him to die.' I told him I would bear him in my arms into the Kingdom of God if I could, but I couldn't. Then I tried to preach the Gospel. He only shook his head and said:

"'He can't save me; I have sinned all my life.'

"My thoughts went back to his loved ones in the North, and I thought that even then his mother might be praying for her boy. I repeated promise after promise, and prayed with the dying man, but nothing I said seemed to help him. Then I said that I wanted to read to him an account of an interview that Christ had one night while here on earth—an interview with a man who was anxious about his eternal welfare. I read from the third chapter of John, how Nicodemus came to the Master. As I read on, his eyes became riveted upon me, and he seemed to drink in every syllable. When I came to the words, '*As Moses lifted up the serpent in the wilderness, even so must the Son of Man be lifted up: that whosoever believeth in Him should not perish, but have eternal life,*' he stopped me and asked:

" 'Is that there?'

" 'Yes,' I said.

" 'Well,' he said, 'I never knew that was in the Bible. Read it again.' Leaning on his elbow on the side of the cot, he brought his hands together tightly, and when I finished he exclaimed:

" 'That's good! Won't you read it again?' Slowly I repeated the passage the third time. When I finished I saw that his eyes were closed, and the troubled expression on his face had given way to a peaceful smile. His lips moved, and I bent over him to catch what he was saying, and heard in a faint whisper:

" 'As Moses lifted up—the serpent—in the wilderness,—even so—must the Son of Man be lifted up:—that whosoever—believeth in Him—should not perish,—but have eternal life.'

" He opened his eyes and said: 'That's enough; don't read any more.' Early next morning I again came to his cot, but it was empty. The attendant in charge told me that the young man had died peacefully, and said that after my visit he had rested quietly, repeating to himself, now and then, that glorious proclamation: 'Whosoever believeth in Him should not perish, but have eternal life.' "

The following description of one of the journeys Mr. Moody took to the scene of battle is sent by a friend:

" During the winter and spring of 1861 and 1862 I was a medical student in the city of Chicago, and saw Mr. Moody almost every day as he went hurrying about busily engaged in his good work. That was in the early days of the Young Men's Christian Association, and he was looked upon as one of the most active promoters of that Association. The great battle of Pittsburg Landing was fought on Sunday and Monday, the 6th and 7th of April, 1862; the news reached

Chicago on Tuesday, the 8th, and on Wednesday morning a call came for physicians and nurses for the wounded, for the supply of both was entirely inadequate for the work to be done. Accordingly the Young Men's Christian Association was called upon to send as many nurses as possible, and I, being a medical student, was invited to be one of the company.

"A special train was made up by the Illinois Central Railroad Company, and by five or six o'clock Wednesday evening we were at the depot ready to be off. Our train was a heavy one, carrying about sixty or seventy-five physicians and about three hundred nurses, besides many supplies. I had a seat in the centre of the car, which was comfortably full.

"When we were two or three hours out of Chicago and every one was getting settled down in his seat for the night (we had no sleepers then) I was aroused by a gentle tap on the shoulder and asked if I would not attend Mr. Moody's prayer-meeting, which was then to be held in the front end of the car. I wasn't a Christian then and I didn't go, but nevertheless my conscience gave me a stinging rebuke and I was set to thinking. In the forward end of that car was Mr. Moody, engaged in conducting a prayer-meeting; in the rear end was a company of men playing a game of cards. I couldn't help realizing the wonderful zeal of the man in his great work, and how earnest and how careful he was that no duty be neglected, no opportunity lost. We reached Cairo on Thursday, April 10th, were transferred from our train to the steamer, and soon on our way up the Ohio and Tennessee rivers.

"When evening came the passengers were sitting about in groups in the large cabin. Mr. Moody, with his Young Men's Christian Association assistants, passed through the crowd and again invited the men to attend prayers in one corner of the large room. There again he conducted a service. I don't remember seeing anything more of the card-players. As on the first evening so on the next, I didn't attend prayers, but I remember that among those who didn't there was no effort made to disturb the meeting. Nor was any evidence of disrespect shown as far as I could see.

"On Friday afternoon about three o'clock we reached Pitsburg Landing, and were at once sent to the different steamers that were standing there, loaded with hundreds of wounded soldiers waiting for our arrival, and so were scattered in all directions. I saw no more of Mr. Moody during that trip, but have thought of this circumstance many, many times and of the intense Christian zeal by which he was always impelled."

Many an instance is related of Mr. Moody's enthusiastic admiration of heroism, and this was, of course, accentuated when there was the added quality of outspoken loyalty to Christ. Such a soldier Mr. Moody recognized in Major Whittle, who was then a lieutenant in the Seventy-second Illinois. After the battle of Vicksburg in 1863 this young officer was sent home severely wounded. His popularity in the city called forth a great demonstration in Chicago on his return. The American Express Company, in whose service he had been engaged, sent their employees with a band of music and all their wagons to escort him from the station. A few days later Lieutenant Whittle was asked to make a speech at a patriotic rally, where a number of prominent men had been invited to speak. Referring to this occasion, Major Whittle says:

"I, a boy of twenty-one, was put forward to speak, with Bishop Simpson on the platform behind me waiting to give his address. I was weak from my wound, and felt foolish at being in such a position. Directly in front of me, in the centre of the hall, a sturdy young man jumped to his feet and cried:

"'Give him three cheers!' I recognized the face of Mr. Moody as he led the cheering with great earnestness. This manifestation of sympathy nerved me for the few words that followed, and I have often thought it was a specimen of what his courage, faith, and example have been to me all through his life. When I told him some time afterward of how much good his sympathy had done me that night, and how vividly I remembered his earnest, determined look as he led the crowd, I was rewarded by his reply:

"'I took you into my heart that night and you have been there ever since!'"

While serving with the command of Gen. O. O. Howard, who was in thorough sympathy with his efforts, Mr. Moody's ministry was especially fruitful. General Howard thus speaks of his work in the army:

"Moody and I met for the first time in Cleveland, East Tennessee. It was about the middle of April, 1864. I was bringing together my Fourth Army Corps. Two divisions had already arrived, and were encamped in and near the village. Moody was then fresh and hearty, full of enthusiasm for the Master's work. Our soldiers were just about to set out on what we all felt promised to be a hard and bloody campaign, and I think we were especially desirous of strong preaching. Crowds and crowds turned out to hear him. He showed them how a soldier could give his heart to God. His preaching was direct and effective, and multitudes responded with a promise to follow Christ."

These war-time experiences introduced Mr. Moody to a larger field by bringing him prominently before the whole country. The Young Men's Christian Association noon prayer-meetings in Chicago became a centre, where he and his fellow-workers met and reported on their frequent excursions to the front, and people from all over the Northwest sent in requests for prayer at these meetings, on behalf of husbands, brothers, and sons.

When the Spanish War broke out, and thousands of young men were again gathered into army camps, Mr. Moody's heart went out toward them with the same longing that had urged him on during the Civil War. His experiences in 1861-65 helped him to arouse the churches in this new emergency. He became chairman of the Evangelistic Department of the Army and Navy Christian Commission, whose method of work was fourfold: (1) the preaching of the Gospel by well-known ministers and evangelists, to whom the men would listen; (2) the placing of Young Men's Christian Association tents within reach of every regiment, whither the men might go as a place of resort, and where they would find good reading and writing materials; (3) the free distribution of Bibles, Testaments, hymn-books, and other religious books; and (4) the visitation of the sick and wounded in hospitals. The following letter, which he wrote at this time, resulted in great blessing to thousands of soldiers in the great military camps during the summer of 1898:

"Thirty years ago war clouds gathered over our land, and the church of God was aroused as I have never seen it since in behalf of the young men of America. This interest expressed itself in the formation of the Christian Commission, and everywhere efforts were made for the religious interests of the soldiers. Meetings were held everywhere, and many a camp became the scene of a deep and effective revival, and for more than thirty years I have been continually meeting men who were converted in those army meetings.

"Now the dark shadow of war again rests upon our land. Is it not possible that God intends to use even the darkness of this evil for the blessing of the youth of this land; and while He has called us to become the instrument of His justice may He not have in store a season of revival for those who, brought face to face with danger and in realization of the seriousness of life, may be reached, when at other times careless and indifferent? It seems to me that it is just the nick of time in which to reach thousands of young men with the Gospel, either through a Testament, a good book, or the spoken message. A minister in Philadelphia writes me that there is an excellent opportunity of doing good at Tampa, and I have no doubt that other camps offer equally favorable conditions."

Mr. Moody was preaching in Pittsburg when one of the first regiments started for Cuba. He mentioned that incident at the meeting, and raised several hundred dollars in order to follow these young soldiers with the Gospel. Major Whittle, Dr. A. C. Dixon, Rev. R. A.

Torrey, and others were sent, and an appeal was made for money to send books as well as men. The Young Men's Christian Association also desired to send workers to the front, and the War Department deciding that it could have only one religious body among the soldiers, an Army and Navy Christian Commission was organized, and Mr. Moody was made chairman of the Evangelistic Department. The object of the organization was to reach the soldiers and sailors of the United States, in the army and navy, with the Gospel of Christ. Bibles, religious books, colportage library books, and the new "Army Hymn Book," compiled by Mr. Sankey, were sent in great quantities. Major Whittle gave this incident among many, showing the very important nature of the work done through this agency:

"I called on a dying lieutenant this morning, who said that he was turned to God at the first meeting held in the camp. I did not know about it at the time, but my heart was full of gratitude to God as the dying man's face lit up in recognition of me! His hot hand pressed mine as he drank in: 'Him that cometh to Me I will in no wise cast out,' and other Scripture passages. He told me that he did in his heart trust Christ. We sang to him, 'My faith looks up to Thee,' and commended him to God in prayer. He has a wife and five children. He was a travelling man, and unsaved up to the night of May 27th. The doctor said there was no help and that he would die to-day. If God has been pleased to use my coming here to save that one soul, I will praise Him through eternity."

Another incident is given herewith: "We spend our forenoons going to the hospitals. There are about one thousand men at Chickamauga in the various hospitals, sick with malarial fever and typhoid fever, and every day brings us to the bedside of some hungry, thirsty, dying soldier. One of our workers went to a hospital and asked:

"'May I go in and see the sick? Is there anything I can do?'

"'For God's sake, yes,' said the surgeon; 'go with that woman. She has just arrived from the North, and I can't bear to tell her that her boy won't recognize her; he is dying; he won't live five minutes. Go in with her.'

"So he went in and stood by the cot where this soldier was breathing his last. He couldn't recognize his mother; and this mother, a lady dressed in black, stood there at the foot of the cot watching the last breath of her dying boy. And when at last his soul had gone she turned back the sheet that covered him, and there upon his army shirt was a badge of the Epworth League. He had had it transferred from his soldier's coat to his shirt; he told the nurse he wanted to wear that badge when he was dying.

"As his mother looked upon it she burst into a sob, and the whole tent of sick soldiers and the doctors and nurses sobbed with her. And what a privilege it was for our delegate to tell that mother: 'I was here yesterday and talked with your boy! I had been speaking with this man here about being a Christian, and your son overheard it, and when I came to his side he said: "Oh, dear me. How can that man get along without Jesus?" I said to him: "Are you a Christian?" And with a smile upon his young face he said: "You bet I am," and he turned back the sheet and showed me the badge upon his breast, and I talked with him and prayed with him.'"

CHAPTER IX

Sunday-School Convention Work

AT the close of the war in 1865 Mr. Moody returned to Chicago and again engaged in Sunday-school work. He had made known his purpose to his former associates in the Christian Commission, William Reynolds and B. F. Jacobs, by announcing, "When the war is ended let's give our strength to Sunday-school work."

His mission school in Chicago was a revelation. William Reynolds was carrying on one in Peoria, M. C. Hazard was superintending one in Galesburg, but there may have been others.

Of the work at this time, Mr. Hazard says: "Mr. Moody's mission school was the first large effort in this direction. The reports of it were stimulating. Many made the journey to Chicago to inspect it and find out its methods. Those methods were widely copied, and the success of that school caused the starting of many others. The mission school movement, if it did not originate with Mr. Moody, received a great impulse from him. He popularized it and gave it strength and momentum.

"His methods in getting children to attend it were unique. He made use of many devices to draw them in. In his recruiting excursions his pockets were almost always filled with oranges, candy, maple-sugar, or something toothsome. At one time he offered a squirrel with its cage to the one who would bring in the largest number of scholars within a specified time. He was fertile in expedients to lure in the boys and girls. But having secured them, he was equally inventive in his efforts to retain them. Once on his roll, he looked after them, visiting their homes if absent, and taking such a warm and practical interest in them that they became devotedly attached to him."

But Mr. Moody did not wait for Sunday-school workers to come to Chicago to learn of him—he went out to them. He began holding conventions in behalf of the Young Men's Christian Association work, in which some of his Sunday-school methods and experiences were narrated with telling effect. The organization of the Illinois State Sunday-school Association, however, gave him his great opportunity.

The State soon became enthusiastic on Sunday-school work. Great crowds running up into the thousands attended its conventions. "The Advance" reported the meeting at Duquoin, and fifty thousand copies of the paper were ordered by the State Association for distribution. The reports of some of the subsequent meetings were similarly widely scattered. What was being done in Illinois stimulated other States to imitation. Thus the movement spread from State to State, resulting finally in national gatherings, and they in international assemblies.

The first State convention of the Illinois Sunday-school Union was held in March, 1859, but owing to the Civil War, which engrossed attention by its large needs and opportunities for Christian effort, it was not until 1864 that the second convention could be held.

On learning of the arrangements for this gathering, Mr. Moody at once planned to be present. "The Sunday-school convention is to be held in Springfield, beginning on Tuesday morning," he announced to his friends, Mr. Jacobs and Rev. J. H. Harwood. "Let's go to Springfield on Friday evening and visit all the pastors, superintendents, and choirs, and hold special meetings on Sunday and Monday and see if the convention can be something besides a parade." The proposition seemed practical, and on the Friday evening preceding the convention the three started for Springfield. On their arrival the following morning they went to the hotel, and after breakfast set out in search of some quiet place for their prayer-meetings. The Baptist church near by seemed to offer what they were looking for, and they entered it through the basement. The three delegates seated themselves on the pulpit sofa and used the large Bible on the desk, from which they read. Then they knelt in prayer, and while thus engaged the door opened. When the prayer was ended Rev. N. D. Miner, the pastor, who had entered meantime, came up to them, saying:

"You are welcome, brethren, whoever you may be!"

Arrangements were at once made for special meetings there. The convention was well attended, and at the close of the Sunday afternoon service a number of conversions took place, while the following meetings on Sunday and Monday awakened a deep religious interest in the community. By the time the convention assembled on Tuesday the town was in the midst of a revival, in which the Sunday-school delegates took an earnest part. Many of these were deeply affected and carried the influence of the convention into all parts of the State.

In the fall of that year the Chicago Sunday-school Union decided to perfect its organization; the Rev., now Bishop, John H. Vincent was called from his church and became the superintendent of the Union, and on January 1, 1865, began the publication of "The Chicago Sunday-school Teacher." This proved a bond of strength to the Chicago Sunday-school workers, and in 1866 Mr. Moody became the vice-president of the Union.

At the convention held in Peoria in 1865 Mr. Moody was made a member of the State Sunday-school Executive Committee, which devised a plan for canvassing all the counties and securing their local organization. To this action may be traced the system that now exists in America. The State was divided into districts, and Mr. Moody and others volunteered to attend conventions. He went with an earnest purpose and a burning zeal that were felt everywhere throughout the State.

The reports of his work created a demand for services in other places, which he met, as is indicated in the following extract from a letter to his mother:

"The Lord is blessing my labors, and I think you would say, 'God bless you; go forward.' . . . I was away all last week to Sunday-school conventions. Have got to go again this week, and all of next week, so you see I am driven more than I ever was in my life. I have crowded houses wherever I go. Last week the house was full and the sidewalk outside, so they had to open another church, and I spoke in two houses. The Lord blessed me very much, and the work commenced in good earnest, so they have sent for me again."

"I was invited to go down into a little town in the State of Michigan," he relates of the beginning of a certain revival. "A minister, who was a perfect stranger to me, came to the depot to meet me and took me to his house to dinner. After dinner he took me out to the meeting. There were about twenty-five wives and mothers on their knees, as I went into that house, weeping and praying to God to bless their unconverted children and their unconverted husbands.

"Then he took me off to the other end of the town and introduced me to an old elder of the church. The man was dying with consumption, and now that he had given up and could not get out of the house, he began to realize that he had not been a faithful steward. And yet he must soon give an account before God of his stewardship. There was not a young person in the whole congregation who was a member of the church—not one of the sons or daughters of the officers and elders or members had joined it. There had not been a revival there for a great many years. First he himself began to pray. Then he sent for his brother elders and told them how he felt, and wanted to have them pray. They had become so discouraged and disheartened that they could not. Then he sent for the men of the church and talked to them. They too had become discouraged. Then he sent for the women of the church, and there the dying man pleaded with them to meet together to pray for God to revive His work. This had been going on for two weeks when I got there.

"That night I preached, and it was as if I was preaching against the air. It seemed as if every word came back to me. But about midnight, a boy came downstairs to his father, who was a member of the church and a professed Christian, and said: 'Father, I want to have you pray for me.' The father said he could not pray. He didn't sleep any that night. But the next morning, at the prayer-meeting, he got up and told us about it, and said he wanted to have us pray for him. A father that professed to be a Christian and could not pray for his own boy, who was weeping over his sins!

"Well, we prayed for him, and inside of twenty-four hours there was not a young person upwards of twelve years old whose father or mother was a member of that church that did not give evidence of being converted. God came suddenly to His temple, and there was a mighty work—I think one of the grandest, one of the best works I have ever seen in my life. The work was revived as soon as the church began to pray to God to revive it."

When Mr. Moody belonged to the Executive Committee of the State Sunday-school Association he would often turn a county convention into a prayer-meeting or a revival meeting. At Pontiac, Ill., there was a revival that swept through the county. Several lawyers joined the church, and the court adjourned at ten minutes before twelve to attend the noon prayer-meeting. The revival began by Mr. Moody's going through the town one day and talking to every man, woman, and child he met. Approaching a group of politicians, he heard one of them say of a proposed nominee:

"I think that man could carry the county."

"My friend," interrupted Mr. Moody, "we want to carry this county for the Lord Jesus Christ!"

The politician, with a Westerner's appreciation of a joke, slapped Mr. Moody on the shoulder, burst into a laugh, and cried out: "I am with you there, old fellow!"

Mr. Moody's words became the watchcry of that whole religious movement.

In writing of these early experiences in Sunday-school convention work Mr. Jacobs relates the following incident:

"Perhaps the most dramatic scene that has ever occurred in an Illinois Sunday-school convention was at Quincy in 1870. Philip C. Gillette was chosen president, in opposition to the wishes of a few persons, who, seeing the power of the convention, were trying to turn it into a different channel. Watching for an opportunity, they selected the time when Mr. Moody was answering questions that had been submitted in writing, and dropped into the box an inquiry that reflected unpleasantly upon the Executive Committee.

"Mr. Moody first read the question, and then with great power reviewed the work of the committee, disclaiming credit for himself, magnifying the work of the others. In his own effective way he spoke of the continued blessing that had rested on them, as a token of God's approval. He closed by tendering the resignation of all the members of the committee, and then said: 'Let us pray.' In a prayer of sweetness and power he led the congregation near to God. He remembered those who had made an attempt to turn the convention aside from its great work, and prayed for them too. The effect was indescribable. The audience, estimated at three thousand persons, was greatly moved, and, upon motion, the committee were reëlected by acclamation."

Other States shared with Illinois the benefit of Mr. Moody's help in Sunday-school work. He attended county and State conventions in Michigan, Wisconsin, Minnesota, and Iowa. It was at the Minnesota Sunday-school convention, held in Winona, that Mr. Moody first met Miss Mary V. Lee and Miss Sara J. Timanus. Both were teachers in the Minnesota State Normal School. After hearing them speak and teach, Mr. Moody conferred with others about them, and they went to Illinois and attended county conventions. Following this, Miss Timanus, now Mrs. W. F. Crafts, was employed by Mr. Moody and Mr. Jacobs to superintend the primary classes of their Sunday-schools and attend county Sunday-school conventions. She was for twelve years president of the International Primary Union.

Up to this time the Sunday-school lessons had been entirely a matter of selection with the teachers of individual classes, or at best with the officers of a Sunday-school. Instead of a system of Bible study for everybody each class was following its own course. The possibilities of a general system of Sunday-school instruction now occurred to Mr. Moody and his associates in the State Sunday-school work.

The subject was first agitated in Chicago, where a number of schools were induced to use the same lesson. The advantages of the plan were evident immediately, and Mr. Moody continued to urge its general adoption. Later the system was accepted by the State Sunday-school Union, and in 1868 Mr. Moody, who then published a periodical called "The Heavenly Tidings," induced Mr. Jacobs to contribute brief notes on these lessons. In other State Sunday-school conventions, where he was increasingly in demand, Mr. Moody urged the system of lessons adopted by Illinois. It was widely appreciated, so that in 1869, at the National Sunday-school Convention in Newark, N. J., a committee was appointed to arrange what has since become the International Sunday-school Series of Bible Lessons.

Mr. Moody always retained his deep interest in the work in which he was engaged at this time. Even after he began to devote himself more fully to evangelistic work he frequently attended the conventions of Sunday-school workers. In 1876 he was made president of the Illinois State Sunday-school Union. He took an active part in the Galesburg (Ill.) Convention in 1880, and was a daily speaker at the International Convention held in Boston in 1896. At this latter gathering his old fervor was manifested, and he tried to awaken all the delegates to their personal responsibilities in the salvation of the children intrusted to their teaching.

"Again and again did he plead with the Sunday-school workers to be faithful," writes a friend who was present. "His voice, full of pathos, seems to those who heard it to sound forth even now the solemn words:

"'If I had the trumpet of God, and could speak to every Sunday-school teacher in America, I would plead with each one to lead at least one soul to Christ this year!'"

DWIGHT L. MOODY.

When President of the Chicago Young Men's Christian Association.

THE ORIGINAL FARWELL HALL.

The first Young Men's Christian Association building erected in America.

D. L. Moody's Mother.

From a portrait taken in 1867.

CHAPTER X

Early Evangelistic Efforts

ALTHOUGH Mr. Moody was now engaged in State Sunday-school conventions and Young Men's Christian Association activities, his interest was still strong in the work begun in the North Market Hall. The continuous growth of the school there and the many conversions that had taken place from the first were clear proofs of its success, and the evening gospel services during the week were attended with very encouraging results. In time the demand for the establishment of a permanent church organization grew urgent. Mr. Moody hesitated for some time before considering such a step, urging the new converts to ally themselves with the neighboring churches. He was always averse to multiplying agencies when existing organizations needed support, and preferred therefore to devote his energies to evangelistic work, yielding to the denominational churches the function of indoctrinating the Christian faith.

But it was in this effort that one of his few failures must be recorded. The allegiance to North Market Hall on the part of the converts was stronger than Moody's advice, and those who had come to the knowledge of Christ under the instruction there given could not be induced to leave the school.

It was inevitable, therefore, that a permanent church organization should be formed. This was accomplished in 1863, and a year later the Illinois Street Church, as it was called, was settled in a suitable place of worship. The church building itself was plain, but with ample accommodations for the congregation and Sunday-school, the auditorium having a seating capacity of fifteen hundred, and in addition there were several class-rooms. The Rev. Mr. Harwood was called to the pastorate, and Mr. Moody was one of the deacons.

The church became the centre of various forms of Christian activity. It was open every evening in the week, and gospel services were supplemented by regular church meetings, while special gatherings for mothers and young women, Bible readings, prayer and praise services, missionary rallies, and similar services were of regular occurrence. In the homes of the members cottage meetings were also gathered, while open-air services were held regularly during the summer. Among other services Mr. Moody had children's prayer-meetings. "Some of the happiest nights I ever had were in these children's prayer-meetings," he used to say. "Some people don't believe in early conversion. 'If they have a father or mother they'll take care of them,' they say. Then they complain, 'If you do get a hold on them and they are converted, they won't hold out.'

"Well, that is not my experience. Some of the most active men that I had to help me in Chicago were little barefooted boys picked up in the lanes and by-ways whom I had in my children's meetings.

"I was once sent for by a mother who was on her death-bed; she had been married twice; her second husband abused her son terribly.

"'Now I am dying of consumption,' she said; 'I have been sick a long time, and since I have been lying here I've neglected my boy. He has got into bad company, and he's very, very unkind to me. Mr. Moody, I want you to promise me that when I am gone and he has no one to take care of him that you'll look after him.' I promised that I would. Soon after she died, and no sooner was she buried than the boy ran away. The next Sunday I spoke to the children in my Sabbath-school, and asked them to look for him, and if they found him to let me know. For some time I did not hear from him, but one day one of my scholars told me that he was a bell-boy in a certain hotel. I went to this hotel, found him, and talked with him.

"How well I remember that night! There was no place where we could be alone in the hotel, so I asked him where we could go and not be disturbed. He said the only place he knew of was on the hotel roof. We went together up there, and I spoke to him about Christ and what He had done for him, and how He loved him. The tears trickled down his cheeks; and when I asked him if he wanted to know Christ he told me he did. I prayed with him there, and he became a Christian. Below was the tumult of the city. It was the night before the Fourth of July, and they were firing off cannon and sky-rockets, while there on that roof, at midnight, this boy was praying. Many years later I met him again; he is now an active Christian, superintendent of a Sunday-school, and he comes to Northfield frequently in the summer. *He* has held on and he is leading others."

Mr. Moody's zeal was well known in Chicago. He would not wait for opportunities to be made for seeking to bring men to Christ, but made them himself. It is related how, on one occasion, he accosted a young man, apparently just come from the country, with his frequent inquiry: "Are you a Christian?"

"It's none of your business," was the curt reply.

"Yes, it is," was the reassurance.

"Then you must be D. L. Moody!" said the stranger.

The hostile criticism received in these days was by no means limited to mere scoffing; often he would be directly criticised. But with an ever-ready tact he would turn the thing to his credit with a splendid self-possession.

On one such occasion Mr. Moody was one of several speakers at a convention. A minister who followed him took occasion in his speech to criticise him, saying that his address was made up of newspaper clippings, etc. When he sat down Mr. Moody stepped to the front again, and said he knew it was so; that he recognized his want of learning and inability to make a fine address; he thanked the minister for pointing out his shortcomings, and asked his critic to pray that God would help him to do better.

On another occasion Mr. Moody was subjected to a great deal of annoyance from those who used to attend the open-air services and noon prayer-meetings with the express purpose of making a disturbance. These occurrences continued with a persistence that became almost intolerable. At the close of a prayer-meeting one day Mr. Moody was standing at the door shaking hands with the people as they went out. As an added trial to Mr. Moody's patience the irrepressible disturber himself advanced, extending his hand. For an instant there was a hesitation; then accepting the proffered hand, he said:

"I suppose if Jesus Christ could eat the Last Supper with a Judas Iscariot I ought to shake hands with you."

There were times when his old quick temper broke out again, but even on such occasions it would seem that the momentary weakness was turned to good, so humbly and sincerely did he repent. One evening after an unusually earnest evangelistic appeal Mr. Moody was standing near the door of the inquiry-room, urging the people to come in. The entrance to the room was by the lower landing of the stairs, and Moody was just at the head of a short flight. While he stood there a man approached him and deliberately and grossly insulted him. Mr. Moody would never repeat the insult, but it must have been an unusually bitter one. Instantly he thrust the man from him, and sent him reeling down the remaining steps to the vestibule. Happily the man escaped uninjured, but having given way to a sudden temptation, he was keenly rebuked by his conscience for what might have caused a serious accident. A friend who was present on the occasion and witnessed the scene described what followed:

"When I saw Mr. Moody give way to his temper, although I could not but believe the provocation was extraordinary, I said to myself, 'This meeting is killed. The large number who have seen the whole thing will hardly be in a condition to be influenced by anything more Mr. Moody may say to-night.' But before Moody began the second meeting that night he arose, and with trembling voice made a humble apology.

"'Friends,' he said, 'before beginning to-night I want to confess that I yielded just now to my temper, out in the hall, and have done wrong. Just as I was coming in here to-night I lost my temper with a man, and I want to confess my wrong before you all, and if that man is present here whom I thrust away from me in anger I want to ask his forgiveness and God's. Let us pray.' There was not a word of excuse or vindication for resenting the insult. The impression made by his words was wonderful, and instead of the meeting being killed by the scene it was greatly blessed by such a consistent and straightforward confession."

Mr. Moody never lost an opportunity for reaching those whom others could not reach, and many an incident is related of his thus invading the enemy's country. Once he was invited, as a joke, to the opening of a great billiard hall and saloon. He saw the owners, and asked permission to bring a friend. They consented, but asked who he was. Mr. Moody said it wasn't necessary to tell, but he never went without Him. They understood his meaning then, and protested:

"Come, we don't want any praying!"

"You've given me an invitation, and I'm going to come," he replied.

"But if you come you needn't pray."

"Well, I'll tell you what we'll do," was the answer; "we'll compromise the matter, and if you don't want me to come and pray for you when you open, let me pray for you both now," to which they agreed. Mr. Moody made them kneel down on the instant, and then prayed that their business might go to pieces, but that God would save them!

"The first thing Mr. Moody does with those whom he succeeds in bringing under Christian influence is to turn them to account in pushing on the work," writes the Rev. David Macrae, a Scotch clergyman, in his account of a visit to Mr. Moody's Sunday-school in the early sixties. " No place is too bad, no class too hardened, to be despaired of. He sometimes takes a choir of well-trained children with him to the low drink-saloons to help him attract the drunkards and gamblers to his meetings. On one such occasion which was described to me, he entered one of these dens with his choir, and said: 'Have a song, gentlemen?' No objection was offered, and the children sang a patriotic song in fine style, exciting great applause. Mr. Moody then started them with a hymn, and went around, while they sang, distributing tracts. When the hymn was over he said: 'We will now have a word of prayer.'

"'No, no!' cried several in alarm, 'no prayer here!'

"'Oh, yes, we'll have a word. Quiet for a moment, gentlemen,' and he offered up an earnest petition. Some of the men were touched, and when he invited them to go to his meeting and hear more, about half of them got up and went."

It often required a great deal of tact to adapt a young convert to work best suited to his abilities, but to this Mr. Moody proved himself equal.

" Every man can do something," he said. " There was a Swede converted once in our mission in Chicago. I don't know how. I don't suppose he was converted by my sermons, because he couldn't understand much English. But the Lord converted him into one of the happiest men you ever saw. His face shone all over. He came to me, and he had to speak through an interpreter. This interpreter said that the Swede wanted to have me give him something to do. I said to myself: What in the world will I set this man to doing? He can't speak English!

" So I gave him a bundle of little hand-bills, and put him out on the corner of the greatest thoroughfare of Chicago, and let him give them out, inviting people to come up and hear me preach. A man would come along and take one and see 'Gospel Meeting,' and then turn around, perhaps, and curse the fellow. But the Swede would laugh, because he didn't know that he wasn't blessing him! He couldn't tell the difference. A great many men were impressed by that man being so polite and kind. When winter came and the nights got so dark they couldn't read those little hand-bills, he got a little transparency and put it up on the corner, and there took his stand, hot or cold, rain or shine. Many a man was won by his efforts."

The following extract from an address given at this time on "How to Reach the Poor" illustrates his keen judgment in dealing with men at this early date:

"We don't make our services interesting enough to get unconverted people to come. We don't expect them to come—we'd be surprised enough if they did. To make them interesting and profitable, ask the question, How can this be done? You must wake the people up. If you can't talk, read a verse of Scripture, and let God speak. Bring up the question, What more can we do in our district? Get those who never do anything to say what they think ought to be done, and then ask them if they are doing it. Don't get in a rut. I abominate ruts. Perhaps I dread them too much, but there is nothing I fear more."

D. W. McWilliams, a life-long and intimate friend, writing of his first acquaintance with Mr. Moody at this time, says:

"It is conceded by all who knew him that one of the qualities which made him so useful and successful was his openmindedness in observing surrounding circumstances; coupled with this, and largely developed in him, was his willingness to receive suggestions and alertness in adopting them where the work of blessing others would be promoted.

"It was at the house of a friend in Peoria, Ill., in 1861, that I first met Mr. Moody. Our host had invited several ministers and two laymen to meet him at dinner. When they arrived Mr. Moody was not with the others, but inquiry led to the information that he had come early and was upstairs in a room at prayer with an unconverted friend of the host, who had been induced to call upon Mr. Moody for this special purpose.

"On being introduced to those present Mr. Moody soon turned to one of the ministers and said, 'How do you explain this verse in the Bible?' giving the verse in full. Soon after he turned to another minister, quoted a verse, and asked, 'What does that mean?' The entire conversation that day was exposition of Scripture in reply to Mr. Moody's rapid questions, and a stirring of hearts in the direction of personal work for the salvation of others. The impression made upon the guests that day was of Mr. Moody's love for the souls of others and his intense desire for Bible knowledge.

"Soon afterward I called upon Mr. Moody in Chicago, and was conducted through his parish. We went to what would now be called the 'slums.' Soon a crowd of street gamins, boys and girls of all ages, were following us with loud shouts of 'Oh, here's Moody! Come, here's Moody!' Evidently they all knew him as their best friend. He had candy in both side pockets, and gave it freely. We visited house after house of the poor, sick, and unfortunate. He was everywhere greeted with affection, and carried real sunshine into these abodes of squalor. He inquired for the absent ones by name."

CHAPTER XI

Christian Association Work

"I BELIEVE in the Young Men's Christian Association with all my heart. Under God it has done more in developing me for Christian work than any other agency." This was Mr. Moody's testimony to the influence of the organization for which he gained so many friends and supporters.

From the time he gave up business to devote himself to Christian work Mr. Moody was very enthusiastic in the work of the Chicago Association. This interest was greatly strengthened by his experiences in the Christian Commission work and the Association formed at that time. As secretary and for several years as president he worked earnestly to build up the organization in every department, but more especially did the spiritual needs of the work appeal to him.

The daily noon prayer-meeting had been one of the permanent results of the great revival, and to this meeting he gave his heartiest support. Young as he was, it was not long before he became the leader of the meeting, and side by side with his mission work he carried the steady extension of the Christian Association.

Under his leadership the Association prospered greatly and soon demanded larger accommodations. The board of managers thought, planned, and prayed for a building of their own, but with little or no practical result. Finally it was proposed that Mr. Moody, who had recently been successful in erecting the Illinois Street Church, should be elected president, with John V. Farwell for vice-president. Mr. Moody was considered too radical to head the ticket, however, so the names were reversed. While the election was in progress Mr. Moody was out getting pledges, and before night a building was assured that should contain a hall with a seating capacity for three thousand people, as well as rooms for smaller meetings and offices. Feeling, as he always did, the efficacy of prayer, he had asked B. F. Jacobs and J. W. Dean to unite with him in petition that the way might be opened for such a building. Then with characteristic foresight, believing that his prayer would be answered, he got a charter from the State, exempting the Young Men's Christian Association's real estate from taxation.

A stock company was then formed, and on looking for a location a site originally secured for the city water-works office and tower was decided upon as the most appropriate in size and location. The city had grown so rapidly that the lot was entirely inadequate for the proposed water-works, and the property now belonged to Mr. Farwell. At. Mr. Moody's solicitation, it was donated to the work for young men, being the equivalent of a contribution of $40,000. The first cash subscription of $10,000 was then secured from Cyrus H. McCormick, and others generously aided in the work, until a sufficient sum was secured for " the first hall ever erected in America for Christian Association work," which distinction it claimed. At the dedication of the building, September 29, 1867, a large audience taxed the utmost capacity of the hall, many visitors coming from distant cities. The interdenominational character of the Association was proved by the presence of ministers of all denominations, and this at a time when the work was only beginning, and jealous eyes were watching lest it should prove a rival of the churches.

In his speech on this occasion Mr. Moody recounted the blessings the Association had received and how God had led them from small beginnings to their present position of influence. He made a characteristic plea for an aggressive attack upon the strongholds of sin, saying Christians had been on the defensive too long. He confessed his belief that by the Lord's blessing a religious influence was to go out from this Association that "should extend to every county in the State, to every State in the Union, and finally crossing the waters, should help to bring the whole world to God."

It had been planned by some of the subscribers to the Association building fund that it should be named after Mr. Moody, as it owed its existence to his vigorous efforts. As soon as he learned of this Mr. Moody took the platform, and in a short and vigorous appeal asked the audience to name it Farwell Hall, in honor of the man who was chairman of the building committee and had been so liberal a giver. The proposal was carried by acclamation, although Mr. Farwell modestly insisted afterward that "the audience acceded to the only mistake Mr. Moody ever made in connection with this enterprise."

Within four months after its dedication Farwell Hall burned down, entailing great loss, as it was only partly insured. Mr. Moody took matters in his own hands again, and so promptly that it is said he had secured subscriptions for the new hall before the old one ceased burning. While the ruins were still smouldering he received a telegram from J. D. Blake, of Rochester, Minn., an early friend of the general Association work, offering to take $500 worth of stock in the new building.

"When the costly hall of the Young Men's Christian Association took fire in 1867," wrote the Rev. Mr. Macrae, "the secretary and other officials, as soon as they found the building was doomed, ran about among the merchants in the city for subscriptions. 'Our hall is burning, sir; the engines are at work, but there is no hope. We shall want a new one. Let us have money enough to begin at once!' Thousands upon thousands of dollars were subscribed without a moment's hesitation, and it is said that before the fire was out money enough had been raised to build a new hall in a style of even greater magnificence than the first. This is only a specimen of the lightning Christianity of Chicago.

"The man who may be called *par excellence* the lightning Christian of the city is Mr. Moody, the secretary of the Association referred to, and a man whose name is a household word in connection with missionary work. I went to one of his mission schools, and have rarely beheld such a scene of high-pressure evangelization. It made me think irresistibly of those breathing steamboats on the Mississippi that must either go fast or burst. Mr. Moody himself went about the school seeing that everybody was at work; throwing in a word where he thought it necessary; inspiring every one with his own enthusiasm."

The second Farwell Hall was completed and dedicated in the following year. This building was superior in many respects to the first one, but suffered the fate of its predecessor. The new hall was destroyed in the great Chicago fire of 1871.

The third Farwell Hall was erected while Mr. Moody was in England in 1872-75. But in this also he had a share in raising money to pay for its erection. After the close of his mission in Chicago in 1877 he secured the balance of the money necessary to clear the Association building from debt. This third building was demolished to give place to the present Farwell Hall, which exceeds in value any Association building now in existence.

Richard Morse writes of Mr. Moody's ability in the way of securing subscriptions:

" In every city in which he worked, on both sides of the ocean, his work and words summoned to the Association a group of consecrated laymen, and with them financial resources which everywhere promoted the extension and usefulness of our work for young men.

" In almost every city his effort was always not only to promote the spiritual life of the Association, but also to procure for it better accommodation and appliances and in many instances a building.

" I remember vividly my visit to England late in the summer of 1875, just after Mr. Moody had closed his most remarkable evangelistic tour in the United Kingdom. I visited many cities, and was invariably entertained with cordial hospitality, and I felt that this was due not so much to my being the secretary of the International Committee, as to my being the friend, and to some extent the associate, of Mr. Moody. I found in every city a group of influential laymen who had recently become connected with the Association owing to Mr. Moody's work, and who were giving it leadership and financial resources which greatly increased in every instance the beneficent reach and influence of the organization. It was the spiritual life and at the same time the leadership of the laymen which he contributed in such great measure to the Association movement; the actual money raised, in connection with or as a result of his meetings, was simply one of the signs of this.

"No list of the amounts raised in the various cities can show a total amount which represents to any degree the financial help that came to the Association through his agency.

"In regard to the amount raised in New York as a result of his meetings here in 1876 I would say that at that time there was a mortgage of $150,000 upon the Association building, corner of Twenty-third Street and Fourth Avenue, against which there was a pledge of $50,000 from a friend of the Association, which he had deposited in its safe, to be paid whenever the balance of the mortgage had been subscribed. At the close of Mr. Moody's meetings in the Hippodrome (now the Madison Square Garden) it was proposed to raise $200,000, including the pledge above referred to; $150,000 to be devoted to paying off the mortgage and $50,000 to the work of the Bowery Branch of the Association. This money was happily secured as the result of these meetings."

These facts speak for themselves. But any simple narration of them would be incomplete without some slight comment on this remarkable power that influenced not only men's hearts, but their pockets—perhaps a harder task. He begged for men's money as simply and directly as he begged for their conversion; he trusted implicitly that God would grant him both; and he was rarely disappointed in either. The poor offered him small sums; the rich gave with a magnificent liberality: he accepted both as his Master's due.

In his Association work at this time Mr. Moody seems to have developed the peculiar gift of discerning the special abilities of others. In the noon-day prayer-meetings he was on the watch to discover a new worker or to call upon strangers to take part. Mr. A. J. Bell, an evangelist of San José, Cal., describes the following experience with Mr. Moody at one of the meetings:

"One day the leader assigned did not get there in time, and Mr. Moody came to me, requesting that I take charge. I had just arrived from a journey, hot and dusty. 'Mr. Moody,' I said, 'I am just in from a long absence and am not presentable. Excuse me, please, and at some other time I will lead the meeting.'

"I shall never forget the incident, for it was the turning point in my life. 'I thought you were a Christian soldier,' he said, and added, 'Go forward and we will pray for you.' As soon as the meeting was over he came again and thanked me. 'You did well,' he said. 'But it is all wrong, this holding back! Your duty is clear; keep in front. Be a minute man.'

"In twenty-five years I have not forgotten that expression, and since then I have been at the front in evangelistic work. Had Mr. Moody not pressed me into service then, the probabilities are that I would have never entered the field."

In 1867 a great Young Men's Christian Association convention was held in Pittsburg, which was accompanied by a wide-spread religious awakening. Here again Mr. Moody's presence was felt. "With his characteristic energy, wonderful foresight, and practical good in securing results," says Oliver McClintock, who was president of the Association just organized at that time, "Mr. Moody called a meeting of the leading women who had been impressed by the addresses and events of the convention, and organized them into a Young Women's Christian Association, which grew into a strong and efficient organization. Several large and benevolent institutions now having valuable properties grew out of this movement."

The Rev. James S. Chadwick became city missionary of the Methodist Episcopal Church in Chicago in 1861. His office was in the building in which the Young Men's Christian Association had rooms before the erection of Farwell Hall. With reference to Mr. Moody's labors in behalf of the suffering and needy, he says:

" I have known him to start from the Young Men's Christian Association with baskets of provisions for poor families, many of whom would have been neglected or overlooked but for his timely interest. He always urged those whom he thus relieved to attend church and become Christians. In many instances whole families were thus brought to know and serve the Lord Jesus Christ. In the noon-day prayer-meetings men have arisen and told how Mr. Moody visited their homes with substantial relief for hungry children, and then joined in prayer for all the family.

" Mr. Moody would regularly station himself at the entrance of the Young Men's Christian Association rooms, just before the hour of noon, and distribute to passers-by invitations to go upstairs to the noon-day prayer-meeting. Christians and persons who were not Christians were frequently prevailed upon to spend a few minutes in the helpful and inspiring prayer-service. Many conversions resulted from these invitations."

Direct evangelistic preaching was a prominent feature of these early years of Association work. The most aggressive phase of it was no doubt the " open-air " talks. During the summer months Mr. Moody could be seen every night, if the weather permitted, in what was known as the Court House Square. The steps of the building became his pulpit, a half-dozen young men and women his choir, the passing throng, or as many as could be arrested by the exercises, his audience. A position was usually taken where the prisoners in the long corridors could hear what was going on, and these, crowding to the grated windows, became an important part of the congregation.

To one of less determination such efforts at evangelizing would have been discouraging. Opposition in one form or another was frequent. A certain "free-thinker" appeared regularly for months, often interrupting—always trying to hold the crowd after Mr. Moody had closed, and later following the company that had gone with Mr. Moody and his assistants to the service that was held regularly in the smaller Association hall. Occasionally some half-intoxicated stroller would try to put an end to the open-air service. One evening a large earthen jar was thrown from an upper window of the court-house and, falling within a couple of feet of the speaker, was broken into fragments.

Mr. Moody was a true friend of prisoners, frequently visiting the common jail, and also what was known in Chicago as the "Bridewell," talking, reading, and praying with the inmates.

Experiences gathered in such work—the necessity for ready action in emergencies; the strength acquired in stemming opposition; the growth of character in standing unflinchingly for conviction and duty—all these made for larger equipment in wider spheres of action. It was but a repeated demonstration of the Master's principle of reward. "*Thou hast been faithful over a few things, I will make thee ruler over many things.*"

At a convention in St. Johnsbury, Vt., in 1870, whenever he rose to speak he first read a verse from the Bible. A man who followed him said to Mr. Moody: "I'm glad you keep to your chart."

"There is nothing else to keep to," he replied; "if that goes everything goes."

Ps 91 (Thy lodging) The shadow of His wings (Thy habitation) The most High
(Thy covering) His wings (Thy Shield) His truth (Thy Keepers) His angels

PSALM XCI.

HE that dwelleth[b] in the secret place of the Most High, shall β abide under the shadow[c] of the Almighty.

2 I will say of the LORD, *He is* my refuge, and my fortress: my God; in him will I trust.

3 Surely[d] he shall deliver thee from the snare of the fowler, *and* from the noisome pestilence.

4 He shall cover thee with his feathers, and under his wings shalt thou trust: his truth *shall be thy* shield and buckler.

5 Thou[h] shalt not be afraid for the terror by night, *nor* for the arrow *that* flieth by day,

6 *Nor* for the pestilence *that* walketh in darkness, *nor* for the destruction *that* wasteth at noonday.

7 A thousand shall fall at thy side, and ten thousand at thy right hand; *but* it shall not come nigh thee.

8 Only[k] with thine eyes shalt thou behold, and see the reward of the wicked.

9 Because thou hast made the LORD, *which is* my refuge, *even* the Most High, thy habitation,

10 There[n] shall no evil befall thee, neither shall any plague come nigh thy dwelling.

11 For[o] he shall give his angels charge over thee, to keep thee in all thy ways.

12 They shall bear thee up in *their* hands, lest thou dash thy foot against a stone.

13 Thou[q] shalt tread upon the lion and κ adder; the young lion and the dragon shalt thou trample under feet.

14 Because he hath set his love upon me, therefore will I deliver him: I will set him on high, because he hath known my name.

15 He[t] shall call upon me, and I will answer him: I[u] *will be* with him in trouble; I will deliver him, and honour him.

16 With λ long life will I satisfy him, and shew him my salvation.

PSALM XCII.

A Psalm *or* Song for the Sabbath day.

IT[x] *is a* good *thing* to give thanks unto the LORD, and to sing praises unto thy name, O Most High:

2 To shew forth thy lovingkindness in the morning,[a] and thy faithfulness μ every night,

3 Upon an instrument of ten strings, and upon the psaltery; ν upon the harp with π a solemn sound.

4 For thou, LORD, hast made me glad through thy work; I will triumph in the works of thy hands.

5 O LORD, how great are thy works! *and* thy thoughts[c] are very deep.

6 A brutish man knoweth not; neither doth a fool understand this.

7 When[g] the wicked spring as the grass, and when all the workers of iniquity do flourish, *it is* that they shall be destroyed for ever:

8 But thou, LORD, *art most* high for evermore.

9 For, lo, thine enemies, O LORD, for, lo, thine enemies shall perish; all[h] the workers of iniquity shall be scattered;

10 But my horn shalt thou exalt like *the horn of* an unicorn: I shall be anointed[l] with fresh oil.

11 Mine eye also shall see *my desire* on mine enemies, *and* mine ears shall hear *my desire* of the wicked that rise up against me.

12 The righteous[a] shall flourish like the palm tree; he shall grow like a cedar in Lebanon.

13 Those that be planted in the house of the LORD shall flourish in the courts of our God.

14 They shall still bring forth fruit in old age; they shall be fat and γ flourishing;

15 To shew that the LORD *is* upright: *he is* my rock,[e] and *there is* no unrighteousness[f] in him.

PSALM XCIII.

THE[g] LORD reigneth; he is clothed with majesty; the LORD is clothed with strength, *wherewith* he hath girded himself: the world also is stablished, that it cannot be moved.

2 Thy throne[i] *is* established δ of old: thou *art* from everlasting.

3 The floods have lifted up, O LORD, the floods have lifted up their voice; the floods lift up their waves.

4 The[l] LORD on high *is* mightier than the noise of many waters, *yea, than* the mighty waves of the sea.

5 Thy testimonies are very sure: holiness[m] becometh thine house, O LORD, ζ for ever.

PSALM XCIV.

O LORD η God, to whom[p] vengeance belongeth; O God, to whom vengeance belongeth, θ shew thyself.

2 Lift up thyself, thou judge of the earth: render a reward to the proud.

3 LORD, how long[r] shall the wicked, how long shall the wicked triumph?

4 *How long* shall they utter *and* speak hard[s] things? *and* all the workers of iniquity boast themselves?

5 They break in pieces thy people, O LORD, and afflict thine heritage.

6 They slay the widow and the stranger, and murder the fatherless.

7 Yet they say, The LORD shall not see, neither shall the God of Jacob regard *it*.

8 Understand,[w] ye brutish among the people; and, *ye* fools, when will ye be wise?

9 He[y] that planted the ear, shall he not hear? he that formed the eye, shall he not see?

10 He that chastiseth the heathen,[z] shall not he correct? he[b] that teacheth man knowledge, *shall not he know?*

11 The LORD knoweth the thoughts of man, that they *are*[c] vanity.

12 Blessed[d] *is* the man whom thou chastenest, O LORD, and teachest him out of thy law;

13 That thou mayest give him rest from the days of adversity, until the pit be digged for the wicked.

14 For[f] the LORD will not cast off his people, neither will he forsake his inheritance:

15 But judgment shall return unto righteousness; and all the upright in heart ρ shall follow it.

16 Who will rise up for me against the evildoers? *or* who will stand up for me against the workers of iniquity?

17 Unless[i] the LORD *had been* my help, my soul had σ almost dwelt in silence.

18 When I said, My foot[k] slippeth; thy mercy, O LORD, held me up.

19 In the multitude of my thoughts within me thy comforts[m] delight my soul.

20 Shall the throne of iniquity have fellowship with thee, which[n] frameth mischief by a law?

a Ps. 52. 8. Ho. 14. 5, 6. b Ps. 27. 5. β lodge. c Ps. 57. 1. γ green. d Ps. 124. 7. e De. 32. 4. f Zep. 3. 5. g Is. 52. 7. Re. 19. 6. h Ps. 121. 5, 6. i Ps. 45. 6. δ from then. k Pr. 3. 25, 26. l Ps. 89. 9. m He. 12. 14. Re. 21. 27. n Pr. 12. 21. ζ to length of days, Ps. 23. 6. o Mat. 4. 6. η God of revenges. p De. 32. 35. Na. 1. 2. θ shine forth, Ps. 80. 1. q Job 5. 23. κ or, asp. r Job 20. 5. Je. 12. 1, 2. s Ps. 73. 8, &c. Jude 15. t Is. 65. 24. u Is. 43. 2. λ length of days. v Pr. 3. 2. 22. 4. w Ps. 92. 6. Ro. 3. 11. x Ps. 147. 1. y Ex. 4. 11. z Eze. 39. 21. Hab. 3. 12. a La. 3. 23. μ in the nights. b Pr. 2. 6. ν or, upon the solemn sound with the harp. c 1 Co. 3. 19, 20. π Higgaion, Ps. 9. 16. d Job 5. 17. Pr. 3. 11. He. 12. 5, &c. e Is. 55. 9. Ro. 11. 33. f 1 Sa. 12. 22. Ro. 11. 1, 2. g Ps. 73. 18..20. Mal. 4. 1. ρ be after. h Mat. 7. 23. i Ps. 124. 1, 2. σ or, quickly. k Ps. 38. 16. l 2 Co. 1. 21. 1 John 2. 20. m Ps. 63. 5, 6. 2 Co. 1. 3, 4. n Is. 10. 1.

A PAGE FROM MR. MOODY'S BIBLE.

Ira D. Sankey.

CHAPTER XII

YOUNG MEN'S CHRISTIAN ASSOCIATION CONVENTIONS

DURING his leadership of the Chicago Association from 1865 to 1871 Mr. Moody's influence was felt not only in Chicago, but in the International and State conventions. He was present at the International Conventions in Albany, 1868; Baltimore, 1869, and Indianapolis, 1870.

It was at the Indianapolis convention that Mr. Moody first met Mr. Sankey, who was a delegate from his native town of Newcastle, Penn. The reputation of the Chicagoan had already aroused Mr. Sankey's interest, but as both were seated upon the floor of the hall among delegates his curiosity could not be gratified during the first few days. At the close of the convention it was announced that Mr. Moody would lead an early morning prayer-meeting at six o'clock the next day in a neighboring church. This afforded the opportunity Mr. Sankey had looked for, and he came with a friend.

There was some difficulty in starting the singing until Mr. Sankey's friend urged him to begin a hymn. He began to sing, "There is a fountain filled with blood," in which all the congregation joined. At the close of the service Mr. Sankey was introduced by his friend, and was immediately recognized by Moody as the leader of the singing.

A few inquiries regarding Mr. Sankey's family ties and occupation followed; then the evangelist announced in his determined fashion, "Well, you'll have to give that up! You are the man I have been looking for, and I want you to come to Chicago and help me in my work."

Mr. Sankey was somewhat surprised at this sudden suggestion, and assured Mr. Moody that he could not leave his business, but accepted an invitation to lunch with him that day and learn something of the nature of the work proposed. Nothing definite resulted from this conference, although Mr. Sankey promised to give the matter his prayerful consideration.

Later in the day a card was handed him asking him to meet Mr. Moody that evening at a certain street corner to assist in an open-air service. To this Mr. Sankey responded by writing on the back of the card, "I'll be there." In company with a few friends Mr. Sankey met Mr. Moody at the appointed place, and thus describes the informal service that followed:

"Without stopping, Mr. Moody walked into a store on the corner and asked permission to use a large empty box which he saw outside the door. This he rolled to the side of the street, and taking his stand upon it, asked me to sing the hymn, 'Am I a soldier of the Cross?'

"After one or two hymns Mr. Moody began his address. Many workingmen were just then on their way home from the mills, and in a short time a large crowd had gathered. The address that evening was one of the most powerful I had ever heard. The crowd stood spellbound at the burning words, and many a tear was brushed away from the eyes of the men as they looked up into the speaker's honest face. After talking about fifteen or twenty minutes he closed with a short prayer and announced that he was going to hold another meeting at the Academy of Music, inviting the crowd to follow him there. We sang the well-known hymn, 'Shall we gather at the river?' as we marched down the street.

"It took but a few minutes to pack the lower floor of the Academy, Mr. Moody seeing to it that the laboring men were all seated before he ascended the platform to speak.

"The address was as impressive as the one delivered on the street corner, and it was not until the delegates began to arrive for the evening session of the convention that the meeting was brought to a close. Mr. Moody cut short his sermon, and after a word of prayer dismissed the audience, telling them that they could now go home and get something to eat."

Mr. Sankey was greatly impressed by these two meetings, and, after the convention, went back to Newcastle and told his family of his invitation to Chicago. Some months later he yielded to Mr. Moody's invitation to come for at least a week, and then to decide the question. He arrived in the city early one morning, reaching Mr. Moody's home just as the family were gathering for morning prayers. He was at once asked to sit down at the organ and lead them in a hymn, which he did.

They spent their first day together visiting the sick who were members of Mr. Moody's congregation. Mr. Sankey sang and Mr. Moody read words of comfort from the Word of God and offered prayer for the healing of both body and soul.

The following Sunday a large meeting was held in Farwell Hall. At the close of the service a number of persons arose for prayer, and at the close of the "inquiry meeting" Mr. Moody turned to the singer and said, "You are going home to-morrow, but you see I was right in asking you to come and help me in this work, and I hope you will make up your mind to come as soon as possible."

This wish was granted, for Mr. Sankey soon resigned his business, went to Chicago, and joined Mr. Moody in his work in the Illinois Street Church and also in that of the Young Men's Christian Association.

In 1879, at the International Convention of the Young Men's Christian Association held in Baltimore, Mr. Moody was enthusiastically elected president. At this time he answered several important questions in his characteristic way. One of these was with reference to the work of the general secretary, to which he replied:

"A man cannot be an evangelist and general secretary without spoiling his work in both positions. The secretary, in order to succeed, must take up the work for young men and decide to do this one thing. On this account I gave up the secretaryship to become an evangelist. You cannot do both."

When asked if it were advisable to appoint unconverted men on committees, and if so under what circumstances, he said, "Well, if you want to carry a corpse, put them on. A man that is dead has to be carried. I think one man with Christ in his soul is worth a thousand of those without Christ."

When any one went to him while he was secretary in Chicago, and bored him with some hobby to be worked out in the Association, he would say—if it was good in itself—"Yes, that is a good thing to do. I will appoint you chairman of a special committee to work that out. You fill up the committee with several others, and go to work."

His attitude on "social problems" was determined by experience with men. He had little sympathy with efforts toward amelioration which stopped at giving food. At the same time he had no patience with those who tried to stir up strife between the classes. When asked what he would do for the unemployed or what advice he would give them, he said:

"First of all, to seek the Kingdom of God and His righteousness, believing His promise, which I never knew to fail, that all things will be added to them. Second, to pray to God for work. Third, to be patient as possible during these times of hardship. Fourth, to look earnestly for work. Fifth, to take any honest employment that offers itself. Sixth, to study economy. I think one of the greatest needs of our country is that the laboring men should own their own homes."

"We used to have men coming in all the time," he would say, "asking for work, when I was secretary in Chicago. They would tell me of their sufferings, and how they had no work and wanted help. At last I got a number of cords of firewood and put it in a vacant lot, and got some saws and sawbucks, but kept them out of sight. A man would come and ask for help.

"'Why don't you work?' I would ask.

" 'I can't get any work.'

" 'Would you do anything if you could get any?'

" 'Oh, yes, anything.'

" 'Would you really work in the street?'

" 'Yes.'

" 'Would you saw wood?'

" 'Yes.'

" 'All right.' And then we would bring out a saw and sawbuck and send them out, but we would have a boy watch to see that they did not steal the saw. Sometimes the fellow would say, 'I will go home and tell my wife I have got some work'; and that would be the last we would see of him. During the whole winter I never got more than three or four cords of wood sawed."

He formed friendships in the Association work which continued through life and were of great assistance to him in his evangelistic as well as his educational work. Gen. J. J. Estey, of Brattleboro, became acquainted with Mr. Moody in September, 1867, at the Young Men's Christian Association convention held in Burlington, Vt.

"I shall never forget his coming into the church where the convention was held," says General Estey. "His entrance was an inspiration to every one present, and from that time until the close of the meeting the enthusiasm which prevailed was something remarkable. About six weeks later I visited Chicago, and called upon him. I had simply met him at the convention referred to, but he immediately knew me and called me by name. This I learned afterward was one of the peculiar gifts with which he was endowed, that of putting names and faces together, and rarely making a mistake.

"The following fall I had the pleasure of entertaining him at my home during the Young Men's Christian Association convention, which was held in Brattleboro. We had a number of guests, and when he came he brought one of his brothers with him. I shall never forget one thing which occurred at that time. As we came out of the dining-room after breakfast he whispered to me to ask every one to pray at family devotions, which I afterward learned was his way of getting his brother to offer his first public prayer. The brother repeated the Lord's Prayer as his part of the service.

"The summer following his return from his first trip to Europe he was in Northfield holding meetings, and we used to go down with a carload of people to assist, and not only received a great blessing ourselves, but were able to help in the inquiry-room.

"When the schools were started he invited me to become one of the trustees, which position I have held ever since. Before the Mount Hermon School was begun, he took me over the ground in his buggy, and invited me to become a trustee of that school, which position I very gladly accepted; and during its early days, while he was abroad, I visited the school nearly every week, to straighten out such difficulties as might occur from time to time among the boys. There were then simply the two farm-houses, with twelve boys, a teacher, a matron, and one servant in each house.

"Our relations have been very intimate ever since those days, and I consider it one of the greatest honors of my life to have been in any way associated with him, and to have known him so intimately. I can truthfully assert that he was the most sincere man I ever knew. He was extremely cautious, and has often said to me that I might be able to do such and such things, but that it would not answer at all for him, in his position, to do them. Of all the men I ever knew I think he was the most careful about keeping himself from every appearance of evil."

CHAPTER XIII

First Visit to Great Britain

HIS appreciation of other speakers was one of Mr. Moody's marked characteristics. He was always hunting for some new and well-taught Bible teacher or some successful gospel preacher to address his Illinois Street Church or the Farwell Hall meetings. No minister of any note passed through Chicago without Mr. Moody's learning of his presence in town, and if his orthodoxy was assured, he was certain to receive a pressing invitation to address one or both of the gatherings at the church or Association. This happy faculty of enlisting others brought him into close personal touch with most of the leading Christian workers, clerical or lay, who visited Chicago, including many from abroad.

From these latter friends Mr. Moody heard much of English methods of work, and he felt that a greater knowledge of them would be very helpful. In his abrupt and impulsive way he announced one Sunday, in 1867, to his mission school, that he was going to start for England that week. Mrs. Moody was at that time a sufferer from asthma, and their physician had suggested that a sea voyage, with an entire change of air and scene, was desirable.

There were two men in England whom Mr. Moody had a great desire to hear and meet—Charles H. Spurgeon and George Müller, and with the twofold purpose of affording a beneficial trip for Mrs. Moody and making the acquaintance of these leaders in Christian work, he went abroad.

At that time he was unknown in England except to a few who had visited America. Among these were Fountain J. Hartley, secretary of the London Sunday-school Union, who invited Mr. Moody to speak at an anniversary meeting in Exeter Hall. It was customary for a speaker on such an occasion to be connected with a resolution, as its mover or seconder, in order to give him a right to the floor. Mr. Moody was therefore assigned to move a vote of thanks to the chairman of the evening, who in this instance was the well-known Earl of Shaftesbury.

"Towards the close of the meeting," says Dr. Henry Clay Trumbull in relating this incident, of which he was a witness, "the chairman yielded his chair to the vice-chairman, in order that such a resolution could be offered. The vice-chairman announced that they were glad to welcome their 'American cousin, the Rev. Mr. Moody, of Chicago,' who would now 'move a vote of thanks to the noble Earl' who had presided on this occasion. With refreshing frankness and an utter disregard for conventionalities and mere compliments, Mr. Moody burst upon the audience with the bold announcement:

"'The chairman has made two mistakes. To begin with, I'm not the "Reverend" Mr. Moody at all. I'm plain Dwight L. Moody, a Sabbath-school worker. And then I'm not your "American cousin"! By the grace of God I'm your brother, who is interested with you in our Father's work for His children.

"'And now about this vote of thanks to "the noble Earl" for being our chairman this evening. I don't see why we should thank him, any more than he should thank us. When at one time they offered to thank our Mr. Lincoln for presiding over a meeting in Illinois, he stopped it. He said he'd tried to do his duty, and they'd tried to do theirs. He thought it was an even thing all round.'

"That opening fairly took the breath away from Mr. Moody's hearers. Such talk could not be gauged by any standard. Its novelty was delightful, and Mr. Moody carried his English hearers from that time on."

He soon found his way to the Young Men's Christian Association in Aldersgate Street, and left a permanent impression on English religious life by establishing a noon prayer-meeting. The first meeting was held on May 13th, when nearly a hundred men were present, and the numbers continued to increase until there was a daily attendance of from two to three hundred. Mr. Moody's first text was: "To every man his work." His experiences of gospel work in Chicago were told with a freshness and vigor that captivated all who heard him. The unique and original way in which he pursued his efforts among the rough and lawless children of Chicago was described with thrilling interest. The following letter to his mother is an indication of the impression Mr. Moody received at this time:

"I have at last got started here. I send you an account of the daily union prayer-meeting. It is a great success. They are starting them in different parts of the city, and I am in hopes great good will come from it. They are also starting them in different parts of the Kingdom.

"The great orphan schools of George Müller are at Bristol. He has 1,150 children in his house, but never asks a man for a cent to support them. He calls on God, and God sends money to him. It is wonderful to see what God can do with a man of prayer."

When Mr. Moody was in Bristol, on May 10, 1867, he gave an address to a Sunday-school Bible class, closing with the request that the young men who desired prayer should rise. Fifteen members of the class rose immediately, among them John Kenneth Mackenzie, then a lad of sixteen, who later became a medical missionary in China, and was the means of founding and conducting the first government medical school in that empire in connection with the London Missionary Society.

While Mr. Mackenzie dated his earnest desire for a spiritual life from that occasion, he had not yet fully realized it, and it was not till the anniversary of the day on which he had been impressed by Mr. Moody's address that he rose with several companions at a meeting of the Young Men's Christian Association and avowed himself a follower of the Lord Jesus. Eight years after his college student life he met Mr. Moody in "a never to be forgotten meeting." Mrs. Bryson, his biographer, says:

"It seems to have greatly cheered the heart of the young soldier, who was just putting on the armor for service in the foreign field, to receive words of counsel and blessing from one who some years before had been the instrument in God's hands of leading him to more earnest thought concerning the verities of the unseen and eternal."

It was at this time that Mr. Moody heard the words which marked the beginning of a new era in his life:

"*The world has yet to see what God will do with and for and through and in and by the man who is fully and wholly consecrated to Him.*"

"He said 'a man,'" thought Moody; "he did not say a great man, nor a learned man, nor a rich man, nor a wise man, nor an eloquent man, nor a 'smart' man, but simply 'a man.' I am a man, and it lies with the man himself whether he will or will not make that entire and full consecration. I will try my utmost to be that man."

Being introduced one day by a London friend to Mr. Bewley, of Dublin, the latter asked:

"Is this young man all O and O?"

"What do you mean by 'O and O'?" said the friend.

"Is he Out and Out for Christ?" was the reply.

This remark deepened the impression made, and from that time forward the endeavor to be "O and O" for Christ was supreme.

Before sailing from New York a friend had advised him strongly not to miss meeting the missionary veteran, Dr. Duff, and also to see Dr. Guthrie's work in Edinburgh. Thither, therefore, Mr. Moody went, and while he failed in his special purpose he had the opportunity of speaking one night in the Free Assembly Hall and meeting several prominent religious leaders.

This trip was very helpful to Mr. Moody, and he never ceased to appreciate the associations then formed. In speaking at the annual breakfast of the Young Men's Christian Association in London shortly before returning to America he said:

"It has been my privilege to be in your city two months, and I have thought you were exalted to Heaven with privileges—privileges so numerous that I pity a man who, without hope, goes down to death from the city of London. I have longed to see the founder of the Young Men's Christian Association. Far away in the western part of America I have often prayed for this Association, and my heart has been full this morning as I sat here listening to my friends and looking them in the face.

"I do not know that I shall ever have this privilege again; it is not likely that I shall; next month I return to my home, but I shall always remember this morning. It is said that Napoleon, after his army had accomplished a great victory, ordered a medal to be struck with these words: 'I was there'—that was all. In after years when I am far away in the western prairies of America, and when May comes, I shall think that in 1867 'I was there,' and as the years roll on, if it shall be my privilege to meet in yonder City any that are here this morning, we may there sit down by the banks of the beautiful river of the water of life that flows from the throne of God and talk of this morning. It will give us pleasure then to think that we were together in the fight."

Then Mr. Moody went on to tell of new methods of work in America, especially in Chicago, which moved every one, now to laughter and now to tears. His own visits to the saloons and other haunts of sin developed an ingenuity and tactfulness which showed themselves born of a deep and passionate love for the salvation of souls.

A trip abroad seldom proves so great a success as did this journey, the purpose of its undertaking being perfectly gratified—Mrs. Moody entirely and finally cured, while Mr. Moody met both George Müller and Charles H. Spurgeon. A short visit to the Paris Exposition, the great "world's fair" inaugurated by Napoleon III, was an added pleasure.

On July 1st, on the eve of their return to America, a farewell reception was given to Mr. and Mrs. Moody in London. The appreciation and friendship which the Sunday-school worker, their "brother" from America, had won among Christian workers during this brief visit of three months were widely recognized. In the opinion of one of the speakers:

"Few men who have visited a foreign shore have endeared themselves to so many hearts in so short a time, or with an unknown name and without letters of commendation won their way so deeply into the affections of a multitude of Christian brethren as had Mr. Moody. Few had ever heard of him before, but having talked with him or heard him speak of Jesus, asked for no other warrant to yield him a large measure of their love."

It was on this first visit to Great Britain that he met for the first time R. C. Morgan, then and now the editor of that most influential and widely circulated weekly religious periodical known for years as "The Revival" and later as "The Christian." A warm attachment sprang up at once between these two men who were working, each in his own way, to spread the Gospel.

In later years Mr. Moody referred to his earlier efforts as being in a measure an exhibition of "zeal without knowledge"; but, as he would also add, "There is much more hope for a man in such a condition than for that man who has knowledge without zeal." Mr. Morgan, a careful and thorough Bible student, was drawn to the young American stranger, and from the first gave him sympathy and encouragement, and has ever been a most generous supporter in all his later projects. Before he visited the British Isles again Mr. Moody too was to receive a more perfect knowledge of the Word of God.

CHAPTER XIV

INFLUENCE OF HENRY MOOREHOUSE

A NEW epoch in Mr. Moody's religious experience and preaching was marked by his friendship with Henry Moorehouse. The acquaintance made in Dublin during this first short visit to Great Britain seems to have been but casual.

"I had read in the papers about 'The Boy Preacher,' said Mr. Moody in relating the circumstances of his meeting with Moorehouse, "but I did not know that this was he. He introduced himself to me and said he would like to come to Chicago to preach. He was a beardless boy—he didn't look more than seventeen—and I said to myself, 'He can't preach.' He wanted me to let him know what boat I was going to America on, as he would like to go on the boat with me. Well, I thought he couldn't preach and I didn't let him know. I hadn't been in Chicago a great many weeks before I got a letter saying that he had arrived in America and that he would come to Chicago and preach for me if I wanted him. Well, I sat down and wrote a very cold letter: 'If you come West, call on me.' I thought that would be the last I should hear of him. I soon got another letter saying he was still in the country, and would come to Chicago and preach for me if I wanted him. I wrote again, 'If you happen to come West, drop in on me.' In the course of a few days I got a letter stating that on a certain Thursday he would be in Chicago and would preach for me. Then what to do with him I didn't know. I had made up my mind that he couldn't preach. I was going to be out of town Thursday and Friday, and I told some of the officers of the church, 'There is an Englishman coming here Thursday who wants to preach. I don't know whether he can or not.'

"They said there was a great deal of interest in the church, and they did not think he had better preach then; he was a stranger, and he might do more harm than good. 'Well,' I said, 'you might try him. I will announce him to speak Thursday night. Your regular weekly meeting is on Friday. After hearing him you can either announce that he will speak again the next night or you can have your usual prayer-meeting. If he speaks well both nights you will know whether to announce him or me for the Sunday meetings. I will be back Saturday.'

"When I got back Saturday morning I was anxious to know how he got on. The first thing I said to my wife when I got in the house was, 'How is the young Englishman coming along? How do the people like him?'

"'They like him very much.'

"'Did you hear him?'

"'Yes.'

"'Well, did you like him?'

"'Yes, I liked him very much. He has preached two sermons from that verse of John, "*For God so loved the world, that He gave His only begotten Son, that whosoever believeth in Him should not perish, but have everlasting life,*" and I think you will like him, although he preaches a little differently from you.'

"'How is that?'

"'Well, he tells the worst sinners that God loves them.'

"'Then,' said I, 'he is wrong.'

"'I think you will agree with him when you hear him,' said she, 'because he backs up everything he says with the Bible.'

"Sunday came, and as I went to the church I noticed that every one brought his Bible. The morning address was to Christians. I had never heard anything quite like it. He gave chapter and verse to prove every statement he made. When night came the church was packed. 'Now, beloved friends,' said the preacher, 'if you will turn to the third chapter of John and the sixteenth verse, you will find my text.' He preached the most extraordinary sermon from that verse. He did not divide the text into 'secondly' and 'thirdly' and 'fourthly'; he just took the whole verse, and then went through the Bible from Genesis to Revelation to prove that in all ages God loved the world. God had sent prophets and patriarchs and holy men to warn us, and then He sent His Son, and after they killed Him, He sent the Holy Ghost. I never knew up to that time that God loved us so much. This heart of mine began to thaw out; I could not keep back the tears. It was like news from a far country: I just drank it in. So did the crowded congregation. I tell you there is one thing that draws above everything else in this world, and that is *love*. A man that has no one to love him, no mother, no wife, no children, no brother, no sister, belongs to the class that commits suicide.

"It's pretty hard to get a crowd out in Chicago on a Monday night, but the people came. They brought their Bibles, and Moorehouse began, 'Beloved friends, if you will turn to the third chapter of John, and the sixteenth verse, you will find my text,' and again he showed on another line, from Genesis to Revelation, that God loved us. He could turn to almost any part of the Bible and prove it. Well, I thought that was better than the other one; he struck a higher note than ever, and it was sweet to my soul to hear it. He just beat that truth down into my heart, and I have never doubted it since. I used to preach that God was behind the sinner with a double-edged sword ready to hew him down. I have got done with that. I preach now that God is behind him with love, and he is running away from the God of love.

"Tuesday night came, and we thought he had surely exhausted that text and that he would take another, but he said: 'If you will turn to the third chapter of John and the sixteenth verse, you will find my text,' and he preached again from that wonderful text, and this night he seemed to strike a higher chord still. '*God so loved the world, that He gave His only begotten Son, that whosoever believeth in Him should not perish, but have* '—not going to have when you die, but have it right here, now—' *eternal life.*' By that time we began to believe it, and we have never doubted it since.

"For six nights he had preached on this one text. The seventh night came, and he went into the pulpit. Every eye was upon him. He said, ' Beloved friends, I have been hunting all day for a new text, but I cannot find anything so good as the old one; so we will go back to the third chapter of John and the sixteenth verse,' and he preached the seventh sermon from those wonderful words, '*God so loved the world.*' I remember the end of that sermon: ' My friends,' he said, ' for a whole week I have been trying to tell you how much God loves you, but I cannot do it with this poor stammering tongue. If I could borrow Jacob's ladder and climb up into Heaven and ask Gabriel, who stands in the presence of the Almighty, to tell me how much love the Father has for the world, all he could say would be: "*God so loved the world, that He gave His only begotten Son, that whosoever believeth in Him should not perish, but have everlasting life.*" '

"If a man gets up in that pulpit and gives out that text to-day, there is a smile all over the church."

Mr. Moorehouse taught Moody to draw his sword full length, to fling the scabbard away, and enter the battle with the naked blade.

This first visit to America was repeated in August, 1868, when he again visited Chicago and labored with Mr. Moody for two months, preaching in his church and in Farwell Hall. During this time, accompanied by Mr. Moody, he went to various other cities, holding some seventy-two meetings. In the winter of 1872 he came again to America and conducted services in Chicago, and again in 1878 he assisted Mr. Moody's evangelistic work in a New England mission.

Mr. Moorehouse was among the first to welcome Moody to England in June, 1875, and assisted him at Newcastle-on-Tyne, and other places, taking a leading part in his all-day meetings. The delighted

ILLINOIS STREET CHURCH, CHICAGO.

First building erected by Mr. Moody. Scene of his efforts before Chicago fire.

MOODY'S TABERNACLE.

First building erected after Chicago fire. Occupied for two years. A scene of remarkable evangelistic effort.

D. L. Moody.

From a portrait in oil by Healey. The one relic saved by Mrs. Moody from the Chicago fire.

recognition of each other's strength of character bound them closely together in a strong friendship. Mr. Moorehouse's affectionate nature and devotion to the Master and Mr. Moody's strong common sense and ever-widening influence combined to make them irresistible companions in evangelistic work.

CHAPTER XV

THE CHICAGO FIRE AND ITS RESULTS

IN the spring of 1871, in company with Philip Phillips and the Rev. J. H. Vincent, Mr. Moody went on a trip to California. On his return to Chicago the weather had become very hot, his audience was scattered, and it seemed almost impossible to get them together again. For some time he considered the means of getting hold of them again. At one time he thought he would get up some kind of sacred concert, or secure some one to lecture on historical events, for he feared that the Gospel would not "draw" in such weather.

After praying over it the thought came to him: "Preach to them upon Bible characters." He had some six or eight of these in his mind, and decided to begin with Adam. So he took up Adam and studied the subject, but feared that he could never talk about him for thirty minutes. Then he thought that he would try Enoch. Next he studied Noah, and then came to Abraham, whom he selected as one of the characters. It was not long before Farwell Hall began to fill up, and inside of five weeks he had large congregations.

When he came to the study of Christ he intended to devote six nights to His life. He had been spending four Sunday nights on the subject, and had traced His career from the manger to His arrest and trial. On the fifth Sunday night, October 8th, he preached to the largest congregation that he had ever addressed in that city, having taken for his text, "*What then shall I do with Jesus which is called Christ?*" After preaching—or talking, as he did not call it preaching then—with all his power of entreaty, presenting Christ as a Saviour and Redeemer, he said:

"I wish you would take this text home with you and turn it over in your minds during the week, and next Sabbath we will come to Calvary and the cross, and we will decide what to do with Jesus of Nazareth."

"What a mistake!" he said, in relating the story to a large audience in Chicago on the twenty-second anniversary of the great fire in that city in 1871; "I have never dared to give an audience a week to think of their salvation since. If they were lost they might rise up in judgment against me. I remember Mr. Sankey's singing, and how his voice rang when he came to that pleading verse:

"'To-day the Saviour calls,
For refuge fly!
The storm of Justice falls,
And death is nigh!'

"I have never seen that congregation since. I have hard work to keep back the tears to-day. I have looked over this audience, and not a single one is here that I preached to that night. I have a great many old friends and am pretty well acquainted in Chicago, but twenty-two years have passed away, and I have not seen that congregation since, and I never will meet those people again until I meet them in another world. But I want to tell you of one lesson I learned that night, which I have never forgotten, and that is, when I preach, to press Christ upon the people then and there, and try to bring them to a decision on the spot. I would rather have that right hand cut off than to give an audience now a week to decide what to do with Jesus. I have often been criticised; people have said:

"'Moody, you seem to be trying to get people to decide all at once: why do you not give them time to consider?'

"I have asked God many times to forgive me for telling people that night to take a week to think it over, and if He spares my life, I will never do it again. This audience will break up in a few moments—we may never meet after to-day. There is something terribly solemn about a congregation like this.

"You will notice that Pilate was just in the condition of my audience that night, just the condition that you are in to-day—he had to decide then and there what to do with Jesus. The thing was sprung upon him suddenly, although I do not think that Jesus Christ could have been a stranger to Pilate. I do not believe that he had preached in Judea for months, and also in Jerusalem, without Pilate's having heard of His teachings. He must have heard of the sermons He had preached; he must have heard of the doctrine He taught; he must have heard of the wonderful parables that He uttered; he must have heard of the wonderful miracles that He had performed; he must have heard how Herod had taken the life of His forerunner by having him beheaded, and of the cruel way Herod had treated Him: Pilate was no stranger to Jesus of Nazareth.

"Ever since that night of the great fire I have determined as long as God spares my life to make more of Christ than in the past. I thank God that He is a thousand times more to me to-day than He was twenty-two years ago. I am not what I wish I was, but I am a good deal better than I was when Chicago was on fire."

The year 1871 was a critical one in Mr. Moody's career. He realized more and more how little he was fitted by personal acquirements for his work. An intense hunger and thirst for spiritual power were aroused in him by two women who used to attend the meetings and sit on the front seat. He could see by the expression on their faces that they were praying. At the close of services they would say to him:

"We have been praying for you."

"Why don't you pray for the people?" Mr. Moody would ask.

"Because you need the power of the Spirit," they would say.

"I need the power! Why," said Mr. Moody, in relating the incident years after, "I thought I had power. I had the largest congregations in Chicago, and there were many conversions. I was in a sense satisfied. But right along those two godly women kept praying for me, and their earnest-talk about anointing for special service set me to thinking. I asked them to come and talk with me, and they poured out their hearts in prayer that I might receive the filling of the Holy Spirit. There came a great hunger into my soul. I did not know what it was. I began to cry out as I never did before. I really felt that I did not want to live if I could not have this power for service."

While Mr. Moody was in this mental and spiritual condition Chicago was laid in ashes. The great fire swept out of existence both Farwell Hall and the Illinois Street Church. Sunday night after the meeting, as Mr. Moody went homeward, he saw the glare of flames, and knew it meant ruin to Chicago. About one o'clock Farwell Hall was burned and soon his church went down. Everything was scattered. At midnight the fierceness of the fire seemed to be waning, and it was thought that the fire department could gain the upper hand, as they had done the night before. The family retired, but within an hour a loud call was made to all the residents of their street to hasten their escape. The fire had crossed the river and was rapidly advancing.

It was too late to think of saving much more than could be carried in the hands. A neighbor took Mr. Moody's two children in his already crowded carriage, and made his escape north. A few articles of silver and some valued tokens of friendship were hastily placed in a baby cart. But there was one article Mrs. Moody's heart was set upon saving. This was a portrait in oil of Mr. Moody by the artist Healy, which hung on the wall of their parlor. It was a gift from the artist, presented to Mrs. Moody after their return from the first trip to Europe in 1867. A free lease of this home, completely furnished, was presented to Mr. Moody at that time by his Chicago friends, and this portrait Mrs. Moody prized above anything the house contained.

A stranger who had entered the room assisted in taking it from the wall. Calling Mr. Moody, his wife urged him to save it for her. The ludicrous side of the situation at once appealed to him, notwithstanding the terror of that awful night.

"Take my own picture!" he said. "Well, that would be amusing! Suppose I am met on the street by friends in the same plight as ourselves, and they say:

"'Hello, Moody, glad you have escaped; what's that you have saved and cling to so affectionately?'—wouldn't it sound well to reply:

"'Oh, I've got my own portrait?'"

No entreaty could prevail on Mr. Moody, but the canvas was hastily knocked out of the heavy frame, and carried off by Mrs. Moody herself—the one relic rescued from their home. A bruised face was part of the price paid for this effort, for once on the street there was a constant struggle with the terrific wind. Love won, but only after a fierce battle. This portrait now hangs on the walls of the Northfield home, a reminder of that night of fiery ordeal.

As soon as his wife and family were safe with friends Mr. Moody devoted himself to relief work. Before long he started for the East to raise money for the homeless, and also for the new church. George H. Stuart and John Wanamaker, of Philadelphia, and other friends in the East raised $3,000, and a temporary building, 75 by 100 feet, was immediately reared on a lot not far from the site of the former church. On December 24, 1871, just two months and fifteen days after the fire, this building, known as the North Side Tabernacle, was dedicated.

When in New York he heard there was a rich man in Fall River who was very liberal. So he went to him, and secured a check for a large amount. His new friend, who was Mr. R. K. Remington, took him in his carriage to the houses of other rich men in the city. When they parted at the train Mr. Moody grasped his hand and said:

"If you ever come to Chicago, call on me; and I will try to return your kindness."

Said Mr. Remington, "Don't wait for me; do it to the first man that comes along."

During this Eastern visit the hunger for more spiritual power was still upon Mr. Moody.

"My heart was not in the work of begging," he said. "I could not appeal. I was crying all the time that God would fill me with His Spirit. Well, one day, in the city of New York—oh, what a day!—I cannot describe it, I seldom refer to it; it is almost too sacred an experience to name. Paul had an experience of which he never spoke for fourteen years. I can only say that God revealed Himself to me, and I had such an experience of His love that I had to ask Him to stay His hand. I went to preaching again. The sermons were not different; I did not present any new truths, and yet hundreds were converted. I would not now be placed back where I was before that blessed experience if you should give me all the world—it would be as the small dust of the balance."

When Mr. Moody returned to Chicago his mission work at the new tabernacle went forward successfully, and within a year steps were taken to erect a permanent building. The lot on which the present church stands was secured. Contributions came in from all quarters, thousands of Sunday-school children contributing five cents each to place a brick in the new edifice. For two years the basement of the present building was roofed over temporarily and used for meetings, and finally, as a subsequent chapter will explain, means were provided for the completion of the structure which has since been known as the Chicago Avenue Church.

Five years after the great fire, when he had returned from his work abroad, Mr. Moody wrote the following letter to the members of the Chicago Avenue Church, whom he loved so dearly:

"I need not tell you how much I would like to be with you on Fast-day, but God has ordered it otherwise. As I am alone to-day with none but my blessed Master, waiting in this hotel for the Sabbath to pass, so that I can get on to my home, where I can see and try to help cheer my heart-broken mother (he had just received word of the sudden death of a brother), I feel that I must tell you some of the thoughts that have been passing through my mind.

"For fifteen years I have been especially burdened for three objects: the church, the Young Men's Christian Association, and a dear brother, who is now in Heaven. God has answered my prayer for him, saved him, made him useful to others, and now taken him to Himself. That burden is gone. The Young Men's Christian Association has been blessed of late, too. But how is it with my first love? For years I seldom get on my knees in private but I think and pray for the dear church in Chicago, and of late you have been on my mind and heart far more than usual. Are you going to let this time of blessing pass without a blessing to you?

"The only way any church can get a blessing is to lay aside all difference, all criticism, all coldness and party feeling, and come to the Lord as one man; and when the church lives in the power of the thirteenth chapter of First Corinthians I am sure that many will be added daily to the flock of God. I would like to have the church read that chapter together on their knees on Thursday and, as you do so, pray God to apply it with power. Of late my earnest prayer to God has been that He would help me to save more, and I cannot tell you how wonderfully He has answered my prayer. It seems as if you were all much nearer and dearer to me than ever. My heart goes out to you, and I long to see you all coming constantly to God for a fresh supply of love.

"I found a verse in I Peter, iv. 8, to-day. I never saw it before: '*Above all things put on love.*' Think much of that one expression. Put it at the head of the list. Faith is good, but this is above it. Truth is good: it is a beautiful sight to see the church of God study the Word, but what are we if we do not have love? May the dear church get such a flood of love from on high that it will fill all our hearts. The last night Jesus was on earth, before they crucified Him, He said to His disciples: '*This is My commandment, that ye love one another as I have loved you.*' Let us think on these solemn words, and may the love of Christ draw us all together so we will be as one man."

Enclosed in this church letter, Mr. Moody wrote the pastor, the Rev. Dr. W. J. Erdman:

"I do hope you will hold the people to the thought of love. I am sure that is where the churches have all gone astray. We must have it above all things. See how Paul and Peter agreed in this. Let us put that first. If the church is sound in love I think it will be sound in everything else. That God may be with you and bless you in a wonderful manner is my earnest and constant prayer."

CHAPTER XVI

First Extended Mission in Great Britain

SO great was the interest at the tabernacle that the work went on unabated during Mr. Moody's absence while working in behalf of the new building. Finding, therefore, that he could be spared from Chicago, and desiring to learn more of the Bible from English Bible students, Mr. Moody determined to cross the sea again. He started for a short trip in June, 1872. This visit calls for special consideration on account of one incident that undoubtedly marked another turning point in Mr. Moody's career.

He was determined not to get into work, if he could help it; but one day, at the close of the service in the Old Bailey prayer-meeting, the Rev. Mr. Lessey, pastor of a church in the North of London, asked him to preach for him the next Sabbath. Mr. Moody consented.

The morning service seemed very dead and cold. The people did not show much interest, and he felt that it had been a morning lost. But at the next service, which was at half-past six in the evening, it seemed, while he was preaching, as if the very atmosphere was charged with the Spirit of God. There came a hush upon all the people, and a quick response to his words, though he had not been much in prayer that day, and could not understand it.

When he had finished preaching he asked all who would like to become Christians to rise, that he might pray for them. People rose all over the house until it seemed as if the whole audience was getting up.

Mr. Moody said to himself:

"These people don't understand me. They don't know what I mean when I ask them to rise." He had never seen such results before, and did not know what to make of it, so he put the test again.

"Now," he said, "all of you who want to become Christians just step into the inquiry-room."

They went in, and crowded the room so that they had to take in extra chairs to seat them all. The minister was surprised, and so was Mr. Moody. Neither had expected such a blessing. They had not realized that God can save by hundreds and thousands as well as by ones and twos.

When Mr. Moody again asked those that really wanted to become Christians to rise, the whole audience got up. He did not even then know what to do, so he told all who were really in earnest to meet the pastor there the next night.

The next day he went over to Dublin, but on Tuesday morning received a despatch urging him to return, saying there were more inquirers on Monday than on Sunday. He went back and held meetings for ten days, and four hundred were taken into that church.

After some time what was, perhaps, the secret of this marvellous manifestation of the Spirit's working was revealed. There were two sisters belonging to that church. One was strong, the other was bedridden. One day as the sick woman was bemoaning her condition the thought came to her that she could at least pray, and she began to pray God to revive her church. Day and night her prayer went up to God.

One day she read in a paper an account of some meetings Mr. Moody had held in America, and, though she did not know him, she began to pray that God would send him to her church. On the Sunday Mr. Moody preached, her sister went home and said:

"Whom do you think preached this morning?"

She suggested the names of several with whom her pastor was in the habit of exchanging.

Finally her sister told her, "It was Mr. Moody, from America."

"I know what that means," cried the sick woman; "God has heard my prayers!"

Mr. Moody believed that it was this revival that carried him back to England the next year.

Among other meetings he attended the Mildmay Conference, and thus records his impression of the Rev. William Pennefather, the founder of Mildmay:

"I well remember sitting in yonder seat looking up at this platform and seeing the beloved Mr. Pennefather's face illuminated as it were with Heaven's light. I don't think I can recall a word that he said, but the whole atmosphere of the man breathed holiness, and I got then a lift and impetus in the Christian life that I have never lost, and I believe the impression will remain with me to my dying day. I thank God that I saw and spoke with that holy man; no one could see him without the consciousness that he lived in the presence of God."

It was the first and last time they ever met; but Mr. Pennefather was strongly impressed with the conviction that Mr. Moody was one for whom God had prepared a great work, and after his return to America he wrote him, telling him of the wide door open for evangelistic work in London and elsewhere and promising him a warm welcome if he would ever come over and help them. Other invitations equally cordial were received about the same time from Cuthbert Bainbridge, of Newcastle-on-Tyne, and Henry Bewley, of Dublin. These were accompanied with the promise of funds to meet the travelling expenses of Mr. Moody and his party.

After arranging for the work in which he had been engaged in Chicago it was decided to accept these invitations and return to England for a short visit. Philip Phillips, a warm personal friend of Mr. Moody, was at this time the leading gospel singer in America, and Mr. Moody at once urged him to accompany him. This he was not able to do, and P. P. Bliss, whose reputation as a gospel solo singer and composer had created a demand for his services on all sides, was then invited. He had been associated with Mr. Moody on several occasions, and both men were closely attached to each other. But in this he was also disappointed, as it seemed impossible for Mr. Bliss to leave home.

It was Mr. Moody's first idea to leave Mr. Sankey in Chicago to continue the work in the mission church and in the Association. Finally, however, he decided that the British call was of sufficient importance to take Mr. Sankey from his work for a few months at least.

Mr. Moody had at that time about $450, which he had loaned to a friend to be invested during his absence, as all his expenses on the mission were to be met by those who had invited him. Steamship passage for Mr. Moody and his family and Mr. Sankey had been engaged, but the promised funds failed to come. Within a day or two of the time for departure Mr. Moody had to request the return of his loan to meet travelling expenses. On reaching Liverpool, on June 17, 1873, the cause for the non-receipt of the promised funds was at once apparent. All three of the cordial and devoted friends on whose invitation Mr. Moody had depended for moral and financial support had been called to be with their Lord.

After reading the letter announcing the death of these friends, Mr. Moody turned to Mr. Sankey and said: "God seems to have closed the doors. We will not open any ourselves. If He opens the door we will go in; otherwise we will return to America."

On their arrival at Liverpool they went to an hotel, where they spent the evening. Mr. Moody then discovered in one of his pockets an unopened letter which he had received, just before leaving New York, from Mr. Bennett, the secretary of the Young Men's Christian Association at York, England. Mr. Bennett said that he had heard of his work in America among young men, and he hoped if he ever came to England he would come there and speak at the Association.

"This door is only ajar," Mr. Moody exclaimed, "but we will consider the letter as God's hand leading to York, and we will go there."

After spending one night in Liverpool Mr. Moody, with his family, took the train for London, and Mr. Sankey went to Manchester to the home of the one man whom he knew in England—Henry Moorehouse. On receiving Mr. Moody's despatch that he was ready to begin his meetings in York, Mr. Bennett replied that everything was so cold and dead in the town that it would take at least a month to prepare for the intended mission. The despatch concluded by asking Mr. Moody to name a date when he could consult him regarding the proposed meetings. With his usual promptness this telegram was sent in reply:

"I will be in York to-night." At ten o'clock that evening he reached the city, where no one except his friend, Mr. Bennett, had ever seen him and very few had ever heard his name.

The situation was not encouraging, but after looking it over carefully Mr. Moody declared that every man must make his own way and that he was ready "to go in at once." Mr. Sankey was telegraphed for, and the meetings opened immediately. The next morning application was made to several ministers of the town for the use of their pulpits on the coming Sabbath, and two Wesleyan, a Baptist, and a Congregational church were placed at their disposal.

It is interesting to look through the files of the religious papers for the two years that covered Mr. Moody's campaign in Great Britain. In some of the later issues double numbers were published, the extra pages being devoted entirely to articles concerning the great meetings. In contrast with these extensive reports is the following modest little notice in one corner of "The Christian," entitled, "Mr. D. L. Moody in England":

"Mr. Moody has just arrived in England with his family, and is accompanied by a Christian brother who leads the singing at his meetings, after the manner of our well-known and much-loved friend, Philip Phillips. Mrs. Moody and her children remain with her sister in the neighborhood of London while her husband is holding meetings in the provinces. Last Lord's Day he preached in Independent and Wesleyan chapels in York, and we believe that he intends to continue a while in the North of England and then go to Scotland. He prefers preaching in chapels, and so strengthening existing causes, to commencing a new work in public halls, etc. Any friends who desire his help, especially in the north, should write to him at once, Young Men's Christian Association, York. We will notify change of address from week to week, as we receive it from him."

The clergy at first were strongly inclined to look upon the newcomers with suspicion and disfavor, and the attendance was small to begin with, but gradually the meetings grew in interest, the clergy cooperated, and both preaching and singing became the subject of public conversation throughout the community.

Mr. Moody wrote from York, on June 30th, to Mr. Farwell, of Chicago, as follows:

"You will see by the heading of this note that I am in York. I began here one week ago yesterday (Sunday) and have had splendid success so far. Yesterday we had four meetings. They were large and I think very profitable. God was with us. I preached in the morning on '*They that be wise shall shine*'; in the afternoon on *No difference*,' and in the evening from the text, '*The spirit of the Lord is upon me because He has anointed me to preach the Gospel.*' Sankey sang the hymns finely; all seemed to be much pleased with him. I think he is going to do much good here. All the chapels are open to us, and invitations are coming from all over the country; I think we shall have all we can do here. I think of you all and get fearfully homesick at times.

"Keep me posted in regard to the Young Men's Christian Association building and all about the stock. I should like to see a good building go up there. I do not see any better opportunity to work for Christ than in that field. I do not know what is to become of the Young Men's Christian Association in England and America if something of the kind is not done. I send you some flower seeds. I think the one marked 1-6 is beautiful, and never have seen anything in America like it. I hope you will have success with them. Remember me to Wells and all your own family. Yours thro' the Grace of God."

"Yes, I have known Mr. Moody ever since a memorable Monday morning in 1873," writes the Rev. F. B. Meyer, who was among the first to associate himself with the movement. "I can see him now, standing up to lead the first noon prayer-meeting in a small, ill-lit room in Coney Street, York, little realizing that it was the seed-germ of a mighty harvest, and that a movement was beginning that would culminate in a few months in Free Assembly Hall, Edinburgh, and ultimately in the Agricultural Hall and the Royal Opera House, London. It was the birth-time of new conceptions of ministry, new methods of work, new inspirations and hopes.

"What an inspiration when this great and noble soul first broke into my life! I was a young pastor then, in the old city of York, and bound rather rigidly by the chains of conventionalism. Such had been my training, and such might have been my career. But here was a revelation of a new ideal. The first characteristic of Mr. Moody's that struck me was that he was so absolutely unconventional and natural. That a piece of work had generally been done after a certain method would probably be the reason why he would set about it in some fresh and unexpected way. That the new method startled people was the greater reason for continuing with it, if only it drew them to the Gospel. But there was never the slightest approach to irreverence, fanaticism, or extravagance; everything was in perfect accord with a rare common sense, a directness of method, a simplicity and transparency of aim, which were as attractive as they were fruitful in result.

"The first ten days of his meetings were only moderately successful, and he gladly accepted my invitation to come to the chapel where I ministered, and there we had a fortnight of most blessed and memorable meetings. The little vestry there—how vividly I remember it!—was the scene of our long and earnest prayers as we knelt around the leather-covered table in the middle of the room. Two

D. L. Moody, in his Forty-fifth Year.

DWIGHT L. MOODY AT 45. PORTRAIT TAKEN IN PARIS.

Presbyterian students, brothers, from Dr. McKay's church in Hull, often used to pray with us, and I remember that Mr. Moody, at the great Free Trade Hall, Manchester, referred to that little room as the fountain from which the river of blessing for the whole country had sprung.

"Many recollections of those days come back as I write: How in the midst of tea at home Mr. Moody suddenly felt that he should preach his afterward famous sermon on Heaven, and started off on a three miles' walk to fetch his notes; how Mr. Sankey went over to see Mr. Rees, of Sunderland, the sailor-preacher, of whom I had spoken to them, and proved his singing powers in the little back parlor of W. D. Longstaff, to the entire satisfaction of both minister and elder; how we had our all-day meeting, the first of its kind in England; and how the fire of God burnt hot in all our hearts. Ah, blessed days! that will live as long as memory endures, days of Heaven, of wonder, of a new and brilliant constellation in one's sphere, of the beginning of a lifelong devotion to another man, which has only ripened and deepened with every succeeding year."

The first public report of the meetings in York appeared in "The Christian" for July 10th, in a letter from Mr. Bennett, who said:

"The following notes of our brother D. L. Moody's evangelistic labors in this city will doubtless be welcomed by your readers. On Sunday morning, June 22d, Mr. Moody preached in Salem Congregational Chapel to Christian workers; in the afternoon, in the Corn Exchange, to about a thousand persons, and in the evening in Wesley Chapel. Many were impressed. Every evening during the following week Bible lectures were delivered in various chapels, each service resulting in the saving of souls, but especially in the quickening of believers. Formality and apathy are to a great extent dissipated, and Christians have been led to pray and work for the conversion of sinners.

"During the past week the Lord has greatly blessed us in the ingathering of souls. On Sabbath day, June 29th, Mr. Moody preached in two other chapels, and also twice in the Corn Exchange, to audiences numbering about a thousand each. Every week evening service is preceded by a service of song, conducted by Mr. Moody's colaborer, Mr. Sankey, whose hymns, tunes, and voice (like those of Philip Phillips) have drawn and impressed many. Mr. Moody preaches the Gospel and Mr. Sankey sings it. Prayer-meetings have been held every noon at the rooms of the Young Men's Christian Association, and many there have offered themselves and others for the prayers of God's people.

"Though this is the summer season, and we were under a disadvantage in consequence (through the miscarriage of letters to and from Mr. Moody) of not having notice, and, therefore, were unprepared for his visit, when Mr. Moody dropped down on us on the Saturday morning, arrangements were made and bills printed all in a few hours, and from the first the Lord has greatly blessed our brothers' labors in the strengthening and stimulating of Christians and in the bringing of many out of darkness into light; their visit will long be remembered in this city. The congregations have from the first been increasingly large; all denominations have opened their chapels and given us their presence and help. Many of the clergy have also heartily bidden them 'God-speed.'

"P. S.—Sunday evening, 11 P.M. Just before posting this, let me add that this afternoon a large chapel was filled to hear Moody; a deep impression was made. I have just come from the evening service, where every aisle and standing place, the vestries and lobbies, even the pulpit stairs, were crowded nearly half an hour before the evening service commenced. The Holy Spirit worked mightily, sinners in all positions in life sought the Lord earnestly, and Christian brothers and sisters of the Church of England, Friends, and of every denomination, were constrained without invitation to speak and pray with them. I don't know how many, but over fifty gave their hearts to Christ. Mr. Moody will (if the Lord will) proceed to Scarborough shortly."

Writing again from York, July 14th, Mr. Bennett said that the American evangelists were still there and that every meeting during the week just passed had been attended with great blessing. "One distinguishing feature of our brother's meetings," he said, "is the Bible lectures which he gives on such subjects as 'The Blood of Christ,' 'Walking with God,' etc. The passages of Scripture are previously selected and read out by friends in various parts of the audience. The chapel was crowded long before the service last evening, and many sought and found the Saviour. We have had most refreshing seasons at our noon prayer-meetings: we hope to continue them. Let me ask the Lord's children to pray that these meetings may become an institution in this city and be greatly used of God in the binding together of Christians of every name, in the deepening of their spiritual life and fervor, and in the establishment of a great rallying centre for organization and aggressive effort."

Each public service was followed by an inquiry meeting, which at first was considered a novelty, but gradually became a great power in the work. Mr. Moody's manner of expounding the Scripture at once attracted attention. The Bible readings, which he had given in Brooklyn and other cities, were continued with great effect. Believers were aroused to a new interest in the Sacred Word. Bibles were seen at every meeting and new methods of Bible study were suggested. Mr. Meyer thinks that no one has given a greater impulse to Bible study than Mr. Moody.

"During the time of his meetings in Great Britain the Bagster publishing house could hardly keep pace with the demand for Bibles which he created," he says. "He knew his Bible as very few have done, and was always wearing out Bibles, covering the margins with references and notes, and allowing them to pass freely among his friends. His Bible school and the Chicago seminary have filled hundreds of young minds with the same enthusiasm. In my earliest acquaintance with him I remember how eager he was that I should tell him any new thing I had discovered in the Word of God. How interested he was, for instance, when I said that the use of the article in Acts, i. indicated that the scene of Pentecost was the same upper room where the Apostles had prepared the Passover!"

The first all-day meeting which Mr. Moody held in England was arranged by Mr. Meyer and himself as they walked up and down Coney Street, York. It began at eleven A.M. and lasted six hours, and an evening service followed. From its novelty it attracted great attention, and it commended itself heartily to all who attended the services. First, there was an hour for confession and prayer; second, an hour for praise; third, a promise meeting, which consisted of testimonies on the part of believers to the fulfilment of promises in their own experiences; fourth, a witness meeting, which was a succession of public confession of Christ by young converts; fifth, a Bible lecture by Mr. Moody, and, finally, a communion service conducted by Mr. Moody and four ministers.

After five weeks of meetings in York, resulting in the professed conversion of several hundred people, Mr. Moody went to Sunderland. Here the meetings were even more largely attended. The chapel in which the services were held soon became too small for the audience, finally necessitating the use of one of the largest halls in the North of England.

Mr. Rees, who invited Mr. Moody to Sunderland, was an open-communion Baptist, the pastor of the Bethesda Chapel, where the inquiry meetings were held after the first meeting in the Victoria Hall. The week-day meetings were held in such chapels as could be secured, for there was more or less criticism to be overcome. It was said that there was only one minister heartily in sympathy with the revival movement; all the other clergymen were half-hearted or even active in opposition.

During the Sunderland mission a committee from the Young Men's Christian Association called upon Mr. Moody and asked him to speak before the young men. The invitation was readily accepted. The committee then apologized for not joining earlier in the work, explaining that their delay was not due to lack of sympathy, but to the fear that the Association *would be injured* if its officers seemed to favor a sectarian work. When they came to a better acquaintance with him they were frank to acknowledge how little they knew at that time of the spirit of the preacher.

In Sunderland, as in York, special stress was laid upon the noon prayer-meeting and upon the afternoon meetings. Here, also, an all-day meeting was held. It is interesting to read the impression which Mr. Rees had after working for a month with Mr. Moody and Mr. Sankey:

"1. Both these brethren are genuine to the backbone.

"2. They are as disinterested as they are zealous, and their zeal is extraordinary.

"3. Mr. Moody is the 'Mercurius' of the pair. Mr. Sankey is not the 'Jupiter,' but the 'Orpheus.' The former is not eloquent, but very fluent; not poetical or rhetorical, but he never talks twaddle and seldom utters a sentence that is not well worth hearing. He is a rapid, too rapid a speaker; nevertheless, what he does say is sensible, forcible, and to the point and not too long, which is a great advantage. He is American to the core, in speech, intonation, and vigor. His anecdotes are superabundant and, for the most part, the acquisition of his own experience; they are always apt, often most pathetic, and sometimes appalling. His earnestness is intense, his energy untiring, his courage leonine, his tact uncommon, and his love for souls most tender."

After the Sunderland mission Mr. Moody began a new work in Newcastle-on-Tyne. He had now gained the sympathy of nearly all the ministers of the several denominations, except those of the Established Church, who, learning that he was not ordained, refused in any way to countenance the work.

After a few weeks of very successful meetings the editor of "The Newcastle Chronicle," a Mr. Cowen, then a member of Parliament for that district, described the meetings in his paper, speaking of them as a "wonderful religious phenomenon." On the whole it was a friendly review and criticism of the work. This was an unusual notice for such a prominent secular paper, and Mr. Cowen's article created a profound impression throughout England, resulting in invitations to hold services in other cities.

Mr. Moody had been slowly overcoming the prejudice against his preaching and Mr. Sankey's singing at York and Sunderland, but when he accepted an invitation to visit Newcastle, the home of the Mr. Bainbridge at whose invitation partly he was in England, he did so with the determination to stay there long enough to settle for all time the questions which had arisen as to their methods and motives. He knew that he could accomplish nothing among the people until he had their confidence, and this would be won most easily when he had the coöperation of the clergymen. "On this line and in this place if it takes all summer," was his spirit, if not his motto.

The meetings were held in the Rye Hill Baptist Chapel, seating some sixteen hundred people, and while they were not large at first, they increased rapidly.

"Mr. Moody preaches," wrote a friendly critic at the time, "but the conventional use of the word 'preaching' does not convey any notion of Mr. Moody's talk. He is a business man and he means business; every word he speaks is meant to lead to a definite business; if it does not do that, he regards it as thrown away. Most people believe that there is a life beyond the grave and that there is some way of salvation and some way of being lost forever; and this is rather important business after all. Mr. Moody goes into the heart of this matter at once and he puts it in a business way. He says he himself has salvation, in fact is saved forever by the Son of God, and that every soul that wants it may have it too, at once, and know it, and go home with it, and be as happy as he likes. A good many, if not all, of the really earnest ministers of all denominations indorse, as perfectly true, what he says, although it is put in a new way. But better than all, he takes his stand by the Bible and proves it. I think this ought to be more widely known."

Here at Newcastle the same increasing interest that had been experienced at Sunderland attended the mission. The meetings were transferred from a church to the Music Hall, and there Mr. Moody and his friend, Henry Moorehouse, who had joined him, preached to the great congregations which gathered there. Educated people were among the first converts; those who had known the Scriptures from childhood decided definitely for a religious life; and the work thus started went down through all classes of society, and influenced the surrounding towns.

The inquiry-room work was thorough, every inquirer being known by name and residence. As rapidly as possible ministers and experienced Christian workers only were allowed to have a hand in this important part of the meetings, and they were admitted by ticket.

When an all-day meeting was announced to be held at Newcastle on November 12th, many anticipated failure, but those who had felt the reviving power and the love of God and had made this meeting a matter of earnest prayer knew that it could not fail. Not only did the people from Newcastle attend in large numbers, but visitors from Sunderland, Shields, Jarrow, and neighboring towns came in by train and filled the church and galleries. Business, home cares and work, pleasure and idleness had been left behind by the hundreds of earnest Christians who came to worship God and to hear His Word.

An hour was given to prayer and Bible reading, and a second hour to promises, Mr. Moody leading during this part of the service. Another hour was set apart for experience and exhortation, which was followed by an address by Mr. Moorehouse on "Separation." The sixth and last hour was devoted to a sermon on "Heaven," preached by Mr. Moody. In the evening a gospel service was held, Moody and Moorehouse speaking. The chapel was filled to overflowing.

After this all-day meeting the work seemed to grow steadily. Mr.

Moorehouse speaks in this connection of four things which he had observed " about dear Moody's work," as he called it:

" 1. He believes firmly that the Gospel saves sinners when they believe, and he rests on the simple story of a crucified and risen Saviour.

" 2. He expects, when he goes to preach, that souls will be saved, and the result is that God honors his faith.

" 3. He preaches as if there never was to be another meeting, and as if sinners might never hear the Gospel sound again: these appeals to decide *now* are most impressive.

" 4. He gets Christians to work in the after-meetings. He urges them to ask those who are sitting near them if they are saved. Everything about their work is very simple, and I would advise the workers in the Lord's vineyard to see and hear our beloved brothers, and, if possible, learn some blessed lessons from them in soul-winning."

At one of the inquiry meetings at Newcastle Mr. Moody had an interview, which he often related in later years, as illustrating the need of confession and restitution.

The inquirer complained that every time she began to pray, five bottles of wine came up before her mind, which she had stolen when serving as housekeeper for a gentleman. She had never been able to pray since. In reply to her request for advice Mr. Moody said without hesitating, " Pay for them."

" But the person is dead," she said.

" Are not some of the heirs living? "

" Yes; a son."

" Then go to that son and pay him back."

" I want to see the face of God," she said, " but I could not think of doing a thing like that. My reputation is at stake."

She went away, and came back the next day to ask if it would not do just as well to put that money in the treasury of the Lord.

" No," was the reply, " God doesn't want any stolen money. The only thing is to make restitution."

For several days she struggled with her pride, but finally went into the country, saw the son of her former employer, made a full confession, and offered him a five-pound note. He said he didn't want the money, but she finally persuaded him to take it, and came back at peace with God and the world.

CHAPTER XVII

Birth of the "Moody and Sankey Hymn-book"

NEWCASTLE was the birthplace of the "Moody and Sankey Hymn-book," for it was during this mission that the demand for its publication first became urgent. The hymns and tunes used in the British churches and chapels were not adapted to evangelistic services, and neither Mr. Moody nor Mr. Sankey was familiar with the books in use. They therefore adopted for use in their meetings Philip Phillips' book, "Hallowed Songs," containing many American hymns and a few English tunes. Mr. Sankey used such hymns from his private collections as he had been singing in Chicago and elsewhere, and which were not contained in this book.

Some of these became very popular, and in a short time frequent requests were made for their publication. With the view of meeting the many inquiries as to where the hymns could be procured, Mr. Sankey wrote to the publishers of the book they had adopted, offering to supply a dozen or more of the songs he was singing, provided they would print them in the back of their own book. This offer was not accepted, and when urged again later it was definitely declined. As the requests for the publication of the hymns continued, Mr. Moody determined to publish the hymns on his own responsibility, and arranged with Messrs. Morgan and Scott to issue a pamphlet of sixteen pages, personally guaranteeing the cost of the plates. This collection of hymns was known as "Sacred Songs and Solos," and sold in large quantities at sixpence a copy. For several months it was used in the services as a solo-book, in connection with the larger book originally adopted.

From time to time additions of new songs were made to the smaller collection, and several months later a small book of "words only" was published and sold for one penny (two cents) per copy, after which the larger hymn-book first adopted was discontinued.

Mr. Moody's faith in the power of sacred song was fully rewarded, for he lived to see these songs make their way into the hearts of millions of people, and afford the means of establishing and maintaining churches, Christian Associations, educational institutions, and Biblical schools.

The first advertisement of "Sacred Songs and Solos" appeared in "The Christian" of September 18, 1873, which gave it a much wider circulation than would have been possible through its use in the meetings alone, and it soon found its way into all parts of the British Empire and later on into every Christian land. The copyright of the book was not taken out by Mr. Moody or Mr. Sankey, but by the publishers.

On reaching Ireland it was rumored that Mr. Moody was growing rich by the royalties from the hymn-books. This he publicly denied, together with other reports of a like character to the effect that P. T. Barnum, the great showman, was behind the whole movement. On the occasion of the visit to London, preparatory to their great meetings held there, Mr. Moody stated in a large public meeting of ministers and others that the royalties from the hymn-book, then in the hands of the publishers, together with what might afterward accrue, would be placed in the hands of a committee of well-known business men, of which Mr. Hugh M. Matheson, of London, was chairman, which committee would dispose of the royalties as they saw fit.

At the close of the London campaign and shortly before Moody and Sankey returned to America, the statement of Morgan and Scott, the publishers of the hymn-book, showed that the sum standing to the credit of the evangelists was about £7,000 ($35,000). Word was sent to the committee that this amount was at their disposal, to be used as they might elect. The committee refused to dispose of the fund for general purposes, asserting that they did not propose to have Mr. Moody pay this large sum for the privilege of preaching in London.

Mr. Moody's church in Chicago had been only partially rebuilt after the fire, for, owing to the panic which followed in 1873-74, a good portion of the pledges made for its erection had grown worthless, and the work stopped with the completion of the first story only. A temporary roof had been placed over this, however, and services had been held here while Mr. Moody was abroad. A friend from Chicago, who was interested in the church, was in London at this time, and hearing that there was no one who would take the hymn-book money, he suggested to the committee that it be forwarded to Chicago to complete that building. This suggestion was adopted, the money paid over, and the splendid edifice at Chicago Avenue and La Salle Street, which has been a centre of spiritual activity for more than twenty-five years, was completed and dedicated free of debt.

While Mr. Moody and Mr. Sankey were abroad P. P. Bliss, who was then associated with Major D. W. Whittle in evangelistic work, brought out for use in their meetings a small volume of hymns and tunes under the title of "Gospel Songs," mostly of Mr. Bliss's composition. When Mr. Moody returned to America in August, 1875, it became necessary to arrange for the publication of a new collection of hymns, composed largely of those which had been in use abroad. It was decided to unite in making the book, and after some discussion as to a name, the title "Gospel Hymns and Sacred Songs" was adopted.

The first book became very popular, and a large number was sold during the great meetings held in Philadelphia, New York, Chicago, and Boston. Since Mr. Bliss, Mr. Sankey, Mr. McGranahan, Mr.

Stebbins, and others continued writing new hymns and tunes as Mr. Moody's work went on, it was natural that there should be subsequent compilations, and "Gospel Hymns," No. 1, was followed by Nos. 2, 3, 4, 5, and 6.

The royalties from these books were at first paid over to a committee of prominent business men of Philadelphia, Chicago, and New York, of which William E. Dodge, of the last-named city, was chairman, and were distributed by them for the benefit of religious, philanthropic, and educational purposes in many parts of the United States. At Northfield, East Hall, a dormitory of the young ladies' seminary, and Stone Hall, a recitation hall of the same institution, together with Recitation Hall at Mount Hermon, were erected from this fund. At the present time all royalties are paid directly to the trustees of the schools of Northfield and Mount Hermon.

The following statement from Mr. Dodge, chairman of the American trustees, is of special interest in this connection:

"Mr. Moody was greatly pained when in Great Britain to find that those who were opposed to the new religious life had circulated reports that large sums of money were made from royalties on the hymn-book, and that the meetings were really carried on for the purpose of selling it, thus increasing the income of those conducting them.

"On his return to America, and before visiting the great cities of the country, he felt the need of a book of hymns and tunes adapted to his use here, and determined to arrange its publication so as to avoid all possible criticism.

"He invited me to visit Northfield to confer with him on the subject, which he felt to be of great importance. I met there Mr. Sankey and Mr. Bliss, and found a most delightful and unusual spirit of Christian self-sacrifice on their part. They were willing to contribute their own hymns and tunes and the copyrights which they held, and joined with Mr. Moody in giving up all possible claim to any benefits which might arise from their publication.

" Mr. Moody urged me to act as trustee, to arrange with the publishers for a royalty, and to receive any money which might come from this source and distribute it at my discretion for religious and benevolent purposes. I declined to act alone, but promised Mr. Moody that if two other gentlemen were selected I would gladly serve with them, and suggested the names of George H. Stuart, of Philadelphia, and John V. Farwell, of Chicago; a board of trustees was thus formed.

" The sale of the first editions of the books greatly exceeded our expectations, and, although the royalty was, on a single copy, small, as trustees we received up to September, 1885, the large sum of $357,-388.64. All of this was carefully distributed among various religious and educational institutions. It was finally determined to be wise and right that as the schools at Northfield had become so firmly established, and were doing such great good, the entire royalties of these books should be turned over to the trustees of these schools, and this was accordingly done under careful legal advice.

" During all these years neither Mr. Moody nor Mr. Sankey had any fixed income. Mr. Sankey, especially, had given up copyrights that would have brought him in a large sum yearly and opportunities to hold musical institutes and conventions which would have added largely to his income. Neither of them during the whole continuance of the trust received one dollar of personal advantage, and as they had no definite means of support the self-sacrifice and the unselfishness of this course, in order to prevent the slightest breath of scandal and not weaken the influence of their personal work, were very remarkable and very beautiful. I have never known anything like it.

" In closing the trust, which was a peculiar one, after getting full legal advice, I submitted the opinions to a lawyer of very high national reputation—the leader of the bar in New York in all matters of consultation. He was greatly interested in the form of the trust, though he had but little sympathy with the religious work. He gave a large amount of time and thought to the matter, and after giving his opinion

I asked him to be kind enough to send me a memorandum, so that I could personally send him a check, which I supposed would necessarily be a large one. He told me that under no possible circumstance would he accept a cent; that the unselfishness and splendid quality of men who could make such a sacrifice was a revelation of human nature that made him feel better disposed toward mankind.

"I have ventured to go into this matter somewhat at length, because while Mr. Moody and Mr. Sankey have not received a cent of personal benefit from the royalties on the hymn-books, unkind and ignorant assertions have been made to the contrary in some quarters."

In the later editions of "Gospel Songs" the services of George C. Stebbins and James McGranahan should receive special mention. Both these gentlemen were closely associated with Mr. Moody in his evangelistic work in Great Britain and America, and were prominent in the Northfield conventions and Bible schools.

"My acquaintance with Mr. Moody began in 1871," writes Mr. Stebbins. "I used to see him in the noon meetings in Chicago, where I occasionally went to help in the singing, but it was not till the summer of 1876 that I came more directly in touch with him. In August of that year, at the request of Major Whittle, whom I met in Boston, I went up to Northfield to spend a Sunday with him and Mr. Moody, to assist them in some services that had been arranged for that day. This was the first time I had seen Mr. Moody since the night he left Chicago for his work in Great Britain, which was destined so soon to make him known throughout the Christian world. And yet, though he was then at the height of his fame, and conceded to be one of the great religious characters of his time, he was still the same unassuming and unaffected man that he was before his work had brought him into such prominence before the world.

"He was spending the summer at his home, ostensibly for rest, as he had just concluded his great campaigns in Brooklyn, New York, and Philadelphia, but even then he could not keep still; he was preaching two or three times every Sunday in some of the smaller towns or cities among the New England hills, and during his days at home he was always trying to interest the neighbors and the country people in something besides their daily round of toil, always having their spiritual welfare at heart. I remember very well an instance of this:

"During the few days that I was visiting him he drove about the country and invited the people to his house to hear some music. The day set was very hot and sultry, but the people crowded the rooms to suffocation, and he, taking a place by an open window in full view of the audience and the performer, gave directions as to what should be sung, occasionally making some encouraging or humorous remark to keep up the interest. Any one with such a keen sense of humor as his must have been much amused to see the singer sweltering in the heat while doing his best for an hour or more to entertain the guests.

"During that visit Mr. Moody induced me to enter evangelistic work, and my connection with him and Mr. Sankey dates from that time. My first work was to organize and drill the choir of eight hundred singers for his great tabernacle work in Chicago, which began in October of that year and continued till the end of December.

"During the years that have followed it has been the privilege of Mrs. Stebbins and myself to be associated with Mr. Moody in several of his great campaigns, both at home and abroad, all of which have been memorable as indicating the extraordinary hold he had on the affections of the people of all classes.

"Mr. Moody not only loved nature, but art and poetry also, and the latter more especially as it was found in the poetical books of the Bible. He would sometimes ask for a chapter, and after listening intently to its close he would break the spell by saying, 'Beautiful!' then drop on his knees and pour out his heart to God in thanksgiving and prayer.

"His thoughtfulness for others, especially for those working with him, was very marked. It was not uncommon for him, at the close of

The Chicago Avenue Church, Chicago, as Occupied for Two Years.

Completed later by means of English hymn-book royalties.

Chicago Avenue Church, Chicago.

Buildings of Ladies' Department, Bible Institute, adjoining at the right.

a hard day's work, to say, just before he began his last address, 'You slip out and go home. I'll get on. I want you to be fresh for to-morrow.'

"In this connection I might speak of another trait of his that may not be generally known; that is, his disposition to make others as little trouble as possible on his account. I have known him to put up with annoying things, and positively suffer discomforts rather than inconvenience others or indulge in faultfinding.

"Some interesting illustrations of his conscientiousness in regard to accepting compensation for his services in evangelistic work came under my notice while spending a winter with him in the West. We had held a mission in one of the large cities for five weeks, having three meetings a day. At the close a representative of the finance committee came to his hotel and handed him a check for $1,500 for himself and his assistant. He immediately handed it back, saying that it was too much. A day or so afterward the gentleman went again to the hotel, and not seeing Mr. Moody, left the same check for him. Finding it awaiting him on his return, he took it back to the gentleman, who, in telling me about it afterward, stated that Mr. Moody told him in very plain terms that he meant what he said when he first returned the check, and he would not accept it. A thousand dollars was afterward given him: this he accepted. This decision was made in consideration of the fact that he had then well under way plans for establishing the Bible Institute in Chicago, and also that he needed money all the time to carry on his schools at Northfield. Immediately after this a ten days' series of meetings was begun in a city near by, at the close of which the committee handed him $500, which he accepted, but at the last meeting, when a collection was taken up to pay off the debt of the Young Men's Christian Association, he contributed the whole amount that had been given him for his services.

"The last time we heard Mr. Moody preach was at the church in Northfield in September, 1899, the first Sabbath after the opening of the seminary. There were no flowers in the church, and he remarked upon it, saying that he wished the senior class of the seminary to act as a committee to see that there were flowers every Sunday. He then said, 'I preached in Plymouth Church, Brooklyn, last Sunday and there were no flowers. One of the papers said the next day that the usual flowers were omitted from the pulpit because it was understood Mr. Moody did not like flowers.' Turning to me, he said, 'Stebbins, you tell them when you go back to Brooklyn how I love flowers.'"

Mr. and Mrs. McGranahan were associated in evangelistic work with Major Whittle, but frequently assisted Mr. Moody in his conventions, at his meetings, and at his schools, and were often in his home. "No one could know him without loving him," says Mr. McGranahan, "nor be with him without being benefited. Once in a Western city some twenty years ago a number of people had gathered in his room and were discussing some knotty question with a good deal of warmth and earnestness. Conflicting opinions were freely and emphatically expressed. Mr. Moody looked on, a silent spectator. When all had gone I shall never forget his remark nor the spirit it revealed: 'Mac, the world is in great need of peace-makers.' I trust I may never lose the desire I then felt to be among that number.

"Untiring in his own labors, his consideration for others was as tender as a father's. When we were holding a series of meetings at Auburn, N. Y., Mr. Moody came during the closing week to conduct a convention. I found it difficult to continue to lead the singing and do the solo work that was expected; but as I had often done before, I decided to stand by the choir until I could do no more. Mr. Moody said, 'No, it is not required of you to attempt what you are not able to do. Your voice is of too much importance to injure knowingly. *We do not serve a hard Master.* When health is at stake and matters beyond our control interfere, our duty is plain. Go at once and leave the convention with the major and me. Care for your voice, and have it for use as long as you live.'

"Mr. Moody has always been an inspiration to me in preparing hymns for gospel work; not that he was a musician or claimed to be, but I soon learned to prize his judgment as to the value and usefulness of a hymn for our work. What moved him was sure to move others, and what failed to do so could be safely omitted. I have esteemed it one of my highest privileges to share in preparing songs for his work, and, now that he has gone, how lonely it seems!"

CHAPTER XVIII

THE AWAKENING IN EDINBURGH

THE success of the American evangelists in the North of England led to an investigation of their methods, and after some hesitation they were invited to Edinburgh, and held their first service in the Music Hall, the largest in the city, on Sunday, November 23, 1873. Mr. Moody was indisposed that evening and Rev. J. H. Wilson and Mr. Sankey conducted the meeting, and the next day Mr. Sankey's organ was broken, and Mr. Moody conducted alone. At the opening service not only was the hall densely packed in every cranny, but the lobbies, stairs, and entrance were all crowded, and several thousand people went away, unable to obtain admission.

On the weekdays following, the evening service was held in Barclay Free Church, and every foot of standing room in that large edifice was occupied every night by attentive crowds. The attendance at each meeting must have exceeded two thousand. On the evening of the second Sunday, special services were held in three churches: the Barclay Church, beginning at six o'clock; the Viewforth Church, at seven o'clock, and the Fountainbridge Church, at eight o'clock. Long before the time appointed all three churches were filled to overflowing and hundreds were turned away. The second week the meetings were held in the Broughton Place United Presbyterian Church, and the numbers continued to increase.

"The part of the service toward which all the rest tends, and in which the power culminates," said a writer in "The Edinburgh Daily Review," "is the address of Mr. Moody, in which, in simple figures and telling language, he holds up before men the truth as it is in Jesus and makes most earnest and powerful appeals to heart and conscience. Mr. Moody is strikingly free from all pretence and parade; he speaks as one who thoroughly believes what he says and who is in downright earnest in delivering his message. His descriptions are characterized by a remarkable vividness and graphic power. He has a great wealth of illustration, and his illustrations are always apposite, bringing into the clearest light the point which he intends to illustrate, and fixing it forever into the memory. There is very little excitement; there is no extravagance; but the effect of the services is seen in the manifest impression produced on the audience, generally in the anxious inquirers (varying in number from about forty to upward of seventy), who remain for spiritual conversation and prayer after every meeting, and also in the hundreds of persons in all grades of the social scale scattered through Edinburgh and the neighborhood, who are more or less awakened to realize the importance of eternal things and are burdened with the sense of sin and a longing to obtain salvation. Not a few also profess to have been brought out of darkness into marvellous light, and to be going on their way rejoicing."

In Edinburgh, as in every city where missions were held, the daily noonday prayer-meeting was established. The deep interest manifested in this meeting was shown in two ways: First, in the number of requests for prayer sent in by persons seeking a blessing for themselves or others, of which more than a hundred were handed in at every meeting, representing the burdens, the cares, the longings of many a heart, with requests for thanksgiving and praise for former prayers answered and blessings bestowed. Second, by the large attendance, more than five hundred persons being present the first day, this number steadily increasing until, at the end of the first week, the Queen Street Hall was found to be too small.

For a time there was some difficulty in fixing on a suitable place. The Rev. Alexander Whyte, of Free St. George's, offered his church for the prayer-meeting, but finally, on account of its central situation, the Free Church Assembly Hall was selected. The attendance soon reached a thousand, and often exceeded that number. The first half of the hour was employed in singing part of a psalm or hymn, reading briefly the requests for prayer, and praying, followed by a few remarks by Mr. Moody on some passage of Scripture. During the second half of the meeting any one could speak or pray or call for a hymn.

Many ministers and laymen of the various evangelical denominations in Edinburgh and Leith gladly welcomed Mr. Moody on his arrival in the city, and threw themselves heartily into the work. Others who at first had difficulties and stood somewhat aloof found their objections melting away with personal contact, and identified themselves cordially with the work. It was delightful to witness the unbroken unity and brotherly love that prevailed among all engaged in the movement. Denominational differences were for the time lost sight of.

The Rev. Andrew Thomson, pastor of the Broughton Place United Presbyterian Church, thus expressed himself:

" There is nothing novel in the doctrine Mr. Moody proclaims. It is the old Gospel—old, and yet always fresh and young, as the living fountain or the morning sun—in which the substitution of Christ is placed in the centre and presented with admirable distinctness and decision. It is spoken with most impressive directness, not as by a man half convinced and who seems always to feel that a sceptic is looking over his shoulder, but with a certainty of the truth of what he says, as if, like our own Andrew Fuller, ' he could venture his eternity on it '; as if he felt that ' if he did not speak the very stones would cry out.'

" I would not for the wealth of the world have the recollection of what I have seen and heard during the past week blotted out from my memory. When Howe was chaplain to Cromwell at Whitehall he became weary of the trumpery and pomp of the palace and wrote to his ' dear and honored brother,' Richard Baxter, telling him how much he longed to be back again to his beloved work at Torrington. 'I have devoted myself,' he said, 'to serving God in the work of the ministry, and how can I lack the pleasure of hearing their cryings and complaints who have come to me under conviction?' I have shared with many beloved brethren during the past week in this sacred pleasure, and it is like eating angels' bread, first to hear the cry of conviction and then the joy of reconciliation and peace. I was much struck by the variety among the inquirers. There were present from the old man of seventy-five to the youth of eleven, soldiers from the castle, students from the university, the backsliding, the intemperate, the sceptic, the rich and the poor, the educated and the uneducated, and in how many cases were the wounded healed and the burdened eased!"

The fourth week of special meetings began in St. Stephen's Established Church on Tuesday evening, December 16th, where the services were continued for three evenings. Admission was by ticket, and the church was crowded in every part, two thousand people being present at each meeting. St. Stephen's congregation is composed largely of the upper class, many of whom attended and were deeply impressed by the preaching and singing. The Rev. Dr. Nicholson presided, and every evening there were present ministers of all denominations from all parts of the country, while representatives of the nobility, professors from the university, and distinguished lawyers and Parliamentary leaders were also in evidence.

The Free Assembly Hall was crowded one Sunday morning with Sunday-school teachers. Every one present felt that his work among the young called for absolute consecration and a high level of Christian life. In the evening the same building was filled with students. Around the platform were professors from nearly all the faculties in the university and several professors from the Free Church College. Hundreds applied for admission in vain, and the Free High Church was opened and services conducted there as well as in the Assembly Hall.

Professor Blaikie thus referred to the blessing which had come to the ministers of the city:

"It would be difficult to enumerate the ministers who have taken a prominent and most hearty interest in the movement. The utter absence of jealousy, the cordial coöperation of the clergy of all denominations in the work, has been extremely striking. They have gained in no ordinary measure the esteem of the laity by their cordiality, seeming to think nothing of the fact that strangers from another country have been the instrument; all other feelings being apparently swallowed up in thankfulness for the blessing that has come. At the same time there is a very general feeling that the wonderful work is due in a large degree to the faithful labors and earnest prayers of the clergy and Christian people of Edinburgh, although the peculiar gifts of the strangers have been especially blessed.

"It is amusing to observe how entirely the latent distrust of Mr. Sankey's 'kist o' whistles' has disappeared. There are different ways of using the organ. There are organs in some churches for mere display, as some one has said, 'with a devil in every pipe,' but a small harmonium designed to keep a tune right is a different matter, and is seen to be no hindrance to the devout and spiritual worship of God."

The interest manifested in Edinburgh attracted the attention of Scotland generally, and brought invitations for missions in other cities. Requests, sent not only by ministers, but by provosts, councillors, and leading citizens, were received daily from towns large and small, and the desire for Mr. Moody's services seemed to be remarkably serious and earnest. It was not to gratify curiosity, but to promote spiritual and eternal good that his presence was sought; even remote rural parishes in Scotland met to pray for a blessing on his labors, and the belief prevailed that what was then going on in Edinburgh would spread over the country. "Never, probably," said Professor Blaikie, "was Scotland so stirred; never was there so much expectation."

The meetings increased in numbers and in spiritual interest as the weeks went by. One Sunday morning Mr. Moody preached to the young men in the Free Assembly Hall at nine o'clock. The place was filled to overflowing, though the admission was by ticket. At the close of the service a gentleman appealed to him for another effort among the young men. Mr. Moody replied that if those present would get up another meeting for unconverted young men he would address them, and he asked all those who were willing to work to stand up. The whole audience rose, and the second meeting was held on Friday evening. On Sunday evening the Free Assembly Hall, the Established Assembly Hall, and the Free High Church were all filled to overflowing, as well as Free St. John's Church. All denominational differences were forgotten. Professor Charteris spoke in the Free Church; Professor Blaikie spoke in the Established Church. Brethren from all parts of the country came together in the unity of a common need and a common Saviour. So deep was the spiritual awakening that the following circular letter was sent to every minister in Scotland:

"Edinburgh is now enjoying signal manifestations of grace. Many of the Lord's people are not surprised at this. Ministers and others have been for some time discerning tokens of special interest and expectation attending the ordinary ministrations of the Word; and in October and November last many Christians of various denominations met from time to time to pray for it. They hoped that they might have a visit from Messrs. Moody and Sankey, of America, but they very earnestly besought the Lord that He would deliver them from depending upon them or on any instrumentality, and that He Himself would come with them or come before them. He has graciously answered that prayer, and His own presence is now wonderfully manifested among them. God is so affecting the hearts of men that the Free Church Assembly Hall, the largest public building in Edinburgh, is crowded every evening with meetings for prayer, and both that building and the Established Church Assembly Hall overflow whenever the Gospel is preached. But the numbers that attend are not the most remarkable feature. It is the presence and power of the Holy Ghost, the solemn awe, the prayerful, believing, expectant spirit, the anxious inquiry of unsaved souls, and the longing of believers to grow more like Christ—their hungering and thirsting after holiness. The hall of the Tolbooth Parish Church and the Free High Church are nightly attended by anxious inquirers. All denominational and social distinctions are entirely merged. All this is of the grace of God.

"Another proof of the Holy Spirit's presence is that a desire has been felt and expressed in these meetings that all Scotland should share the blessing that the capital is now enjoying.

"It is impossible that our beloved friends from America should visit every place, or even all those where they have been urged to go. But this is not necessary. The Lord is willing Himself to go wherever He is truly invited. He is waiting. The Lord's people in Edinburgh, therefore, would affectionately entreat all their brethren throughout the land to be importunate in invoking Him to come to them and to dismiss all doubt as to His being willing to do so.

"The Week of Prayer, from the 4th to the 11th of January next, affords a favorable opportunity for combined action. In every town and hamlet let there be a daily meeting for prayer during that week and also as often as may be before it. In Edinburgh the hour is from twelve to one o'clock, and where the same hour suits other places it would be well to meet together in faith at the throne of grace. But let the prayers not be formal, unbelieving, unexpecting, but short, fervent, earnest entreaties, with abounding praise and frequent short exhortations; let them entreat a blessing on all the means of grace enjoyed by our native land, and let them also embrace the whole world, that '*God's way may be known upon earth, His saving health among all nations.*' If the country will thus fall on its knees, the God who has filled our national history with the wonders of His love will come again, and surprise even the strongest believers by the unprecedented tokens of His grace. '*Call upon Me and I will answer thee, and show thee great and mighty things, which thou knowest not.*' "

While the Holy Spirit was daily and hourly approving the work of the evangelists the powers of darkness were not idle. A Scotchman in Chicago, a lawyer by profession, sent a scurrilous letter to a prominent clergyman in Scotland attacking both the commercial honesty and the religious character of Mr. Moody. Unsupported by the slightest evidence, the charges were made that he had sold information regarding the interest of one of his employers to a business rival; and, further, that he was insincere in his attitude toward the doctrines so dear to Scotch hearts.

The letter was widely distributed in manuscript copies in places where it would do the greatest possible harm and where it would be most difficult to counteract its influence. At last a copy fell into the hands of the Edinburgh Committee, and steps were taken to ascertain the truth or falsity of the statements made.

Mr. Moody was deeply exercised over the letter for the sake of the work in Scotland, although perfectly conscious of his rectitude. He trusted his reputation implicitly to his Heavenly Father and demanded that the committee who had invited him to Edinburgh give the matter a thorough investigation.

The Rev. John Kelman, of Free St. John's, Leith, the secretary of the Edinburgh Committee, and the man who had gone to Newcastle to see Mr. Moody's work, and who was in a large measure responsible for his visit to Scotland, sent a copy of the letter to Mr. Farwell in Chicago, saying:

"The friends of religion who have been associated in Christian work with Mr. Moody in this country are anxious that there should be a thorough investigation of the truth or falsity of these charges. I have been requested to apply to you in the hope that you would be kind enough to furnish me at your earliest convenience with whatever information you can obtain as to the facts in the case."

The following communication, signed by thirty-five clergymen, educators, editors, and secretaries who had known Mr. Moody and his work in Chicago, was sent to the Edinburgh Committee:

"We, the undersigned pastors of the city of Chicago, learning that the Christian character of D. L. Moody has been attacked, for the purpose of destroying his influence as an evangelist in Scotland, hereby certify that his labors in the Young Men's Christian Association, and as an evangelist in this city and elsewhere, according to the best information we can get, have been evangelical and Christian in the highest sense of those terms; and we do not hesitate to commend him as an earnest Christian worker, worthy of the confidence of our Scotch and English brethren, with whom he is now laboring, believing that the Master will be honored by them in receiving him among them as a colaborer in the vineyard of the Lord."

Later C. M. Henderson, the nephew of his former employers, the successor to the business and the head of the house at the time the criticism was made, said: "For fifteen years since Mr. Moody left us I have watched him, assisted him, and believed in him," and until the death of Mr. Henderson a few years since he was a frequent contributor to Mr. Moody's work.

Severe as had been the test of faith and bitter as had been the experience during two or three months before this slander was run down and killed, the outcome gave Mr. Moody a hold upon Scotland which it is doubtful he could have secured if all men had spoken well of him.

Along with the Edinburgh meetings services were held in Leith, in the Free North Leith Church (Dr. Macdonald's) and in the Free St. John's (the Rev. J. Kelman's). These meetings were important from the fact that the large shipping interests of the town attracted people from almost all parts of the world. Many seafaring men attended the services, and the influence extended not only throughout the great population of Scotland, but was carried in the ships around the world.

Toward the end of the Edinburgh meetings Dr. Horatius Bonar

sent a letter which, although not intended for publication, had been so frequently requested by the public that it was printed, and an extract is given herewith. After referring to the meeting in the Corn Exchange with its great crowd of listeners, most of them from the Grassmarket and the Cowgate, he said:

"These American brethren bring to us no new Gospel, nor do they pretend to novelty of any kind in their plans, save perhaps that of giving greater prominence to the singing of hymns, conveying the good news to their hearers through this instrumentality. We may trust them. They fully deserve our confidence; the more we know of them in private the more do we appreciate them and the more do we feel inclined to cast in our lot with them. We ask for soundness in faith, and we do well. These men are sound. We ask for a consistent humble life, and we do well. These men are consistent and humble. We ask for self-denial, and we do well. These men are self-denying, hard-working men, who are spending and being spent in a service which they believe to be not human but divine. We ask for definite aims, an ultimatum in which self shall have no place, and we do well. These men have the most definite of all definite aims—winning souls to everlasting joy, and they look for no fame and no reward save the Master's approval: the recompense in reserve for those who turn many to righteousness. They have in view no sinister nor sordid motives, as their past history shows, as every one who associates with them must feel. Besides all this, it is vain to try to stop them. They will work and they will speak, whoever shall say nay. Let us work along with them. Rowland Hill was once asked the question: 'When do you intend to stop?' 'Not until we have carried all before us,' was his answer. So say our brethren from Chicago. We say, Amen. This needy world says Amen. Human wickedness and evil say Amen. Heaven and earth say Amen. The work is great and the time is short, but strength is not of man but of God."

The most remarkable meeting, perhaps, held in Edinburgh was that held during the closing hours of the year 1873. There were many misgivings as to the possibility of keeping a large audience together from eight o'clock until twelve on the last night of the year. Mr. Moody's expectations, however, were justified by the crowd which filled the Free Assembly Hall for five hours on that evening. Many of all ages and classes stood all the evening, or exchanged places occasionally with those who had seats near them. Mr. Moody entered the hall at eight o'clock accompanied by many ministers and laymen. The congregation had already been waiting for them an hour. After singing and prayer, he announced that the order for the evening would be: "The utmost irregularity. In fact, anything that is worship will be in order; and when I am speaking, if any one has an illustration to give, or would like to sing a hymn or offer prayer, let him do so." This singular invitation was at once accepted and acted upon by many speakers, and gave constant variety to the meeting, so that the interest never flagged. Mr. Sankey and the Fisk Jubilee Singers sang hymns frequently. Soon after eleven o'clock Bible study ceased, and the remainder of the session was given to prayer.

During the Week of Prayer the services continued, with remarkable results. On January 14th Mr. Moody presided at an all-day Christian convention held in the Free Church Assembly Hall, which was largely attended. The Tolbooth Established Church and the Free High Church were equally crowded. The people from the surrounding country poured in by hundreds, and some were there who had come fifty, a hundred, and two hundred miles. Dr. Bonar opened the proceedings with an address on "Personal Effort." Reports were received from Newcastle and other places where Mr. Moody had held meetings, showing that the work which had been started had gone on after they left the place. An hour was devoted to the question drawer, which Mr. Moody conducted. The services closed with an address by him on "Works."

Donald McAllan, the chairman of an Infidel Club in Edinburgh, for many years had given great trouble to the Carrubber's Close workers. He went to a meeting in the Free Assembly Hall to have an argument with the evangelist. Instead of arguing with him Mr. Moody dealt with him as with a man needing salvation, asking if he had ever heard or known of any one who wished to be saved by Jesus and had come to Him and been refused. Reluctantly he admitted that he did not know of any such case.

"No," said Mr. Moody, "the Scripture cannot be broken. Do you know we are praying for you—and you will yet be converted!"

Later on, in the town of Wick, Mr. Moody met this man again, and saw that the Spirit was dealing with him. On his return to Edinburgh McAllan was attending a meeting which was being addressed by James Balfour, when he suddenly became converted.

American newspapers heard of this story and denied its truth, but at a meeting subsequently held in the Free Assembly Hall Mr. Moody told the story of the conversion and its denial, adding:

"I understand that this former infidel is present in this meeting. If so, will he kindly rise and bear witness to the fact of his conversion?"

Mr. McAllan rose near the spot where Mr. Moody had first dealt with him, admitted that he had been the infidel who had formerly opposed the Gospel so bitterly, and declared what great things the Lord had done for him.

During these Edinburgh meetings Mr. Moody took occasion to reply to some criticisms which had appeared in the daily papers. These were to the effect that he had cast a slight on the educated ministry in one of his addresses at the recent all-day conference in Glasgow. Mr. Moody asserted that he had said he did believe in an educated ministry, and appealed for corroboration to those present who had heard him.

"Many young men enter on Christian work far too late in life for them to go through the regular college course. The church ought to take these men in hand and give them the opportunity for doing that for which they are fitted. Peter, the unlettered fisherman, did work as good as Paul, the man of education. Of course Paul did some special duties better because of his education. But there are some kinds of work that men, whether educated or not, are not fitted for. Why should not devoted Christian women be trained to hold mothers' meetings, cottage prayer-meetings, and to teach young mothers cooking, dressmaking, and so forth? That is a practical kind of Christianity for which only consecrated and trained women are fitted. The churches ought also to train helpers to go around among the people and get hold of the non-churchgoers, and in that way supplement the regular ministry. The time has come to call out the volunteers. In Scotland there are piety and education and money enough to evangelize the whole world. If a man has a desire for a university education let him have it by all means, but it is not necessary for every one to know Latin, Greek, and Hebrew." As a finishing stroke on this point, Mr. Moody quaintly observed that he regretted exceedingly he had never had a college education himself; but he did not get it, and he was doing the best he could without it.

Free Church Assembly Hall, Edinburgh.

Farewell Meeting at Botanical Gardens, Glasgow.

CHAPTER XIX

In Glasgow and the Scottish Towns

GLASGOW was visited after the Edinburgh mission closed; in fact preparations began as soon as the Edinburgh work started. In the middle of December a meeting was held in Glasgow to arrange for the visit of the Americans, which was attended by more than a hundred ministers and laymen of all the evangelical churches. At the first of a series of union prayer-meetings in St. George's Established Church on January 5th, Mr. Moody spoke briefly, returning to Edinburgh for the evening meeting. After beginning their work in Glasgow, he returned to Edinburgh two or three times to assist in special meetings. Berwick-on-Tweed, Melrose, and Dundee were visited, and meetings lasting a few days each were conducted there after the Edinburgh mission closed.

The Glasgow meetings had been going on uninterruptedly for more than a month when Moody and Sankey reached there on February 7th, and began their labors on the following morning, February 8th. At nine o'clock a stirring meeting of Sabbath-school teachers was held in the City Hall, attended by about three thousand. The evening evangelistic service was held at half-past six, but more than an hour before that time the City Hall was crowded, and the great multitude outside were drafted off to the three churches nearest, which were soon filled. The next day prayer-meeting began in the morning in the United Presbyterian Church.

Dr. Bonar thus referred to the meetings not long after they were started:

"There have been not a few awakened of late, and the interest is deepening. The ministers of all denominations take part most cordially. Men are coming from great distances to ask the way of life, awakened to this concern by no directly human means, but evidently by the Holy Spirit, who is breathing over the land. It is such a time as we have never had in Scotland before. The same old Gospel as of aforetime is preached to all men: Christ who was made sin for us, Christ the substitute, Christ's blood, Christ's righteousness, Christ crucified; the power of God and the wisdom of God unto salvation; but now the Gospel is preached '*with the Holy Ghost sent down from Heaven*,' and amid all this the enemy is restrained, so that we are reminded of Revelation, vii. 1-3, the time before the coming of the Lord, when the four angels are charged to let no storm burst in, nor to allow the wind of Heaven to ruffle the sea's smooth surface or move the leaf of any tree until the seal of the living God has been put upon His elect. Is not this sealing going on daily among us? Are not the four angels looking on? Surely it is the time to seek the Lord that He may rain righteousness upon us."

From Glasgow as a centre, occasional meetings were arranged in adjoining towns, and Helensburg, Greenock, and Paisley were visited, while the ministers of Glasgow and other cities took the regular meetings during the absence of Mr. Moody.

On Thursday, April 16th, a convention of ministers, office-bearers, and other Christians from all parts of Scotland and the North of England was held in the Crystal Palace Botanical Gardens. Five thousand people were present, the larger proportion being men. Professor Charteris, of Edinburgh, read a paper showing how the revival movement could be advanced and directed into the ordinary church channels. Professor Fairburn, of the Free College, spoke upon the great doctrines which had been emphasized during the meetings. Dr. Cairns, of Berwick, Mr. Van Meter, of Rome, and others took part.

One of the most impressive gatherings during this mission was a meeting held in the Kibble Crystal Palace especially for warehouse girls, of whom there are probably more than twelve thousand in the city. Tickets were issued, and while five thousand were seated in the building and several hundred standing, outside was a crowd of more than a thousand girls. On the following evening the meeting was for young men, when nearly six thousand were brought together. A service was held for children also, and another for young women.

The final meeting was held in the Botanical Gardens on the following Sunday. Mr. Sankey found his way into the building and began the service with six or seven thousand, who were crushed together there, but so great was the crowd outside, estimated at twenty or thirty thousand people, that Mr. Moody himself could not get inside. Standing on the coachman's box of the carriage in which he was driven, he asked the members of the choir to sing. They found a place for themselves on the roof of a low shed near the building, and after they had sung Mr. Moody preached for an hour on "Immediate Salvation." So distinct was his voice that the great crowd could hear him without difficulty. The evening was beautiful, the air calm, the sun near its setting; the deep green foliage of the trees that enclosed the grounds framed the scene. Writing of this, a witness said:

"We thought of the days of Whitefield, of such a scene as that mentioned in his life, when, in 1753 at Glasgow, twenty thousand souls hung on his lips as he bade them farewell. Here there were thirty thousand eager hearers, for by this time the thousands within the Crystal Palace had come out, though their numbers quietly melting into the main body did not make a very perceptible addition to the crowd; and many onlookers who knew something of such gatherings were inclined to estimate the number much higher."

After the sermon Mr. Moody asked all those who wished to attend the inquiry meeting to enter the palace. Those who could remain were requested to gather in the neighboring church, Kelvinside, for prayer. In a few minutes the Crystal Palace was filled, and when

Mr. Moody asked for those who were unsaved and yet anxious to be saved, two thousand people rose to their feet.

"It was a strange and solemn sight, so many unsaved and yet seeking salvation," said a spectator. "It made the heart yearn in an intense desire for them, and assuredly it was of the Lord that these two thousand should thus appeal to the Lord's people for help at the very moment when these special meetings were brought to a close. It was a sight that summoned the Lord's people to continue every effort in their behalf, hastening with sharpened sickles to the fields ready for the harvest."

Thursday, May 24th, being the Queen's birthday and a general holiday in Edinburgh, a farewell meeting was held on the grassy slopes between Arthur's Seat and Salisbury Craig above Holyrood. Here Mr. Moody preached to an audience of twenty thousand, and the scenes witnessed in Glasgow the previous Sunday were repeated.

From Glasgow Mr. Moody went to the north of Scotland. In Dundee, where he was holding meetings, he was taken to visit a bed-ridden cripple, and the conversation he held there left a lifelong impression upon him, and in after years frequently figured as an illustration in his sermons. The sufferer had fallen and broken his back when he was a boy of fifteen. He had lain on his bed for about forty years, and could not be moved without great pain. Probably not a day had passed in all those years without acute suffering, but day after day the grace of God had been granted to him, and his chamber seemed as near Heaven as one could get on earth.

"I can imagine that when the angels passed over Dundee they had to stop there for refreshment," said Mr. Moody. "When I saw him, I thought he must be beyond reach of the tempter, and I asked him: 'Doesn't Satan ever tempt you to doubt God, and to think that He is a hard Master?'

"'Oh, yes,' he said, 'he does try to tempt me. I lie here and see my old schoolmates driving along in their carriages, and Satan says: "If God is so good why does He keep you here all these years?

You might have been a rich man, riding in your own carriage." Then I see a man who was young when I was walk by in perfect health, and Satan whispers: "If God loved you, couldn't He have kept you from breaking your back?"'

"'What do you do when Satan tempts you?'

"'Ah, I just take him to Calvary and I show him Christ and I point out those wounds in His hands and feet and side, and say, "Doesn't He love me?" and the fact is, he got such a scare there eighteen hundred years ago that he cannot stand it; he leaves me every time.' That bedridden saint had not much trouble with doubts; he was too full of the grace of God."

At Aberdeen no building could accommodate the audience, and on Sabbath afternoon, June 14th, the meeting was on the links in the natural amphitheatre of the Broadhill, where a platform had been erected for choir and speakers. Some ten thousand people were around the platform long before the hour of the meeting, and when Mr. Moody spoke on "The Wages of Sin is Death," it is estimated that from twenty to twenty-two thousand people heard his words.

Montrose, Brechin, Forfar, Huntley (where more than fifteen thousand people were gathered in the open-air service), Inverness, Arbroath, Tain, Nairn, Elgin, Forres, Grantown, Keith, Rothesay, and Campbelltown were some of the places visited during the summer.

An employer was converted at one of the meetings in another part of Scotland. He was very anxious that all of his employees should be reached, and he used to send them one by one to the meetings. But there was one employee who wouldn't attend. The moment he heard of his employer's desire he made up his mind he wouldn't go. If he was going to be converted, he said, he was going to be converted under some ordained minister; he was not going to any meeting that was conducted by unordained Americans. He believed in the regular Presbyterian Church of Scotland, and that was the place for him to be converted.

"After we left that town and went away up to Inverness," said Mr.

Moody in relating the incident, "the employer had some business up there, and he sent this man to manage it.

"One night, as I was preaching on the bank of a river, I happened to take for my text the words of Naaman: '*I thought*.' I was trying to take men's thoughts up and to show the difference between their thoughts and God's thoughts. This man was walking along the bank of the river. He saw a great crowd, and heard some one talking, and wondered what that man was talking about. He didn't know we were in the city, so he drew up to the crowd and listened. He heard the sermon and became convicted and converted right there. Then he inquired who was the preacher, and he found out it was the very man whom he had said he would not hear—the man he disliked. The very man he had been talking against was the man God used to reach him."

An all-day meeting was held at Inverness on August 27th. Mr. Moody with a few friends then went down the Caledonian Canal to Oban, where much preparatory work had been done during the two preceding months by Drs. Horatius and Andrew Bonar. After a few hours' rest at the home of Sir William McKinnon at Ballinakill he concluded his stay in Scotland by a mission to Campbelltown.

A year after the evangelists left Glasgow Dr. Andrew A. Bonar said:

"We in Glasgow who have watched this movement and taken part in it are aware that our testimony cannot have much influence on those to whom we are strangers, but to any of those who will listen we should like to testify to the permanence of the work among us, and any who will come and see for themselves will at once discover how extensive and sincere this work has been. Personally I can say, and many of my brethren are prepared to make the same statement, that the fruit of last year has been as satisfactory in every way as at any period in my ministry, while it has also had some new features of special interest. There have indeed been cases of backsliding, but what of that? Is not the parable of the sower true in all ages?"

In his biography of Henry Drummond, Dr. George Adam Smith states that the power of the revival movement in Scotland at this time spread beyond the congregations immediately gathered, and that one of its most striking features was the social and philanthropic work it stimulated.

"Like all religious revivals," he says, "this one had its origin among the merely well-to-do classes, and at first offered some ground for the sneers at bourgeois religion which were cast upon it. But Mr. Moody, who had a knowledge of the city, and the power to bring up before others the vision of its needs, inspired the Christians of Glasgow to attempt missions to the criminal classes and the relief of the friendless. The lodging-houses were visited, with every haunt of vagrants about the brick-kilns upon the south side and elsewhere. Temperance work was organized, and although there were, as always in that work, very many disappointments, a large number of poor drunkards were befriended and reformed.

"A huge tent was raised on the Green, and afterward replaced by a hall, which became the scene of a Sabbath morning breakfast to the poor and the centre of a great deal of other philanthropic activity. New interest was aroused in industrial schools, and, on the advice of Sheriff Watson, a veteran in this line of education, an industrial feeding-school was established for ill-fed and ill-clad children. At Saltcoates a house was bought and furnished for orphans; new impulses were given to the Orphan's Home of Scotland, founded in 1871 by Mr. Quarrier, who, with his fellow-workers among the poor of Glasgow, has given inestimable assistance to Mr. Moody's mission. A boarding-house for young women was opened in Glasgow.

"Mr. Moody gave great attention to the Young Men's Christian Associations, and at the height of the movement secured very large subscriptions for their foundation or expansion. He felt strongly that they had been conducted upon methods which were either too vague or too narrow, and that for their success 'clear and liberal views were needed.' He defined their aim—to promote the spiritual instincts and look after the temporal welfare of young men. Each ought to be a nursery of Christian character, a most efficient evangelistic agency, a centre of social meetings, and a means of furthering the progress of young men in the general pursuits of life. But along with liberality in your aims you must have thoroughness in details. The spiritual must be distinctly dominant. Do not, however, put the Association in place of the church; it is only a handmaid and a feeder of the church. For every man it must find some work, and use every particle of power in the young convert."

Professor Smith has not been able to trace with exactness how Henry Drummond was drawn into the movement by Mr. Moody. But from the first, he says, Drummond felt Mr. Moody's sincerity and the practical wisdom of the new methods. The aim at the individual, the endeavor to arouse and secure him—this was what he had missed in ordinary church methods and now found. The inquiry meetings bridged the gap between the preacher and the hearer, and brought them together, man to man, before God. On his side, Mr. Moody was feeling the need of a young man to take charge of the meetings for young men, and it is a tribute to his insight that he chose one whose style and tastes were so different from his own. At first Drummond was employed, like other students, only in the inquiry-room. From working in the inquiry-rooms he began to address meetings.

After some time Mr. Moody sent him to continue the work among young men at places which he had visited. In Sunderland alone one thousand persons gave in their names as converts, the Rev. James Stalker and the Rev. John F. Ewing working with Drummond. Newcastle and other towns in which Mr. Moody had held meetings were in turn visited by the three Scotchmen. "The Sunderland mission made Drummond a man," says Professor Smith. "He won from it not only the power of organizing and leading his fellowmen, but that insight into character and knowledge of life, on its lowest, as on its highest, levels, that power of interest in every individual he met, which so brilliantly distinguished him and in later years made us who were his friends feel as if his experiences and his sympathies were exhaustless."

The Rev. Dr. John Watson (Ian Maclaren) recently made this reference to Mr. Moody's relations with Professor Drummond:

"As soon as Moody came to Edinburgh, Drummond allied himself with the most capable, honest, and unselfish evangelist of our day, and saw strange chapters in religious life through the United Kingdom. This was the infirmary in which he learned spiritual diagnosis."

W. Robertson Nicoll, editor of "The British Weekly," in his introduction to Drummond's "Ideal Life," speaks as follows regarding the awakening in Scotland, and the relation to it of Moody and Drummond:

"A crisis was sure to come, and it might very well have been a crisis which would have broken the church in pieces. That it did not was due largely to the influence of one man—the American evangelist, Mr. Moody. In 1873 Mr. Moody commenced his campaign in the Barclay Free Church, Edinburgh. A few days before, Drummond had read a paper to the Theological Society of his college on 'Spiritual Diagnosis,' in which he maintained that preaching was not the most important thing, but that personal dealing with those in anxiety would yield better results. In other words, he thought that practical religion might be treated as an exact science. He had given himself to scientific study with a view of standing for the degree of Doctor of Science. Mr. Moody at once made a deep impression on Edinburgh, and attracted the ablest students. He missed in this country a certain religious provision for young men, and he thought that young men could best be moulded by young men.

"With his keen American eye he perceived that Drummond was his best instrument, and he immediately associated him in the work. It had almost magical results. From the very first Drummond attracted and deeply moved crowds, and the issue was that for two years he gave himself to this work of evangelism in England, in Scotland,

and Ireland. During this period he came to know the life histories of young men in all classes. He made himself a great speaker; he knew how to seize the critical moment; and his modesty, his refinement, his gentle and generous nature, his manliness, and, above all, his profound conviction, won for him disciples in every place he visited. His companions were equally busy in their own lines, and in this way the Free Church was saved."

CHAPTER XX

Irish and English Cities

ON the conclusion of the Scotch mission, efforts were made to induce Mr. Moody to visit London. The interest awakened in Scotland had attracted the attention of the Christian public throughout Great Britain, and it was felt that a mission in London would be attended with marked results. When asked to conduct a mission he always insisted upon the necessity for unity among the ministers, and as London at this time was not ready for a "union" movement among the representatives of all denominations, he decided to accept the many urgent invitations to visit Ireland.

His first mission was in Belfast, where he began on Sunday, September 6, 1874, with a service at eight A.M. in Dugall's Square Chapel. This meeting was exclusively for Christian workers, and long before the hour named the chapel was crowded. Mr. Moody discussed the necessity of entire devotion to the work and unwearied labor for the Lord. In the evening the third meeting for the day was held in the largest church in the city, capable of holding two thousand people, but here again the streets were crowded with those unable to secure admission.

The daily noon prayer-meeting was begun in Dugall's Square Chapel, but the room was so overcrowded that it seemed advisable to adjourn to a building seating fourteen hundred people. Here, as elsewhere, this noon meeting became the centre of the movement and proved a great blessing to the work and workers. Evening meetings began the first day in the Rosemary Street Church, but the crowds were so great and caused so much inconvenience that Mr. Moody changed his plans somewhat and held a meeting at two P.M. exclusively for women, and a meeting in the evening in another church for men.

As the work went on the interest increased rapidly. The audiences consisted mostly of young men, and the number of strangers who visited Belfast from long distances was very large. Within ten days after the first meeting the movement spread to Bangor, ten miles distant, where Henry Moorehouse, Rev. H. M. Williamson, and others preached.

Soon after the meetings began Mr. Moody published the following letter, calling upon the Christians throughout Great Britain to hold daily noon prayer-meetings:

"During the revival of God's work in America in 1857 and 1858, in nothing was the power of God's Spirit more manifest than in the gatherings that came together at twelve o'clock in the day for prayer and praise. Many of the meetings commenced at that time are still continued, with an almost constant and visible result attending them.

"In hearing from time to time of the blessings connected with these noon prayer-meetings in America, a strong desire for similar meetings in their own towns has come to the hearts of many, and the thought has occurred to us that if such meetings were started in the different towns of the kingdom, similar to those in Edinburgh and Glasgow, they might be the means of a very great blessing. Could no such meetings be started?—commenced on the 1st of October, and continued until January 1st, making three months of united prayer for a blessing on the country at the noontide hour? May not the results be beyond our estimation? The noon prayer-meetings at Newcastle, Edinburgh, and Glasgow are still kept up, and if God blessed these places, as we believe, in answer to prayer, is He not able and willing to bless others?

"The question may arise, How can these meetings be started? I would suggest that a few Christians, clerical or lay, should get a suitable room which will be comfortable and easy of access. Then select the leader for each day a week in advance, with a request that he open the meeting at the half-hour, advertising not only the leader for each day, but also the subject for prayer and thought at the meeting.

"If these meetings are thrown open for any one to speak or pray as he may feel led, with an occasional psalm or hymn, sung from the heart, I believe many would be glad to attend, and, doing so, would go away refreshed.

"After starting the meetings let them be well made known; let the notice of them not only be given from the pulpit and from the weekly church prayer-meetings, but also advertised constantly in the newspapers, with the names of the leaders and the subject for the day.

"There may be occasionally a person who will take up more time than he ought; but if such a thing should occur, or if any one whose character is known to be doubtful should be prominent, let one of the brethren go to such a one privately and in a spirit of love expostulate with him.

"Again I urge, will not God's children all over the United Kingdom meet at the noon hour and unite their prayers with those of Christians in different towns for the mighty blessing? He says, '*Call unto Me, and I will answer thee and show thee great and mighty things.*'

"Has not the time come for the church of God to arise and call on our God for a blessing? Thousands of our young men are fast passing to a drunkard's grave, while many of our young women are being drawn into the whirlpool of worldliness. Will not the fathers and mothers, if there is no one else to meet, come together at the noontide hour and ask for a blessing on their children?

"I trust there may be a united cry going up to God for a blessing all over the land. Surely God will answer the cry of His children. Shall we say, '*There are yet four months, and then cometh the harvest,'* or shall we arise now, and, with prayers, put in the sickle and gather?

"If He is with us, we are able to possess the land, and no giant, however great, can hinder."

When in response to this letter the central noon meeting was established in Moorgate Street Hall, London, Mr. Moody sent this telegram:

"Daily meeting of Belfast sends greeting to the Christians of London. Our prayer is that the meeting may become a great blessing to many. *'He must increase, but I must decrease.'*"

Open-air meetings were held on Sunday afternoons, attended by the thousands who could not get into the churches or halls. The first Sunday Mr. Moody spoke upon the text: "*Go ye into all the world, and preach the Gospel to every creature,*" following this by a meeting for inquirers only in the Ulster Hall, the largest public building in the city.

Not the least gratifying feature of the Belfast meetings was the bringing together of all evangelical denominations. Presbyterians, Episcopalians, Methodists, and Baptists mingled without distinction. One night in Rosemary Street Church the Rev. Mr. Dickson, of the Mariners' Episcopal Church, was one of the busiest among the inquirers, and on another evening an Episcopal clergyman occupied the pulpit of the Eglinton Street Presbyterian Church.

At the close of the Edinburgh mission it was said that fourteen hundred people had professed conversion. People who did not believe in the work, however, asserted that eleven hundred of these were women, hinting that this kind of thing could only make progress among women and weak-minded men. When he arrived in Glasgow, therefore, Mr. Moody made a special prayer that he might be able to refute this notion by being honored in the conversion of young men, and this wish was so far gratified that when he was about to leave the city, and held a meeting of those who believed they had been brought to Christ since his coming, out of the thirty-two hundred who attended sixteen hundred and thirty were men. Baffled in this matter, the enemies of the work now found a new cause of faultfinding. They could not deny that many men had been blessed, but they suggested that these were not of a class which most needed conversion—the abandoned class of the community. When coming to Belfast, therefore, Mr. Moody prayed that he might be specially able to do good to this class. His prayer had so far been answered that the first three converts who rose to tell that they had become changed men were formerly drunkards.

An open-air meeting was held October 8th, one of the largest ever seen in Ireland. Mr. Moody addressed a vast multitude on the words: "I pray thee have me excused."

The last meeting in Belfast was on the evening of October 16th. It was designed for those who had reason to believe that they had become converted during the meetings. Admission was strictly by ticket, received only on personal application, and twenty-one hundred and fifty tickets were given out.

Londonderry was next visited. The meetings were largely attended by young and old of all classes from this and surrounding districts. Excursion trains brought many, while hundreds walked and drove many miles. The attendance steadily increased to the close, while a noticeable feature in connection with the meetings was the large number of clergymen present.

The prevailing characteristic of all the meetings was intense earnestness and solemnity without, however, any undue excitement. The services seemed to awaken the liveliest interest in the public mind and to produce a marked impression. The inquiry meetings after the first night were very well attended—large numbers remaining for conversation and prayer with Mr. Moody and the Christian workers.

The work in Dublin had been preceded by a general prayer-meeting made up largely of members of all evangelical denominations of the city, the clergymen working cordially together without the least shade of envy or party spirit. The Rev. Dr. Marrable, of the Church of Ireland, presided at the first service, supported by Presbyterians, Wesleyans, and others. On the following day the management secured the use of the Exhibition Palace, the largest and most commodious building which had up to that time been placed at Mr. Moody's disposal, and here, as elsewhere, the same general interest was at once awakened.

A correspondent of "The Christian," of London, writing at this time says:

"The inhabitants of Dublin are becoming alive to the fact that we are now in the enjoyment of a great time of refreshing, and that our gracious God is working powerfully among us by the instrumentality of these, His honored servants. Such a sight has never been witnessed here as may now be seen every day—thousands flocking to the prayer-meeting and to the Bible reading, and, most of all, to the evening services in the great Exhibition Palace. It fills the heart of a child of God with deepest emotion to stand upon the platform from which Mr. Moody preaches, and to cast one's eye over the vast concourse of people hanging on the speaker's lips as in burning words he discourses of life and death, and 'Jesus and His love.' One cannot but ask the question, 'What is the magic power which draws together these mighty multitudes and holds them spellbound?' Is it the worldly rank or wealth of learning or oratory of the preacher? No, for he is possessed of little of these. It is the simple lifting up of the cross of Christ—the holding forth the Lord Jesus before the eyes of the people in all the glory of His Godhead, in all the simplicity of His manhood, in all the perfection of His nature, for their admiration, for their adoration, for their acceptance.

"As an Episcopal minister I am most thankful to see so many of the dear brethren in my own church, as well as of the other evangelical churches, attending and taking part in these happy services. May each of us receive a blessing, and in turn be made a blessing to our flocks. An able and godly minister stated a day or two ago that by attendance at these services he seemed to have returned to the

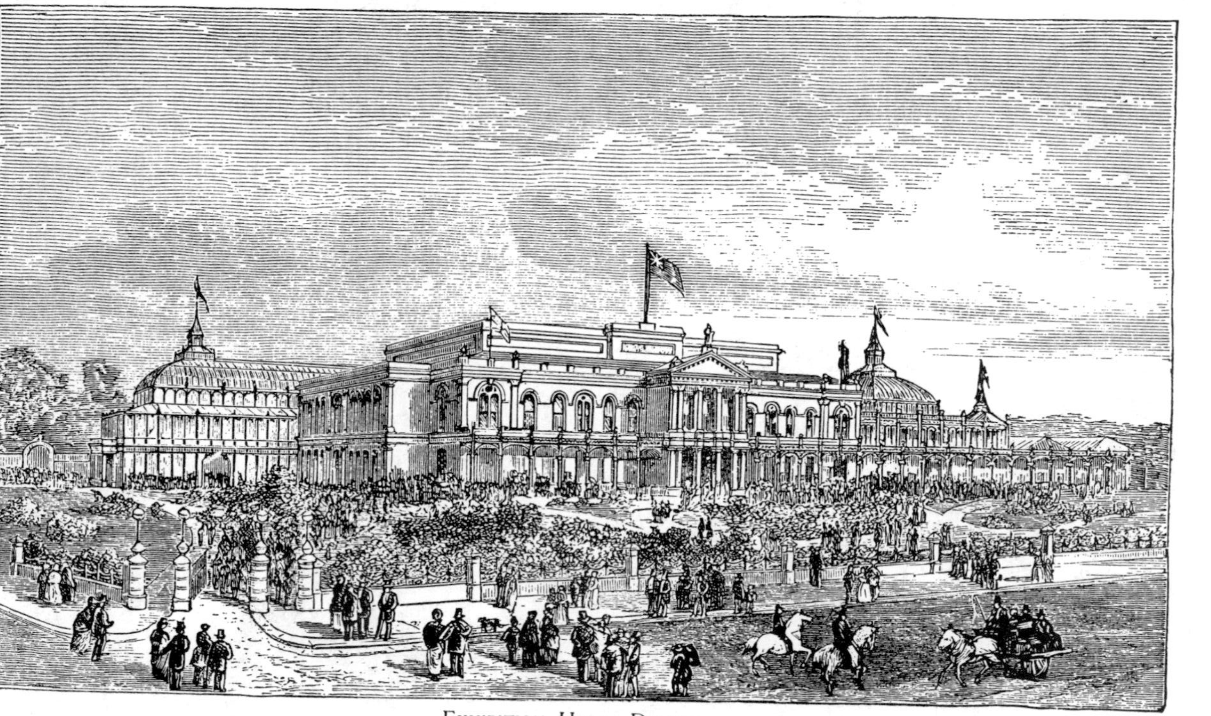

EXHIBITION HALL, DUBLIN.

Occupied for the great mission in that city.

Bingley Hall, Birmingham, England.

'freshness of his spiritual youth,' a sentiment worthy of a noble man and a generous heart."

The active coöperation of the Episcopalians and the respect and tacit sympathy manifested by some of the Roman Catholics were notable features of Mr. Moody's work in Ireland at this time. The leading Roman Catholic paper of the city gave full information respecting the work, and was extremely friendly toward it. In "The Nation" an article appeared entitled "Fair Play," in which the editor informed his constituents that "the deadly danger of the age comes upon us from the direction of Huxley and Darwin and Tyndall, rather than from Moody and Sankey. Irish Catholics desire to see Protestants deeply imbued with religious feeling rather than tinged with rationalism and infidelity, and so long as the religious services of our Protestant neighbors are honestly directed to quickening religious thought in their own body without offering aggressive or intentional insult to us, it is our duty to pay the homage of our respect to their conscientious convictions; in a word, to do as we would be done by."

Mr. Moody now returned to England, and visited Manchester, Sheffield, Birmingham, and Liverpool with marked success. In Manchester particularly he did much for the Young Men's Christian Association. After a stirring appeal for a building fund he took up a collection of £1,800 for the purpose.

In speaking of the definite results of the meetings in Manchester, the Rev. W. Rigby Murray wrote to "The Christian":

"If one class has been blessed more than another during these past weeks, it has been the regular Christian ministers. I am sure I voice the sentiment of all my brethren who have thrown themselves heart and soul into the movement, when I say that we have received nothing less than a fresh baptism of the Holy Ghost. Our souls have been quickened; our faith in the adaptation of the glorious Gospel of the blessed God to the wants and longings of the human spirit has been deepened; our sense of the magnitude and responsibility of our offices as Heaven's ambassadors, charged with a message of reconciliation, and love for the guiltiest of the guilty and the vilest of the vile, has been greatly increased. Mr. Moody has demonstrated to us in a way at once startling and delightful that, after all, the grand levers for raising souls out of the fearful pit and the miry clay are just the doctrines which our so-called advanced thinkers are trying to persuade the Christian world to discard as antiquated and impotent. These are, the doctrine of the atoning death of Jesus Christ; the doctrine of a living, loving, personal Saviour, and the doctrine of the new birth by the Spirit and the Word of Almighty God.

"One of the ablest ministers at the noon prayer-meeting on the last day of the year solemnly declared that, whereas the first of these cardinal verities had not been fully realized by him before these services commenced, he now felt it to be a spring of joy and satisfaction to his soul such as language could hardly express. And then how shall I speak of the gladness which filled our hearts as we heard, almost from day to day, of conversions in our congregations, of parents rejoicing over sons and daughters brought to Jesus, of young men consecrating their manhood and strength to God, and of converts offering themselves for all departments of Christian service? If our dear friend Mr. Moody had accomplished nothing more than the quickening of the ministers of this great centre of population and the stirring us up to greater devotion to our glorious calling as laborers together with God, his visit would not have been in vain. Give us a revived ministry and we shall soon see a revived church."

"What is to be done for the unsaved masses?" Mr. Moody asked while in Sheffield. In answering his own inquiry he said that he had found a spiritual famine in England such as he had never dreamed of. "Here, for instance, in this town of Sheffield," he said, "I am told that there are one hundred and fifty thousand people who not only never go near a place of worship, but for whom there is actually no church accommodation provided, even if they were willing to take advantage of it. It seems to me if there be upon God's earth one blacker sight than these thousands of Christless and graceless souls, it is the thousands of dead and slumbering Christians living in their very midst, rubbing shoulders with them every day upon the streets, and never so much as lifting up a little finger to warn them of death and eternity and judgment to come. Talk of being sickened at the sight of the world's degradation, ah! let those of us who are Christians hide our faces because of our own, and pray God to deliver us from the guilt of the world's blood. I believe that if there is one thing which pierces the Master's heart with unutterable grief, it is not the world's iniquity, but the Church's indifference."

He then argued that every Christian man and woman should feel that the question was not one for ministers and elders and deacons alone, but for them as well. "It is not enough," he said, "to give alms; personal service is necessary. I may hire a man to do *some* work, but I can never hire a man to do *my* work. Alone before God I must answer for that, and so must we all."

On the last day of the old year—1874—the meetings at Sheffield were begun. The first meeting was held in the Temperance Hall at nine P.M., beginning with the new hymn, afterward so famous, written by Dr. Horatius Bonar:

"Rejoice and be glad, the Redeemer has come."

Just before the hour of midnight Mr. Moody asked all those who desired the prayers of Christians to rise. For a time none were willing to do so, but soon a few stood up, and the Christians were asked to pray for them. Just then the bells began to ring in the new year, and with a prayer by Mr. Moody one of the most solemn meetings of the series was closed.

Following the Sheffield mission Mr. Moody held a two weeks' series of meetings in Birmingham. The Town Hall, Carr's Lane Chapel, and Bingley Hall were found none too large for the audiences which attended. During the first eight days of their stay in that city the total attendance at the three halls was estimated at one hundred and six thousand. Dr. W. R. Dale was at first inclined to look with disfavor on the movement and stood aloof. As the interest continued, however, he became more impressed and attended the meetings regularly.

"Of Mr. Moody's own power," he said, "I find it difficult to speak. It is so real and yet so unlike the power of ordinary preachers, that I hardly know how to analyze it. Its reality is indisputable. Any man who can interest and impress an audience of from three to six thousand people for half an hour in the morning and for three-quarters of an hour in the afternoon, and who can interest a third audience of thirteen or fifteen thousand people for three-quarters of an hour again in the evening, must have power of some kind. Of course, some people listened without caring much for what he said, but though I generally sat in a position which enabled me to see the kind of impression he produced, I rarely saw many faces which did not indicate the most active and earnest interest.

"The people were of all sorts, old and young, rich and poor, tradesmen, manufacturers, and merchants, young ladies who had just left school, cultivated women, and rough boys who knew more about dogs and pigeons than about books. For a time I could not understand it—I am not sure that I understand it now. At the first meeting Mr. Moody's address was simple, direct, kindly, and hopeful; it had a touch of humor and a touch of pathos; it was lit up with a story or two that filled most eyes with tears, but there seemed nothing in it very remarkable. Yet it told. A prayer-meeting with an address at eight o'clock on a damp, cold January morning was hardly the kind of thing—let me say it frankly—that I should generally regard as attractive, but I enjoyed it heartily; it seemed one of the happiest meetings I had ever attended: there was warmth and there was sunlight in it. At the evening meeting the same day, at Bingley Hall, I was still unable to make out how it was that he had done so much in other parts of the Kingdom.

"I listened with interest, and I was again conscious of a certain warmth and brightness that made the service very pleasant, but I could not see that there was much to impress those who were careless about religious duty. The next morning at the prayer-meeting the address was more incisive and striking, and at the evening service I began to see that the stranger had a faculty for making the elementary truths of the Gospel intensely clear and vivid. But it still seemed most remarkable that he should have done so much, and on Tuesday I told Mr. Moody that the work was most plainly of God, for I could see no real relation between him and what he had done. He laughed cheerily, and said he should be very sorry if it were otherwise.

"Scores of us could preach as effectively as Mr. Moody, I felt, and might, therefore, with God's good help be equally successful. In the course of a day or two, however, my mistake was corrected. His preaching had all the effect of Luther's; he exulted in the free grace of God. His joy was contagious. Men leaped out of darkness into light and lived a Christian life afterward." Dr. Dale did not believe much in evangelists, but he had a profound respect for Mr. Moody, and considered that he had a right to preach the Gospel, "because he could never speak of a lost soul without tears in his eyes."

After the work in Birmingham came a mission in Liverpool, where the blessed experiences of the preceding weeks were repeated. In this case no suitable auditorium could be secured, and a wooden structure one hundred and seventy-four feet long and one hundred and twenty-four feet wide, capable of accommodating ten thousand people, was erected at great expense. This was called Victoria Hall. The building was erected in forty days.

At the close of the mission a convention was held, where the rousing addresses of Dr. Chown, of Bradford, Newman Hall, of London, Dr. Dale, of Birmingham, Mr. Fletcher, of Dublin, and other men of large experience produced a profound impression. An important feature of the convention was Mr. Moody's hour with the "Question Drawer."

One little observed but important part of the meetings was the gathering of children every Saturday at noon in nearly every town and city visited. This was usually organized into a permanent institution. While they were still in Great Britain many of these meetings were held every week, and after a time the Edinburgh children conceived the idea of opening a friendly Christian correspondence between the various meetings and set the example by sending a letter to the children of Dublin.

One of the most interesting meetings at Liverpool was the children's service, where Mr. Moody and Mr. Sankey were both present. Some of the papers put down the number in Victoria Hall at twelve thousand, with an overflow meeting of about two thousand in the Henglers Circus. Mr. Moody gave an address founded on a book with four leaves, black, red, white, and gold, a sort of running interchange of simple yet searching questions and answers. Responses were very promptly given. Mr. Sankey's singing was especially enjoyed by the young people, who joined in the choruses with great heartiness.

Mr. Moody made an impressive appeal in Victoria Hall to merchants, employers, and friends of young men, the meeting being in connection with the special appeal for funds in behalf of the new Young Men's Christian Association building. The audience was one seldom seen even in Liverpool. There were men of very different beliefs and nationalities: High Churchmen, Broad Churchmen, Low Churchmen, Orangemen, Wesleyans, Unitarians, Baptists, Presbyterians, Roman Catholics, Jews, Greeks, Spiritualists, and others. Different phases of commercial life were represented. There were present also clergymen; town councillors, Liberal and Tory; leading members of the Dock Board and the Select Vestry, millionaire shipowners, dealers in every kind of produce, timber merchants, sugar merchants, tea merchants, corn merchants, provision merchants, brokers, shopkeepers, and many women.

When Mr. Moody rose to speak he said that he was often asked whether he believed in the Young Men's Christian Association. He wanted to say that he did with all his heart. Because they did not have Associations in the days of the fathers, he said, a great many churches now thought they were not needed, but that was no fair criterion.

"Fifty or one hundred years ago young men lived at home. They lived in a country home, and did not come to these large cities and centres of commerce as they do now. If they did come, their employers took a personal interest in them. I contend that they do not do so now!" and at this sturdy utterance of opinion there was a subdued but perceptible "Hear, hear!" from various parts of the hall.

"Since I have come to Liverpool," he added, "there is hardly a night that in walking from this hall to my hotel I do not meet a number of young men reeling through the streets. They may not be *your* sons, but bear in mind, my friend, they are *somebody's* sons. They are worth saving. These young men who come to large cities want somebody to take an interest in them. I contend that no one can do this so well as the Christian Association. Some ministers claim that Associations are doing the church harm—they draw young men away from the church. That is a mistake. They feed the church; they are the handmaids of the church. They are not tearing down the church; they are drawing men into it. I know no institution which helps to draw churches so much together as these Young Men's Christian Associations."

Later, on the completion of the building for which Mr. Moody had made so strong a plea, he was requested by Alexander Balfour, the president of the Young Men's Christian Association of Liverpool, to place the memorial tablet of the new structure, which bears the inscription: "This memorial stone was laid by D. L. Moody, of Chicago, March 2, 1875."

One who was present at the Liverpool meetings thus describes the deep impression made upon the public:

"Men who wrote and spoke against the movement, men who laughed at it, went to hear and came away with changed thoughts—six thousand people at the midday prayer-meeting, six thousand at the afternoon Bible lecture, and ten thousand at the evening meeting, with the inquiry-rooms full, is something that even 'The Exchange' has to admit. But beyond this there is the mighty power of God's spirit, working and acting, which no tables can register, no numbers record."

Following Mr. Moody, Henry Drummond held meetings for young men in Liverpool, with an average attendance of fourteen hundred nightly. Of Mr. Drummond it was said: "His gentleness is only surpassed by the earnestness with which he carries out and controls this most successful service."

CHAPTER XXI

The London Campaign

MR. MOODY turned a deaf ear to all the invitations that poured in from London during his first two years in Great Britain, for the spirit of unity in the earlier calls that would indicate the coöperation of all denominations was at first lacking, and until this was assured he did not feel that the time was ripe.

When he was in Edinburgh Hugh M. Matheson, a London business man, made the trip to the Scottish metropolis to hear him. It was the last day of the meetings; there was the usual large attendance, and Mr. Matheson found no opportunity to present the invitation that he had brought with him. Afterward he went to Thurso, where they had a delightful interview. They discussed London and the best means of preparing for a mission there, should he see his way to undertake it.

During all the missions in Scotland and Ireland, as well as in the large manufacturing centres, the work had been fully reported in "The Christian," of London. Thousands of copies of this paper had been sent to the clergymen of Great Britain, and the movement had been closely followed by the Christian public. Appreciating the benefit of such a medium, Mr. Moody wished to distribute the paper still more widely over England, and Mr. Matheson agreed to raise a fund of £2,000, to circulate the paper gratuitously for three months to thirty thousand clergymen and nonconformist ministers all over England. The accounts which it gave of the remarkable movement in Scotland stimulated the desire for a similar work in London.

While the evangelists were in Dublin the final arrangements were made, and the central noon prayer-meeting at Moorgate Street Hall, London, adopted the following resolution:

"That, in accordance with the suggestion of Mr. Moody, it is hereby determined to arrange for special evangelistic work in London during four months of next year; namely, March, April, May, and June; that a fund of not less than £10,000 be placed in the hands of the treasurer, and that men of distinguished evangelistic gifts heartily interested in the work be invited not only from other parts of England, but also from America, Scotland, and Ireland, to assist in the movement."

Four centres were selected for preaching-places: Agricultural Hall at Islington in North London, seating thirteen thousand seven hundred persons, with standing room for four or five thousand more; Bow Road Hall in the extreme east, with ten thousand sittings; the Royal Opera House in the West End, in the aristocratic quarter of Westminster, and Victoria Theatre in the south, and, later, Camberwell Green Hall.

The need for evangelistic services in London at that time may be gathered from statistics which were published shortly before Mr. Moody went to the metropolis. The promoters of special services in theatres and music halls made the following statement concerning the city's need, in the report of their fifteenth series of services:

"117,000 habitual criminals are on its police register, increasing at an average of 30,000 per annum;

"More than one-third of all the crime in the country is committed in London;

"23,000 persons live in its common lodging-houses;

"Its many beer shops and gin palaces would, if placed side by side, stretch from Charing Cross to Portsmouth, a distance of 73 miles;

"38,000 drunkards appear annually before its magistrates;

"It has as many paupers as would occupy every house in Brighton;

"It has upward of a million habitual neglecters of public worship;

"It has 60 miles of shops open every Lord's day;

"It has need of 900 new churches and chapels, and 200 additional city missionaries."

All through the months of January and February extensive preparations were made for the intended meetings. No movement within the memory of those then living had so bound together the clergymen and Christian workers of various denominations. Had the meetings not been held, the preparations for them would, in themselves, have been a great blessing.

On Friday, February 5, 1875, Free Masons' Hall in London was crowded with ministers and other Christian workers from all parts of London and its suburbs to confer with Moody in reference to the services soon to begin. There were nearly two thousand persons present at one of the largest and most varied meetings of the ministerial order ever held for any purpose in England. Representative men from all the evangelical churches were there, and there was besides a contingent from the ritualistic clergy, who had scarcely been expected. Prebendary Auriol and Mr. Kitto headed a strong phalanx of evangelical churchmen; Dr. Moffat, Dr. Stoughton, Mr. Hannay, Dr. Llewelyn Bevan, and Mr. Braden were among the Congregational ministers who answered to the summons; the venerable Charles Stovel was one of the many Baptists; the Presbytery sent a formidable array, among whom were Doctors Edmonds, Fraser, Dykes, Paterson, and Thain Davidson; while the various branches of the great Methodist body attended in great numbers.

The chair was occupied by Mr. Stone, of Blackheath, a London merchant. Mr. Moody made a brief statement. There were, he said, many obstacles to the proposed work in London, which could be put out of the way if they could only meet together and come to an understanding. He found some of the very best men kept out of the work because they heard this and that. Perhaps some things they heard were true and some not; and if they only had a "fair and square" understanding, he thought it would be helpful. He spoke frankly to his new friends, telling them that the great difficulty with which they had to contend was prejudice, and he urged the ministers to come into sympathy with the work at the beginning, and invited questions from every one.

He spoke of the prejudice of some people against the inquiry-room, and explained in detail the method, that those who were present might judge for themselves. A charge of undue excitement in the meetings had been made. This was also erroneous. Very often in a room with a hundred inquirers one could hear scarcely a whisper. Concerning the sale of the hymn-books he said:

"A great deal has been said about our making a fine thing financially out of this movement from the sale of the hymn-books, organs, etc. Now I desire to say that up to the 1st of January we received a royalty from the publishers of our hymn-books, but from that date, when the solo book was enlarged, we determined not to receive anything from the sale, and have requested the publishers to hand over the royalty upon all our hymn-books to one of your leading citizens, Mr. H. M. Matheson, who will devote the same to such charitable objects as may be decided upon.

"In regard to the organ question, I want to say, once for all, that we are not selling organs—that is not our mission, nor are we agents for the sale of organs; nor do we receive a commission or compensation in any way whatever from any person or persons for the organ that Mr. Sankey uses at our meetings.

"I hope now that no one here will think that I have made these statements to create financial sympathy in our behalf. We do not want your money; we want your confidence, and we want your sympathy and prayers, and as our one object in coming here is to preach Christ, we believe we shall have them, and that with God's blessing we shall see many brought into His fold. If we make mistakes, come and tell us. Then I shall not fear for the result."

Many questions were asked Mr. Moody, and many misstatements

corrected. One clergyman wished to know whether the work had the effect of estranging people from the communion. If so, he could not uphold the mission without being false to his ordination vows and the Holy Ghost. Mr. Moody replied that his one object was to preach the Gospel, a statement which was greeted with cheers.

The next questioner wanted to know if it were true that a Roman Catholic took the chair at one of Mr. Moody's meetings in Ireland. Mr. Moody said that he was not responsible for the chairman, and added, amid laughter, that his meetings were attended by "Jew, Greek, and barbarian."

One clergyman asked Mr. Moody to print his creed before he came to London.

"My creed is in print," was the ready response.

"Where?" was the general inquiry, as many people reached for their note-books.

"In the fifty-third chapter of Isaiah," was the reply.

His answer was entirely satisfactory, and there was no further question as to Mr. Moody's orthodoxy.

The opening meeting at Agricultural Hall was held on Tuesday evening, March 9th, and the noon meeting at Exeter Hall on the following day. The house-to-house visitation committee had been actively at work, and in the noon prayer-meeting at Moorgate Street Hall there was a decided increase of interest and fervor. Prayer-meetings had also been held in Agricultural Hall for a month, attended by more than a thousand people.

The campaign was an unquestionable success from the outset. Many of the leading evangelical ministers and laymen of London were on the platform at the first service. The hall was quickly filled, seats and standing room, and thousands went away disappointed, though seventeen thousand people were crowded into the great building.

Mr. Moody won all hearts in the very beginning by asking the vast audience to "praise God for what He was going to do in London." He added that he had received despatches from many cities in Great

Britain saying that the Christians were praying for London, and then he prayed with great fervor that a blessing might come upon the city, thanking God for the spirit of unity among the ministers and praying that there might be no strife among them.

In his address he expressed his early fear that if he should come to London many people would be led to trust too much to the excitement of the great meetings, at the risk of having their eyes turned away from God. Those who had come expecting to hear a new Gospel would be disappointed. He had the same old story to tell that the ministers whom he saw before him had preached and were preaching in their churches and chapels. Referring to the men, weak in the estimation of the world, whom the Lord had used to do a great work for humanity, he said that it was not good preachers that were wanted in London, for probably at no time had the city possessed so many great preachers as then.

The belief of every individual Christian should be, not that "God *can* use me," but "He *will* use me." What was wanted was that they should be out and out on the Lord's side, heart and brain on fire for Him, ready to use every power and every opportunity for service. He also spoke of the necessity for perfect unity in carrying on the work, and expressed a hope that ministers, Sabbath-school superintendents, teachers, and parents would all be found working and praying for the success of the movement.

The first Sunday afternoon the great hall was nearly filled with women, and in the evening it was crowded to its utmost capacity with men. In order to reach different classes of people, Mr. Moody began to repeat his afternoon sermon in the evening, in the hope that those who came to one service would stay away from the other to make room for different audiences.

The noon meetings in Exeter Hall were crowded day after day, and reports of the work throughout the Kingdom were received and many requests made for prayer. But the enthusiasm was not confined to Mr. Moody's meetings. At the East End Tabernacle the

Rev. Archibald G. Brown had the pleasure of seeing two thousand members of his evening congregation remain to an after-meeting, and instead of the churches and chapels declining in interest, as it was feared, they were filled as they had not been before. The best of the work was in the inquiry-room, where earnest workers found plenty of scope for their zeal and more for their wisdom and tact.

From the outset attention was directed to Christians, Mr. Moody saying that "he would rather wake up a slumbering church than a slumbering world," and that "the man who does the most good in the world is not the man who works himself, but the man who sets others to work." He was able to help people more in a few minutes in the inquiry-room than he could in a whole sermon.

"You have had enough of pulpit preaching," he said, "and very good preaching too; what we want now is hand-to-hand work, personal effort, individuals going to people and pressing on them the claims of Christ."

One woman, eighty-five years old, asked for a part in the house-to-house visitation. She said:

"I must do something; I am getting old, but I will take a district."

"Only think of that," was Mr. Moody's comment. "This old lady, who has lived fifteen years on borrowed time, has taken a district and started out."

She went to one house where the people were Roman Catholics, and wanted them to take a leaflet announcing the meetings, but they pushed it away.

"Well," she said, "if you won't read it I will read it to you," and she did.

"Of course they couldn't put out a woman eighty-five years old," said Mr. Moody. "Nobody could think of doing that. It stirred me greatly. It ought to shame us all. Every young man and woman who is not at work ought to be ashamed." He concluded his address by calling for a thousand men and women who would join him in an effort to win one soul to Christ during the week, and in answer to his question: "Who will join me?" the greater part of the congregation stood up.

It must not be supposed that Mr. Moody was entirely free from criticism. The infidel in the street and an occasional editor in his office vented his spite against religion by attacking those who came to proclaim it. As the crowds gathered for the opening service false handbills were distributed, pretending to describe the sermons that were about to be delivered.

The "Vanity Fair" outside the great hall in the evening has been described by an eye-witness:

"Many policemen to keep the way; multitudes of young men full of fun and joking; multitudes also of evil women and girls, gaily dressed, joining in the ribaldry; the two together forming a mass of well-dressed but disreputable blackguardism, proving to demonstration that the American evangelists had come at last exactly where they were sorely needed. Omnibus-men, cabmen, tramcar-men, board-men, and loafers of every description took part in the universal carnival. Oaths, jests, slang, and mockery were all let loose together; but not one serious face, not one thoughtful countenance, not an idea of God's judgment or of eternity in all the vast changing multitude outside.

"After the service inside had ended, and partly during its continuance, detachments of choirs belonging to the neighboring missions had stationed themselves near the hall and occupied themselves in singing the 'Songs and Solos' and delivering addresses of the briefest character. But all seemed in vain; the very spirit of mockery seemed to possess the great majority. There was nothing like spiteful opposition, much less of interference; the singers and speakers were merely regarded as amiable enthusiasts, who had rashly delivered themselves to the merciless mockery of a London mob."

The mob was not the only form of opposition. "The Saturday Review" expressed surprise that "so many persons go to hear the Americans. As for Moody, he is simply a ranter of the most vulgar

MR. MOODY IN 1884.

From an oil painting by Clifford. Presented to Mrs. Moody in London at close of second British campaign.

AGRICULTURAL HALL, ISLINGTON, LONDON.

The largest hall ever occupied by the evangelists.

type. His mission appears to be to degrade religion to the level of the 'penny gaff.'"

"The New York Times," at that time, was nearly as strong in its opposition to the evangelists. In its issue of June 22, 1875, in an editorial column, this statement occurred:

"We are credibly informed that Messrs. Moody and Sankey were sent to England by Mr. Barnum as a matter of speculation."

The London society papers devoted a great deal of attention to Mr. Moody on this visit. Caricatures of him and Mr. Sankey appeared in "Vanity Fair." The tone of the articles and paragraphs describing the meetings was at first contemptuous, but as eminent leaders of society began to attend, it became more sympathetic and respectful. "Mr. Moody," says one writer, "is a heavy-looking individual, with a nasal twang and a large fund of (to English ears) slightly irreverent anecdote."

Curious reports of Mr. Moody's provincial tour went before him to London. "The World" said: "In many large English towns they (the evangelists) had the satisfaction of throwing females into convulsions, and have been lucky enough to consign several harmless idiots to neighboring lunatic asylums." Those who attended the meetings bore testimony that this element of violent excitement was totally absent from them.

A penny biography of Mr. Moody sold widely in the London streets that spring. Everything that could be done to counteract his influence and prejudice the public against him was attempted by certain papers. Londoners were told that, "judged by the low standard of an American ranter, Mr. Moody is a third-rate star." His reading of Scripture was severely blamed. "Mr. Moody, with a jocular familiarity which painfully jarred on our sense of the reverential, translated freely passages of the Bible into the American vernacular. The grand, simple stories of Holy Writ were thus parodied and burlesqued." But in spite of all the hostility of the press, it soon became manifest, not only that the "common people heard him gladly," but that society itself was moved and deeply impressed by his preaching. One of the first to attend the meetings was Lord Cairns, then Lord Chancellor in Mr. Disraeli's government. He occupied a prominent seat in the Agricultural Hall, Islington. Very soon nearly all the leaders of society had followed his example. The epithets "pernicious humbugs," "crack-brained Yankee evangelists," "pestilential vermin," "abbots of unreason," with which the anti-Christian press pelted the preachers, gave way to much more polite language when the highest in the land were numbered among their hearers.

The London papers had asserted that Moody and Sankey were financially interested in the sale of the cheap photographs sold on the streets, although these were uniformly little more than caricatures. A photographer in one of the largest provincial towns, seeing these criticisms, wrote a letter to "The Times" stating that he had offered Moody and Sankey £1,000 (about $5,000) if they would sit for a photograph and allow him to copyright it, but that the offer was refused. The publication of this letter had a remarkable effect in establishing confidence.

In striking contrast with this flippant attitude was a leading article in "The London Times," which referred pleasantly to Mr. Sankey's singing, and then added:

"But people would not come together for weeks merely to hear expressive singing, nor to yield to the impulse of association. They come to hear Mr. Moody, and the main question is: What had he to say? Is any Christian church in this metropolis in a position to say that it can afford to dispense with any vigorous effort to rouse the mass of people to a more Christian life? The congregations which are to be seen in our churches and chapels are but a fraction of the hundreds and thousands around them, of whom multitudes are living but little better than a mere animal existence. If any considerable proportion of them can be aroused to the mere desire for something higher, an immense step is gained; if the churches are really a higher influence still, Mr. Moody will at least have prepared them better material to work on."

A striking incident connected with this campaign was the publication of a letter written by the Archbishop of Canterbury to a friend, in which he said he took the deepest interest in the Moody and Sankey movement, and that, having found an opportunity for consulting some of his Episcopal friends on the subject, his own view was very much strengthened by what he heard from them; that the great truths of the Gospel should be urged on the people's consciences was no innovation, and he heartily rejoiced that the movement was conducted on so great a scale and with such apparent success. At the same time he made it clear that he did not *officially* sanction the work.

"Many of our parochial clergy, as you are aware," he wrote, "have been present at the meetings in question, and those who have stood aloof have not done so from any want of interest, but because they have felt that, greatly as they rejoiced that simple gospel truths were urged on their people's consciences, there were circumstances attending the movement to which they could not consistently give their approval. If there is a difficulty in the clergy's giving their official sanction to the work, you will at once see that in the case of the bishops there are greater difficulties in the way of any direct sanction, which, coming from them, could not but be regarded as official and authoritative; and I confess that the objections I originally felt still remain in full force now that we have had time to examine and to learn from various quarters the exact nature of the movement.

"But looking to the vast field that lies before us, and the overwhelming difficulties of contending with the mass of positive sin and careless indifference which resists on all sides the progress of the Gospel, I, for my part, rejoice that, whether regularly or irregularly, whether according to the Divine Scriptural and perfect way or imperfectly, with certain admixtures of human error, Christ is preached and sleeping consciences are aroused."

The inquiry meetings in connection with the Agricultural Hall services were held in St. Mary's Hall, a large concert-room. Mr. Moody divided the inquirers, leaving the women in the basement and sending the men into the gallery, and directed the workers to divide in the same way. All around the gallery were men in twos and threes, to the number of two or three hundred—each couple or three separated from their neighbors, and earnestly engaged in their own work, without taking any notice of those near and around.

Here, for instance, was a couple discussing a difficulty in the way; there another couple earnestly reading passages of God's Word; next was one pleading with another; here a worker was praying for the light to come; there another, pressing the inquirer to pray for himself, and others praying earnestly together.

Bow Road Hall, in the East End of London, was the second place of meeting. It was patterned somewhat after Bingley Hall in Birmingham. An American spending a few weeks in London at the time sent this description of the building and one of the meetings in it to a home paper:

"The Bow Road Hall is a capacious frame building, sheathed with corrugated iron, which was erected for these meetings in the East End of London; it is in easy reach of a vice-infected, poverty-stricken district which Mr. Moody thinks 'comes nearer hell than any other place on earth.' A thick carpeting of sawdust, laid upon the ground, forms the floor. It is seated with cane-bottomed chairs, of which, I am told, it holds over nine thousand. Scripture texts in white letters two feet high, on a background of red flannel, stretch along the several walls. A choir of one hundred young men and women occupies a part of the platform.

"The preaching begins at eight o'clock. At half-past seven every chair in the hall is filled. Late comers, who cannot be packed upon the platform or find standing room out of range of those who are seated, are turned away by the policemen at the entrances. The choir fills the time with hymns familiar to American Sunday-schools and prayer-meetings:

"'Sweet hour of prayer,'
"'When He cometh,'
"'Come to the Saviour,'

but mostly unknown here until Mr. Sankey sang them into notice and favor.

"A Christian cannot look into the faces of this serious, hushed, expectant audience of eight or ten thousand people without being deeply moved by the thought of the issues that may hang on this hour. Most of them seem to belong to the class of shopkeepers and thrifty working people. But here and there a diamond flashes its light from richer toilets, while some of the faces evidently belong to the very lowest classes. Hundreds, if not thousands, of them have come from other quarters of the city, from five to ten miles away. They sit so closely packed that the men wear their hats. Ushers, carrying their tall rods of office, are thickly scattered along the entrances and aisles. In a great tent at the rear a prayer-meeting is going on for the blessing of God on the evening's service.

"Promptly at eight Mr. Moody steps out and plants both hands on the rail that runs along the front of the platform and forms his pulpit. He has grown stout since leaving America, and wears a flowing beard, but there is no mistaking the man as soon as he opens his mouth. He sees too many people, he says, whose faces are getting familiar at these meetings. 'It's time for Christians to stop coming here and crowding into the best seats. It's time for 'em to go out among these sailors and drunkards and bring them in and give *them* the best seats.' Mr. Sankey sits at his cabinet organ close by—that 'kist o' whistles' which so scandalized some of the good Scotch brethren last year—and Mr. Moody calls on him to sing

"'Jesus of Nazareth passeth by.'

It is plain enough, before the first verse is finished, that this movement owes much of its success to Mr. Sankey. He has a voice of unequalled clearness and power, which sounds through the hall like a trumpet. Each word is articulated with great distinctness, and there is a soul in the singing that is something more and higher than mere art. The hymn tells at once, as any one can see by the intent eyes that are everywhere focussed on the singer. A prayer by Mr. Moody, brief, ejaculatory, fervent, and Mr. Sankey sings

"'There were ninety and nine,'

with great effect. Mr. Moody, aptly turning the Whitsunday commemoration of the day of Pentecost to account, reads a part of Peter's address on that occasion, and announces that he proposes to take the same text and topic—the crucified Christ.

"The sermon that follows is simply the story of the closing scenes in the Saviour's life, beginning with the gathering of the little company of thirteen at the Last Supper. It is told in the photographic way of one who has studied it so intently that the whole scene stands out in clear detail and intensely real before him. And he makes it seem very real and present to his audience. There are Moodyish touches to the picture, here and there, that are very characteristic and effective. 'Judas made great professions. He got near enough to the Son of God to kiss him. But he went down to perdition.' His words tumble over each other in the haste of his utterance. He has a surprising faculty for such grammatical mistakes and illiteracies as 'The Spirit done it,' ''Tain't no use,' 'Git right up,' 'He come to him,' etc. But these minor blemishes sink out of notice in the tremendous earnestness with which he speaks. That is the preëminent characteristic of the discourse. The noiseless, rapt attention of the vast congregation is wonderful. Hundreds are in tears.

"In the very midst of one discourse, and the height of its interest, two or three quickly succeeding shrieks came from the centre of the audience. Mr. Moody stopped as if at a signal, and, with Sheridan-like promptness, said: 'We'll stand up and sing,

"'"Rock of ages, cleft for me,"

and the ushers will please help that friend out of the hall. She's hysterical.' There were no more 'hysterical' demonstrations during the evening, and the congregation scarcely realized that there had been any interruption in the service.

"At the close of the address, which was something less than an hour long, those who wished to become Christians were invited to stand up, and several hundred arose. While they remained standing all Christians present were asked to rise. Apparently not a tenth of the audience kept their seats under both invitations. The congregation was then dismissed, but with an urgent request to stay to the second meeting, for conversation and prayer with inquirers. Many remained, perhaps twelve or fifteen hundred, but much the larger part were Christians. As there were opportunity and occasion, they scattered about the hall, talking and praying with those who had asked for prayers. The interest in this second meeting did not, somehow, seem to match that of the preaching service. But it would be manifestly unfair to measure the influence of the latter by such a test. It was as well calculated to quicken Christians as to awaken the impenitent; to set them at work elsewhere and everywhere as in Bow Road Hall. It was spoken of at the noon prayer-meeting the next day as the best, so far, of the London meetings.

"Nothing is clearer than that London has been remarkably stirred by the labors of these two evangelists. The windows of every print store are hung with their pictures. Penny editions of Mr. Sankey's songs are hawked about the streets. The stages and the railway stations are placarded to catch the travellers for their meetings. The papers report their services with a fulness never dreamed of before in reporting religious meetings. Yet it is doubtful whether, with services held almost every day since about the 1st of March, five per cent. of the people of this great city have ever heard them, or fifteen per cent. ever heard of them."

While Mr. Moody was reaching the tenement-house population in the crowded East End he was also holding services in the fashionable

West End. The Royal Opera House was secured, and, in addition to the noon prayer-meeting and a Bible lecture in the afternoon, he preached twice every evening except Saturday, being driven rapidly from the Opera House to Bow Road Hall. One Sunday he arranged to preach four times. Ignorant of the distances, he was obliged to walk sixteen miles besides delivering the sermons, as he would not use a public conveyance on Sunday.

"I walked it," he announced later when preaching on the Fourth Commandment, "and I slept that night with a clear conscience. I have made it a rule never to use the cars, and if I have a private carriage, I insist that horse and man shall rest on Monday. I want no hackman to rise up in judgment against me."

In a later visit to Scotland a committee went to a livery-stable keeper, without Mr. Moody's knowledge, to secure a carriage to take him to a distant meeting on the following Sunday.

"It will hurt him less to walk," said the owner of a thousand horses, "than to drive a horse and carriage four miles through the Decalogue." Mr. Moody was greatly pleased with the reply and often repeated the incident, remarking that he wished more employers were as careful of the interests of their men as well as their dumb animals.

Among those who attended the London meetings was Mr. Gladstone, who entered heartily into the service. At the close of the meeting Mr. Moody was presented to him. The conversation was characteristic in its abruptness, and in reply to an inquiry as to its nature, Mr. Moody said, "Oh, he said he wished he had my shoulders, and I said I wished I had his head on them."

Although Mr. Moody was always utterly indifferent to rank and title as such, his influence was no less effective on the highly educated and socially eminent. Lord Shaftesbury thanked God publicly that Mr. Moody had not been educated at Oxford, "for he had a wonderful power of getting at the hearts of men, and while the common people hear him gladly, many persons of high station have been greatly struck with the marvellous simplicity and power of his preaching." Lord Shaftesbury added that the Lord Chancellor of England a short time before had said to him, "The simplicity of that man's preaching, the clear manner in which he sets forth salvation by Christ, is to me the most striking and the most delightful thing I ever knew in my life."

Mr. Moody received no more hearty support from any one in London than that given by the Rev. Charles H. Spurgeon. Addressing his own audience, Mr. Spurgeon said that "some of my hearers have probably been converted under the influence of the services conducted by my dear friends, Moody and Sankey, at Agricultural Hall." He implored them, if they professed to have found Christ, not to make a sham of it, and said that their salvation, if it were worth anything, should be a salvation from sin. Salvation from hell was not the salvation they ought to cry after, but salvation from sin, and that would bring salvation from hell. A thief might want to get salvation from going to prison, but the only salvation for him that was worth anything was salvation from thieving.

One of the most enthusiastic services, and in many respects one of the best, was held in Spurgeon's Tabernacle. It was designed for the benefit of the students of Mr. Spurgeon's college and the Baptist ministers in town for the April anniversaries, but the scope of the meeting was widened and tickets were issued to the Sunday congregation. In his address Mr. Moody was dwelling on the passage, "*Prepared unto every good work,*" and he said:

"I wonder how many of you would rise if I should ask every man and woman to do so who is ready to go and speak to some anxious soul—I wonder how many would rise and say, 'I am ready for one.'" He paused. "Some one behind me says, 'Try it,' but I am rather afraid." He paused again. "Well, suppose we do try it. How many of you are ready to go and talk to some soul?"

The students and ministers on either side of the platform at once rose in a body, and their example was quickly followed by members throughout the congregation. Equal to the occasion, Mr. Moody said:

" Well, now you have risen, I want to tell you that the Lord is ready to send you. Nothing will wake up London quicker than to have the Christians going out and speaking to the people. The time has come when it should be done. We have been on the defensive too long."

CHAPTER XXII

THE LONDON CAMPAIGN CONTINUED

AT the opening of the mission in Camberwell Green Hall Mr. Moody received the valuable assistance of Rev. W. H. M. Hay-Aitken and Rev. Charles H. Spurgeon.

Special children's services were begun here, and the exercises were adapted to their tastes and needs. On one occasion between six and seven thousand children from the various charitable institutions of London gathered to hear Mr. Moody's anecdotes, to answer, as they readily did, the simple questions, and to listen with delight to Mr. Sankey's beautiful hymns. From shoeblacks' homes, doorstep brigades, newsboys' societies, boys' and girls' refuges, industrial schools, schools for the blind and for cripples, and homes for orphans, the waifs and strays came trooping up to swell the lilliputian host. Forty-seven such Christian nurseries sent their contingents, and as the entire army rose to sing "Hold the fort," the sight was most touching and beautiful. The uniforms of the several brigades, the costumes of the girls, varying from bright scarlet to black, came out most effectively, and their singing was well worth walking miles to hear. The galleries and spare floor space were filled with parents and friends of the girls and boys, with an extensive intersprinkling of children, who enjoyed the treat as much as their more favored contemporaries in the body of the hall.

Among Mr. Moody's most valued assistants and closest friends, men who gave him most valuable aid at this time and never lost their warm associations with him during his life, were Dr. Andrew Bonar, of Glasgow, and Henry Drummond. The London meetings were thus described by Drummond in a letter to his father: " Everything is bright outside and inside, and I only wish you were here to share the enjoyment. How would you like to see an acre of people? That is exactly the size of the audience to which Mr. Moody preaches every night in the East of London. Here is his programme: A three miles' drive to noon meeting; lunch; Bible reading at 3.30, followed by inquiry meeting till at least five; then five miles' drive to East End to preach to twelve thousand at 8.30; then inquiry meeting; five or six miles' drive home. This is every day this week and next—a terrible strain, which, however, he never seems to feel for a moment. The work is coming out grandly now, and I think the next two months will witness wonderful results. It is deepening on every side, and even London is beginning to be moved. Mr. Moody said 'Sunday was the best day of his life.' "

The following extract from Dr. Andrew Bonar's diary at this time is also of special interest:

" Have been with Moody again in London. Immense crowds, wonderful sight, and more wonderful impression. Had time to-day for prayer. Saw how simple confidence in Christ had helped me very often in the past, and sought to be able to have this always, as well as often. There is great talk about higher life and much movement in that direction, and, though there is error mingled, this may be the Lord's way of answering the prayers which some of us have sent up, asking in our lives more likeness to Christ.

" At Camberwell Hall not less than nine thousand assembled, morning, noon, and night. In the morning, before eight o'clock, I was summoned away to the overflow in the neighboring church. But the most remarkable part of the day was our Bible reading with Mr. Moody in the forenoon; about thirty Christian friends present. We were like Acts, xx. 7, talking for two hours and then dispensing the Lord's Supper. Mr. Moody closed with prayer. Most solemn scene, never to be forgotten.

" The last of Mr. Moody's meetings here, an assembly of ministers and friends at Mildmay: I thought upon Rev. vii. 1-3."

John Wanamaker, of Philadelphia, presided at a noon meeting, and spoke of the deep interest that was felt in America in the great religious movement going on in London. One afternoon about three thousand children, with a thousand adults, came together, when Henry Drummond presided and gave a delightful address, which was well suited to the young audience.

During the mission in London a number of conventions were held, notable among which was a convention for young men held one evening at Mr. Moody's request. The special attraction was the presence of three presidents of Young Men's Christian Associations in America. Henry Drummond read a part of the " Sermon on the Mount," Mr. Moody gave a sketch of the origin and progress of the Association movement in Great Britain and America, and then called upon William E. Dodge, president of the Young Men's Christian Association in New York, to speak. He was followed by John V. Farwell, the president of the Association in Chicago, and John Wanamaker, the president of the Philadelphia Association.

Professor Drummond conducted the meetings for young men, bringing with him a large and varied experience, besides being especially gifted with many qualifications for this special work. He ruled the meeting with a firm and yet gentle hand, and possessed a happy knack of putting every one at his ease and making him feel that he was one of a circle of friends met for the common welfare.

Another convention was held the following week in the Haymarket Theatre, in which reports of the work in various parts of Great Britain were presented. The question of the unchurched masses and other practical topics occupied one day. Sunday-schools, the inquiry-room, and work for young men were taken up on the second day.

As the end of the series of meetings approached, still another conference was held, this time with the house-to-house visitors and superintendents, and later a meeting of ministers of the Gospel for praise and thanksgiving before Mr. Moody's return to America.

The last week that Moody and Sankey were in London they received an invitation to hold a service on grounds adjacent to Eton College, so that those boys who were anxious to attend might have an opportunity of doing so. There were upward of nine hundred boys at this well-known school, almost under the shadow of the royal palace at Windsor. Notwithstanding his already overfilled time, Mr. Moody accepted the invitation, and arrangements were made for a meeting in a tent erected outside the college grounds. The headmaster of Eton, who had absolute jurisdiction in such matters, agreed not to put any obstacle in the way of the boys attending.

Just before the meeting was to be held Mr. Knatch Bull-Hugessen, a member of Parliament, took steps to prevent the meeting, and published a correspondence of his with the provost of the college. No little excitement was caused by this unexpected turn of affairs, and the matter was discussed in the House of Lords. Mr. Moody, with those who had arranged for the meeting, saw no reason to change their plans, and went to Windsor shortly after noon on Tuesday. When they reached there they found that they could not meet in the tent, and tried to secure the use of the town hall, but were disappointed in this also. Mr. Caley, a leading townsman of Windsor, generously offered the use of his garden, and this offer was accepted.

Shortly after three o'clock some two hundred Eton boys appeared, and when the meeting proper began the garden was well filled with a standing audience of about a thousand. After the singing of the "Hundredth Psalm" and a prayer by Lord Capan, Mr. Moody, standing upon a chair under the shade of a large chestnut tree, surrounded by attentive groups of Eton boys, delivered an address, in which he dwelt with his usual earnestness on the value of the Gospel, which, he said, had removed from his path the bitterest enemies with which he had ever had to contend—the fear of death, judgment, and sin. Mr. Moody departed little, if at all, in his discourse from his usual line of argument, exhortation, and illustration. He expressed the hope that, as many of them might occupy in the future high positions in the State, they should do their utmost, by the early cultivation of Christian virtue, to qualify themselves to fill those positions worthily and to merit the glorious hereafter which was promised to those who conformed to the will of God.

At the closing service in London Mr. Moody said:

"For two years and three weeks we have been trying to labor for Christ among you, and now it is time to close. This is the last time I shall have the privilege of preaching the Gospel in this country at this time. I want to say that these have been the best years of my life. I have sought to bring Christ before you and to tell you of His beauty. It is true I have done it with stammering tongue. I have never spoken of Him as I would like to. I have done the best I could, and at this closing hour I want once more to press Him upon your acceptance. I do not want to close this meeting until I see you all in the ark of refuge. How many are willing to stand up before God to-night and say by that act that they will join us in our journey to Heaven? You that are willing to take Christ now, will you not rise?"

Many rose to their feet and were led in prayer by Mr. Moody, who besought the power of the Holy Ghost to fall equally upon those who had risen and upon those who had not, and with a closing hymn, "Safe in the arms of Jesus," the work of the evangelists for that campaign was at an end.

A farewell and thanksgiving meeting was held the next day, July 12th, at Mildmay Conference Hall. The hall was crowded with ministers and laymen, the three galleries containing many ladies. Of the ministers present at this memorable meeting there were 188 belonging to the Church of England, 154 Congregationalists, 85 Baptists, 81 Wesleyan Methodists, 39 Presbyterians, 8 foreign pastors, 8 United Methodists, 7 Primitive Methodists, 3 Plymouth Brethren, 2 Countess of Huntingdon's Connection, 2 Society of

Friends, 3 Free Church of England, 1 Bible Christian, and upward of 20 whose denominational connections were not discovered. These figures are taken from the official statement supplied at the meeting, and show the catholic and unsectarian character of the services, as well as the universal esteem with which the evangelists were regarded by all sections of the Church of Christ in Great Britain.

Mr. Moody said that they were met to give thanks to God and not to honor men, and he very emphatically requested that nothing should be said about the human instruments of the mission's success. Dr. Andrew A. Bonar, of Glasgow, gave an interesting address, and the Rev. Archibald Brown, Dr. Donald Fraser, the Rev. Marcus Rainsford, Rev. W. H. M. Hay-Aitken, Henry Varley, Lord Shaftesbury, and others spoke.

It will be remembered that Lord Shaftesbury was "the noble Earl" who presided at the first meeting which Mr. Moody attended in London in 1867, and to whom he declined to move a vote of thanks (saying that there was no more reason for doing so than for thanking the audience). "Nothing but the positive command of Mr. Moody," he said, "could have induced me to come forward on the present occasion and say but a very few words in the presence of so many ministers of the Gospel; but as Mr. Moody has asked me to speak of what has occurred during the past four months, I do so with the deepest sense of gratitude to Almighty God that He has raised up a man with such a message, to be delivered in such a manner. Though Mr. Moody has forbidden us to praise him and his friend, yet if we praise God for sending us such men we do no more than express our admiration for the instruments He has raised up, while we give Him all the glory.

"I have been conversant for many years with the people of the metropolis, and I might say that wherever I go I find the traces of the work, of the impression that has been made, of the feeling that has been produced, which I hope will be indelible. Only a few days ago I received a letter from a friend, a man whose whole life has been

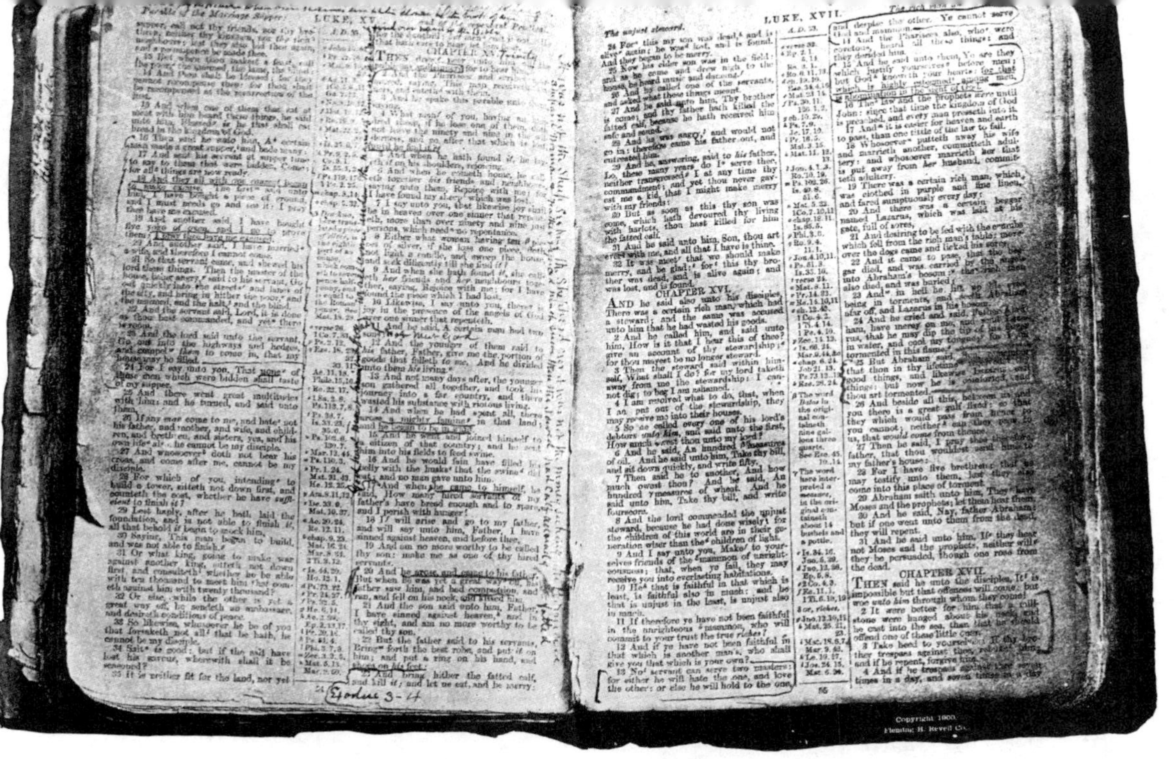

MR. MOODY'S OLD BIBLE.

Saved from the Chicago fire, and in constant use for over twenty years.

Mr. Moody Preaching in the Opera House, Haymarket, London.

Portable Hall.

Two of which were used during the later London campaign. Seating capacity, 6,000 each.

given to going among the most wretched and the most abandoned of the populous city of Manchester, who speaks of the good that had been effected there by Mr. Moody and Mr. Sankey. A correspondent in Sheffield has also written me that he could not begin to satisfy the wants of the people, that they are calling for tracts and anything else to keep up the religious feeling that has been aroused. He says: 'For God's sake, send me tracts by thousands and millions.' Even if Messrs. Moody and Sankey had done nothing more than to teach the people to sing such hymns as 'Hold the fort, for I am coming,' they would have conferred an inestimable blessing on Great Britain."

During the four months of the London mission the work accomplished is shown by the following statistics:

In Camberwell Hall, 60 meetings, attended by 480,000 people; in Victoria Hall, 45 meetings, attended by 400,000; in the Royal Haymarket Opera House, 60 meetings, attended by 330,000; in Bow Road Hall, 60 meetings, attended by 600,000; and in Agricultural Hall, 60 meetings, attended by 720,000; in all, 285 meetings, attended by 2,530,000 people. The mission cost £28,396 19s. 6d., nearly all of which was subscribed before the close of the meetings.

After leaving London Mr. Moody went for a short rest with the Rev. Mr. Aitken and Mr. Balfour, of Liverpool, to the country residence of the latter at Bala, Wales. Even here he was not allowed complete rest, as he was called upon to give three gospel addresses and several Bible readings during his short vacation.

As he had to pass through Liverpool to sail for America he was urged to conduct two or three more services in that city before leaving the country, and on August 3d a Christian conference was held in Victoria Hall, and in the evening a farewell meeting. In addition to Mr. Moody's sermon, addresses were made by clergymen and Christian workers, including Henry Drummond and James Stalker, of Edinburgh. Mr. Moody spoke again in the evening to the young men.

The last service held in England by Mr. Moody was on the morning of his departure. The doors were opened at seven o'clock, and when he rose to speak there were between five and six thousand people present. He repeated the watchword he had given the day before, "Advance." He then offered to shake hands with all the people present, "in the person of the president of the Association."

Mr. Moody left England August 14th, and on his arrival in New York he was greeted by many friends, including Messrs. D. W. McWilliams, William E. Dodge, Jr., George H. Stuart, and J. V. Farwell.

Some of the direct results of this English tour, covering more than two years, have been summarized by one writer as follows: "A spirit of evangelism was awakened that has never died away. A large number of city missions and other active organizations were established. Denominational differences were buried to a remarkable extent. The clergymen of all denominations were drawn into coöperation on a common platform, the salvation of the lost. Bibles were reopened and Bible study received a wonderful impetus. Long-standing prejudices were swept away. New life was infused into all methods of Christian activity. An impetus was given to the cause of temperance such as had not been experienced in Great Britain before. No attempt was made to proselytize, but converts were passed over to existing churches for nurture and admonition in the things of the Lord."

"Since Mr. Moody made his way across the ocean twenty-three years ago," wrote a prominent Scotch minister in 1896, "an American preacher has been a welcome visitor here."

With reference to this work, the late Rev. Dr. Philip Schaff, of New York, made the following remarks in an address in London some years ago:

"One of the most interesting and remarkable facts in the history of these days is the wonderful effect produced among you by the efforts of two laymen from America. It was a greater marvel to us than to you, and the only way to account for it is to refer it at once to the grace of God! Such a movement the world has not seen since the days of Whitefield and Wesley, and it is wider in its results than the work of those two honored men. It is most unsectarian in its character, and, I may add, the most unselfish movement known in our common history. It was for the purpose of winning souls to Christ and of extending His Kingdom, without regard to denominational boundaries, that these two men came to England, and every church may reap the benefit. . . . We in America had no idea these two men could have produced such a commotion among you all; but it is just the old, old story of the simple fishermen of Galilee over again."

Subsequently he said of his countrymen: "They have proved the power of elementary truths over the hearts of men more mightily than all the learned professors and eloquent pastors of England could do. As the Methodist revival, more than a hundred years ago, stopped the progress of deism, so these plain laymen from America turned the tide of modern materialism and atheism. It is the grace of God behind these men which explains the extraordinary religious interest they have awakened all over Scotland and England. The farewell service given to the American evangelists on the 12th of July, in London, furnished abundant testimony to the fruits of their labors from the mouths of ministers and laymen of all denominations. It was a meeting which will not easily be forgotten."

CHAPTER XXIII

Return to America

THE reports of the deep religious awakening in Great Britain had preceded Mr. Moody to America, so that on his return he was as well known there as in Great Britain. A little over two years before he had left his country, known only to a comparatively small circle of Sunday-school workers and Young Men's Christian Association friends. In Chicago his name was more prominent than elsewhere, but to the general public his work was not familiar. It may be said, then, that Mr. Moody was introduced to America by Great Britain, as he, in turn, is said to have introduced several Englishmen to their own country.

Immediately on his return he received many invitations to visit the leading cities in America. In some cases these were sent to him before he left London. In several places committees had been formed to arrange for a series of meetings, which he was asked to conduct. It must have been most gratifying as well as flattering to find at once such a widespread expression of appreciation, but with a characteristic spirit of humility he turned aside from all these invitations, ostensibly to rest, but in reality to study and to wait upon God for guidance as to his future plans.

On arriving in New York Mr. Moody with his family went directly to Northfield to spend several weeks with his aged mother. Here he gave much time to a careful preparation for the work of the coming winter. Mornings were devoted to reading and the preparation of addresses, as he had had little opportunity during the busy months abroad to acquire new material.

Mr. Moody's Mother, Died 1896, in Her Ninety-first Year.

View of Connecticut River Valley from D. L. Moody's Residence.

It was at this time that he purchased the small farm which later became his home. A barren little tract of twelve acres near his mother's place was offered for sale at this time at a moderate price, and Mr. Moody bought this, purposing to hold the land for his mother and to spend a few summers there for the sake of his children. For several summers he retreated to the quiet seclusion of this country home, where he could study and prepare for the arduous missions during the winter months. Gradually his interests in Northfield increased, until the home he planned for rest and quiet became the scene of his greatest activities and most lasting work.

Soon after arriving at Northfield he was again besieged with the most cordial and urgent invitations to visit different American cities. Among others was one from Washington, brought by the Rev. Dr. John P. Newman, who was delegated by the pastors of that city to go to Northfield and secure a positive answer to the question:

"Will you conduct a campaign in Washington this fall?"

Dr. Newman found Mr. Moody busily engaged in farm duties. He listened attentively to the distinguished preacher, later a bishop of the Methodist Episcopal Church, but he was not prepared to give a definite answer.

"I don't know yet where the first meetings will be held. I am waiting to see where I am led." This was all that he could be induced to say.

Dr. Cuyler, of Brooklyn, also visited Northfield, "to hear from Mr. Moody's own lips the thrilling story of what God had wrought in Great Britain." The two friends talked frankly of the meetings abroad, and of those soon to begin in America.

"At the farmhouse table of his venerated mother," writes Dr. Cuyler, "he related some of his experiences. When I asked him who had helped him most, he replied: 'Dr. Andrew A. Bonar and Lord Cairns. The first one helped me by inspiring hints of Bible truth for my sermons; the other one by coming often to hear me, for the people said that if the Lord Chancellor came to my meetings they had better come too.' He might have added, if his characteristic modesty had allowed, that Cairns had said that he 'gave him a new conception of preaching.'

"The next morning Moody told me that as he had had but few educational advantages in his boyhood, he was thinking of starting a school of a decided Christian character for boys and girls in Northfield. And lo! into what a goodly tree has that seed-thought grown —and how God has watered it! Many other reminiscences crowd upon me; but I restrain my pen, for if all his friends should tell all they know a volume would swell into a library. Of one thing I feel sure, and that is, if another book of the Acts of Christ's faithful Apostles were to be written, probably the largest space in the record of the nineteenth century would be given to the soul-saving work of Charles H. Spurgeon and Dwight L. Moody."

Another visitor who gave and received a great blessing was Major Whittle, his former associate and lifelong fellow-worker. Several years before, while walking home from a meeting in his tabernacle in Chicago, stopping near a lamp-post where their ways were to part, Mr. Moody opened his Bible to II Timothy, iv., and in reply to something his friend had said as to what could be done to rouse the people, read, "Preach the Word; be instant in season, out of season; reprove, rebuke, exhort with all longsuffering and doctrine," adding, "This is our commission, Whittle."

Nothing more was said then, but there came to his friend the conviction, which never from that time left him, that God might call him to some form of gospel work.

"As I look back now," writes Major Whittle, "it was a wonderful manifestation of the presence of the Spirit of God, and I bless Him for His goodness in sending the call through Mr. Moody to me."

The following extract from Major Whittle's diary of September, 1875, gives a picture of the daily life at Northfield during the preparation for the first gospel campaign in this country:

"Bliss and myself received a letter from dear Moody to come at once to Northfield, Mass., and confer with him about the work for the coming winter. We left Chicago together Monday evening, September 6th. Arrived at South Vernon, Vt., Wednesday noon. Dear Moody was at the station with a carriage to meet us, and received us with much joy. Over two years ago we parted with him in Chicago. Since that time he has been used to arouse the Christian world, to lead thousands of souls to Christ, and to stimulate scores, as he did in the cases of Bliss and myself, to go out into the vineyard.

"I love him and reverence him as I do no other man on earth. To me he has seemed for years a man full of the Holy Ghost. The only change I see in him now is a growth of conscious power and an ability for speaking with added weight and deeper conviction. He is wholly and thoroughly conscious that it is all of God. Praying alone with him, I found him humble as a child before God. Out in the work with him I found him bold as a lion before men. No hesitation, no shrinking, no timidity; speaking with authority, speaking as an ambassador of the most high God.

"Two weeks we passed in this beautiful mountain home of our brother. We met his widowed mother, his three brothers, his wife and children. We were made part of the family and taken over all the haunts of Moody's boyhood; up the mountain where he used to pasture the cows and pick berries and gather chestnuts, and where he passed the last Sunday alone with God before he sailed for England upon his last memorable visit.

"We went with him to take dinner with his uncle Cyrus, over the Connecticut River, and as we were crossing the beautiful stream, the valley sloping down on either side and the blue hills and mountains beyond, Bliss and Sankey sang together, 'Only waiting for the boatman,' and 'There is a land of pure delight.' Moody was helping the ferryman. We all thought the crossing very slow. After the third or fourth song Sankey looked around and discovered Moody holding on to the wire and pulling back while the ferryman pulled forward; his object being to get in a good many songs, not only for his own enjoyment, but for the good of the ferryman, a boyhood friend for whose conversion he was interested. Moody greatly enjoyed Sankey's discomfiture, and, after a hearty laugh from us all, we joined in the song, 'Pull for the shore,' and by keeping a watch on Moody reached the shore as we closed.

"One beautiful day we took luncheon in baskets and, driving out four or five miles, climbed the highest of the hills and had a picnic on its top. We could see for miles up and down the Connecticut Valley. The village of Northfield was at our feet, Brattleboro just at the north, and all around us grand old granite mountains. Mount Monadnock, the largest of these, was at our right as we faced the valley. Upon this mountain Moody asked which of the mountains of the Bible was dearest to us. His was the mountain in Galilee where Christ met the disciples after He had risen. (Matt. xxviii. 16.) Bliss and Sankey both chose the Mount of Transfiguration; Samuel Moody, the mount where Christ preached His sermon; George Davis, Calvary; my own choice, Olivet. We had a precious season of prayer upon this mount, asking for power for the work before us and praising the same Lord for meeting us here Who met His disciples in Galilee.

"I spent the rest of the day with Moody, driving up the valley to Warwick—a most beautiful ride—and back to Northfield. Moody told me much of his experience in Great Britain. I asked him if he was never overcome by nervousness and timidity because of the position in which he stood. He said no; that God carried him right along as the work grew. He had no doubt that, had he known when he reached England what was before him, he would have been frightened. But as he looked back all he could think of was Jeremiah's experience—that God gave him a forehead of brass to go before the people. He had such a consciousness of the presence of God in his meetings in London, that the people—lords, bishops, ministers, or whoever they were—were as grasshoppers.

"It troubled him somewhat in going to London that his sermons and Bible talks would all be reported, and his entire stock, the same that he had used in other places, would thus be exhausted, but as he expressed it, 'There was no help for it, so I just shut my eyes and went ahead, leaving it with God.' He told me he spent but comparatively little time in secret prayer and had no experience of being weighed down and burdened before God. He did not try to get into this state. His work kept him in the spirit of prayer and dependence upon God, and he just gave himself wholly to the work. For a year or more before he left Chicago he was continually burdened and crying to God for more power. Then he was always wanting to get a few people together for half a day of prayer, and would groan and weep before God for the baptism of the Spirit. He did not seem to be in this state now.

" I wanted such a season while with him, feeling my own need, but he was as one who had passed through that experience, and had just put himself wholly in God's hands, received the baptism of the Holy Ghost, and was being led in all things by Him. His prayers while I was with him were as simple as a child's, full of trust, humility, and expectation that God would not disappoint him. There seemed to me an understanding established between the servant and the Master which made long prayers or the importunity of repetition unnecessary. During our stay with Moody, services were held in the Congregational Church every night with very blessed results. The whole population attended, and hundreds came from surrounding towns. Dear Moody's mother and two brothers, connected with the Unitarian Church, were much blessed. I shall always thank God for the blessed experience of these two weeks. Many brethren from different parts of the country came and went while we were there, among them Stuart, of Philadelphia; Rowland, Dodge, and McBurney, of New York; Remington, of Fall River; Moore, of Boston; Fairbanks, of Vermont, and others.

" While together we arranged for the compilation of hymns for our common use. We all agreed that it would be best to distribute our forces in different parts of the country and not to be in the same locality."

Nothing was more characteristic of Mr. Moody than his longing for retirement in the country from the press of his work. Though his life-work lay for the most part in great cities, he was born a country lad, and for him the everlasting hills possessed a wealth of meaning and a marvellous recuperative power. Some instinct drew him back to the soil, some mysterious prompting impelled him to solitude, away from the crowds that absorbed so much of his strength; then, after a little respite, he would return with new strength and new vitality.

CHAPTER XXIV

Brooklyn, Philadelphia, and New York

"HOW is it that while you and other like men are all but inaccessible, fenced in by closed doors and guarded by polite but immovable private secretaries, Dwight L. Moody sees you at any time?" was asked of a certain prominent financier.

"He is one of us," was the reply.

From the very first of his evangelistic work in America Mr. Moody's sound judgment inspired the confidence of men of affairs. While his loyalty to the Gospel in all its simplicity, without championing theological fads, recommended him to the ministers who believed in evangelistic efforts, he also earned the support of laymen who were able to give him the opportunity for large enterprises. This had been demonstrated in the work in Great Britain, and on his return to his own country the same general support was afforded in the larger American cities which had extended to him the heartiest invitations. These invitations were readily accepted, for, as Mr. Moody expressed it, "Water runs down hill, and the highest hills in America are the great cities. If we can stir them we shall stir the whole country."

The first American campaign was begun in Brooklyn, October, 1875. Preparations had been made for these meetings, not only by providing places of assemblage and arranging a programme for the exercises, but by the union of various denominations in holding meetings for prayer and conference, and pledging one another to a cordial cooperation in the effort of the evangelists, upon whose work in Great

Britain the Divine blessing had so signally rested. A rink was engaged for a month and chairs for five thousand persons were provided.

As the interest in the services grew, greater efforts were put forth to reach more people by increasing the number of meetings. The help of local ministers and prominent laymen was enlisted, and overflow meetings and special services in churches and halls widened the scope of the work.

The influence of the mission extended beyond Brooklyn. The "New York Tribune," commenting editorially on the work, said:

"There is a common-sense view to be taken of this matter as of every other. In the first place, why should we sneer because a large part of the multitudes crowding into the Brooklyn Rink are drawn there only by curiosity? So they were when they followed Christ into the streets of Jerusalem or the wilderness, yet they went to the healing of their souls. Or that a still larger part already profess Christianity, and believe all that Moody and Sankey teach? There is not one of them who will not be the better for a little quickening of his faith, and, we may add, of his movements too. In the second place, with regard to the men themselves, there can, we think, be but one opinion as to their sincerity. They are not money-makers; they are not charlatans. Decorous, conservative England, which reprobated both their work and the manner of it, held them in the full blaze of scrutiny for months, and could not detect in them a single motive which was not pure. Earnest and sincere men are rare in these days. Is it not worth our while to give to them a dispassionate, unprejudiced hearing? Thirdly, in regard to their message. They preach no new doctrine, no dogma of this or that sect; nothing but Christ and the necessity among us of increased zeal in His service. Which of us will controvert that truth? If the Christian religion is not the one hope for our individual and social life, what is?

"And lastly, with regard to the method of these men in presenting Christ and His teaching. Men of high culture or exceptional sensitiveness of taste shrink from the familiarity of words and ideas in

Scene in the Brooklyn Rink.

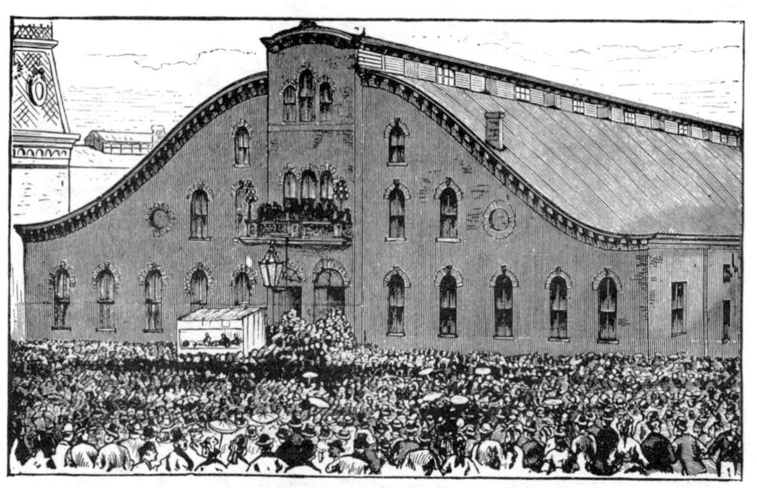

The Brooklyn Rink.
Awaiting the opening of the doors.

EXTERIOR OF OLD PENNSYLVANIA RAILROAD DEPOT, PHILADELPHIA.

INTERIOR OF OLD PENNSYLVANIA RAILROAD DEPOT.

Scene of the great meetings in Philadelphia.

which a subject they hold as reverend and sublime beyond expression is set forth to the crowd. They call it vulgarizing and debasing the truth. Granting that their opinion is right, from their point of view —what is to be done with the crowd? They cannot all be men of fine culture or exceptional sensitiveness; they are not moved to believe or trust in Jesus through philosophic arguments, or contemplation of nature, or logical conviction, or appeals to their æsthetic senses; by classical music, stained glass, or church architecture; they are plain, busy people, with ordinary minds and tastes; yet certainly, as Christ died to save them, it is necessary that they should be brought to Him by some means and persuaded to live cleaner, higher, more truthful lives.

"Christianity is not a matter of grammar for libraries and drawing-rooms, refined taste, or delicate sensibility. It was not to the cultured classes that Christ Himself preached, but to the working people, the publicans, fishermen, tax-gatherers; and He used the words and illustrations which would appeal to them most forcibly. If Messrs. Moody and Sankey, or any other teachers, bring Him directly home to men's convictions and lead them to amend their lives for His sake, let us thank God for the preacher, and let his tastes and grammar take care of themselves."

In Philadelphia a no less notable series of meetings was conducted in the recently abandoned freight depot of the Pennsylvania Railroad, which has since become the widely known Wanamaker Store. This building was provided with seats to accommodate thirteen thousand persons and was otherwise adapted to the needs of a large mission hall. Here, as in Brooklyn, the leading ministers gave their hearty support to the work and in every way expressed their approval of the effort. Separate meetings for different classes of hearers were started early in the work. Mr. Moody said that he was going to have the meeting for young men limited to those under forty, as that would just take him in. His fortieth birthday was celebrated near the close of the campaign.

One meeting was set apart especially for intemperate men and women. At Mr. Moody's request a large number of people who had been regularly attending the meeting remained away that their seats might be occupied by those for whom the meeting was especially designed. The audience has been described as follows by a witness:

"Here and there could be seen the bloated faces of blear-eyed drunkards, glancing wildly around as though the strangeness of the situation was so overpowering that it required a great effort of will to remain; not a few were accompanied by mothers, wives, sisters, or friends, who, having exhausted human means, had determined to lay their burden upon the Lord.

"The great majority of those gathered in the Depot Tabernacle yesterday afternoon were as sad-faced and tearful a collection of humanity as it would be possible to assemble in one place. Those who had not directly suffered by intemperance grew at once into sympathy with the hundreds about them whose heavy sighs told stories of unutterable anguish, and this influence increased until a cloud of terrible depression seemed to hang over the entire congregation. Every class of society was represented in this throng, united so closely by such painful bonds. Close to the half-starved, long-abused yet faithful wife of some besotted brute was seated the child of fortune and culture—child no more, but an old, old woman whose only son, still in his youth, had fallen almost to the lowest depths of degradation.

"Next her was a man whose every feature showed nobility of soul and rare talents, but whose threadbare coat and sunken cheeks betrayed him to all observers as the lifelong victim of an unconquerable appetite. Just behind this group was a young girl whose face, sweet as an angel's, was already furrowed by grief. Beside her was her father, who, broken down in health and almost ruined in mind by the excessive use of liquor, seemed at last to have resigned himself to hopeless ruin. He gazed about in a half-asleep, half-childish way, and several times attempted to get up and leave his seat, but the hand of the child-woman held his very tightly, and each time he would conquer his restlessness and sit down. By far the larger proportion of the congregation were women, almost all of whom had evidently clutching at their hearts the agonizing image of some past or present experience with woe in its most terrible form.

"It was interesting to see the change that gradually came over the audience as Mr. Moody declared over and over again that the God who had once cast out devils could do it then, and would do it if only asked; and as fervent prayers for immediate help were offered, the cloud seemed to rise from their hearts, while the noonday sun poured upon them its blessed rays of hope, and eyes long dimmed by tears beamed with a new light."

Among the laymen who were prominent in this work were John Wanamaker and George H. Stuart. Mr. Wanamaker's special meetings for young men were largely attended at this time.

As on former occasions, Mr. Moody observed the closing of the old year with a special service, which Dr. Henry Clay Trumbull thus describes:

"The central figure on the platform that New Year's eve was one whose appearance and bearing were most impressive. The Rev. Dr. William S. Plumer, then a professor of the Columbia Theological Seminary in South Carolina, and who nearly forty years before was moderator of the General Assembly of the Presbyterian Church, was a figure that would compel reverence and regard in any gathering. Massive in frame, towering in stature, venerable in appearance, with snowy hair and flowing beard, he suggested Michael Angelo's Moses.

"Mr. Moody was on this occasion represented, not as the teacher, but as the inquirer. Dr. Plumer stood out as the teacher, to whom the younger Moody came with his questionings of heart. Few men, if any, in the world better knew the anxious cravings and doubts of the inquiring soul than Moody, as he had met with them in his varied evangelistic labors. Few trained theologians could have more wisely and simply answered those inquirers than the large-brained, large-hearted, large-framed, venerable patriarch before whom Moody stood.

"The whole scene evidenced the simplicity of trust in God as the sinner came to him through Jesus Christ, in his need and in his confidence. The theologian could give the answer that the anxious soul longed for. Mr. Moody and Dr. Plumer were at one in this interview. A few specimen questions and answers will illustrate.

"Mr. Moody: 'Is any given amount of distress necessary to genuine conversion?'

"Dr. Plumer: 'Lydia had no distress—we read of none. God opened her heart, and she attended to the things spoken by Paul. But the jailer of Philippi would not have accepted Christ without some alarm. If you will accept the Son of God, you need have no trouble. There is nothing in trouble that sanctifies the soul.'

"Mr. Moody: 'Well, Doctor, what is conversion?'

"Dr. Plumer: 'Glory be to God there is such a thing as conversion. To be converted is to turn from self, self-will, self-righteousness, all self-confidence, and from sin itself, and to be turned to Christ.'

"Mr. Moody: 'Can a man be saved here to-night, before twelve o'clock—saved all at once?'

"Dr. Plumer: 'Why not? In my Bible I read of three thousand men gathered together one morning, all of them murderers, their hands stained with the blood of the Son of God. They met in the morning, and before night they were all baptized members of Christ.'

"Mr. Moody: 'How can I know that I am saved?'

"Dr. Plumer: 'Because of the fact that God is true. "Let God be true, but every man a liar." If I accept Jesus Christ, it is not Mr. Moody's word, nor Mr. Sankey's, nor Dr. Newton's; it is the Word of the living God, whose name is Amen. "*He that believeth on the Son hath everlasting life.*"'

"Mr. Moody: 'What if I haven't got faith enough?'

"Dr. Plumer: 'Glory to God, if I can touch the hem of my Saviour's

THE "HIPPODROME," NEW YORK.

INTERIOR VIEW OF THE "HIPPODROME."
During the New York mission.

D. L. Moody's Private Study.

D. L. Moody's Library.

garment I shall be saved. A little faith is as truly faith as a great deal of faith. A little coal of fire in the ashes is as truly fire as the glowing heat of a furnace.'

" Mr. Moody: ' I don't feel that I love Christ enough.'

" Dr. Plumer: ' And you never will. To all eternity, you never will love Him as much as He deserves to be loved.

> " ' " Had I ten thousand tongues,
> Not one should silent be;
> Had I ten thousand hearts,
> I'd give them all to Thee." '

" As the hour of midnight approached, the appeals of Mr. Moody, following this illustrative inquiry meeting, grew more and more earnest, and the solemnity of the service deepened. Just before twelve o'clock he asked all present to join in silent prayer.

" While all heads were still bowed the profound stillness was broken by Mr. Sankey's singing of ' Almost persuaded.' Then the closing moments of the passing year were given to earnest prayer, especially for those who had risen to ask for it at Mr. Moody's call, and were now urged to a final decision.

" When at midnight the sounding out of the bell of Independence Hall was the signal for all the bells of the city and the steam-whistles on every side to greet the incoming year, Mr. Moody wished all a ' Happy New Year,' and that never-to-be-forgotten watch-night service closed. Its echoes are still resounding in many hearts on earth and in heaven, and their gratitude is now deeper than ever to dear Mr. Moody and his fellow-worker on that sacred occasion."

The late George H. Stuart thus spoke of the Philadelphia meetings a few weeks after their close:

" In October last we attempted a great work for God in our city. Some had high expectations that it would redound largely to the glory of Heaven. They saw a deep spirit of prayer among the clergymen and members of the churches; and what has been the result? It has far exceeded the highest hopes of the most sanguine. We had little thought to see a hall filled to overflowing day after day with from seven thousand to thirteen thousand people who came to hear the old, old story of Jesus and His love. God heard our prayer, and His work has been continued in all our churches.

"In my own church—an old Scotch church which has been little disposed to unity in such religious movements—I have seen what I had never seen before during the forty years that I have known it. At the morning meetings in the Depot Church and on Sundays the early hour at which people came was remarkable. The watchman told me that he saw men gathering there as early as 4.30 A.M., and at six o'clock on cold mornings in January the throng was so great that he was obliged to open the doors. My church has had two pastors in seventy-five years; on Sunday next it will hold a special communion service, something it has not known in years, and twenty-five new communicants will be there. Two-thirds of them are young men."

During the Philadelphia mission a number of Princeton students attended the evangelistic meetings and were greatly impressed. Returning to their college, they began working for an invitation to Mr. Moody to come and preach to the students. The work inaugurated at that time developed later into organizations that have continued fruitful not only among American students, but throughout the world.

The last notable mission of that winter was conducted in New York. At a meeting of clergymen and laymen in June, 1875, while Mr. Moody was still in London, a temporary organization was formed, of which the late Rev. Dr. John Hall was chairman. By the unanimous vote of all present a cordial invitation was extended to the evangelists to hold a series of religious meetings in New York as soon as their engagements would permit. On the acceptance of this invitation a permanent organization was formed, and careful preparations were made for the proposed meetings. William E. Dodge was president of the general committee; George H. Andrews, Bowles Colgate, and Henry Oakley, vice-presidents; and more than thirty clergymen, representing nearly all the Protestant denominations, and as many laymen, were members of this committee. The executive committee consisted of Nathan Bishop, chairman; John C. Havemeyer, secretary; and William E. Dodge, Jr., the Rev. Dr. S. Irenaeus Prime, S. B. Schieffelin, Elliot F. Shepard, Morris K. Jesup, and R. R. McBurney. The committee obtained a lease of the Hippodrome, on the site of the present Madison Square Garden, at Madison Avenue and Fourth Avenue, between Twenty-sixth and Twenty-seventh Streets, as the most central and suitable building for the meetings. The auditorium was divided into two large halls, each capable of seating about seven thousand persons, and a call was issued by the committee for a private guarantee fund to meet attendant expenses. In the call it was stated that "it must be distinctly understood that Messrs. Moody and Sankey refuse to receive any payment for their own services; thus no part of the above fund will be paid to them."

While the committee were attending to the business details, Christian people were not idle in the churches. There was an increased interest in meetings for prayer and religious conference. The daily prayer-meeting uptown, at Lyric Hall, was largely attended, while the Fulton Street meeting felt the fresh impulse of revival preparations. Again the same hearty coöperation and unity of the pastors of the leading churches were experienced, and this sympathy on the part of the churches found expression in the denominational papers. "The New York Observer" thus voiced the sentiment of the Presbyterians:

"The men who have been invited to New York have given full proof of their efficient ministry by their labors in other places, and our pastors know whom they are addressing when they ask their aid. These evangelists have been proved by the ministers and churches, who of all others were most likely to condemn them if their doctrines and measures had not been in harmony with the Word of God and approved by sound judgment. They have been in the midst of the most orthodox and well-instructed religious communities in Great

Britain. Excellent, learned, thoughtful pastors and the most eminent laymen, statesmen, jurists, and bankers have attended their meetings and given their favorable opinion in writing. Presbyteries, Synods, General Assemblies, dignitaries in the Church of England, and officers under government, men who are not emotional or enthusiastic, who are the furthest removed from religious fanaticism, testify to the great value of the labors of these evangelists.

" Their discourses have been published and widely read by those who disapprove of such labors, as well as by their audiences. 'I have found no fault in them ' is the general verdict. They are simple, scriptural calls to the unconverted. God has followed them with His blessing, and has made them useful in turning sinners from their wicked ways and in bringing them to Christ. We have also personal testimony from wise men who have been on the ground after the evangelists had been away for a year, and they assure us that the work of grace goes forward with no unhappy reaction and with every evidence of continued good."

The papers, secular and religious, published long accounts of the meetings; in some instances giving verbatim reports of the addresses. The following vivid description of an early Sunday morning service is from the pen of William Hoyt Coleman:

" It is ten minutes after seven, and at the Madison Avenue entrance there is a compact crowd extending to the curbstone, awaiting the opening of the doors for the eight o'clock lecture. A well-dressed, good-humored crowd, that stamps its feet and chats pleasantly; one or two men are giving tickets to those who have come unprovided. Across the street a lady is accosting several rough-looking young fellows, apparently inviting them to the meeting, but without success. Five minutes later a door slides back, a gratified ' Ah! ' goes up, and the crowd moves in—slowly—as the door is partly open. Through a wide passage we emerge into a space filled with chairs, surrounded by a low gallery, backed by a huge white board partition, and overhung by an arched roof broken by many skylights.

"A high K-shaped platform runs from one gallery to the other along the white partition; at its centre is a railed projection for the speaker and his assistants, the rails running back to the partition, where there is a doorway with a crimson screen. The right-hand section of the platform holds a melodeon and the choir; the left-hand section the special-ticket holders.

"The hall is nearly full—a mixed assemblage of all classes; some very poor, a few not very clean. Many black faces dot the congregation. A large part of those present are evidently Sunday-school teachers. One wonders how so many can come at so early an hour. A man near by says: 'I built a fire and got my own breakfast.' At 7.40 the choir begins to sing and the congregation joins in. Nearly all have brought their little hymn-books, and, the tunes being simple and spirited, they sing in good time.

"Promptly at eight o'clock two men take their places, one within the rail, the other at the melodeon. As the former rises, after a moment of silent prayer, you see a short, stout-built, square-shouldered man with bullet-shaped head set close on the shoulders, black eyes that twinkle merrily at times, and a full but not heavy beard and mustache. The face expresses fun, good-humor, persistence. The coat is closely buttoned, with a bit of stand-up collar seen over it. Such is D. L. Moody, the leader of the Hippodrome work. As he stands with hand resting on the rail, you are conscious that it is to see, not to be seen. Like an engineer with his hand on the throttle, like a physician with his finger on the patient's pulse, his mind is on the work before him. A quick, soldierly bearing marks every movement.

"He gives out a hymn so rapidly that we scarce catch the words, and then we look at Sankey. A man of larger build, clear-cut features, and shaven chin; a voice clear, melodious, powerful. Easier and gentler in bearing than Moody, he has enough force and fire in speech and song to hold an audience in perfect quiet; and when he sings alone you hear every word and catch from face and voice the full meaning of the song. Both men impress you as honest and good, hearty and wholesome in body and mind, and thoroughly in earnest.

"After the hymns and a prayer comes a solo by Mr. Sankey, and then Mr. Moody lectures on 'Jacob.' Headlong talking would better describe it. His voice is rough, pitched on one key, and he speaks straight before him, rarely turning to the sides. But how real he makes the men! How visibly the deceiving, scheming Jacob stands before us! And how pointedly he applies the lessons of the patriarch's life to the men and women before him! His gestures are few but emphatic—the hand flung forcibly forward with palm open, both hands brought down, hammer-like, with closed fists. But the Bible is too much in his hands to allow frequent gestures. He continually refers to it, reads from it, and keeps it open on the stand beside him. His sermon or lecture is little more than an exposition of a Bible truth, or a dramatic rendering of a Bible story, with continuous application to his hearers.

"There is an occasional slip of speech—'done' for 'did,' 'come' for 'came,' 'Isrel,' etc.—but the Bible knowledge, experience of life, and dead earnestness of the speaker sweep every petty criticism out of sight. Though under full headway he sees all that happens. Toward the close of a sermon a rough young man comes down the aisle, going straight up to the platform steps. 'Usher will take care of that case,' interjects Mr. Moody, and goes quietly on. He ends abruptly, prays briefly, pronounces the benediction, and when you lift your head he is gone."

By the same keen observer a no less interesting description is given of an evening service:

"Imagine yourself on the platform of the Madison Avenue Hall at 7.15 P.M., five minutes before the opening of the doors. Platform and near gallery are already well filled by the choir, Christian workers and their escorts, and special-ticket holders; the floor of the house is unoccupied, save by knots of ushers with their wands, no one being allowed to sit there until the doors are opened. In the railed inclosure, just back of the speaker's place, is a telegraph operator, usually a lady. Near by sits the chief superintendent, with aids at hand to transmit orders. At the other end of the hall sit another superintendent and operator. These control the lighting and heating and the seating of the audience.

"'Ting! ting! ting!' goes a distant bell ten times—attention! 'Ting! ting!' again, and the outer and inner doors slip back at three points, and three streams of people pour into the hall. The foremost enters at a run that would become disorder did not the usher check it, divide the stream, direct it into the front and middle seats, and when a section is filled bar the way with his wand. In ten minutes five thousand persons are seated. The galleries fill more slowly, and when all parts are full the doors are closed, and no one is allowed to stand in the aisles or along the gallery front save a few blue-coated policemen, whose services seem rarely called for.

"The half-hour before meeting time passes quickly. One studies the vast throng before him with unceasing interest. The bright light of the many reflectors falls full upon the faces of all sorts and conditions of men—to say nothing of women and children. A more mixed multitude it would be hard to find. At the four o'clock meetings women are the leading element, next to old people, some of them so feeble as almost to be carried to their seats. But at night all classes and ages are present. There is a quiet stir everywhere, but no noise or levity. At 7.45 Mr. Thatcher leads the choir in singing, and shows great skill in managing both choir and congregation in combined and separate parts and in producing tender and powerful effects. One reason is, he has capital music to do it with. The 'Moody and Sankey Hymn-book' is the best for congregational use ever printed. Its words are full of the Gospel, its tunes express the thoughts they are allied to, and are so simple and yet positive in character that any one can sing them after once hearing them. When this vast congregation sings, 'Safe in the arms of

Jesus' or 'I hear Thy welcome voice,' one gets a new idea of the power of sacred song.

"Eight o'clock, and Mr. Moody is at his post. It is a pleasant night, and though every seat is filled there is a large crowd outside. Announcing a hymn, he says:

"'Now, won't a thousand of you Christians go into the Fourth Avenue Hall and pray for this meeting and let those outside have your seats?' Here is a practical application of Christian self-denial not pleasant to those who have fought for good seats. However, a few go out.

"'Not half enough,' says Mr. Moody at the end of the first verse. 'I want a great many more to go out. I see many of you here every night, and if I knew your names I'd call you out.' So, after much urging, quite a number leave, the doors are opened, and the empty seats are again filled. The platform does not escape.

"'Now, some of you go,' and a few retire. 'Will the ushers please open the windows?' is the next order. Mr. Moody is autocratic in his demands for fresh air.

"'Fresh air is as important as the sermon,' he says. 'We've got to keep these people awake, and they're half asleep already.' All very true, but opening the top back windows throws cruel draughts in the galleries, so it isn't long before the windows are shut, and very soon Mr. Moody is calling for fresh air again.

"How he preaches has already been described. The evening sermon is usually of a bolder offhand character than that of the afternoon, which is intended more specially for Christians. He makes a marked distinction between preaching the Gospel and teaching Christians. His afternoon sermon on the Holy Spirit seemed meant for himself as well as for others, and at the close his voice trembled with emotion as he said: 'I want more of this power. Pray for me, that I may be so filled with the Holy Spirit when coming on this platform that men may feel I come with a message from God.' The quiet of the audience during Moody's preaching and Sankey's singing is remarkable. Even the rough young fellows who crowd the gallery passages make no sound. At the close Mr. Moody announces a men's meeting in the other hall, a boys' meeting in one of the smaller rooms, and the usual work in the inquiry meeting. Those attending these meetings are requested to go to them while the last hymn is being sung.

"The Hippodrome work is a vast business enterprise, organized and conducted by business men, who have put money into it on business principles, for the purpose of saving men. But through all the machinery vibrates the power without which it would be useless—the power of the Holy Ghost. Of course it is successful. Men are being saved day and night, and a moral influence is felt round about the building itself. Two Sundays ago the police returns of that precinct showed no arrests—a thing before unknown—and a recent statement says that in spite of increased destitution among the poor this winter there has been no increase of crime.

"Christians have been warmed, 'limbered up,' and taught to work as they have never worked before; taught how to study their Bibles and how to use them for the good of others; how to reach men simply, naturally, and successfully; how to live consistently and whole-heartedly themselves. The easy-going church life of multitudes has been sharply rebuked by these laborious evangelists. Worshipping in the rude-walled Hippodrome, sitting on wooden chairs, led in song by a man with a melodeon, and preached to by a man without a pulpit, they have learned that costly churches, stained windows, soft cushions, great organs, and quartette choirs are not necessary to the worship of God, and tend to drive away the poor, leaving the rich to enjoy their luxuries alone.

"Congregational singing has received a great impetus. The little 'Moody and Sankey Hymn-book' is crowding out the bulky collections of twelve hundred and fourteen hundred hymns, some of them one-third unsingable and one-third padding. Containing only pieces, new and old, that the people can sing, the people have found it out, and are singing them all over the land and beyond seas in Europe, Asia, and Africa, until five million copies and twenty different translations give some idea of the popularity of this little book. With it goes a new idea—that of singing the Gospel, for many of these pieces are not hymns at all, but simply gospel songs, and they have been the means of converting many souls.

"Ministers of the Gospel have freely acknowledged that Mr. Moody has taught them valuable lessons in their own work: how to make Bible truths and Bible characters more real; how to use the Bible more freely in preaching, instead of taking a text for a peg on which to hang their own ideas; how to bring the truth into close contact with all sorts of people and make it stick; how to set old Christians and young converts to work. And the whole church is now giving heed to Mr. Moody's ideas about church debts, church fairs, church choirs, and other supposedly necessary evils of modern church life."

Mr. Moody's wisdom in accepting invitations to the largest American cities was immediately apparent, for the interest awakened in Philadelphia and New York gave him entrance into still larger fields of service. The support of the large secular papers of the East greatly added to his influence in every effort in Christian work in later years. Although in some quarters the tendency was to refer slightingly to the meetings, many able correspondents expressed their sympathy with the work even if they did not accept the message that was given.

"In the Hippodrome Mr. Moody has gathered day by day the largest audiences ever seen in this city," said one of the ablest of the secular journals. "Lawyers, bankers, merchants, some of whom scarcely ever enter a church, are just as much a part of his congregations as are the second-rate and the third-rate boarding-house people mentioned so conspicuously in a recently published analysis. All classes and conditions of men have been represented in these great revival meetings. Mr. Moody is a man of such persistent consistency that it is scarcely more possible that he should change himself than that—to use a Biblical figure—a leopard should change his spots. Indeed, there is no prospect that he will ever conform either himself or his style to the demands of propriety or to the requirements of grammatical rules.

"Let us frankly confess as we bid him good-by that we are heartily glad that he is what he is. We would not change him. Make him the best-read preacher in the world and he would instantly lose half his power. He is just right for his work as he is, original, dashing, careless.

"Mr. Moody reaches the masses more surely and widely because he is one of them himself, and because he has not been made eloquent and faultless by the trimming and restraining processes of a liberal education. His very solecisms sound sweetly in their ears. His familiarity and conversational manner please them. They like his directness and his earnestness. He is driving a bargain with them, and he talks sense. He is trying to comfort them when 'from the world's bitter wind they are seeking shelter,' and he fills their souls with the assurance of a Father's love. There they sit and listen—the poor, the distressed, the afflicted, the sorrowful—taking 'their fill of deep and liquid rest, forgetful of all ill.' Life becomes pleasanter to them; the future assumes a hopeful aspect. Mr. Moody touches more chords than the ordinary preacher on Sunday; he comes nearer home; he nourishes them more; his society is more refreshing. They go away from the Hippodrome brightened and strengthened. They like Mr. Moody, and so does almost everybody; hence we would not on any account have him change himself. We enjoy his rude simplicity and his pell-mell earnestness, his downright individuality and his uncalculating naturalness."

An interesting incident occurring at this time is related by Prof. George P. Fisher, of the Yale Divinity School, as illustrating Mr. Moody's sincerity and courageous frankness as well as his kindness. Says Professor Fisher:

"I once passed an evening in company with Mr. Thurlow Weed,

who was long a leader in the politics of New York, and in the Civil War was sent abroad on a kind of unofficial embassy to confer with men of power in England. In the course of a long conversation Mr. Weed asked me if I knew Mr. Moody, and added that Mr. Moody wrote him an excellent letter, which he would like me to read. It was an acknowledgment of a very generous contribution from Mr. Weed to defray the expenses of the meetings held in New York. Mr. Weed did not himself mention the occasion of the letter, but he afterwards sent me a copy of it. This is the letter:

" 'Mr. Weed.

" 'My dear Friend: Yours of the 20th of March with check came to hand yesterday, and I am at a loss to know what to do. I am afraid you may put it in with some other good deeds and they may keep you from coming to Christ as a lost sinner. I wish you knew how anxious I am for you and how I long to see you out and out on the Lord's side. I thank you for the money, but what would you say if I should treat your gift as you have the gift of God and send it back to you—would you not be offended? Now as I take your gift, will you not take God's gift and let us rejoice together? I cannot bear to leave the city and leave you out of the Ark that God has provided for you and all the rest of us. Hoping to hear soon of your conversion, I remain your friend and brother (I hope) in Christ,

(Signed) " 'D. L. Moody.' "

When the meetings were in progress, "The Tablet," a Roman Catholic paper, devoted two columns in one issue to the work of the evangelists, saying in its review:

"This work of Mr. Moody is not sin. It cannot be sin to invite men to love and serve Jesus Christ. It is irregular, unauthorized, but it may be bringing multitudes to a happier frame of mind, in which the Church may find them better prepared to receive her sublime faith."

"Whatever philosophical sceptics may say," said "The New York Times," "the work accomplished this winter by Mr. Moody in this city for private and public morals will live. The drunken have become sober, the vicious virtuous, the worldly and self-seeking unselfish, the ignoble noble, the impure pure, the youth have started with more generous aims, the old have been stirred from grossness. A new hope has lifted up hundreds of human beings, a new consolation has come to the sorrowful, and a better principle has entered the sordid life of the day through the labors of these plain men. Whatever the prejudiced may say against them, the honest-minded and just will not forget their labors of love."

Years after this series of meetings was ended it was not an uncommon question for the critics to ask: Where are the converts of the Hippodrome? Without making any effort to investigate the matter themselves, they demanded data forthwith from those who expressed their confidence in the efficacy of special evangelistic effort. The Christians in many of the churches in New York and other cities who first made their profession of faith at these meetings had no distinguishing mark by which they could be at once recognized by the casual observer. But there was hardly a city that Mr. Moody visited during the remaining twenty-five years of his evangelistic career where he did not come across those who had first come to a knowledge of Christ in the old Pennsylvania freight depot of Philadelphia, or in the Hippodrome in New York in the winter of 1875-76. The following testimony of a New York pastor, writing twenty years later, is but one of many that Mr. Moody frequently received:

"It has been said by some of the pastors of the more wealthy churches in this city that but little permanent good resulted to their churches from the series of meetings held by you in this city in 1876. This may be true so far as the churches named are concerned, but it certainly is not true regarding my own church. In 1876 there were received one hundred and thirty-nine persons. Of this number one hundred and twenty-one came on confession of their faith in Christ, and the larger part of them were brought to Christ directly through the influence of the great revival meetings in that year. These converts have worn well; only a very small percentage have fallen away. Never since that day have we received so large a number in any one year.

"The greatest blessing that could come to this city at this time would be such a work as was then carried on so successfully. What this city needs more than anything else is the preaching of the old Gospel. It has lost none of its power. All substitutes have failed, and it is time to come back to the simple teaching of the Gospel of the Cross of Christ. You are doing a great work in Cooper Union and in Carnegie Hall now, and may God bless you and encourage you and give you more and more the baptism of the Holy Spirit."

CHAPTER XXV

Chicago and Boston

IT was not till the fall of 1876 and after the missions in Brooklyn, Philadelphia, and New York that Mr. Moody again visited Chicago to conduct a special evangelistic campaign there. A large tabernacle had been erected for the occasion, with a seating capacity of over ten thousand. Ministers who had known Mr. Moody in earlier years gave their hearty support to the work, and it was most gratifying for him to feel that, in his case at least, it could not be said that a prophet is without honor in his own country. In Chicago Mr. Moody was better known than in any city in the world, and in the mission begun in October, 1876, he received the heartiest cooperation of clergy and laity he had ever known.

It was during this Chicago mission in 1876 that Mr. Moody sustained the loss of a warm personal friend, as well as of an invaluable helper, in the sudden death of Mr. P. P. Bliss. Although comparatively a young man, Mr. Bliss's name was a familiar one in every Sunday-school in America, and the "Moody and Sankey Hymn-book" owed much of its original popularity to his contributions. A musical genius of unusual promise, he had been willing to sacrifice his taste for higher lines of composition to write music that would prove effectual in carrying the gospel message to the greatest numbers. As a hymn-writer as well as a composer he was equally successful, as "Hallelujah, what a Saviour!" "More holiness give me," "I know not what awaits me," and "Wonderful words of life" testify. His personality was most lovable, and the strong attachment between him and Mr. Moody made the bereavement a deep one. Mr. and Mrs. Bliss had been spending Christmas with their family in Tonawanda, and were on their way to join Mr. Moody in Chicago when they met death by a railway accident, their train crashing through the Ashtabula bridge and falling seventy feet into the river below. Mr. Moody never ceased to miss their aid in his work, and often spoke in warmest appreciation of their beautiful ministry.

The Chicago mission of 1876 was not only attended with manifest and sustained interest, but resulted in a material increase in church membership, for Mr. Moody never failed to urge the immediate affiliation of young converts with some regular church, and devotion to the strengthening of existing Christian agencies. At the close of the mission a farewell service was held for those who professed to have been brought to Christ during the mission, for which admission was secured by ticket only. Applications were made for six thousand of these tickets, and before the meetings closed local churches reported over two thousand accessions on profession of faith.

Of late, critics have occasionally intimated that Mr. Moody no longer received the same cordial support in Chicago that characterized the earlier missions of twenty years ago. When, therefore, in 1897, it was announced that Mr. Moody was to conduct a series of meetings in the Auditorium, the largest hall in the city, with accommodations for six thousand, many asserted that he would be unable to fill the hall mornings and afternoons.

Mr. H. R. Lowry, representing "The Chicago Times-Herald," thus describes the meetings at this later date:

"It made a scene without precedent; a preacher on the platform said it was like nothing so much as the host which sat at the foot of the mountain for the model sermon. Six thousand more men and women were standing in the streets after the management had ordered the doors closed. This multitude would not accept the announcement that the vast hall was packed from ceiling to pit. It swept around the corners and in the avenues until traffic was blocked.

View in Main Street of Northfield.

View in Main Street of Northfield.

A Forest Convention at Kinsman, Ohio. Home of Mr. James McGranahan.

The cable-cars could not get past. They insisted that there must be some mistake, as there had never been any prayer-meeting in Chicago since Moody went away where there had not been room for more people than cared to attend. A line of policemen tried to argue, but the crowd would not be reasoned with. An hour before the time for opening there had been a stampede. The men at the entrances were swept from their posts by the tide. The overflow waited patiently during the service, and a small fraction of it was able to get inside after Mr. Moody had finished his sermon and Dr. Torrey started the call for volunteers in the service.

"Mr. Moody was one of the first men on the stage at the morning session, pacing up and down the front. He saw the throng pouring in. Hundreds of singers were coming through the back entrance and climbing into places in the tiers of seats, which ran back like the side of a pyramid. He gave orders like a general. There must be a good beginning. He said a good beginning meant half the battle. He urged the choir to sing as if it meant it. He did not want any lagging. The organist must make the organ thunder. He told the two hundred preachers who sat on the stage that they were there for work—not for dignity. He was going to turn the battery towards Sinai."

Chicago was always dear to Mr. Moody's heart, and here he always counted on the sympathy of many friends. As in 1876 and in 1897, the same cordial welcome always waited for him in the city of his earlier Christian activities.

On the close of the Chicago campaign Moody began a mission in Boston that in many respects presented peculiar difficulties. The "hub" of New England's culture and refinement is the centre of every new philosophy and fad, while materialism and rationalism are widely spread. The idea of a revival in Boston was repugnant to many people, and on many sides he was subjected to hostile criticism and false reports, often of a personal nature. But if he experienced strong opposition from such sources, he received, on the other hand, no less hearty support from others. Among these were many who became his confidential advisers in later projects, including, among others, Mr. Henry M. Moore, than whom Moody had no more valued supporter or closer friend; Mr. Henry Durant, whose counsel was of such great value in the founding of the Northfield schools, and Dr. A. J. Gordon, whose assistance at the Northfield conferences was of inestimable value.

In Boston, as in Chicago, a large temporary building was erected for the mission, with a seating capacity of six thousand. A representative committee of prominent ministers and laymen of all denominations supported the work, and from the first great interest was shown. The following appreciation of the Boston work was given at the close of the mission by Dr. Joseph Cook, in prefacing one of his Monday lectures:

"It will always stand uncontrovertibly that a structure which holds from six thousand to seven thousand people has been opened in Boston for religious audiences, and that week after week, for two months, on every fair day, and often twice or thrice a day, when an undiluted Christianity has been proclaimed there, this building was filled to copious overflowing. What other cause would have filled it as often and as long? This is the large question which Edinburgh and London, Chicago and San Francisco, will ask.

"As a help to an interior view of Massachusetts and its capital, it it not improper for me to state what the evangelists themselves could not, perhaps, with propriety say publicly, that their notion is that in Boston the average result of their work has been better than it was in Edinburgh.

"In one particular this revival certainly surpasses that under Whitefield in this city in 1740—namely, in the extent to which the press has been enlisted in the work of sending religious truth abroad. All the leading respectable newspapers of Boston have favored the revival. In the next place, it deserves to be mentioned that religious visitation from house to house, and especially among the perishing and degraded, is now going forward in a hopeful manner in this city. And we have yet to speak of the prayer-meetings among the business men, which have not yet attained the height of their influence.

"Let me mention, as a fourth prominent result of this revival, the great effort made for temperance. We have done more in that particular than was done in Boston in Whitefield's day, for in his time men were not awake to that theme."

The five missions conducted in Brooklyn, Philadelphia, New York, Chicago, and Boston during the years 1875, 1876, and 1877 may be properly termed the beginning of an evangelistic mission in America covering a period of over twenty years. To recount the hundreds of cities visited, not only in the United States but in Canada, and extending even to Mexico, would be very largely a repetition of previous incidents and methods of work. North, South, East, and West, Mr. Moody visited all the leading cities of the continent. In some cases he devoted an entire winter to work along evangelistic lines and in Bible readings among Christians. This was the case in Baltimore, St. Louis, and San Francisco, in each of which he stayed from five to six months. Often his missions would close with a short convention for Christians, the purpose being to awaken greater interest in church work and evangelistic effort, and there would always be the same earnest appeal to young converts to do what they could to show their gratitude in working for the church.

In later years Mr. Moody was often criticised for devoting so much time and energy in preaching to Christians. His special gift, it was asserted, was to evangelize, and it was unwise for him to turn from the unconverted masses to try to arouse Christians. Others claimed that the earlier missions had not left a permanent result in the communities where they had apparently aroused greatest interest and had the largest attendance. This twofold criticism could have been refuted readily had any one accompanied him to any town in which he had ever before been engaged in sustained effort. His repeated experience was that in any average church or hall in such places many who had been led to Christ through his ministry, or Christians who had been themselves helped or had had relatives converted under Mr. Moody, would constitute a large portion of the audience. They would come early to the place of meeting and take the nearest seats, and those for whom he specially sought to preach the Gospel would be either crowded out or find places only in a remote part of the hall. Thus his very success in God's work became, in many places, an actual hindrance to preaching the Gospel to those who had never accepted Christ.

It was for the same reason that Mr. Moody was frequently unable to conduct an inquiry meeting. Although firmly believing in personal dealing, he was confronted in many places with the twofold difficulty of being unable to secure efficient Christian workers sufficiently familiar with God's Word to lead inquiring souls to the Master, and the interruptions he would be subjected to himself when dealing personally with those who wanted his help. On such occasions it would often seem more like a testimony meeting than an inquiry-room, as one after another would come forward to tell Mr. Moody how they had been led to Christ through him during some former mission.

Even in cities remote from the scenes of earlier missions he would receive these testimonies. During his last extended tour on the Pacific coast in the winter of 1899 he was continually meeting those who dated their Christian life from missions he had conducted years before in some city in the Eastern States or in Great Britain.

For these reasons Mr. Moody was always looking for new fields, and on the tour just mentioned he accepted invitations to the newly settled towns of Colorado, New Mexico, and Arizona. After spending a number of weeks in Denver and Colorado Springs he began a series of short missions in places he had never before visited. In some of these there was little support to be counted on, as the Christian portion of the population was inconsiderable among the large number of fortune-seekers attracted to the country solely by the idea of money-making or adventure. But here he doubled his energies, and was richly rewarded. Speaking of the difficulties in this work, he said: "Last fall I prayed God to send me to a hard field, and He has answered my prayer." But difficulties were always an incentive to harder work in his case, and he spoke longingly of the possibilities of a longer mission than he was then able to make in these places. His work was more than once successful in bringing a prodigal to himself. In one town in the new country he received a hurriedly written note from a wanderer after a sermon on "Repentance," stating that he had left the service that night during the sermon, convicted of his sin, and was leaving by the midnight train for his home in Philadelphia, to seek his parents' pardon for his cruel treatment and desertion.

Striking as is the impression produced by great bodies of men yielding to a common emotion, there is something almost equally forcible in these picturesque, individual incidents. In reading accounts of thousands turned away from crowded halls, and of thousands converted by certain definite missions, one is liable to forget that these crowds are all made up of single souls, and that men are gained one by one. Mr. Moody was much given to the man-to-man method; he was especially interested in the inquiry-room, and always laid great stress on the necessity for competent helpers in this work. "Let every one of us try to get one soul!" was his constant appeal. And how many he won personally in this way cannot possibly be estimated.

Nor, indeed, did he care to estimate them. He was intolerant of that kind of statistics. When a minister recently asked him how many souls had been saved under his preaching, he answered, "I don't know anything about that, Doctor. Thank God, I don't have to. I don't keep the Lamb's Book of Life."

In reviewing the work of these months and comparing the missions held in Great Britain and in America, Prof. W. D. Mackenzie said recently:

"It is a strange fact, and one that strikes a kind of awe into the soul whenever it is contemplated afresh, that Mr. Moody's career of evangelism reached its height in America during a period of extraordinary material prosperity, and in Great Britain during a period of extraordinary intellectual scepticism and religious depression, the two conditions most hostile to faith. In the face of the claims of the world, he preached the claims of the living God and His Gospel. He went from end to end of this land calling multitudes away from mere earthliness of interest, and from the greed for wealth and prosperity, to the problem of individual salvation and the concerns of everlasting life. In England he found himself in communities where philosophy and science had almost tied the tongues of many preachers and chilled the devotion of multitudes of the most intelligent classes. He did not attempt to reconcile science and religion, nor to meet the terrific onslaught of a revolutionary philosophy upon the Christian faith. Simply and powerfully and in the Holy Spirit he preached the Gospel, and compelled an amazed people to see that the might of that Gospel is as unquestionable and divine as ever. Moody's work was one of the most powerful influences in stemming the tide of doubt which was flowing over England in the 70's.

"In Scotland he rendered the same service, and also another, for vast portions of Scotland had remained invincibly Christian, but the Christianity of those days was stiff and formal, severe and ungenial. Few churches used hymns, and fewer still had organs. The Established Church had begun to recover popularity, and its empty buildings were beginning to fill; but it lacked the warmth of true evangelism. The Free Church had lost most of its fervent and brilliant leaders of earlier days, and a new class of men were growing up, scholarly and powerful but again inclined to formality of preaching, and many doubted."

CHAPTER XXVI

Second Extended Mission in Great Britain

THE memory of Mr. Moody's work in Great Britain was a great inducement to him to accept a most urgent invitation to return for a similar mission in the fall of 1881. In many respects the work of this visit was like that of the first; many of its experiences were repeated in the cities visited on this occasion; it almost seemed that he took up the work just where he had left it six years before. From the first he met the heartiest support from ministers of all denominations, and the same general interest was evinced everywhere. As on the previous occasion, the mission began in the North of England, this time in Newcastle-on-Tyne, where Mr. Moody conducted meetings during the latter part of October and the first two weeks of November.

Edinburgh was then visited, and a six weeks' mission was held, and this was followed by five months' work in Glasgow and the immediate vicinity. In this city Prof. Henry Drummond again assisted Mr. Moody in his work, and the friendship begun during the earlier visit became more deeply rooted. Saturday, which Mr. Moody observed as his day of rest, was usually spent with his family, and Drummond was often a welcome addition to the small circle. Mr. Moody would turn continually to him in those days for advice and fellowship, and their attachment deepened into the warmest love.

In Edinburgh and Glasgow Mr. Moody introduced a new feature into his work, by conducting Saturday morning meetings for children. On these occasions he would give "illustrated sermons" to the little ones, presenting the gospel truth through sight as well as hearing.

"Altogether it was a novel and a pretty sight," says a writer in describing one of these services, "the mingling of white-headed and venerable fathers with bright little children, some of them not more than five years old. For example, Mr. Sankey was quite surrounded with little people; Dr. Cairns, too, was besieged, and it would be hard to decide whether the esteemed Principal or his youthful neighbors appeared the happier. William Dickson and several other gentlemen acted the part of attentive and kindly monitors.

"Mr. Moody began his address to the children by reading from the Sermon on the Mount three verses, beginning: '*Ye are the light of the world.*' After speaking about the light of the world, he showed that children may be lights, and by a series of questions brought out the idea that children should be obedient. Accepting this answer, he told the story of Adam's fall because of his disobedience.

"Suddenly he called upon Mr. Dickson to produce a candle, to place it on the table, and to clear the table of everything else, so that everybody might see the light. The burning candle was placed in the centre of the table.

"'Now,' he added, 'we will call that light Obedience. Remember that. Mr. Dickson, put Obedience under a bushel.' Immediately Mr. Dickson covered the candle with a bushel.

"'Is that right?' asked Mr. Moody. 'No; for neither do men light a candle and put it under a bushel; but on a candlestick and it giveth light to all that are in the house.' He ordered the bushel raised again, and Obedience was once more seen 'giving light to all that were in the house,' this time placed not under, but on the top of the bushel. 'Adam,' Mr. Moody proceeded to remark, 'when he sinned, hid himself, and was thus like the candle under a bushel.'

"As he proceeded, he had other candles lighted, giving to each a name, and now and again asking all the children to repeat them, occasionally telling anecdotes applicable to the matter in hand and asking for illustrative texts. The list of lights when completed was as follows: Obedience, Kindness, Forgiveness, Truth, Peacemaking, Temperance, Faith, Mercy, Patience, Cheerfulness, Love. The meeting passed all too quickly for the little people, who thought that Mr. Moody was one of the best ministers they had ever heard."

Dr. Andrew A. Bonar, who had worked with Mr. Moody in the first campaign in 1874, and had also been with him in Northfield in 1881, made this entry in his diary on June 9, 1882:

"This week Mr. Moody closes his five months' work among us. And, on looking back, I think it was the Lord who inclined me to go last season to America and thus help to engage him to come to us. I thank the Lord for my being used in some way to help him in the knowledge of the Word and truth. It seems to me plain that the Lord shows His sovereignty by making that man a vessel through which the converting power of God may be poured out on various classes of men. The drunkards have had their day of visitation, and many others of the working men especially. I can now see in the great blessing before us an answer to my prayers on board the ship in my journey to and from America; Jeremiah, xxxiii. 3 has been fulfilled in me. He has shown me great things which I knew not. One marked effect upon ministers here has been the state of expectation in which they now are; they are looking for real results."

Closing his work in Glasgow in June, having held meetings there for five months, Mr. Moody made short visits to some of the large centres of Scotland, holding conventions and organizing evangelistic work.

During the winter a large number of invitations had been continually coming to Mr. Moody to visit different English cities, as well as Ireland and Wales. In order to perfect arrangements for the coming year, a committee of seventy gentlemen, representing the different cities that wished Mr. Moody to visit them, met him in London. In this conference plans were made for visiting the leading cities of the South of England and Wales. Mr. Moody made a characteristic address, saying that he could not visit in a lifetime all the places from which invitations had come. He did not intend to spend the remainder of his days in England, for he felt that his work lay more in America. He thought that if he devoted some months to the principal towns of Scotland, then gave a year to England, with a visit to Paris and Ireland, that a year in London would finish his mission in that country. The latter was referred to a London committee, and the programme outlined by Mr. Moody was practically carried out.

Mr. Stebbins, who accompanied Mr. Moody on his mission at this time, writes as follows:

"We had the pleasure of accompanying Mr. Moody and Professor Drummond on a short visit to many of the larger towns and cities throughout Scotland. This tour Mr. Moody enjoyed to the full. The change from the crowded and smoky city to the fresh and invigorating air of the Scottish hills, covered with heather and dotted over with grazing herds of sheep and cattle, was a constant source of delight to him. In this campaign we took in many of the small towns as well as the large cities. Often they were near together, so we four would drive from place to place instead of going by rail. Mr. Moody was always troubled because the parks or landed estates, with their beautiful castles and gardens, were surrounded by high stone walls that shut in all their beauty. How he enjoyed those drives! He noticed every babbling brook, and not a lark soaring to heaven nor a hedge-row escaped his attention. Flowers were always a source of pleasure to him, and often he would stop the carriage, and Professor Drummond would jump out to pick them, and then tell us the names, and point out to us new beauties of shape or color."

After a fortnight's rest with his family in Switzerland Mr. Moody began the winter's mission by visiting Swansea, Cardiff, Newport, Plymouth, and Devonport during September and the first week in October; then a fortnight in Paris, a week in Bristol, a week each at Cambridge and Oxford, and meetings lasting from three days to a week in Torquay, Exeter, Southampton, Portsmouth, and Brighton through October, November, and December. The month of January, 1883, he spent in Ireland; the month of February was divided between Birmingham, Leicester, and Nottingham; and two weeks' meetings were held each in Manchester, Leeds, and Liverpool.

In this work in Great Britain there was the same programme as on the previous visit, the evangelistic campaign ending in a London mission. On the conclusion of the meetings in Liverpool in the latter part of April Mr. Moody returned to America. At this time the Northfield Seminary and Mount Hermon School were in their infancy, and needed his presence for several months' supervision and personal care. In the fall, however, he returned to Britain, remaining in Ireland for a month's work before beginning that memorable eight months' mission in London.

Great as had been the success of the meetings in London in 1875, Moody's second visit in 1883 was marked by still greater preparations. A large committee was formed in the early spring composed of many of the leading Christian men in London; Hugh M. Matheson, to whom Mr. Moody had committed the hymn-book royalty in 1875, was elected chairman. The committee took charge of the erection of large buildings of corrugated iron and wood in London. This work devolved chiefly upon Robert Paton and Mr. Matheson, who had to select the sites, arrange with the architects of the buildings, and generally manage the whole business. Concerning this campaign, in which he took such an active part, Mr. Matheson said:

"We were discussing with Mr. Moody, at a large meeting, the method to be followed in London, using a plan which I prepared on the spur of the moment while occupying the chair, and which defined the order to be followed in the missions in the various districts north and south of the Thames, and the dates of each. To the amazement of the committee, this was accepted absolutely by Mr. Moody, and the programme was followed in the minutest detail all through the London campaign, with a success that was quite remarkable. Two halls were built—one at Islington, in the grounds of the Priory, and the other at Wandsworth. When the Islington meetings were finished and we went to Wandsworth, the Islington hall was taken down and erected at St. Pancras, and while St. Pancras was being occupied, the Wandsworth hall was removed to Clapham, and so on; north and south being occupied alternately for three weeks in each place, until practically the entire city had enjoyed the opportunity of being present at the services. It was a wonderful time and made a very deep impression.

"The whole mission cost over £20,000, and this sum was raised by special contributions. The royalty on hymn-books was arranged very much as on the former occasion, save that this time Messrs. Quintin Hogg and Robert Paton were associated with me, and shared the responsibility. We arranged in detail with Messrs. Morgan and Scott the royalties to be paid upon each edition of the book, and at the end I was able to remit to America, to trustees for the Northfield schools which Mr. Moody was desirous of founding, and which have since attracted so much attention, no less a sum than £10,000 (about $50,000)."

On November 4, 1883, the long campaign in London was begun. Hall No. 1 was called Priory Hall, and was erected in Upper Street, Islington. The hall had a seating capacity of five thousand, and the inside appearance was pleasing to the eye, while in the matter of acoustics it was as nearly perfect as possible.

At the opening meeting Mr. Moody said:

"I have come to London with high hopes and great expectations. I have about one hundred times more faith than I had when I came here eight years ago. Some people have said that the former work in London hasn't lasted. I want to say that since then I have been preaching all through America—from Maine to the Pacific slope—and that wherever I have gone I have found the fruit of that London work; it is scattered all over the earth."

At this time the Bishop of Rochester addressed a letter to the vicar of St. John's, Blackheath, expressing his desire that the vicar "should give counsel and sympathy to our kinsmen, the American evangelists, who propose to help us with our overwhelming work in South London this winter." He said that these men were personally known to him. "More than once I have come across their track in their own country, and I have heard nothing but good of them. To call them schismatics is to trifle with language; to suspect them of sectarian motives is to do them a great injustice. Their religious services are simple, reverent, and deeply impressive. Their recent labors, not only in our largest towns, but also in our two great English universities, are standing the hardest test, that of time. Should any one doubt if their doctrine is pure or their works solid, let him do what I myself have done and hope to do again—hear and judge for himself. My own desire is that God will raise up ten thousand such men to proclaim His redeeming love."

In referring to the meetings the first week, "The Pall Mall Gazette" said:

"Cultured society will blush to know anything about Messrs. Moody and Sankey and others of their crowd. Revivalism in religion, and American revivalism in particular, is desperately vulgar, but unfortunately the same might be said with equal truth of every popular movement, religious and irreligious, of all kinds. Almost every religion has its origin among men of low degree, and the sons of fishermen and carpenters who create or revive the faiths and superstitions of mankind are, as a rule, very objectionable persons in the estimation of the men of light and leading of their time. It is only when the first fervor of the new faith begins to cool, and its vitality to disappear, that polite society condescends to investigate its origin and to study the phenomena, sociological or otherwise, which it presents. The enchantment of distance renders it possible for self-respecting sons of culture to study, after the lapse of a century, religious revivals which, to their contemporaries, were too vulgar to be noticed except with a passing sneer.

" It is somewhat irrational, however, to subject the scoriæ and lava of extinct volcanoes to the most minute analysis while craters in full eruption are treated as non-existent; nor can a plain man see the sense of poring over dreary tomes, describing the enthusiasm of some preaching friars of the Middle Ages, often as dirty and bigoted as they were vulgar, while the labors of such latter-day friars as the American revivalists who have now pitched their tent—in this case a portable iron building capable of holding five thousand persons—in the North of London are disregarded.

" Moody and Sankey are not, it is true, graduates of any university. They are men of the people, speaking the language and using the methods not of the refined, but of the generality. Yet they have probably left a deeper impress of their individuality upon one great section of English men and English women than any other persons who could be named. Whatever we may think of them, however much their methods may grate upon the susceptibilities of those who have at length succeeded in living up to their blue china, these men are factors of considerable potency in the complex sum of influences which make up contemporary English life. As such they merit more attention than they have hitherto received from the organs of public opinion, and for that reason a full account of the American revivalists and of their services last night, which we publish in another part of the paper, may be studied with interest by some of our readers, and passed over—let us hope without too great a shock to their feelings—by the rest."

In the first London campaign in 1875 great crowds gathered at a few large halls, but in the second series of meetings the halls were taken to the crowded districts, the object being to get nearer to the people who could not or would not go to the larger and more central halls, and that object was admirably secured. In the Nazareth synagogue the Saviour quoted the prophecy from Isaiah that "*the poor have the Gospel preached unto them.*" While no class was excluded during these series of meetings, the poor especially were reached.

The Rev. J. Guinness Rogers wrote to "The London Congregationalist" at the time:

"Mr. Moody's conduct of the entire meeting was a remarkable manifestation of the way in which the fervor of his zeal is helped by his extraordinary sagacity, and by the tact of a shrewd man. Sanctified common-sense is characteristic of the man everywhere, and quite as much in his management of the proceedings as in his own address. He understands how much depends on details, and great care is given to the veriest trifle. He remembers, too, what many of those who claim to be scientific forget, that men have bodies as well as souls, and that these two act and react upon each other, and he does his utmost to guard against the discomfort and weariness which may so easily mar the effect of the best sermon. His one aim is to get that into the hearts of the people, and if he sees anything which seems to hinder him in this, he spares no effort to get it out of the way."

During the mission that winter meetings were held in all parts of London, as may be judged by the fact that the temporary buildings were erected on eleven different sites, from Hampstead Heath on the north to Croydon on the south, and from Stepney on the east to Kensington on the west. During these months Mr. Moody spoke in crowded halls at least twice a day, and on several occasions four or even five times. It was estimated that during the London mission he spoke to over two million people. At many of the meetings entrance was by ticket only, of which over four million were issued during the eight months.

On May 27th a three weeks' mission was begun on the Thames Embankment, in the hall situated on the vacant ground near Temple Gardens. The opening service at Temple Gardens Hall was the beginning of the end. Since the work had included the outlying portions of the metropolis during the previous seven months, it was fitting that the great campaign should terminate in the very heart of the city. The attendance was very large, embracing all grades and sections of the community, from peers of the realm to the poorest of the poor.

Mr. Sankey was obliged to return to America before the London meetings closed, as his health necessitated his taking a rest. The additional burden thrown upon Mr. Moody by his colleague's absence only served to bring out into stronger relief his wonderful powers of adjustment and endurance. From early morning until late at night, and practically all day on Sunday, he was busy speaking, active in the inquiry meetings, in conference with committees concerning the work, and conferring individually with those who needed personal help.

The closing of this mission by a conference for Christians was in line with other campaigns, and June 17-19 was set as the date for this feature of the work. In the afternoon the Lord's Supper was observed, after an address on the Holy Spirit by Mr. Moody. In his invitation to the congregation to remain to the memorial feast, he emphasized the fact that only those who had received Christ and were in communion with the Lord could rightly observe the ordinance, so that all who should remain would do so as a confession of faith in Christ. The sight of the thousands who gathered around the sacred emblems was deeply touching when one remembered the divergence of thought on minor matters that was represented here.

At the close of the mission Mr. Moody accepted an invitation to spend a few days for rest and recreation at the country house of T. A. Denny, and later at the home of his brother, Edward Denny. With him were also invited a score or more of those who had assisted in the work in London, including, among others, Professor Drummond, who had returned from this tour into the interior of Africa in time to be present during the closing weeks of the meetings. Those were very delightful days for Mr. Moody, who, free from the care and strain of his great work, gave himself up to the relief of social life, enjoying particularly the young people's games.

On one occasion during this period of rest Mr. Moody succeeded

The Northfield Home of Mr. Moody.

ROUND TOP: THE BURIAL PLACE.

A place especially sacred to Mr. Moody during his lifetime.

in making a rich discovery for the Christian world by his persistent attempts to draw from Drummond a little of the wealth of information that he possessed. It was on a beautiful Sunday afternoon in June, when they were together at the home of Mr. Edward Denny, not far from Tunbridge Wells, whence, thirteen years later, after months of painful suffering, Drummond entered upon his reward. In those days, however, he was at the zenith of physical strength and, although standing before the world as the suddenly famous author of "Natural Law in the Spiritual World," one of the most modest and unassuming of God's noblemen. An urgent request was made of Mr. Moody to give an informal address.

"No," was the response, "you've been hearing me for eight months, and I'm quite exhausted. Here's Drummond; he will give us a Bible reading."

With characteristic reluctance Drummond consented, and taking from his pocket a little Testament, he read the thirteenth chapter of First Corinthians, and then, without a note and in the most informal way, gave that beautiful exposition which has since become so widely known to thousands under the title of "The Greatest Thing in the World." Three years later, when visiting Northfield at Mr. Moody's special request, the same exposition was repeated, both at the Students' Conference and the August Conference, and in response to Mr. Moody's urgent plea it was later published in its present booklet form. Mr. Moody often said that he wished this address to be read in the Northfield schools every year, and that it would be a good thing to have it read once a month in every church till it was known by heart.

Professor Drummond was only twenty-two when in 1873 he began his work with Mr. Moody in Scotland. When, in later years, the fires of criticism were kindled about Drummond, his great-hearted friend stood by him. He believed in the man with all his heart, even though he might not follow him in all his theories. He knew him to be a Christian "who lived continually in the thirteenth chapter of First Corinthians." Is it a wonder that the affection between these broad-minded, loving-hearted men became a bond that could not be severed? To those who knew both it was not a matter of surprise that, speaking to Dr. Henry Clay Trumbull alone, at different times in the same day, each should say of his friend:

"He is the sweetest-tempered Christian I ever knew."

CHAPTER XXVII

Later Missions in American Cities

THE campaigns of 1875-76 and 1876-77 in the larger American cities were repeated in many other places in succeeding years. Similar records of great meetings in Baltimore, Cleveland, Cincinnati, St. Louis, Denver, San Francisco, Richmond and other cities might be given. Aside from the years 1881-84 and 1891-92, when he was abroad, Mr. Moody filled as many engagements from September till May as could be crowded into eight months of each year.

Burlington, Manchester, Providence, Springfield, Hartford, and New Haven were among the cities in which large and profitable meetings were held in the fall and winter of 1877-78. All New England is said to have felt the influence of the work of that season.

The work in Baltimore in 1878-79 was particularly successful. One of the converts was Todd B. Hall, a detective who went to one of the meetings to arrest a criminal. While waiting for the service to end, that he might take his man without causing a commotion, he says, "I was forced to accept Christ as my Saviour." He went directly to the office and told the chief of the detective force and his associates what he had done; then he went home and told his wife, and she, too, accepted Christ. For more than a score of years he has been a faithful Christian officer and a great blessing to many poor fellows whom he has arrested.

St. Louis was the scene of the evangelist's labors for six months in the winter of 1879-80. An incident from that winter's work made a deep impression upon him:

"There was an old man who had been leading an ungodly life, but who in early manhood had professed Christianity. He came into the inquiry-room, literally broken down. About midnight that old man yielded to God and found peace. He wiped away his tears, and started home. The next night I saw him in the audience with a terrible look in his face. As soon as I had finished preaching, I went to him and said:

"'My good friend, you haven't gone back into darkness again?'

"Said he: 'Oh, Mr. Moody, it has been the most wretched day in my life.'

"'Why so?'

"'Well, this morning, I started out as soon as I got my breakfast. I have several married children in this city, and they have families. I have spent all the day going around and telling them what God has done for me. I told them how I had tasted salvation, and, Mr. Moody, I hadn't a child that didn't mock me!'"

It was during this mission in St. Louis that Valentine Burke, a notorious prisoner, was convicted of sin through reading in a daily paper one of Mr. Moody's sermons which a reporter had entitled "How the Jailer at Philippi Was Caught." Burke had passed through a town called Philippi, in a neighboring State, and, supposing the jailer of that town had been arrested, was curious to learn how it happened. Nine times in that sermon he came across the words, "Believe on the Lord Jesus Christ and thou shalt be saved." He gave his heart to God and became a changed man. Within ten years he had been appointed treasurer of the sheriff's office and was an active Christian worker. He lived a consistent life in a public position of usefulness until his death in 1895.

In the winter of 1880-81, Mr. Moody was on the Pacific coast. Concerning the revival in California, it was admitted by those who knew the spiritual condition of the State that such religious interest as was then manifested had never before agitated California. Its human causes were not single or simple. "The spiritual stagnation, the sordid worldliness, the frivolous pleasure-seeking, the purblind compromising of the Church," to use the words of a Methodist editor, had produced a state of alarm among all who truly feared God. The masses were sleeping. It was deemed expedient to do something to arouse them. Mr. Moody was invited to the coast, and most encouraging results followed his mission.

Concerning the work in San Francisco, "The Pacific" said:

"The great evangelistic work with which our city has been blessed for the last five months is now drawing to a close. Day after day, week after week, the interest has been unabated; and not through one church alone, but through all, the thrill of spiritual life has run, awakening the drooping graces of the members and kindling a new hope in Christian hearts. Backsliders have been restored; the hearts of older Christians, who have long borne the burden and heat of the day, have been gladdened; pastors who have labored on, sowing much and reaping little, have had the joy of welcoming new-born souls into the household of faith, who have brought with them new, fresh life and vigor—and, it may be added, new responsibilities also. As yet many of the new converts are ignorant of religious truth; but, in the weekly prayer-meetings, in the Bible classes, they will receive that spiritual nourishment that they must have to grow. Many valuable helpers are also added to the band of Christian workers already laboring, in season and out of season—new teachers in Sunday-school and helpers in other benevolent work. To God be all the praise for this blessed shower of grace, which we, in this very worldly city, had long desired to see.

"Perhaps the event which will mark this year more signally than any other is the lifting of the great debt of the Young Men's Christian Association. Would any other man have had the faith and courage to undertake such an apparently hopeless task? For three weeks and more Mr. Moody has labored with unwearied persistence and faith in this great undertaking. His great heart has been moved with the clear view of the needs of San Francisco—its multitude of young men that haunt the myriad places of vice and crime in our midst, by night and by day; the lonely, sick, and friendless among the 'wandering boys,' whose only safeguard is the mother's prayers going up from some distant home. Our friends in the country have an equal interest in this institution, for it is their boys that we are seeking to meet with Christian influences, as they come in such numbers to our city. And now the work, which in Eastern cities interposes such benign influences between the mighty powers of evil and the young men of a great city, may go on unhindered and accomplish what its founders designed."

In the midst of the campaign of 1881-84 in Great Britain, Mr. Moody came home to rest during the summer of 1883. Before returning to Europe, a three-days' convention was held in Chicago, in September, similar to those held earlier in New York, Boston, and Philadelphia. Farwell Hall was thronged at every session with clergymen, city missionaries, Association secretaries, Sunday-school officers and teachers, including many devout women.

During the seasons of 1884-85 and 1885-86, Mr. Moody bestowed his attention upon the smaller cities of America. His plan was to arrange a tour including a chain of cities across some important belt of territory, remaining about three days in each place. During those three days he preached, perhaps, three sermons a day, endeavoring to concentrate what he had found by experience to be his most effective arguments and appeals. Whatever time was not thus occupied was for the most part spent in inquiry work. Other evangelists preceded and followed him, and in each place the ministers garnered the harvest and utilized the spiritual awakening. Within two years he was able to visit cities of from ten to one or two hundred thousand population in all parts of North America.

In the fall of 1895, when the Atlanta Exposition was drawing thousands of spectators, Mr. Moody was invited to that city and preached for several weeks in the Tabernacle, which seated several thousand people.

So great was the blessing received by the New York churches in 1890, that a committee was appointed six years later to invite Mr. Moody to visit the metropolis again that fall. He hesitated for some time, assuring the committee that he considered New York to be the hardest city to reach that he had ever visited; that he was unable to get hold of non-churchgoers there. As soon as the doors of any church or hall were opened, the seats were filled by church members who had been in every meeting that he had held.

" I am not blind to facts, nor troubled with mock humility," he said. " Reputation is a great injury in many places, for we cannot get the people that we are after."

It was finally decided to accept the invitation from the New York ministers, and Cooper Union was engaged. The meetings began early in November, and lasted until the holidays. Overflow meetings were held for a part of the time, and evangelistic meetings were started in several churches and chapels, speakers being sent from the main meeting. Once or twice, while the New York campaign was in progress, Mr. Moody went to Philadelphia, and also to Boston, his place at Cooper Union being taken by friends.

January and February, 1897, were spent in Boston, the evangelist holding two meetings each day except Saturday. Although in the close of his sixtieth year, he appeared indefatigable, his enthusiasm had not in the least cooled, nor the intense earnestness which was so great a power with his audiences. As of old, the Boston meetings drew together all classes and conditions of society.

One day, after the meeting in Tremont Temple closed, a fine-looking gentleman in middle life went up to the evangelist and said:

" Mr. Moody, you do not know who I am, but I feel I must speak to you, as I leave for California to-night, and we shall probably never meet again. Twenty-five years ago you were speaking in London, and I and two other rough young fellows wandered in to hear you. We were moral lepers and had gone far in all kinds of sin. The Spirit of God touched our hearts through your words that night. We did not stop to speak to you, but when we came out of the house onto the walk we shook hands and said quietly to one another: 'From this night we begin a new life.' One of the three died in Egypt at the head of his regiment, an earnest Christian soldier. The second is a heroic missionary in Africa, and I am the third."

While in Boston he celebrated the sixtieth anniversary of his birth. This was the occasion of the international present which made it possible to build the chapel at Mount Hermon. At this time an interview with him appeared in the press, in which he was asked what event influenced his becoming an evangelist.

"No special event," he replied. "I entered upon active Christian work in Chicago, and the more I did the more I seemed to have power to do. It was a chain of events beginning with the first Sunday-school work. When a man knows the power of the Gospel of Jesus Christ and His love, he ought to tell it."

"What was the principal event for good in your life?"

"Well, a good many events have been for good, but perhaps none better than the surrender of my will to God."

"What advice would you give, Mr. Moody, to young men?"

"'Seek first the Kingdom of God and His righteousness, and all these things shall be added unto you.'"

"What would you advise them to do to change their mode of living if the life be not pure?"

"Be cleansed by the blood of Christ, and drive impurity out by pure thought and holy influence."

Speaking of his birthday anniversary, Mr. Moody said: "I don't realize that I am growing old, and I have been too busy to pay special attention to anniversaries. As I have often said, I have found life better and better as it passes."

During the visit to Cañon City, Colo., in 1899, the Governor of the

State, hearing that Mr. Moody was to speak at the Penitentiary on Thanksgiving Day, wrote him, inclosing a pardon for a woman who had already served about three years. Seven years more were before her. Mr. Moody was greatly pleased to be the bearer of the message. The woman was quite unaware of the prospective good fortune. At the close of the address, Mr. Moody produced the document, saying: "I have a pardon in my hands for one of the prisoners before me." He had intended to make some further remarks, but immediately he saw the strain caused by the announcement was so severe that he dared not go on. Calling the name, he said: "Will the party come forward and accept the Governor's Thanksgiving gift?"

The woman hesitated a moment, then arose, uttered a shriek, and, crossing her arms over her breast, fell sobbing and laughing across the lap of the woman next her. Again she arose, staggered a short distance, and again fell at the feet of the matron of the prison, burying her head in the matron's lap. The excitement was so intense that Mr. Moody would not do more than make a very brief application of the scene to illustrate God's offer of pardon and peace.

Afterward he said that should such interest or excitement be manifest in connection with any of his meetings—when men and women accepted the pardon offered for all sin—he would be accused of extreme fanaticism and undue working on the emotions. Strange that men prize more highly the pardon of a fellow-man than the forgiveness of their God.

While in California Mr. Moody was invited to visit New Zealand and Australia. Writing from Los Angeles, on February 27th, he said that if his own personal pleasure could have been consulted he would at once have cabled his acceptance, but there were several obstacles which prevented his going. One was the schools, which had become an important part of his life-work. He also felt it difficult to leave his own country, as conditions here seemed to call for greater labor and activity on his part than ever before. The third objection to accepting the invitation was that by the advice of his doctors he avoided a long and especially a warm ocean voyage. He had planned to visit India and China in a trip around the world, but was obliged to give it up, on the urgent counsel of those whose advice he was accustomed to follow.

CHAPTER XXVIII

NORTHFIELD SEMINARY

"THE reward of service is more service" was a favorite saying of Mr. Moody's, and, indeed, it perfectly indicated his life-work. One day, soon after returning to his native town, he was driving with his brother, Samuel Moody, over one of the mountainous roads near Northfield, when they passed a lonely cottage, far distant from any town or neighbor. Sitting in the doorway were the mother and two daughters, occupied in braiding straw hats. The father was paralytic, and could do nothing for the support of the family; thus the burden rested on the women. But though the father was physically helpless, he was an educated man, and his daughters had an ambition that reached beyond their present narrow horizon.

The limitations of their condition and the apparent hopelessness of their future deeply impressed Mr. Moody. The sight of those women braiding hats in that lonely, out-of-the-way place resulted in his determination to meet the peculiar needs of just such girls in neighboring hills and communities.

His brother Samuel undoubtedly added impulse to this purpose. Mr. Moody had a peculiar love for this brother, who was the youngest in the family. He was not strong physically, and his interests were necessarily limited. He read law for a time, and gave promise of making a good attorney. Like his older brother, he was fond of young people, and was instrumental in starting a debating society in Northfield. He constantly regretted the limited opportunities the local schools afforded his twin sister for her mental betterment, and often expressed the wish that something more advanced might be available.

In 1876 Samuel died, but not before he had fostered in his brother's soul a yearning to put such educational advantages within reach of girls living among the New England hills as would fit them for a broader sphere in life than they could otherwise hope for.

Another probable source of suggestion as to purpose and method was Henry F. Durant, of Boston. Mr. Moody made this gentleman's acquaintance in the sixties, and with him visited Mount Holyoke Seminary. During his Boston campaign in 1878 he was a guest at Mr. Durant's home. The latter had just founded Wellesley College, and naturally his daily conversation was full of his plans. Mr. Moody was taken to visit the college several times, and became a trustee.

Mr. Durant's aim for Wellesley was to have a college founded on the Bible, and to give advanced education, while always giving Christ and the Bible preëminence. Recognizing the benefit of industrial duties, as well as of intellectual training, he insisted on the students sharing in the domestic work of the institution. Mr. Moody saw this plan in operation, and at once adopted it in starting the Northfield Seminary.

The purchase of a school site was characteristic of Mr. Moody. One day in the fall of 1878 he stood discussing the project with Mr. H. N. F. Marshall, of Boston, when the owner of sixteen acres of adjoining land passed them. They asked him if he would sell, and learning his price, invited him into the house, made out the papers, and before the owner had recovered from his surprise the land had passed out of his hands. Three or four adjoining lots were bought out in the course of a year, all without their respective owners realizing that their barren farm-lands had any special value. These purchases increased the estate to one hundred acres, the greater part being bare, sandy hillocks, useless even for pasturage, but suitably located, and commanding a pleasing view of the Connecticut Valley.

In the spring of 1879 the erection of a recitation hall intended for one hundred students was begun. With characteristic promptness and energy, Mr. Moody could not wait for a dormitory to be built, but altered his own house to accommodate the students. Instead of the eight pupils as expected, twenty-five appeared. With these, the Northfield Seminary for Young Women was formally opened on November 3, 1879, classes being held in the dining-room of Mr. Moody's home until the recitation hall was completed the following December.

The two girls he had seen in the mountain home were among the first students. So intelligent were they that they soon justified Mr. Moody's efforts in their behalf.

Ground was broken for the first dormitory, East Hall, in April, 1880. It was completed the following August, and was used to accommodate those who attended the first Christian Workers' Conference during the first ten days in September. On the last day of this conference, at the close of one of the morning meetings, Mr. Moody invited those present into the chapel of East Hall for the purpose of dedicating the building. After singing one or two hymns, Mr. Moody spoke as follows:

"You know that the Lord laid it upon my heart some time ago to organize a school for young women in the humbler walks of life, who never would get a Christian education but for a school like this. I talked about this plan of mine to friends, until a number of them gave money to start the school. Some thought I ought to make it for boys and girls, but I thought that if I wished to send my daughter away to school I should prefer to send her to an institution for girls only. I have hoped that money might be given for a boys' school, and now a gentleman who has been here for the last ten days has become interested in my plans, and has given twenty-five thousand dollars toward a school for boys.

"And now as we dedicate this building to God, I want to read you the motto of this school." Then, turning to Isaiah, xxvii. 3, he read:

"'I the Lord do keep it; I will water it every moment: lest any hurt it, I will keep it night and day.'"

And it would seem that this promise has been more than fulfilled, for during the twenty years which have elapsed since then the Seminary has been remarkably blessed.

In the cornerstone of each of the school buildings proper has been placed a copy of the Scriptures. This is symbolic of the place that God's Word holds in the life of the schools. It is, indeed, foundation, cornerstone, and capstone of Mr. Moody's whole system. He recognized that all studies have their value, but believed their importance is increased if pursued in right relation to central truths.

The curriculum of the seminary offers three courses of study. The college preparatory course enables the student to enter any of the leading colleges on certificate. The general course offers the same advantages in Latin, but affords more scope in electives. The English course, by omitting the languages, gives an opportunity for more extended work in sciences, history, and literature. In all branches the student is stimulated to independent thought and investigation. Great emphasis is laid on the foundations of education; hence, for those who are unable to pass a good examination in the fundamental branches, a preparatory department has been planned, which furnishes two full years of elementary instruction.

One line found in the school catalogue which attracts much attention and causes a great deal of pondering is this: "The students perform all the work of the house." To the uninitiated, the hour's domestic work to which she is immediately introduced sometimes seems appalling; but whether or not the task is to mean drudgery depends almost entirely upon the attitude of the student and the spirit in which the work is done. Merry hours are often spent in the kitchen with congenial companions in the cheerful performance of duties which are not always considered the most pleasant. A girl's experience in domestic science is widened, especially if the work falling to her lot be varied—if, in other words, she is a "miscellaneous girl." The schedule of domestic work is arranged largely with reference to the individual's convenience and capabilities, and so as not to conflict with study and recreation hours.

It is not the idea of the Seminary to pay exclusive attention to the training of the mind and soul, but rather to develop a symmetrical womanhood. At least half an hour of outdoor exercise must be taken daily by all, the beautiful and extensive campus offering rare incentives for the fulfilment of this pleasant task. The finely equipped gymnasium is a much-frequented spot. Basket-ball and tennis are favorite sports, impetus being given to games by friendly rivalry between the halls and by challenges between the different classes. Wanamaker Lake, a picturesque sheet of water, often witnesses gay groups of skaters in the winter months, and on beautiful afternoons in June and September is the scene of merry boating parties. Long walks and climbs about the surrounding country are other enjoyable forms of recreation.

There are also lectures, concerts, and various sorts of entertainments which help to brighten the winter evenings and to develop the social life of the school. Receptions and class entertainments are other pleasant features. Often on festive occasions the unique social evenings in the different halls blend brightness with routine and draw friends more closely together. The Current Events Club aims to keep its members informed in regard to living history as it is being enacted and recorded from week to week. The Young Women's Christian Association has in charge the various departments of Christian activity, and keeps students in sympathy with the larger movements to make the world better.

Last June (1899), in a memorable reunion, the twentieth anniversary of the Seminary was celebrated. Words of love and gratitude reached the founder's ears on every side. Well might he rejoice in its almost incredible growth, from a modest beginning twenty years ago, to the present enrollment of nearly four hundred students, with a staff of teachers and matrons numbering thirty-nine. The school property now embraces five hundred acres of land, nine dormitories, a gymnasium, a library, a recitation hall, an auditorium, and farm buildings. The effects of a Northfield training are lasting, as hundreds of former students testify. Many who came to obtain enough education merely to get along better in life, or to fit themselves for some lower sphere, have had their whole course and purpose changed. Instead of leaving the Seminary the irritable, self-centred girls that entered, they have gone out consecrated, self-sacrificing Christians, who have found the joy and happiness that come in the service of Christ.

NORTHFIELD SEMINARY.

MOUNT HERMON CAMPUS FROM "TEMPTATION HILL."

Showing Recitation and Science Halls. Northfield in the distance.

CHAPTER XXIX

Mount Hermon Schools

NO sooner was the Seminary under way than a corresponding school for boys suggested itself. Mount Hermon School for Young Men was therefore started on similar principles. The first purchase of property was made in November, 1879, when a farm of one hundred and seventy-five acres was secured by Mr. Moody. When, a little later, Mr. Hiram Camp, of New Haven, Conn., agreed to contribute $25,000, some adjoining land was bought, and the school started with an estate of about two hundred and seventy-five acres and two farmhouses. At Mr. Camp's suggestion the name Mount Hermon was adopted, "*for there the Lord commanded the blessing, even life for evermore.*" (Psalm cxxxiii. 3.)

The first boys arrived at the school on May 4, 1881. At that time the ages varied from eight to twelve years, Mr. Moody's aim being to give them home life and help, of which they knew little, but before long a change in this direction was adopted. Applications began to pour in from young men whose early education had for various reasons been meagre. Three years later, believing that younger boys had more opportunities to secure schooling elsewhere than the older class of applicants, and realizing that too wide a range in age would not be feasible from the view-point of discipline, the age limit was raised, and it was decided to accept no applicants under the age of sixteen.

Mr. Moody had not mere charity in view; hence his schools do not offer their privileges gratuitously. But he knew that raw material of the most promising kind is often to be found among people of little or no educational attainments, who cannot afford the usual expense of academy life, and in order to open the doors to such, the annual fee of the Northfield schools was fixed at $100 a year, or about half the cost of board and tuition. In other words, Mr. Moody proposed to give tuition and training free to such as would provide their own living expenses.

The system of manual labor common to all Mr. Moody's institutions is best developed at Mount Hermon. Here there is no aristocracy. Every student, big or little, senior or preparatorian, must do a certain amount of manual labor every day, the work being adapted to his physical ability, but entirely regardless of any social standing. This, alone, is enough to keep away that class of young men who go to school for fun and not for work, and the proportion of those who have already formed a strong purpose in life, and who really "mean business," is correspondingly large. Each student is marked according to his faithfulness and efficiency in this department. Thus a basis for the estimation of character is afforded, which Mr. Moody and the teachers have regarded as valuable as that of the class-room.

That there is little chance for loafers may be judged from a glance at a sample of the daily programme, which is tolled out by bells, that remind the students of the remorseless flight of time and opportunity:

6.00 A.M. Rising bell rings.
6.15 A.M. The officer of the floor (a student) makes a tour of the rooms to make sure that no one has forgotten to get up.
6.30–6.50 A.M. "Silent time" for private devotions.
7.00 A.M. Breakfast, after which beds are made, rooms cleaned, etc.
7.40–11.50 A.M. Study and recitation periods.
11.55 A.M. Chapel exercises, lasting about half an hour.
12.30 P.M. Dinner.
1.20–3.20 P.M. Work-time.
3.20–4.30 P.M. Study, or other school duties.
4.30–6.00 P.M. Recreation.
6.00 P.M. Supper; evening devotions being held just before the meal.

7.00–9.30 P.M. Study hours.
9.30–10.00 P.M. Evening "silent time."
10.00 P.M. Lights out, and inspection by the floor officer.

The school remains in continuous session, the calendar year being divided into three terms of four months each. Under this system the school plant is in use in the summer, when expenses are at a minimum.

The regular intellectual routine of school work is adapted in an extraordinary degree to the individual needs of the pupil. Some who have had early advantages prepare for college, or take a thorough course in English branches, adding in each case a course in Bible study. Other men, well on in years, who have been deprived of early advantages, and have a larger knowledge of life and wider acquaintance with the Scriptures, struggle with the multiplication table, and knit their brows over the grammatical structure of simple sentences.

The preparatory course provides instruction in the elementary branches. The classical course of four years gives adequate preparation for admission to any college, and the school certificate admits, without examination, to many well-known colleges. The scientific course affords preparation for the best schools of technology, or secures a good practical education for those who go to no higher institution. An elective course is offered to those whose circumstances demand more freedom in the choice of studies than the other courses allow.

Three societies have been organized for the purpose of debating and other literary work. Friendly rivalry runs high between these societies in the contests for the numerous prizes offered by the school.

Great importance is attached to the spiritual discipline of the students, and in this the home life in the various dormitories is a most important factor. Intercourse with others teaches them to live peaceably and unselfishly. Angularities of character are smoothed and softened, and lessons in forbearance and patience are daily learned—lessons not noted in the catalogues, but as important as mental culture in the preparation for a useful career.

At Northfield and Mount Hermon "chapel" and "silent time" are part of the day's programme. Mr. Moody often said that no infidel had any right to partake of the advantages of the school, knowing that its declared purpose is Christian. Though many who are not Christians are accepted as students, a sincere effort is made to lead them all to Christ, and a very small percentage leaves unconverted. But forcing in this matter is never allowed.

One immediate result of this home life is a happy, contented feeling among the students. Visitors are constantly impressed with the evident unity and cheerfulness of the school.

The Mount Hermon Church directs the Christian activities of the students. This church is homed in Memorial Chapel, the last building added to the school plant before Mr. Moody's decease. The chapel is built upon a prominence that he playfully called "Temptation Hill," hinting that some friend might be tempted to give the money necessary to erect a chapel. But as the hint had not been taken, the sixtieth anniversary of his birthday (1897) was made the occasion of an effort to provide this much-needed building, which, it was presumed, would give him as much happiness as any present made to him personally. Accordingly the funds necessary were raised in England and America by the voluntary contributions of friends who wished to share in this tribute of love and gratitude. Rev. F. B. Meyer, of London, and H. M. Moore, of Boston, were responsible for this suggestion and its consummation.

This commodious chapel has seating capacity for one thousand. Although built expressly as a memorial of Mr. Moody's sixtieth birthday, he would not allow this fact to be mentioned on the bronze tablet in the vestibule, which reads as follows:

"This chapel was erected by the united contributions of Christian friends in Great Britain and the United States, for the glory of God and to be a perpetual witness to their unity in the service of Christ."

OVERTOUN HALL, MOUNT HERMON.

MOUNT HERMON BUILDINGS.

Mount Hermon Chapel.

The Old Mount Hermon Ferry Across the Connecticut.

In both these Northfield schools the end in view has been to impart knowledge, not so much as an accomplishment, but as a means of making men and women more serviceable to society. While the common and even the advanced courses of academic work have all received thorough recognition, it is the Bible that takes preëminence as the real source of spiritual education. Every course includes Bible training, and in both the Northfield Seminary for Young Women and the Mount Hermon School for Young Men each of the eight hundred students receives Bible instruction twice a week.

In the twenty years that have elapsed since these two schools were first established nearly six thousand students have felt the influence of the work, and hundreds have given their time and talent to the proclamation of the Gospel they heard at Northfield. Others have entered various occupations, where their quiet influence is doubtless felt at home or in business.

Rev. Alexander McGaffin, of Brooklyn, a former student in the school, thus writes of the spirit of the place, which he terms *hermonology*:

"I went to Mount Hermon as a mere boy without any particular aim in life or any serious religious convictions. There I came upon a species of Christianity altogether new to me, and an educational training tempered by an earnest religious spirit. One did not study merely for learning's sake, nor was one religious merely for religion's sake. A great purpose was constantly held up, towards which we boy learners were to struggle, and pure motives were inculcated as the ever present power of our lives.

"We were taught that the present was the means and the future the end; that in that future dwelt God and humanity, and that our work would have to do with them.

"The great need of the Eternal One was the cry of His heart for the world; and the great need of man was his undefined longing for God.

"The italicised words in the vocabulary of God, we were taught, are 'the world' and 'redemption.' There is a divine voice, they told us at Mount Hermon, a divine voice speaking, in divine language from Heaven, a message to man, and a human voice speaking in human language, disconnected and wandering, uttering incoherent cries, the cravings of the soul.

"We were to be mediators who could hear the voice from Heaven, could understand the divine language, and could repeat the message over again in words that man might catch, in tones that would reach his heart.

"This was to be the practical religion and constant duty of every one of us, whatever our avocation in the world. We might not all preach in the 'regular way,' but we could preach in the 'irregular way,' as Mr. Moody said. We could learn to understand the two languages and be interpreters thereof to men. This is a sublime mission in the world, and one which was constantly presented to us at Mount Hermon. All our training, educational and religious, was intended to fit us for this work.

"Our religious life, as I look back upon it now, seems to me to have approached in its spirit and activity nearer to the New Testament type than any I have since seen. In the various spheres in which we move one does not often have the privilege of witnessing such a combined and consistent exhibition of this kind of Christianity as could be seen at Mount Hermon. After years of absence and further training, one's heart often turns back to those days of smaller knowledge and higher living. Indeed, it was easy to be a Christian at Mount Hermon, and though the life there had its own temptations, yet, for some of us, the struggle for existence has come later, and no surer anchor did we find than the truths and convictions which embedded themselves in our hearts during those earnest years.

"It was no mean training in itself, apart from the daily instruction and practice, which we received by meeting the eminent leaders of religious thought and activity who so frequently visited the school and addressed the students. It gave us insight such as no reading of books or personal effort could possibly have given us in the same time or with greater power. As experience has come to us in these after years the counsel of those days has remained as the touchstone of good and evil, and without it we might easily have erred.

"Indeed, I cannot see how any one who had spent from two to four years at Mount Hermon as a sincere seeker after religious truth could ever be permanently diverted from the lines of evangelical and aggressive Christianity. Though such an one may temporarily be so blinded as to lose the proportion of things, when thinking out for himself the earlier beliefs of his boyhood, yet I believe and know that, sooner or later, he will turn again to the living truths taught and testified to at Mount Hermon, as a man, staggered and made cynical by the mystery of life, turns again to the love of his mother. I know that what I say has been true of some, and that others, just as candid and thorough in their dealings with 'science falsely so called,' find themselves still walking in the old pathway, the shadows dispelled and the light shining brighter and brighter still.

"Of the men whom I know to be in darkness and doubt to-day the majority of them are those who never have been rightly instructed, or who have never seen the religion of Jesus rightly lived. No one can have been a student at Mount Hermon and have missed either. I speak feelingly and I speak with knowledge. Mount Hermon was the gateway of Heaven for me, and never did it let go its grip until I was able to stand upon my own feet and fight my own religious battles. It helped me to cherish every lofty desire. It inspired me with courage against every evil tendency. It placed before me a holy ambition, and when it launched my little craft out into deep water, there were a compass and pilot aboard—and I have not yet run aground.

"I have said nothing thus far of the educational value of Mount Hermon. It is certainly unique. After seven years' study since leaving the school, I can sincerely say that the best teacher I have ever had was she with whom I began my studies in Greek. For thoroughness, painstaking care, and inspiration, I have never met her equal.

Her teaching, like that of all the others, was characterized by an earnestness of purpose and purity of motive which I have seen in only a few instances since.

"Teaching was regarded at Mount Hermon as a sacred privilege, and was pursued in that spirit which marks sincere religious service. It is my own opinion that more good students are made at Mount Hermon than at most institutions of secondary education. It was not a matter of surprise to those who knew the school, though it was astonishing to some who did not know it, that two of its graduates were the only members of a freshman class in one of the three great colleges of the East who were first honor men in every subject. Nor does it seem strange that three other students had imbibed at Mount Hermon such a love for learning that during the greater part of their college career they lived on a dollar and a quarter or less each per week, cooking their own food in an attic room. One of them declined in bodily vigor. I saw the change; but lately he entered a Western theological school, the winner of a Hebrew prize and a victor over circumstances.

"Two of our men from the same class at Hermon have been valedictorians of their respective classes at college, while a third was the holder of the historical fellowship at another university. These are a few instances of winning work of which I have personal knowledge; there are many others in and out of college of which I am ignorant.

"If I were beginning my education again and, in view of what I now know of preparatory institutions, had to choose a school, I would select Mount Hermon.

"There is one other characteristic of the school which must not be forgotten. It is what might be called the man-making quality. This is an indefinable something distinct from the religious and educational training. There is a sturdiness cultivated there which one feels every day, and which soon works itself into the fibre of every student who enters into the spirit of the place. There is a democratic independence rampant which is bound to affect the most indolent.

The school is not for rich men's sons. They have no right there. There can be no aristocracy of wealth. Every student knows that he must carve out his own future, and that the 'other fellow' is doing the same. This produces a feeling of brotherhood which tones down and Christianizes the 'struggle for life.' The only dependence recognized is interdependence. The only qualities which give leadership are goodness, grit, and skill. Words do not count, but accomplishment. The Past has perished, the Present is all-important.

"Thus would I indicate what seems to me to be the manliness of the life at Hermon; the spirit that asks only for a fair chance and no odds, believing that he who does right will do well.

"The four years spent at Mount Hermon were very happy years, the most critical and formative of my life as I have since learned. For what they mean to me nothing that I can now imagine could compensate, and if life were to be lived over again I would not like to have those four years left out."

CHAPTER XXX

The Bible Institute for Home and Foreign Missions

A LETTER is on file at the women's department of the Institute that intimates Mr. Moody's thought regarding this school:

"East Northfield, Mass.,
"December 16, 1895.

"My dear Miss Strong:

"I want to get my two granddaughters into the women's department the first of the year 1916. They will be about the same age, and I would be glad to have them room together. I want them to understand how to visit from house to house. You might have their names put down, so that if the building is full at the commencement of the fall term they will not be crowded out. Their names are Irene Moody, born at Mount Hermon, August 22, 1895, and Emma Moody Fitt, born at East Northfield, December 16th.

"It is my wish that when they have gotten through the Northfield Seminary they spend two years at the Bible Institute; and as I have taken some interest in the society, I hope you will give my application a favorable consideration. I do not ask for a free scholarship. I only want to make sure to get them in. I should like to have them do some housework. I find it is so much better for young ladies to care for a house, so if they ever have one of their own they will know how to look after it.

"Yours truly,
"D. L. Moody."

"I believe we have got to have 'gap-men'—men who are trained to stand between the laity and the ministers," was a common expression of Mr. Moody's. He felt the great need for more lay Christian workers. On the one hand he found many consecrated men and women ready and anxious to do God's will, and on the other hand he saw that there was plenty of opportunity for them to go to work if they only had the necessary skill and training. His effort was to solve this problem, and he made urgent appeals for funds wherewith to open a training school. Responses to this appeal came heartily, the money was pledged, the preliminary steps were taken, and the new enterprise was chartered under the name of "The Chicago Evangelization Society."

On December 31, 1886, Mr. Moody began a four-months' campaign of evangelistic services in Chicago, going from one church to another, and utilizing the great roller-skating rinks. Every noon a large meeting was held in old Farwell Hall, the audience-room of the Young Men's Christian Association building, which had been the scene of many former experiences in Mr. Moody's life. Each Monday noon reports were heard from the various churches and missions.

During these four months, plans for the "Training School," as it was then called, were being brought into shape, but unexpected hindrances appeared. At the last noon meeting of his stay Mr. Moody asked:

"How shall this work be carried on when I am gone?" and some one called out:

"Get a tent."

"All right," said Mr. Moody; "I'll give the first hundred dollars. Who next?" Money was at once raised for the object, and a gospel tent, eighty feet in diameter, was secured and pitched in a district so wicked that it was known as "Little Hell." The tent was manned by an evangelist with a corps of assistants, Bibles in hand. After a few weeks the tent was moved elsewhere; and so, summer and winter, the meetings went on, the winter services being held in churches, missions, and theatres, and the summer meetings in the tent; the barroom of a small theatre was once used as an inquiry-room, with beer kegs for seats. Multitudes were brought to Christ from the lowest strata of society, and thus was found one solution of the problem: "How shall we reach the masses?"

Training was given the workers in a series of brief "Bible Institutes," when excellent Bible teachers expounded the Scriptures and gave practical methods of Christian work. In May, 1889, the "Institute" was held in the Chicago Avenue Church, and Mr. Moody found nearly two hundred persons present where he had looked for twenty. As a result of that conference the Chicago Bible Institute was formed, and formally opened in the fall of that year.

Land and buildings adjoining the Chicago Avenue Church were purchased at an outlay of $55,000. The three dwellings on La Salle Avenue, included in the original purchase, were fitted up for the home of the women's department, to which three others, costing $36,500, have since been added. On Institute Place $50,000 was expended in the erection of a three-story brick building, one hundred by one hundred and twenty-five feet in dimensions, built about a hollow square having the rare advantage, in the heart of a closely built region, of light and air on all sides. Two more stories were added, just before the World's Fair, at an additional cost of $15,000. This building contains the necessary class-rooms, offices, and dormitories for two hundred men, with dining-hall, kitchen, and laundry. Over $20,000 was spent in furnishing the various departments.

The Institute was formally opened with a week's conference, beginning September 26, 1889. The Rev. Mr. Torrey, superintendent of the Congregational City Missionary Society of Minneapolis, a graduate of Yale College and Seminary, and who had also studied at the universities of Leipsic and Erlangen, was called to the position of superintendent.

Students have come to the Institute from all quarters, till, to-day,

BIBLE INSTITUTE, CHICAGO: MEN'S DEPARTMENT.

PORTION OF LADIES' DEPARTMENT, BIBLE INSTITUTE, CHICAGO.

(Showing south section only.)

there is not a race, and but few nations, which are not represented on its register. The system embraces a thorough doctrinal, analytical, and book study of the English Bible under the tuition of resident instructors. Added to this, lectures are given by the best Bible teachers from both sides of the water on topics to which they have individually given the closest attention. While spiritual exposition is emphasized, all is based upon the most careful and scholarly study of the Word. Two years of twelve months each are required for the course, but, as it proceeds in a circle, students can enter at any time and by remaining two years complete the full course.

Mr. Moody always recognized the power of gospel song, and no education for Christian service would be complete in his eyes without it. Hence a musical department was a necessity. Those gifted in that direction receive careful training in the art of singing the Gospel, a branch of vocal culture to which special attention is not usually given.

The morning hours are spent in the class-room, and the afternoons and evenings are divided between study and practical work among the unconverted. Rescue mission work, house-to-house visitation, children's meetings, women's meetings, jail work, inquiry-meeting work, church visitation—every form of effort which can be developed in the heart of a great and wicked city is here supplied. For several years two and three large tents have been utilized during the summer, and many street meetings are held. When cold weather approaches, the people interested are gathered into cottage meetings, varying in attendance from eight to fifty. At one time thirty-five cottage meetings were being held every week.

The result of the first decade's work of the Institute strongly testifies to its success. In this time several thousand have been in attendance, of which number 202 are in home, city, and rescue missions; 180 in evangelistic work as preachers and singers; 38 in educational and philanthropic work; 64 are superintendents of city missions; 368 are pastors, pastors' assistants, and church visitors; 58 are Sunday-school missionaries; 25 are Christian Association secretaries; 32 are colporteurs, and 186 are foreign missionaries.

The institution at present owns land and buildings which exceed $300,000 in value. It is cosmopolitan in character, receiving students of many tribes and nations from beyond our shores, and sending out men and women with the message of the Gospel to all lands. The Bible Institute has been called the "West Point" of Christian work. It endeavors to embody all the principles which characterize successful Christian workers. Study and work go hand in hand.

Mr. Moody's desire to place deserving students in training for Christian effort both in Chicago and Northfield, and at the same time give consecrated men and women of wealth an opportunity to share in this work, is seen from the following letters sent to trusted friends in New York:

"MY DEAR ———: Can or will you and your wife take one student each in our schools out here for 1891? It will only cost $150 each, and they can report to you every thirty days how they are doing. I have found a good many who have gone through college or seminary, especially ladies, who have no money—for they have spent all at school and have nothing to come here; but $150 will keep them hard at work for three hundred and sixty-five days, and they will do much good, and be learning all the time. My wife and I are each going to take one, and I am going to see if I cannot get two hundred others to do the same, and then it will not come heavy on any of us.

"I am thankful to tell you that I have not found our church in such a good condition in fourteen years. God is using this society to stir up the city. They had the grandest summer that Chicago has seen for many years, and I am in hopes of keeping things moving. I shall want to start in with the workers in 1891, and if you can see your way clear to come in with us I shall be glad."

Under date of February 24, 1890, he wrote to a friend relative to the work of the institution as follows: "I am thankful to tell you that I have some splendid men and women in the field. My school work will not tell much until the century closes, but when I am gone I shall leave some grand men and women behind. I am thankful to tell you I am gaining all the time on the endowment. . . . I hope you will give me the lever. If you cannot, do not cut me off from your list of beggars."

Three special classes of students whose needs the Institute specially aims to meet may be briefly mentioned:

1. Graduates of colleges or theological seminaries who wish to supplement the valuable education received at these schools by a thorough study of the English Bible and methods of aggressive Christian work.

2. Ministers, evangelists, returned missionaries, and other Christian workers who have had actual experience in the field, and who wish to give some time to further study and preparation for larger usefulness.

3. Men and women who do not intend to devote their entire time to gospel work, but who desire a larger acquaintance with the Bible and methods of Christian effort, that, while pursuing their secular callings, they may also work intelligently and successfully in winning others to Christ.

A week before Mr. Moody's health broke down he was pointedly asked:

"Do you consider the Bible Institute a success? If you were starting over again would you follow the same plan?"

"Yes," replied he; "it has been a great success and a wonderful blessing. I would do the same again."

The preceding winter, when he was in Colorado, he wrote:

"It is cheering to come out here and find our boys doing so grandly. It pays for all we have done, and I feel as if I wanted to do far more in the future. It is a blessed thing to just put live men into the work, for they set others to work."

In further testimony to the practical nature of his ideas as embodied in the Institute, it is only necessary to state that institutions on precisely similar lines have sprung up in various parts of the land. Toronto, Canada, and Glasgow, Scotland, sent representatives to Chicago to study the institution; and now both cities have Bible Institutes after Mr. Moody's model. He lived to see his ideas agitated among prominent educators; for more study of the English Bible, and systematic practical instruction of the precise nature that Mr. Moody has given his students for the past ten years, are the two main reforms that President Charles Cuthbert Hall, President Harper, and others, are seeking to bring about in theological seminaries.

THE GOSPEL ON WHEELS: A BIBLE CARRIAGE.

PORTION OF LADIES' DEPARTMENT, BIBLE INSTITUTE, CHICAGO.

Three other buildings to the left do not appear here.

Mr. Moody with College Students.

CHAPTER XXXI

Among College Students

WHATEVER success had attended Mr. Moody's missions in large cities, and whatever influence he had acquired over thinking men as individuals, work in the college communities was the one field for which he considered himself preëminently unfitted. The college spirit is by its very training extremely critical. Inaccuracies of speech are quickly detected, and an attitude of reverence rarely distinguishes the average student. This was perfectly apparent to Mr. Moody, and for some time he avoided and declined college invitations. Occasionally he had accepted invitations to Yale or Princeton, and the results had been deeply gratifying, but there was ever present the feeling that his mission was not to those whose educational privileges had been so much greater than his own. In this estimate of a college audience Moody was doubtless correct, but he made one serious error, owing to his ignorance of the deeper life of the student body. Critical it truly is, but deep below the superficial criticism of the student is an appreciation of genuine sincerity that is equalled by few audiences. Let college men be convinced of a speaker's real worth and unflinching courage, and he will receive a more sympathetic response than from most audiences. This explains largely the influence Moody exerted upon the religious life of many institutions of learning, where the direct and fearless deliverance of his message was received eagerly, with evident results. And if he won a cordial response from the student body, it was because of the thorough sympathy existing between audience and speaker;

for, if the colleges heard him gladly, Mr. Moody certainly enjoyed addressing young men more than any other class.

The first important work among students began in Cambridge, England, during his mission in Great Britain in 1883-84. As has already been stated, Mr. Moody on a few occasions had visited some of the American colleges—notably Princeton in 1876 and Yale in 1878—with most gratifying results. But it was in England that he was truly introduced to the student world.

The notable indication of Mr. Moody's change of attitude was his response to the petitions of the students of Cambridge and Oxford to visit their universities. Among those who were greatly interested in this work, and by their influence contributed largely to its success, were Mr. J. E. K. Studd and Mr. W. H. Stone, at that time undergraduates. The latter, now the Rev. W. H. Stone, M.A., Vicar of St. Mary's, Kilburn, thus describes, in a recent letter, the mission to the University of Cambridge:

"There lies before me a little book with this inscription: 'To my friend, W. H. Stone; D. L. Moody, Cambridge, November 12, 1882.' And now, after seventeen years, that book seems to recall with wondrous vividness the incidents of that memorable week.

"On returning to Cambridge after the long vacation, I was invited by J. E. K. Studd and the Cambridge Christian Union to join the subcommittee in carrying out the arrangements for a mission conducted by Mr. Moody at the invitation of the Union. The Corn Exchange was secured for the Sunday evening meetings and the gymnasium in Market Passage, now the Conservative Club, for the week-day evenings. A large choir of university men met regularly under the direction of G. E. Morgan, of St. John's, to practise those hymns which were likely to be required. A committee, including members from nearly all the colleges, handed a personal invitation to every undergraduate member of the university. The daily prayer-meeting was well attended by the men; all was now ready, and on Sunday evening, November 5th, we proceeded to the first meeting in the Corn Exchange.

"The great building and annex had been seated to hold some twenty-five hundred persons. On the platform, in front of the choir, were the Rev. H. G. S. Moule, John Barton, James Lang, Henry Trotter, and a few others. Seventeen hundred men in cap and gown were counted entering the building. Every one was provided with a hymn-book. In they came, laughing and talking and rushing for seats near their friends. Little attention seemed to be paid to the preliminary hymn-singing of the choir. A firecracker thrown against the window caused some disturbance.

"Then Mr. Moody asked a clergyman on the platform to pray, but men shouted 'Hear, hear!' instead of Amen, and Mr. Sankey's first solo was received with jeers and loud demands for an encore. The reading of the Scripture was frequently interrupted, and Mr. Moody's address was almost unheard by reason of the chaffing questions and noises which came from all parts of the Exchange. Still the evangelist persevered with the most perfect good temper, until a lull in the storm enabled him for five minutes to plead with 'those who honored their mothers' God' to remain for a short prayer-meeting. After the singing of another hymn, during which many left the building, some four hundred remained for a brief prayer-meeting, amongst whom many of the rowdiest men were seen to be quiet, impressed, and apparently ashamed of their recent behavior. With heavy hearts we took our way to our respective colleges, but Mr. Moody seemed undaunted and full of hope for the ultimate success of the mission.

"On Monday we assembled in the gymnasium, and the sight was enough to depress the spirits of the most sanguine, for only a hundred came to the meeting. After the address, Mr. Moody spoke to every man in the building. When, on asking a man if he were a Christian, he received the answer, 'No, but I wish to be one,' we saw that the effort was not to be in vain, for on that night one who was afterwards to row in the 'varsity boat, and then to become a missionary in Japan, decided to serve the Lord Christ. A few more came on Tuesday night. On Wednesday a letter appeared in 'The University Review,' written by J. E. K. Studd, reminding the members of the university that Messrs. Moody and Sankey had been invited by certain undergraduates to conduct the mission, and that they were entitled to the treatment usually extended to invited guests. This letter had an excellent effect throughout Cambridge, and some two hundred came to the evening meeting.

"On Thursday afternoon Mr. Moody gathered a meeting of some three hundred mothers of the town of Cambridge in the Alexander Hall to pray for university men as 'Some Mothers' Sons.' Mr. Moody described this meeting as unique in his long experience. Mother after mother, amidst her tears, pleaded for the young men of the university.

"That night the tide turned. Who that was privileged to witness it will ever forget the scene? I may remind old Cambridge men that there is a gallery in the gymnasium used as a fencing-room, and approached by a long flight of steps from the gymnasium below. The preacher's subject was 'The Marriage Supper of the Lamb.' At the close of his address he asked any who intended to be present at that marriage supper to rise and go up into the gallery—a terrible test. Amidst an awful stillness a young Trinity man rose, faced the crowd of men, and deliberately ascended the stairs. In a moment scores of men were on their feet, following him to that upper room. Many that night made the great decision. Some of the men who then received the Lord Jesus Christ as their personal Saviour are known to me to-day as honored servants of God in positions of great importance. On Friday night there was an increased audience, but no meeting on Saturday.

"What would happen on the last Sunday night was the question in every one's mind. Eighteen hundred men assembled in the Corn Exchange for the final service. In perfect stillness the great gathering listened to a simple address on 'The Gospel of Christ.' The annex was arranged for the after-meeting, and one hundred and sixty-two men gave in their names at the close as desirous of receiving a little book which might prove useful to those who were seeking to know the power of the Gospel of Christ.

"Many men came to see Mr. Moody at his hotel, some to criticise, some to apologize for the unseemly behavior of the first night, and some to receive that help he was so fitted by God to give to those who were seeking the way of peace.

"The impress of this mission still rests upon the religious life of Cambridge. Its influence is felt in many parishes at home and in many of the dark places of heathendom. No one who took any part in this mission could have been tempted to glorify the human agents or ascribe its success to them. It was the work of God. Mr. Moody had none of those qualifications which would mark him out as specially fitted to influence the members of an English university; unlettered and ignorant of the customs of university men, by the power of God which rested upon him he accomplished a work of which no adequate account will be given until the Day of Christ."

From Cambridge the evangelists went to Oxford. The mission opened on Monday evening, November 13th, with a general meeting in the Corn Exchange. The crowd speedily overflowed that building and more than filled the hall close by. As Moody began to read a chapter from the book of Ezekiel, some of the audience began to stamp and shout "Hear, hear!" Mr. Moody immediately closed his Bible, and rebuked them sharply.

"You had better play with forked lightning or meddle with the most deadly disease," he said, "than trifle with the Word of God."

He then asked those gentlemen to rise who wished him to continue, and the whole assembly, with the exception of a few young men, instantly did so. The result was striking and effective, and there were no more interruptions during the evening. The second and third nights there was still a manifest intention to make fun of the services. The second evening Mr. Moody preached on "Repentance," and the third night on "Sowing and Reaping." He had not proceeded far in his discourse on Wednesday evening before it was evident, from the audible adverse criticisms, that there were many present who were not inclined to give the speaker a fair hearing.

A large company returning from a champagne supper attended the meeting, and their boisterous conduct made it difficult for the speaker to be heard. Hymns were applauded, and derisive "amens" accompanied the prayers. This company intent on mischief, attended the second meeting for the students and undertook to break it up.

Mr. Moody found himself in the midst of a group of young men, most of whom had been among the disturbers on the previous occasion. With that readiness of resource which so often stood him in good stead, he seized the opportunity, and proceeded in the plainest, though most courteous, terms to tell the young men what he thought of them and their reprehensible conduct. Addressing them simply as those who, like himself, would lay claim to the title of "gentlemen," he said that they owed him an apology for the treatment which he had received at their hands. He had been invited by their fellow-students to come and speak to them, and the least they could have done would have been to give him a respectful hearing.

"I have always heard of the proverbial love of the English gentleman for fair play," he said. "As an invited guest to Oxford I expected at least to receive a fair chance to be heard. I am here at the invitation of your fellow-collegians, and your condition after a champagne supper is the only explanation I can give of your conduct."

The inference was too much, and several demanded if Mr. Moody meant to say they were drunk.

"Well, gentlemen, I can only say that the less said about that the better. The wine supper seems to me to be the most charitable explanation of your conduct. Now," he said in conclusion, "you owe me an apology, and to show you mean it I expect that you will all be present at the meeting to-morrow night and give me a fair hearing."

They assented to all he said, and offered a verbal apology for having so transgressed the rules of common civility. Mr. Moody accepted this apology as far as he was concerned, but he said they ought to make further reparation by taking prominent seats in the meeting the next night and listening quietly to his remarks.

The result entirely justified his line of action. Having thoroughly earned their personal respect, he succeeded in gaining a hearing for the message he had to deliver, and the next night the band was present in full force, taking prominent seats and giving the closest attention throughout. From this time the strength of the opposition was broken, and on the following evening the Clarendon Assembly Room had become too small for the growing numbers of undergraduates that attended, and they met in the Town Hall. Mr. Moody's subject was the value of moral courage in a bold confession of Christ before men, and many instances from the Scriptures illustrated this. Having dismissed the first meeting and gathered a large number of men near the platform, Mr. Moody mounted one of the seats and adopted a more colloquial form of address.

"It will be a cross to you," he said, "to confess Christ to-night, but the best thing to do is to take it up. If you intend to see the Kingdom of God, you will have to take up the cross. It will never be easier than now. '*Whosoever therefore shall confess Me before men, him will I confess before My Father which is in Heaven.*' Think of Jesus Christ confessing you, and saying, 'This is My disciple.' Is there not some one here who is willing to take up the cross and say right out, 'I will'?"

One voice sounding forth the response gave courage to others, and a stream of "I wills" came thick and fast.

"Thank God!" said Moody, "I like those 'I wills.' Young men, you don't know how cheering this is; it is worth a whole lifetime of toil. This is joy that fills me full. Thank God for giving you courage to speak out. Is there not another here who will take a bold stand for Christ? Perhaps some of you will say, 'Why can't I do it at home?' So you can, but it is a good thing to do it here.

"I remember the first time I stood up to testify for Christ. My knees smote together and I trembled from head to foot; my thoughts left me; I spoke a few words and then sat down; but I got such a blessing to my soul that it has followed me until now. It helps a man wonderfully to take a bold stand and let the world—both friends and enemies—know that you are on the Lord's side. It is so easy to serve Him after you have taken your stand. If a number of you were to come right out for God together, you would change the whole tone of this university. I could stand all night and hear those 'I wills.' They are about the sweetest thing one can hear outside of Heaven."

Mr. Moody had taken a strong stand from the outset, and he knew that he had won the day. It would have been easy to stop here, but those who knew him could not expect to have the matter end simply with a confession of Christ. He hazarded a further test, though he said he had some hesitation in doing it. He suggested that those sitting on the first three seats in the front should vacate them, and that those who had just spoken should come, and, kneeling there, dedicate themselves to the Lord. The request was scarcely uttered before some five or six rows of seats were filled with a solid phalanx of kneeling figures.

"We have seen a good many of Mr. Moody's and other evangelistic meetings," wrote a correspondent for "The Christian," "but if we can trust our memory we have never seen any like this. The power of God seemed to be present in such a degree that these young men, many of them the flower of the rising intellect of our land, seemed to be swayed at his will like the ripe standing corn before the breezes of heaven. We could but exclaim in our hearts: '*It is the Lord's doing, and is marvellous in our eyes.*'"

In the mission which followed in London during the succeeding winter many of Mr. Moody's most efficient helpers came from the universities visited at this time. Doubtless this did much to influence him in his work among students, and his special interest in the Young Men's Christian Association student work dates from this period. His coöperation in this effort was enlisted early in its history, and for several years he raised by personal solicitation the necessary funds for the support of this department of the work. It was in response to his earnest appeal that J. E. K. Studd, of England, and Henry Drummond visited the leading American colleges in the winter of 1886 and the fall of 1887.

In the establishment of the Northfield "Students' Conference" Mr. Moody contributed as largely as in any other way to the religious life of the American colleges. In the winter of 1886, while travelling in the Southern States, he met one of the early secretaries of the college department of the Young Men's Christian Association, and in a conversation regarding the needs of the work Mr. Moody urged a greater prominence for Bible study among students. The counter-suggestion was then made that he should give a daily course of Bible instruction to a number of college men during the month of July, to which he acceded, on condition that the management of the details for the entertainment of the guests should be assumed by the secretaries of the Association. Plans were made at once for the first of those gatherings of students which have since become so prominent a feature of the Northfield work. The invitation to Northfield met with an acceptance far more general than had been anticipated, and it was decided to hold the meetings at the Mount Hermon Boys' School during the month of July.

On July 7th the conference opened with an attendance of two hundred and fifty students, representing eighty colleges in twenty-five States. Mr. Moody presided at the morning meetings, which were devoted to Bible study, in which informal teaching was given the preference over regular discourses. Questions were freely asked and answered. The afternoons were given up to athletic sports and quiet study, either alone or in groups. A peculiar tenderness of feeling prevailed during the closing days of the meeting.

The most prominent outward result of this conference was the attention given to foreign missions. Sons of missionaries and natives from foreign lands spoke at some of the meetings, and before the conference broke up nearly one hundred students announced their intention to become foreign missionaries whenever fitted and required. From this small beginning the Student Volunteer Movement has grown to be recognized as one of the strongest factors in the missionary work of the church to-day.

Although he was deeply interested in the missionary cause, as the results of his work everywhere show, the Volunteer Movement did not at first receive Mr. Moody's indorsement. The enthusiasm of the leaders he felt to be unwise, as it brought undue pressure to bear upon young people and led them to decide impulsively to pledge themselves to a work which no one should enter upon without the clearest call, not from man only, but directly from God. His attitude was invariably consistent: all that could be urged upon any one was *willingness* to do what God called him to do; but, as he himself expressed it, "It is a great pity for young men to place themselves under a pledge to enter any form of Christian work before God calls them, and He never calls a man until he is ready." The wisdom of this has since been recognized by many ardent students of missions, and the large number of unfulfilled pledges and candidates unadapted to missionary endeavor testify to his knowledge of human nature.

The success of this conference at Mount Hermon School effectually dissipated Mr. Moody's doubt of his call to work for the colleges, and he heartily agreed to repeat the Northfield conference the next year. From this time he frequently conducted evangelistic meetings in colleges, and further manifested his interest in Christian work among students, as is shown by his having raised tens of thousands of dollars for the support of the administrative work of the Students' Christian Association.

The attendance has steadily increased at these gatherings, and now there are about seven hundred registered delegates each year. In addition to this there are nearly as many guests, who come to Northfield especially to attend the platform meetings, which are open to all. Missionaries from many lands, presidents and professors of colleges, pastors of leading churches, and other Christian workers address the students, who gather from nearly every leading college and university in this country, Canada, and Great Britain, and such speakers as Henry Drummond, John Mott, Robert E. Speer, Alexander Mackenzie, R. A. Torrey, Francis L. Patton, and Henry Clay Trumbull have been prominent at these annual gatherings in past years.

CHAPTER XXXII

NORTHFIELD CONFERENCES

THE Northfield Christian Workers' Conference, or, as it is more commonly known, the Northfield Bible Conference, to distinguish it from the Students' Conference held in the month of July, was the first of the summer gatherings assembled at Mr. Moody's home. This conference is of special interest as it expresses the spiritual development of the leader himself during the last twenty years of his ministry, and has proved to be one of the most permanent results that he achieved for the Christian church.

In making Northfield his home Mr. Moody had a twofold object in view. As a father he was always watchful of the physical as well as the moral welfare of his children. In the wholesome country life in which he had himself laid the foundations of a rugged constitution he hoped to have his children equally benefited. The quiet of a small New England village, he thought, would also give him ample time for study, which he could not pursue while actively engaged in missions, and so, to bring about these two results, he decided to spend a few weeks each summer in his native town, at the same time visiting his mother.

But public services had become a second nature to him, and even during this short season of relaxation he was soon arranging meetings. On Sundays he was usually away from home, preaching in neighboring towns, and the sight of Mr. Moody driving his old gray horse " Nellie Grey " was a familiar one to all the villages within a radius of twenty-five miles of Northfield. He was also a regular attendant at the mid-week prayer-meeting, helping to build up the local church in every way. During the second summer spent there he began a series of informal Bible readings, to which the neighbors were invited. These gatherings were held in his own house, and the attendance would frequently more than fill the limited accommodations of his dining-room, numbers standing outside on the verandas by the open windows. Usually he would conduct these meetings himself, although sometimes a prominent visitor would be called upon to speak.

In the spring of 1880 Dr. William Blaikie, of Edinburgh, visited Mr. Moody, and a week's series of Bible readings was at once arranged to be held in the new recitation hall, now Revell Hall, of the Northfield Seminary. These were only occasional indications of a deeper purpose, probably very indefinite in his own mind at the time, but ultimately to find expression in the establishment of the Northfield Bible Conferences.

In November, 1879, he began an evangelistic mission in Cleveland, Ohio. The customary conference for Christian workers was held at the close of the series of evangelistic meetings, at which time the Rev. H. B. Hartzler gave an address on "Prayer for the Church," which deeply impressed Mr. Moody, who sat immediately in front of the speaker. As Mr. Hartzler proceeded, Mr. Moody bowed his head in deep meditation for a time, then, as if some plan of action had suddenly commended itself, he raised his head, flashed one quick glance at Mr. Hartzler, and resumed his position. At the close of the service he at once drew Mr. Hartzler aside to the pastor's study and abruptly announced: "I want you to come to Northfield next summer. Will you? I want to have a meeting to wait on God, and want *you*." This was rather too sudden for the other, who could not make an engagement so far ahead.

On August 4th of the following year, however, he received the following letter:

NORTHFIELD, MASS.

"DEAR MR. HARTZLER: Enclosed you will find a circular that will explain itself. [The call for the first conference.] I got a start towards it in your city when you spoke at the convention there about November 1st. Now, will you come? *I want* you above any other man in this *nation*. Do not say me *nay*, but come and let us wait on God together.

"Yours truly,

"D. L. MOODY."

The call, entitled "A Convocation for Prayer," was as follows:

"Feeling deeply this great need, and believing that its reward is in reserve for all who honestly seek it, a gathering is hereby called to meet in Northfield, Mass., from September 1st to 10th inclusive, the object of which is not so much to study the Bible (though the Scriptures will be searched daily for instruction and promises) as for solemn self-consecration, for pleading God's promises, and waiting upon Him for a fresh anointment of power from on high.

"Not a few of God's chosen servants from our own land and from over the sea will be present to join with us in prayer and counsel.

"All ministers and laymen, and those women who are helpers and laborers together with us in the Kingdom and patience of our Lord Jesus Christ—and, indeed, all Christians who are hungering for intimate fellowship with God and for power to do His work—are most cordially invited to assemble with us.

"It is also hoped that those Christians whose hearts are united with us in desire for this new enduement of power, but who cannot be present, will send us salutation and greeting by letter, that there may be concert of prayer with them throughout the land during these days of waiting.

"D. L. MOODY."

Mr. Hartzler accepted the invitation, and was urged by Mr. Moody to assume charge and preside at all the meetings. With this request

—probably the only one he ever refused Mr. Moody—he positively declined to comply, and Mr. Moody was obliged to assume the leadership himself. In later years Mr. Hartzler became one of his most valued helpers at Northfield, both in the Mount Hermon School and at the several Northfield Conferences, and Mr. Moody often referred in terms of warmest appreciation to that convention in Cleveland where he first met this friend.

Over three hundred visitors responded to the first call. Those who could not be accommodated in East Hall, the one dormitory building of the Northfield Seminary at this time, filled the recitation building, and crowded the astonished town, some camping out in tents wherever a sheltered corner was to be found. The village church was scarcely large enough for a meeting-place, and a large tent was pitched behind Mr. Moody's house.

The second convention was held the year following; then, owing to Mr. Moody's campaigns in Great Britain, there was an interval of three years; but since a third gathering, in 1885, they have been held without interruption every successive year during the early part of August.

The meetings of the first conference were largely devotional, study being directed especially to the doctrine of the Holy Spirit. Many prayers were offered in behalf of the new institutions at Northfield, designed, as they were, to be distinctly a place for Christian nurture and a training-school for Christian laborers. The meeetings proved most impressive and fruitful.

"It is safe to say that in modern times no such gathering as the first Northfield conference has been witnessed," writes Mr. Hartzler. "Like the Jerusalem Pentecost, there were present 'devout men out of every nation under heaven.' America, Europe, Asia, and Africa had their representatives. It was interesting to find brethren there from almost every State in the Union; from Mexico, Canada, England, Scotland, Wales, South Africa, Athens, Smyrna, Cappadocia, and many other lands and cities; pastors and evangelists, professors and editors, elders and deacons, devout women and earnest youth, and '*all with one accord in one place*.'

" Another remarkable feature of the convocation was the wide-spread interest and sympathy with the object of the gathering, which was manifested in hundreds of letters and telegrams that came pouring in from all parts of this and other lands. Mr. Moody began to receive these communications weeks before the meetings opened, and they kept coming by scores even to the closing day. Christian associations, colleges, young ladies' seminaries, churches, camp meetings, women's prayer-meetings, individual ministers and laymen, and almost every class and condition of Christian people were in communication with those present. It is especially noticeable that a large proportion of the letters were from ministers of the various denominations.

" At the close of the ninth day there were more than three thousand requests for prayers piled up on Mr. Moody's desk. He had held them until that time, feeling that those present needed first to draw near to God in prevailing prayer for themselves before they began to pray for others. He learned also that meetings for the same object were being held in a number of places. He had no programme for the meeting. At first he took no leading part in the speaking, calling others to the front, but finally he yielded to the general desire to hear him, and preached two or three sermons on the Holy Spirit. The main object of the conference, as set forth in the call, was so manifestly approved of God that it was steadily kept in view from beginning to end. The object was 'solemn self-consecration, pleading God's promises, and waiting on Him for a fresh anointing of power from on high.'

" 'Don't think of your homes, your families, your work, or your churches now,' said Mr. Moody at one of the meetings. 'Don't pray for anything or anybody but yourself. Attend now to your own heart only.'

" One day a man arose who said that he had been five years on the

THE NEW AUDITORIUM, NORTHFIELD. THE CENTRE OF THE CONFERENCES.

On the Northfield Auditorium Platform.

Mr. Sankey at the organ. Mount Hermon Quartette at left.

Mount of Transfiguration. Mr. Moody cast a quick glance upon the speaker and flashed into his face a sharp question:

" 'How many souls did you lead to Christ last year?'

" 'Well, I don't know,' was the astonished reply.

" 'Have you saved any?' persisted Mr. Moody.

" 'I don't know that I have,' answered the man with a depressed air.

" 'Well,' said Mr. Moody, 'we don't want that kind of a mountain-top experience. When a man gets up so high that he cannot reach down and save poor sinners, there is something wrong.'

" Meetings were held in the Seminary chapel and also daily in a large tent on a green knoll near Mr. Moody's house, later known as 'Round Top,' and now the burial-place of the evangelist. The men met in this tent, and the women held their meetings in the Seminary chapel. At the close of the morning meetings in the tent other meetings were held in Bonar Glen, a shady ravine under the trees, and in the Seminary. To many these meetings are still memorable, and will be while life lasts."

Dr. Hartzler refers to one meeting which he considered especially sacred. It was held in a large tent on Round Top.

" Under common impulse the little company of twenty-six clasped one another's hands, stood in a circle, and entered into a solemn covenant of consecration with God and with one another. Some one proposed that each one take a list of the names and addresses of all, and that we pledge ourselves to pray daily for each other till death.

" 'No,' said Mr. Moody, 'don't bind yourselves to do that. Pray for one another, of course, but don't pledge yourselves to do it every day, lest you burden your conscience and make an irksome duty out of what should be a delightful privilege.' "

Some words of caution spoken by Mr. Moody at the close of this meeting may well be recalled at this time:

" Don't go away and talk so much about these meetings as about Christ; the world needs Him.

"Every place where God leads, there is your field.

"Don't talk an inch beyond your experience.

"A holy life will produce the deepest impression. Lighthouses blow no horns; they only shine.

"Confessions should only extend to parties sinned against.

"Look out for the devil at the foot of the mountain."

Among the interesting incidents of that meeting which have been received from friends two are given:

"We were perhaps a hundred men, seated on the clean straw under the tent at noon, on Round Top. Mr. Moody was leading the conversation hour. He sat sturdily against the central tent-pole. Out came the plump question:

"'Brethren, how many of you have so grown in grace that you can bear to have your faults told?'

"Many hands went up. Quick as a flash, but not sharply or insultingly, Moody turned to a young Episcopal minister in front of him and said:

"'Brother, you have spoken thirteen times in three days here, and perhaps shut out twelve other good men from speaking.'

"It was true. The young man had been presuming and officious. Mr. Moody fitted him fairly. He had held up his hand as one willing to be chided for fault, but he could not bear it. He owned no fault or sorrow, but stoutly defended himself—or tried to—only making his case really the worse. Then a real old Yankee vinegar-face on the outer rim of the circle turned loose and sharply berated Moody for his bluntness. The good man blushed, but listened until the abuse was over; then, suggestively covering his face, he spoke through his fingers.

"'Brethren, I admit all the fault my friend charges on me; but, brethren, *I did not hold up my hand!*'"

At one of these meetings for Christian workers Mr. Moody presented a very high ideal for the ministry, and spoke severely of those who failed in their sacred calling. His words were very pointed, and a young theologue who was present winced, and spoke out ingenuously:

"Mr. Moody, I don't see any such ministers as you describe." It was a frank and outspoken remonstrance, but not rude. Quick as a flash came the retort:

"You are a young man yet; you will see many of them. Tarry in Jericho until your beard be grown."

The reply was unjust and it hurt, yet there was too much life in the meeting for stopping. In writing of the scene, a friend says:

"It went on with a clear sense that the evangelist had dropped a little from his standard of loving courtesy to his guests. He could have ignored it; the tide of his eloquence was full. Yet the most eloquent was to come. In my heart has ever since been written a memory which brings moisture into my eyes yet, and ranks itself unquestionably as the greatest thing I ever saw Moody do.

"'Friends,' he said, 'I answered my dear young friend over there very foolishly as I began this meeting. I ask God to forgive me, and I ask the forgiveness of my brother.' And straightway he walked over to him and took him by the hand. That meeting needed no after-meeting. It was dramatically and spiritually made perfect. The man of iron will proved that he had mastered the hardest words of all earth's languages, 'I am sorry.'"

The many testimonials of blessing that resulted from the first Conference led Mr. Moody to call a second gathering the following year, which continued through the entire month of August. Dr. Andrew A. Bonar was the leading speaker on this occasion, and his impressions are thus given in his diary, recently published:

"August 4th. Northfield. Began yesterday, but specially to-day the Conference took shape. Was requested to open, which I did from Exodus, xxxiv., Communion with God. A gathering of God's people from every quarter."

. . . .

"August 13th. Much exercised about getting power from on

high, about which much conversation. I am rather disappointed that there is not more prayer throughout the day, but the atmosphere is delightful—so much brotherly love, so much Biblical truth, so much delight in whatever exalts Christ.

"August 14th. Preached on John, iii. 30. Mr. Moody as kind as possible and most earnest in all work."

When Mr. Moody was abroad in 1892, Dr. A. J. Gordon, of Boston, had charge of the meetings, and the following year, when the World's Fair Campaign engrossed all of Mr. Moody's energies, Dr. Gordon, assisted by H. M. Moore, again conducted the Conference.

In 1891 the Rev. F. B. Meyer, of London, a prominent speaker at the Keswick Conference in England, was present at Northfield, and the subjective side of Christian living received special prominence. There was no advocacy of "sinless perfection," but a clear presentation of the possibilities of a life truly yielded to God and the privilege it afforded of living free from the bondage of sin. The message of this teacher was markedly fruitful in the lives and ministries of many who were present. Mr. Meyer returned in succeeding years, and other English speakers have laid great emphasis of late on this line of teaching, including, among others, Prebendary Webb-Peploe, Andrew Murray, and G. Campbell Morgan.

There again Mr. Moody showed the sound judgment that guided his work, for he refused to limit the Northfield work to any one phase of Christian truth. Northfield was to be representative of all the truth contained in God's Word, and while giving due prominence to the importance of subjective dealing, he accompanied it with lectures from the leading American ministers on methods of Christian work, Bible interpretation, and all the other varied experiences of a wide and charitable conception of Christian thought and activity. Missionary interests have been presented by representatives of all lands, while city, frontier, and evangelistic work have received the due recognition they deserve.

The wisdom of this course is amply proved by the continued

Interior Northfield Auditorium During Conference.

Members of New York Presbytery in Attendance at Northfield Conference, 1899.

MR. MOODY AS HE APPEARED AS CHAIRMAN OF THE NORTHFIELD CONFERENCES.

growth of these Conferences and the many testimonies received from those who have been blessed in attending them.

For years Stone Hall, the recitation hall of the Northfield Seminary, was used as the audience-room for the summer Conferences, but in time this became overcrowded, and in 1894 the beautiful auditorium on the crest of the hill overlooking the campus was erected, primarily for these gatherings.

"I have always tried to build according to my faith," said Mr. Moody on the opening night. "This time my friends think my faith has carried me away. They do not believe that I shall ever see this building full." Within a week, on the first Sunday morning, seats, platform, stairways, and aisles were filled with an audience numbering about three thousand, and this experience has been repeated every year.

The following call, dated June 1, 1899, was the last one that Mr. Moody issued:

"DEAR FRIENDS AND FELLOW-WORKERS:

"The seventeenth General Conference of Christian Workers will be held at Northfield, August 1st to 20th, and all of God's people who are interested in the study of His Word, in the development of their own Christian lives, in a revival of the spiritual life of the Church, in the conversion of sinners, and in the evangelization of the world, are cordially invited to be present.

"I am glad to send out this invitation to my fellow-workers because I believe that such a gathering was never more needed than this year. Many thoughtful men have come to feel strongly that the hope of the Church to-day is in a deep and wide-spread revival. We are confronted with difficulties that can be met in no other way. The enemy has come in like a flood—it is time for those who believe in a supernatural religion to look to God to lift up a standard against him. Oh, for a revival of such power that the tide of unbelief and worldliness that is sweeping in upon us shall be beaten back; that every Christian shall be lifted to a higher level of life and power, and multitudes of perishing souls be converted to God! Why not? God's arm is not shortened, nor His ear heavy. I believe the sound of the going in the tops of the mulberry trees may already be heard.

"The history of revivals proves that such a work must begin at the house of God. Who can doubt that if somehow the Church could be thoroughly aroused—not a mere scratching of the surface of our emotions, but a deep heart-work that shall make us right with God and clothe us with power in prayer and service—the last months of this century would witness the mightiest movements of the Holy Spirit since Pentecost? The whole aim of this conference is to help bring this about.

"Why need any pastor or church fail to share in the blessing? How sad the experience of that worker who sees others greatly used in such a movement and himself passed by—other fields rejoicing with the joy of harvest while his still lies barren and unfruitful! It need not be so. Let us break up our fallow ground, seek a fresh anointing of the Spirit, and then move forward, expecting great things of God.

"We are to have with us some of the most widely known teachers of this country and England—men on whose labors God has already set His seal. There will be the great help that comes from close contact with hundreds of earnest men and women, almost all of them engaged in some form of Christian work. The accommodations for boarding are ample and pleasant, and the expense moderate. I shall be glad to hear from all who are planning to come. May I not ask Christian people to begin now to pray for a special outpouring of the Spirit upon every meeting of the Conference?

"Yours in the Master's service,

"D. L. Moody."

In response to this invitation the largest gathering ever held at Northfield met during the first three weeks of August. The Presbytery of New York engaged Weston Hall, and sixty of its pastors and members were entertained there, several accompanied by their wives. Three or four of the leading pastors of the city were among the speakers at the Auditorium and on Round Top.

During the last August Conference Mr. Moody started a new work in establishing a week's Conference for young people, in which he had the hearty coöperation of John Willis Baer, of the United Society of Christian Endeavor. This gathering aimed to reach young people in the churches, and by informal conference advise the best methods of work.

In another chapter we have alluded to the development of the Students' Conference. The marked results of this gathering, as well as that of the August Conference, led the officers of the Young Women's Christian Association to institute a Conference for young women on lines similar to that for young men. This met for the first time in 1893, and has steadily increased in attendance and influence with succeeding years. The leading women's colleges are represented at this gathering by large delegations, as well as many of the leading Young Women's Christian Associations.

A new feature was introduced in 1899, which gave Mr. Moody great encouragement and suggested a new phase of Northfield work. The Lowell Young Women's Christian Association had sent a large delegation to the Conferences, and in the winter of 1898-99 it was proposed by the secretary, Miss Louise Pierson, to erect a house where twenty-five or thirty young women could live at a slight expense and enjoy the advantages of Northfield. Between the Seminary and the Northfield Hotel, accordingly, "Lowell Lodge" was erected, and opened on August 15, 1899. Twenty-five self-supporting young women occupied this building during the Bible Conference. Some of them boarded themselves, paying a dollar a week for lodging, but the majority had their meals at the Lodge, which cost two or three dollars additional. In his address at the dedication, Mr. Moody said:

"I am more than pleased with what has been accomplished here.

We give the land very gladly because we believe it is going to open up a new plan, which I hope will be a great blessing not only to the town of Northfield, but to the country. If people see that such a house can be put up for $1,000, some of them will duplicate this one. We will furnish the land for nothing. If girls come here from Lowell and get stirred up by God's Spirit so that they go back and carry a blessing to others, we shall be a thousand times repaid for the little paltry land that we give. We don't want a city in Northfield; we want to spread out. There is no reason why the whole mountain-side should not be built up.

"The greatest trouble we have is to entertain the people who come here. You can imagine that to have twelve hundred extra people in a little town like this, as we have had for the last few days, makes somebody work. Now, if people will undertake to put up houses where they can board themselves it will be a great relief. In that way they can get a room and live on bread and milk and blueberries, for about two dollars a week. We don't ask them to come here to pamper the body, but to feed the soul.

"I believe the blessing of God is going to rest upon this building and those who come here. I think Northfield is just about as near Paradise as we can get on earth."

CHAPTER XXXIII

VISIT TO THE HOLY LAND

AS early as January, 1887, Mr. and Mrs. Peter McKinnon, of Scotland, urged Mr. Moody to accompany them to Palestine. That the invitation touched a very sympathetic chord is evident from the response called forth:

"MY DEAR MRS. MCKINNON:

"Yours of January 10th came to-day. I could hardly keep back the tears as I thought of going to Calvary, Gethsemane, and the Mount of Olives with you. My heart is with you, and I cannot tell you what a self-denial it is to me not to go. For years I have wanted to do so, and though I have never left my work for pleasure in my life, I think I should have gone this time if I had not been as I am. For three years they have been trying to get me to go to Chicago, and I told them that if they would do certain things I would give them three months. They have done what I asked them to do, and so I must stay here now until April or May. I do long to take a trip, and would like to go with you and your husband more than with any one else; but I must decline for another thing: Miss Holton * is dying, and I would go to her if I could get away. She is in California, and the letter that came last night says she will not live thirty days—and I cannot go to her! Poor Fannie, how sad it is for her to lay down her work and

* A cousin and for many years a member of his household, Miss Holton was one of Mr. Moody's most efficient helpers in the establishing of Northfield Seminary.

die! But I am glad she is ready, and is not dreading death as she once was. The sting is all gone, but it is so hard to die away from her sisters.

"Remember me to all old friends; think of me and pray for me in the Garden and on Olivet and at Calvary, and take one good look when in Bethany and see if you can see the place where the Master was once seen, and ask Him to come back again.

"Thanking you again for your great kindness,

"Yours as ever,

"D. L. Moody."

In February, 1892, the generous and cordial invitation was repeated. Mr. Moody was then engaged in Scotland, and it was impossible for him to leave his work. This was his response:

"Paisley, Scotland, February 10, 1892.

"My dear Mrs. McKinnon:

"I would be glad to go to Palestine, but there are some reasons that will keep me. First, the work. It would be a pity to leave it now, and I am committed until the 1st of April. Second, in April, when it grows warmer, I come down with headache and suffer a good deal unless I keep where it is cool. Third, my wife says that Palestine is said to be unhealthy, and no one can go there in the spring. So I think, if ever I see the land of Abraham and his children, I shall have to see it when I go in another body, and it may be I will see it with Christ Himself. I cannot tell you how glad I am your husband is better. Tell him I pray for him daily, and trust it will be the will of God to lift him up again. I did not know I loved him so much until I heard he was so sick.

"Mr. Sankey has gone up to London to attend the funeral of Mr. Spurgeon; they wanted me to go, but I could not get away. The churches, halls, etc., were all engaged and this kept me; I am thankful to tell you the work is good here, and I have much to encourage me, yet I get homesick at times and long to see my family. May the blessing of God rest on you and your dear husband is the prayer of

"Your true friend,

"D. L. Moody."

A man of such energetic spirit as Mr. Moody found very little opportunity for holidays. He sacredly tried to observe one day in seven as a rest-day, but otherwise he was almost constantly occupied except when journeying—and even then people recognized him and sought his spiritual advice, and were not denied. Of late years, with the multiplication of his schools, conferences, and other organizations for promoting the cause of Christ, there was less and less opportunity for withdrawing for any length of time from active participation in their control.

Still anxious to carry out their plan, Mr. and Mrs. McKinnon deferred their trip until April, and finally prevailed on Mr. Moody to accompany them.

Taking his wife and his son Paul, he went from Paris to Rome, where he was to join Mr. McKinnon's party. His interest in everything about him was intense, and, as usual, it centred particularly in the people and their methods of life.

The farming on the hillsides specially attracted his attention; to see men living in their little houses perched like crows in a nest on the edge of the snow line, reclaiming patches of land, some of them hardly twenty feet square, excited his wonder. He would frequently say: "Look here! See that hillside farming! That beats all I ever saw. If ever I hear a Northfield man complaining of his farm again, I'll fall on him." This reference to his size caused much merriment.

On their arrival at Rome, Mr. and Mrs. McKinnon joined the party, and after breakfast they made a tour of the city with a guide. Mr. Moody was unusually silent when going through the beautiful churches, speaking only occasionally. The Coliseum proved a great attraction. He sat on a huge column that was lying on the ground and surveyed the amphitheatre, calling up the various historical accounts of the scenes of murder, cruelty, and martyrdom enacted there.

A stalwart peasant passed by one of the corridors, and Mr. Moody stopped him.

"Tell him he is a fine, powerful man," he said to Ortini, the guide. Ortini did so. The peasant beamed on all the party and spoke rapidly in Italian.

"What did he say?" asked Mr. Moody.

"He said he was heavier, but he is losing flesh. He was too poor to drink wine. If he had wine he would look sleek like you."

"Tell him I am a teetotaler," said Mr. Moody. Ortini did so. The man smiled incredulously, as if such a thing were impossible.

"Tell him it is true," said Mr. Moody.

The man, still laughing, said, producing a loaf from beneath his coat, "You may be a teetotaler in drink, but you are no teetotaler in eating."

The peasant said he had only two francs a day for his family of seven children. Mr. Moody advised him to go to America, and then gave him a two-franc piece. As the party passed on, the man called to the guide, and ran back, holding out the piece of money.

"What is the matter?" said Mr. Moody.

"He says it is the Pope's money and is not good in Rome. Will you give him another piece?"

Mr. Moody could hardly realize that the Pope's silver was not good in Rome, but exchanged the piece of money for another.

He was greatly impressed by the places of historical interest. Anything that had a touch of Paul's life in it moved him deeply. Every place that could be verified as being in any way connected with Mr. Moody's greatest Bible hero was carefully sought out. The Rev. J. Gordon Gray took him out to the Appian Way, and when the original pavement was reached, Moody insisted on alighting from the carriage and going on foot over the stones which St. Paul had trodden as he entered Rome. The ruins of Nero's palace on the Palatine Hill had

MR. MOODY PREACHING ON "THE HILL CALLED CALVARY," OUTSIDE JERUSALEM.

Mr. Moody stands at direct angle of the two stars.

THE CHILDREN OF JERUSALEM FIND MR. MOODY A GENEROUS DISTRIBUTER OF "BACKSHEESH."

WITH DAUGHTER AND GRANDDAUGHTER.

far more attraction for him than St. Peter's or any of the spectacles of modern Rome. He seemed to take great delight in the many monuments which Rome had erected to Paul, saying that the emperors who tyrannized the earth were remembered only by ruins.

When he visited St. Peter's he spoke of the sad degeneration of the communion service from the pure faith of the early church.

In the evening Mr. Moody preached in the Presbyterian church, of which Dr. Gray was pastor. About one hundred and thirty people were present. The sermon delivered was the one that he gave on the last afternoon in Kansas City, on "Grace," from the text: "*The grace of God that bringeth salvation,*" etc.

Friday, April 8th, the party started for Naples, and sailed from there for Port Said, which was reached four days later. Writing from Port Said, Mr. Moody said:

"We are now near where the children of Israel passed when they went out of Egypt. The country is sandy and barren, but the canal is a wonder, and it seems strange to be in this land of the Pharaohs, of Moses and Aaron and Joseph."

After coaling the steamer at Port Said they sailed on the Suez Canal to Ismailia. Little sleep was taken that night. About midnight they passed the old Syrian Road at Candara, where the ancient Jews and others travelled from Europe and Asia into Egypt, where, no doubt, Joseph was taken by the caravan. At Ismailia a train was taken to Alexandria through the land of Goshen, full of interest to every Bible student. Mr. Moody's thirst for information was satisfied here, as elsewhere, by an early morning ride with a guide before the rest of the party were up. At Alexandria a boat was taken for Joppa.

The Holy Land was sighted on Good Friday. The landing at Joppa was not made until late in the afternoon, and at about four o'clock the start was made for Jerusalem. Supper was eaten at Ramleh. Mr. Moody finished before the rest, and said he would go out into the air. When the party was ready to start he was nowhere to be seen, and calling failed to reach him. The carriages were entered, and after a while he was overtaken. He had informed the guide that he was going on before, but was now beginning to be frightened, as he had seen several dark-looking Arabs scowling as they passed and spitting at him, and he thought it wiser to take the carriage.

The moon rose brightly over the mountains as the carriages drove on. About one o'clock a cup of coffee was served at Colonieh. Active signs of life were seen along the road. Caravans with camels heavily laden passed many times. Jerusalem was reached at three o'clock Saturday morning, and after a few hours' rest a walk was taken about the city, out to the tomb of David, alongside of which was a little house, where, in an upper chamber, it is said that the Master ate the last supper. Mr. Moody was incredulous on all the traditional sights seen in Jerusalem except the Temple and Calvary. He said that most of the localities were obscure, " but the hills you cannot change nor remove."

Mr. George D. Mackay, of New York, who joined the party on the trip, says of this first day in the Holy City:

" Our walk around Zion Hill finished at the Joppa Gate. Just before reaching it we saw a group of lepers. The sight was pitiful in the extreme. The thought of contamination was uppermost, and we hurried by, anxious to pass such misery. In the afternoon, Paul, Donald [Mr. Mackay's son], and I got donkeys and rode to the top of the Mount of Olives. On the way we passed Calvary."

Mr. Moody took his Bible early Easter morning and went to the Mount of Olives. In the afternoon he preached to a large audience on Calvary under the auspices of the English Church Missionary Society. At least three hundred people were present, largely native and visiting Christians. Some Mussulmans and Jews came to listen, attracted by the crowd. Mr. Moody was in excellent spirits and preached with an emotion that he had rarely, if ever, equalled in any previous sermon. He hardly chose a text, beginning by saying that he had preached for thirty years, but had never felt the awe of God that he did at that moment.

He pointed out the various spots in sight and linked them with their stories in the Bible—Mizpah and Samuel, Moriah and Abraham, the distant hills of Moab and Ruth, Olivet and Jesus. He likened the sacrifice of Isaac to the coming offering up of Jesus, and spoke of how Jesus must have felt as He passed this hill in boyhood, knowing that there He should offer up His life. He spoke of the feasts that Jesus had attended on yonder temple site, and how the burden of His preaching at each one was the new birth in the power of the Spirit; and closed, after saying that the greatest blessing of his life had been the birth in the Spirit, by an appeal to every Christian person to seek God until the baptism of the Spirit should be as fire in their hearts, like that called down by Elijah on the altar of Carmel.

The sermon was preached with a fervor beyond description, and left an ineffaceable impression on all who heard it. A collection was taken at the conclusion for the London Jews' Society School, whose scholars, in number about eighty boys and girls, attended the meeting.

The weekdays were spent in visiting places of interest in Jerusalem and the immediate vicinity. One day was devoted to Hebron. In Jerusalem all the sacred spots, like the Holy Sepulchre, were too uncertain, or else too transformed by tawdriness, to please him.

On Monday the party went to Bethlehem and Solomon's pools. At Bethlehem they drank at the well so dearly loved by David, and photographed a group of Arabs at the curb. There they saw the hills where, no doubt, David tended his flocks and wrote many of the psalms, and also the field of Boaz and the shepherd's field. Later they visited the Church of the Nativity.

Mr. Moody's favorite places were the Mount of Olives, to which he repeatedly returned, and the little village of Bethany, over the brow of the hill. Here, at any rate, he knew he was in the midst of scenes where the Master had often walked.

When he went to Bethany with Mrs. Moody, Mr. and Mrs. McKinnon, and Miss Love, their arrival was celebrated as usual—a horde of children were sent as a general reception committee, to extract from the visitors what "backsheesh" they could in the way of silver, copper, lead, and zinc, which the coin of the Turkish realm furnishes in such infinite and deceptive variety. Some pretended blindness or deafness to work on the visitors' pity; others carried babies, whose little chubby hands were hardly big enough to clutch the coin they held them out for. They immediately surrounded Mr. Moody. He was always generous; on this occasion especially so, because of the unusual nature of the place and its beautiful traditions. He asked if any of them had the name of Mary or Martha, and was agreeably surprised to learn that a number of them had. This opened his pockets again. The news of his generosity rapidly spread through the village, and new faces and hands were quickly added to the crowd; all surging around him in frantic efforts to get the lion's share of the spoils. He was besieged. They swarmed on every side. "Backsheesh!" (gift money) "Backsheesh!" they cried. It was difficult to move. The visit to Bethany was rapidly converting itself into a fight for existence. The case was getting desperate, so he called a truce. He told the dragoman to ask them to be quiet while he made an address. He did so. Then Mr. Moody talked, and the dragoman interpreted. He said in substance:

"I have come six thousand miles to see this little village of Bethany. It was a place my Master loved to visit, and I have come to see it because He loved it. I am very glad to meet you all, and I hope you will grow up to be good men and good women. Now I want to be alone; I have no more 'backsheesh,' and I bid you all good-bye!"

A fine-looking young boy, about sixteen years old, said he wanted to reply to the address. He spoke fluently, and with the grace of an orator. He said:

"We are glad to see the gentleman and his friends who have come

MR. MOODY'S NORTHFIELD HOME.

DINING-ROOM IN MR. MOODY'S HOME.

Mr. Moody Hailing a Friend.

A snap shot.

Mr. Moody as his Townsfolk Knew him.

so far. But the gentleman must not think that his actions are equal to the importance of his visit. Six thousand miles is a long way to come, and the gentleman must have sacrificed much to make the visit. In consequence it is natural for us to expect that he would be munificent in his gifts of 'backsheesh,' which he has not been, and we expect that he will now give a great deal more!"

Mr. Moody, who had regarded with surprise and delight the eloquence and grace of the boy, was so disgusted at the conclusion that he took flight.

"I did think that boy had a soul above 'backsheesh,'" he said.

Some one casually asked Mr. Moody whether he thought any of those children was named Mary or Martha.

"Certainly. Why not?"

"Nothing, only they were all boys."

Mr. Mackay thus describes the visit to the Mosque of Omar:

"In the mosque we all wore felt slippers, which they tied on over our shoes. Mr. McKinnon carried a pair of slippers and put them on. This is necessary, as no heathen foot must touch the sacred floor. Somehow Paul Moody's slippers came off, and, to our consternation, he was discovered by one of the mosque officers to be tramping about with his infidel foot bared to the sole of his shoe. The scene that followed was enough to terrify him. The air was full of Arabic indignation. There were a rushing and a scolding and a wild excitement that were growing decidedly distressing.

"Paul stood holding his foot up so that he would not further contaminate the floor. His mother, pale and nervous, was assisting him, and looking as if she would give anything to get out alive. Arabs began to assemble and jabber ferociously. Meanwhile some wise attendant had got a new pair of slippers, and when Paul was reshod we began to breathe freely, especially as we saw the Arabs were growing calmer and apparently were going to work no vengeance. My own shoe was appearing through the wearing felt, and I began to feel squeamish myself when I thought that the exposure of one-half the sole of my shoe, which was visible every step I took, might repeat the scene we had just gone through."

One morning at five o'clock, in company with Mr. Mackay, Mr. Moody went to the Mount of Olives. It rained, and as they ascended, a beautiful rainbow spanned the city, its base resting on the Temple court at one end and just beyond the Gate of Herod at the other. It looked like a rainbow of promise of the glory to come at Jerusalem. Mr. Moody was surprised when they reached the crest of the mountain, as he had not expected to see such a glorious view of the hills of Judea, the Dead Sea, and the Jordan Valley. He was greatly delighted. Their special quest was the Mount of Ascension, as neither was satisfied with the spot shown. On the Bethany spur of the mountain the two travellers read again the story of Lazarus and the ascension of Jesus. Together they prayed, Mr. Moody pleading with the Lord to come again quickly and to sanctify their visit to that spot by their growth in grace. He was deeply moved, and prayed most fervently. It was fully eleven o'clock when they returned, having been nearly five hours on the mountain. In the afternoon they went to the Jews' Wailing Place and the Pool of Siloam.

When it rained Mr. Moody sent for two members of the London Jews' Society, who called at the hotel, and for two hours he and the rest of the party who wished to do so plied them with questions about the interesting points in Jerusalem.

Once, seeing some poppies on the east Temple wall, he said, "Look there! Drops of blood, a symbol of the blood shed for sin! It seems as though the ground itself is testifying for Christ against the unbelief of the city."

The native children in Jerusalem amused him greatly. On his exit from the hotel he would invariably be surrounded by a crowd of ragged little Arabs, and entertain himself by giving them backsheesh. The older natives interested him also, and he conversed with them constantly, questioning them as to their habits. By the end of the week he was well informed as to the manner of life of the people, the condition of agriculture, the system of government, and a dozen other things.

On his second Sunday in Jerusalem Mr. Moody was up at four o'clock to see the sun rise on the Mount of Olives. He wanted to see the sun come up beyond the hills of Moab. His visit was successful, and he joined his party at breakfast much pleased. He said that he had seen the sun rise and that as he looked over this land of promise, in his imagination he saw Moses' face, surrounded by the sun as a halo. He was in ecstasies over the beautiful eastern view from the Mount of Olives—the Valley of the Jordan, the Dead Sea, the hills of Moab, all seeming only five miles away, although more than twenty. In the afternoon Mr. Moody preached beneath Calvary on the west. There was a rumor that the government had forbidden any Turkish subject to attend the meeting at Calvary under pain of arrest, but there was no truth in it. The Mohammedans had criticised Mr. Moody's preaching from a tombstone in their cemetery the previous Sunday. Mr. Moody said:

"I don't blame them. I wouldn't want any man to stand on my father's grave to preach a sermon." The truth was that the cemetery on Calvary was such a dilapidated affair that the visitors took it for a deserted cemetery, as, indeed, it was.

Mr. Moody preached on "The Good Samaritan" to an audience about as large as that of Easter Day. At the close of the sermon he announced that on the previous Sunday the collection was twenty pounds, although he had only asked for ten. He now wanted ten pounds more for a blind boy to go into the Church Missionary Society's School for a year. The hat was passed, and again twenty pounds was raised.

On Monday morning Mr. and Mrs. Moody and Paul went again to the Mount of Olives, and at noon they started for Joppa. "Thus ends my three weeks with Mr. Moody," wrote Mr. Mackay. "It has been a blessed experience for me."

Mr. McKinnon's party then returned to Egypt. Several days were spent in Cairo, visiting the Pyramids and other points of interest, and in the first week of May the party started for Italy. May was spent in Naples and Florence, the Italian lakes and Switzerland, and by the end of the month Mr. Moody was again in England, having been absent for two months, probably the longest vacation he had ever taken since he had entered business as a boy of seventeen. It was not an unbroken rest, however, for he had preached in Rome, Jerusalem, Cairo, Naples, and Paris, sometimes twice a day, besides conducting numerous Bible readings, to gratify the importunities of English and American friends, who recognized him wherever he went. Moreover, he used to lead the most unlikely people on the most unlikely occasions into direct personal talk regarding their spiritual condition.

" Mr. Moody," said a lady of rank, " no one ever talked to me like this before."

" Then it was quite time somebody did so," he replied, and they remained good friends thereafter.

His visit to the Holy Land remained a vivid, living memory. He constantly referred to it in private conversation and public discourse, regretting on the one hand the present mean condition of Palestine, which, however, he believed was in accord with prophecy, and on the other looking forward with joy to its restoration, when the feet of the Messiah shall once more stand on Olivet.

CHAPTER XXXIV

Capacity for Work

TO those who knew Mr. Moody closely it was not difficult to understand the secret of his capacity for hard work. The magnificent constitution with which he was endowed enabled him to undertake work that demanded continued exertion and special effort. But, beyond this, he was able to throw off all burden of mind when he had done his utmost. "It's worry that kills," he would say, and after the most exacting work he would be able to relieve his mind of all anxiety and rest as quietly as a child. He believed that God would carry on His own work, and after doing all in his power he would cast his burden on the Lord. Thus it happened that he could sleep almost "to order." A few minutes before going to address a large audience he would lie down for a nap, asking some one to waken him in ten or fifteen minutes. Added to this was his genius of generalship, by which he would delegate to others the work they could do, and thus spare himself the trouble of details.

Mr. Moody's evangelistic zeal could never be contented with missions in Great Britain and America. Reports of the great opportunities among English-speaking people in other countries were always a great inducement to accept frequent invitations to visit the great centres of Eastern life. It had been a long-cherished plan of his to make a tour of the world, and in the fall of 1888 Mr. Moody left home with the purpose of going to Japan and China and thence to India. Arriving on the Pacific coast, he found it impossible to obtain release from a tentative acceptance of several invitations to conduct meetings. At this time, therefore, he was unable to take the journey, and during the winter he visited, instead, the cities of the Pacific coast from Vancouver to San Diego. He continued to receive repeated invitations to visit India and China, and in the fall of 1891 he again contemplated the trip. But again it was abandoned, this time after arriving in London, where he was advised by medical men of the danger of such a climate to a man of his age and susceptibility to heat exhaustion. The fact that he suffered from seasickness made the voyages in tropical climates still more objectionable. This was a great disappointment, yet at this time he entered upon a work in Great Britain that for sheer physical endurance must have taxed his strength more than any other mission he ever undertook, with the possible exception of the World's Fair Campaign. A few months before his leaving home, at the time of the Christian Conference, the Rev. John Smith and Dr. Moxey, of Edinburgh, came to Northfield. At one session of the conference Mr. Smith stepped to the front of the platform with a large bundle in his hands, which, he proceeded to explain, was a memorial to Mr. Moody from fifty towns and cities of Scotland, requesting him to make another evangelistic tour in that country. In presenting the petition to Mr. Moody, in behalf of Dr. Moxey and himself, he said that it was the most remarkable memorial ever presented to a Christian worker, at least from Scotland. It was one hundred and fifty feet long and contained twenty-five hundred signatures on its roll, which was nearly a foot thick, including representatives from all the Scotch churches and schools of thought.

Mr. Smith spoke briefly of the special need of Mr. Moody's work in Scotland, saying that the evangelist had the confidence of the churches as no other man had, and that he would bring to many evangelists a blessing which no other man could.

Mr. Moody received the package without a word, put it into the speaker's desk in front of him, and asked the people to engage in silent prayer "that we may be directed in regard to these matters."

No further reference was made to the invitation in public, but a decision was given later, and the tour was undertaken that fall.

Arriving in Scotland late in November, he began a series of meetings that continued till the end of March. An itinerary had been arranged by his old friend, Mr. William Robertson, of Carrubber's Close Mission, Edinburgh, whom he had given *carte blanche* to make appointments for these months. Writing of this four months' work, Mr. Robertson says: "I had a list of the towns drawn out that Mr. Moody visited in Scotland on his last trip. There were one hundred different places, and meetings were held in them all." During this winter he averaged three meetings a day, often in crowded and poorly ventilated halls and chapels.

Mr. Moody had many invitations to spend Christmas with Scotch friends. He preferred, however, to keep the day free in order to give another day to any special place in which there had been much blessing. The meetings in Wick had been exceptionally fruitful, and as the holiday drew near Mr. Moody resolved to return once more to this town for an evening meeting. Relating the experience of the day—a rather typical one as showing his faculty for making the most of time—Mr. Robertson says: "We started to drive across the Ord to Wick, a distance of thirty-seven miles. The sun rose as we left Helmsdale. After a little we got into a gully, from which we again saw the sun rise. Still further on we reached a spot where it again appeared over the hills. Mr. Moody said it would be a memorable Christmas day for him, as he had seen the sun rise three times. As we passed Berriedale, the seat of the Duke of Portland, we found some friends who, hearing that we were to drive that way, had arranged for a short service. In fifteen minutes two prayers were offered, a psalm sung, and Mr. Moody gave a brief Christmas address. At Leibster another halt was made, and another crowded meeting addressed in the Free Church. Wick was reached soon after two, a Bible reading held at three o'clock, and a great mass meeting at night. Early the next morning, train was taken for Elgin." Surely this was a full day's work for a holiday!

It is impossible to go over the work in detail in each place visited. The Scotch mission closed with final meetings in Edinburgh. It was a noticeable fact that at the last afternoon meeting both the moderators-elect of the coming Established and Free Church Assemblies, Professor Charteris and Professor Blaikie, were present, and in consequence of the crowded platform had to share between them the president's chair. This fact was taken as a crowning illustration of the brotherly and thoroughly unsectarian spirit which marked the mission in almost every place where the meetings were held throughout the length and breadth of Scotland.

Later in the year the writer had a personal experience of a similar nature in a six weeks' mission with Mr. Moody in Ireland. Concluding a short mission in Southampton, England, Sunday night, Mr. Moody started for Dublin, Ireland, on a train leaving after midnight, which carried no sleeping-car. Arriving in London before daybreak, he had to drive from Victoria Station to Euston Station to catch the train for Holyhead, where a four hours' passage across the Irish Channel completely prostrated him with seasickness. Dublin was reached by six o'clock in the afternoon, where, after a hasty supper, Mr. Moody addressed a large meeting. Here the audience had been waiting for some time, and the atmosphere was heavy. At the close of the meeting numbers of old friends pressed forward for a handshake and words of welcome, and it was near midnight before Mr. Moody was able to retire. He was entertained by Peter Drummond, who lived some distance out of the city, and he had to take leave of his host early, drive into Dublin, and get the seven o'clock train for Belfast Tuesday morning. It had been arranged that he should conduct a two weeks' mission in the large convention hall in Belfast a week later, and on his arrival the committee of ministers and laymen at whose invitation he had come, met him for conference regarding plans, and lunched with him at the Rev. Dr. Williamson's.

In Londonderry he had time for only a hurried supper after his arrival before going to a crowded meeting that had been awaiting him for over an hour, and it was late that night before he had any opportunity to rest. The remaining days of the week were equally taxing, as he visited six other towns during Wednesday, Thursday, and Friday, often speaking in crowded halls and twice in the open air. The very hospitality which is so characteristic of the Irish added to the demands upon his strength, as in several places, when he felt the need of rest and relaxation, he was entertained at meals where others were invited specially to meet him. Saturday, however, brought a much needed rest at the home of James White, of Fenaghy, and on the following day he began his Belfast mission by addressing ten thousand people in the crowded Convention Hall.

The last three weeks of his mission in Ireland were devoted to holding meetings in the southern counties, where an equally trying itinerary was arranged. Frequently the meetings were conducted in draughty halls, or even in market-places, and the bigotry and superstition of the uneducated masses in some places threatened more than once to make trouble. Never were conditions more trying for him than during that season, and near the close of the mission he began to show the effects of the strain under which he had been working.

In a few meetings that followed in England a heavy cold that he had taken became more pronounced, and on arriving in London to conduct a ten-day mission in Spurgeon's Tabernacle his voice almost entirely failed him. At this time he was accompanied by Mr. Stebbins and his son, and, yielding to their urgent solicitation, consented to see a physician. It was then that Mr. Moody first learned of the heart difficulty to which he finally succumbed. Writing of this occasion, Mr. Stebbins says:

"The third time that I went abroad to assist Mr. Moody was in the fall of 1892. He had engagements to visit several of the larger cities of England, and afterward to hold an eight-day mission in Spurgeon's Tabernacle. He had been suffering somewhat for several days with a throat trouble which gave him considerable anxiety lest it should interfere with his work, so on our arrival in London, with his consent, I sent for Dr. Habershon, a prominent young doctor, afterwards one of Mr. Gladstone's physicians, who made a careful examination of his throat and lungs, and incidentally the action of his heart. Before leaving us the doctor took me aside and told me that he had discovered an irregularity in the action of the heart, asking me if he should tell Mr. Moody.

"'Certainly,' I said; 'he would wish to know of any trouble of that kind.' He informed Mr. Moody of his discovery, and after assuring him that there was no occasion for alarm, but simply necessity for caution lest he should over-exert himself, he expressed the wish that Mr. Moody would allow him to make an appointment for a consultation with Sir Andrew Clarke, one of the most celebrated authorities on such diseases, as he did not wish his own judgment to be relied on wholly in the matter.

"Shortly before leaving London Mr. Moody saw Sir Andrew Clarke, driving immediately to the latter's office from a farewell breakfast given by Sir George Williams and a large number of other friends. After a thorough examination the physician confirmed the opinion of his friend regarding Mr. Moody's condition.

"In reply to Mr. Moody's inquiry regarding what he had done to bring on the difficulty, and how he should avoid increased trouble in the future, the celebrated doctor inquired how many times a day Mr. Moody was in the habit of speaking.

"'Oh, I usually preach three times a day.'

"'How many days in the week?'

"'Five days in the week, and on Sundays four or five times.'

"'You're a fool, sir; you're a fool!' was the brusque response. 'You're killing yourself.'

"'Well, Doctor,' said Mr. Moody, 'I take Saturday to rest. But may I ask you how many hours a day *you* work?'

"'Oh, I work sixteen or seventeen.'

" 'How many days a week?'

" 'Every day, sir; every day.'

" 'Then, Doctor, I think you're a bigger fool than I am, and you'll kill yourself first.'

" And with these pleasantries the two men parted, the celebrated physician to continue his wonderful ministry of healing for little more than a year, while Mr. Moody was permitted to work on for seven years, although with the consciousness that his summons might come at any moment."

CHAPTER XXXV

In Peril on the Deep

AT the close of this unusually trying campaign Mr. Moody passed through an experience that left a most solemn and lasting impression upon his mind. In November, after an absence of over twelve months, he secured passage for himself and his son on the North German Lloyd line, from Southampton for New York. A small company gathered at the station in London to see him off, and in company with two friends and his son he started for Southampton. The journey found Mr. Moody in the best of spirits. To be again on his way home had been a long-anticipated pleasure, and it was expected that a week later would find him back in America.

The last good-byes were said at Southampton, and the party went on board the Spree, at this time one of the fastest vessels of the line.

"When about three days on our voyage, I remember," says Mr. Moody, in describing this event, "I was lying on my couch, as I generally do at sea, congratulating myself on my good fortune, and feeling very thankful to God. I considered myself a very fortunate man, for in all my travels by land and sea I had never been in any accident of a serious nature.

"While engaged with these grateful thoughts, I was startled by a terrible crash and shock, as if the vessel had been driven on a rock. I did not at first feel much anxiety—perhaps I was too ill to think about it. My son jumped from his berth and rushed on deck. He was back again in a few moments, exclaiming that the shaft was broken and the vessel sinking. I did not at first believe that it could be so bad, but concluded to dress and go on deck. The report was only too true. The ship's passengers were naturally aroused, but in answer to frightened inquiries they were assured that it was only a broken shaft.

"The serious nature of the accident soon became evident, however, as other passengers rushed on deck declaring that their cabins were rapidly filling with water. Later it was found that the two fractured ends of the shaft, in revolving, had broken the stern-tube, admitting water into the two aftermost compartments, which were immediately filled. The bulkheads between the compartments were closed at once and braced with beams to resist the pressure of the water. For two days the ship drifted in this helpless condition, in momentary peril from the tremendous force of the water in the flooded compartments, which beat with tremendous force, as the ship rolled, against the next compartment. But for the skill of Captain Willigerod and his efficient engineers, Messrs. Meissel and Baum, the ship would have soon foundered.

"The officers and crew did all that they could to save the vessel. But it was soon found that the pumps were useless, for the water poured into the ship too rapidly to be controlled. There was nothing more in the power of man to do, and the ship was absolutely helpless, while the passengers could only stand still on the poor drifting, sinking ship and look into our possible watery graves.

"All this time, unknown to the passengers, the officers were making preparations for the last resort. The life-boats were all put in readiness, provisions were prepared, life-preservers were brought out, the officers were armed with revolvers so as to be able to enforce their orders, and it was only a question of whether to launch the boats at once or wait. The sea was so heavy that the boats could hardly live in it.

"At noon the captain told the passengers that he had the water under control, and was in hopes of drifting in the way of some passing vessel. The ship's bow was now high in the air, while the stern seemed to settle more and more. The sea was very rough; the ship rolled from side to side, lurching fearfully. The captain tried to keep up hope by telling the anxious people that they would probably drift in the way of a ship by three o'clock that afternoon, but the night closed in upon them without the sign of a sail.

"That was an awful night, the darkest in all our lives—several hundred men, women, and children waiting for the doom that seemed to be settling upon us! No one dared to sleep. We were all together in the saloon of the first cabin—Jews, Protestants, Catholics, and sceptics—although I doubt if at that time there were many sceptics among us. The agony and suspense were too great for words. With blanched faces and trembling hearts the passengers looked at one another as if trying to read in the faces of those about them what no one dared to speak. Rockets flamed into the sky, but there was no answer. We were drifting out of the track of the great steamers. Every hour seemed to increase the danger of the situation.

"Sunday morning dawned without help or hope. Up to that time no suggestion for religious services had been made. To have done that would almost certainly have produced a panic. In the awful suspense and dread that prevailed, a word about religion would have suggested the most terrible things to the passengers. It was necessary to divert their minds, if possible, or they would break under the strain. But as that second night came on, I asked Gen. O. O. Howard, who was with us, to secure the captain's permission for a service in the saloon. The captain said:

"'Most certainly; I am that kind, too.'

"We gave notice of the meeting, and to our surprise nearly every passenger attended, and I think everybody prayed, sceptics and all.

"With one arm clasping a pillar to steady myself on the reeling vessel, I tried to read Psalm xci., and we prayed that God would still the raging of the sea and bring us to our desired haven. It was a new psalm to me from that hour. The eleventh verse touched me very deeply. It was like a voice of divine assurance, and it seemed a very real thing as I read: '*He shall give his angels charge over thee, to keep thee in all thy ways.*' Surely He did it! I read also from Psalm cvii. 20-31. One lady thought those words must have been written for the occasion, and afterwards asked to see the book for herself. A German translated verse by verse as I read, for the benefit of his countrymen.

"I was passing through a new experience. I had thought myself superior to the fear of death. I had often preached on the subject, and urged Christians to realize this victory of faith. During the Civil War I had been under fire without fear. I was in Chicago during the great cholera epidemic, and went around with the doctors visiting the sick and dying; where they could go to look after the bodies of men I said I could go to look after their souls. I remember a case of smallpox where the sufferer's condition was beyond description, yet I went to the bedside of that poor sufferer again and again, with Bible and prayer, for Jesus' sake. In all this I had no fear of death.

"But on the sinking ship it was different. There was no cloud between my soul and my Saviour. I knew my sins had been put away, and that if I died there it would only be to wake up in Heaven. That was all settled long ago. But as my thoughts went out to my loved ones at home—my wife, my children, my friends on both sides of the sea, the schools and all the interests so dear to me—and as I realized that perhaps the next hour would separate me forever from all these, so far as this world was concerned, I confess it almost broke me down. It was the darkest hour of my life.

"I could not endure it. I must have relief, and relief came in prayer. God heard my cry, and enabled me to say, from the depth of my soul, 'Thy will be done!' Sweet peace came to my heart. Let it be Northfield or Heaven, it made no difference now. I went to bed, fell asleep almost immediately, and never slept more soundly in all my life. Out of the depths I cried unto my Lord, and He heard me and delivered me from all my fears. I can no more doubt that God gave answer to my prayer for relief than I can doubt my own existence.

"About three o'clock at night I was aroused from my sound sleep by my son's voice: 'Come on deck, father,' he said. I followed him, and he pointed to a far-off light, rising and sinking on the sea. It was a messenger of deliverance to us. It proved to be the light of the steamer Lake Huron, bound from Montreal to Liverpool, whose lookout had seen our signals of distress and supposed it was a vessel in flames. Oh, the joy of that moment when these seven hundred despairing passengers beheld the approaching ship! Who can ever forget it?

"But now the question was, Can this small steamer tow the helpless Spree a thousand miles to Queenstown? Every moment was passed in the intensest anxiety and prayer. It was a brave and perilous undertaking. The vessels were at last connected by two great cables. If a storm arose these would snap like a thread, and we must be left to our fate. But I had no fear. God would finish the work He had begun. The waves were calmed, the cables held, our steamer moved in the wake of the Huron. There were storms all about us, but they came not nigh our broken ship. Seven days after the accident, by the good hand of our God upon us, we were able to hold a joyous thanksgiving service in the harbor of Queenstown. The rescuing ship that God sent to us in our distress had just sufficient power to tow our steamer and just enough coal to take her into port. Her captain was a man of prayer; he besought God's help to enable them to accomplish their dangerous and difficult task; and God answered the united prayers of the distressed voyagers, and brought us to our desired haven."

As has been said, the experience of those days upon the Atlantic left a lasting impression upon Mr. Moody, but through it all he was thinking of others. His tender heart was torn by the scenes of anguish as mothers wept over their children and fathers pleaded with God to

View of Connecticut Valley from the Stone Chair.

Northfield Seminary.

The Camp at College Conference.

Marquand Hall, Northfield Seminary.

Northfield Seminary Buildings and Campus from the East.

The Connecticut River, with Northfield Seminary in the Distance.

Showing road to South Vernon.

spare them the sight of their sons' destruction. During the first few hours after the danger was known, he had little to say. Once he spoke of the probable outcome of the accident to his son: " I had hoped to have a few more years of work. I had planned to preach the Gospel in Chicago next summer, and I want to do some more work on the schools at Northfield and Chicago. But, if my work is ended, why, it's all right. It's hard for you, though, with your life-work just beginning. If it's God's will, however, it's all for the best." And there he left it.

Strangely enough, this experience apparently cured Mr. Moody of his old enemy, seasickness, and, engaging passage on the Etruria from Queenstown to New York, he was able to enjoy every moment of the trip.

His arrival in America was the occasion for great and sincere congratulation. After a brief interview with the friends gathered to welcome him, Mr. Moody and the members of his family started for home, reaching Northfield that evening. What a reception was accorded him as he approached the scenes so dear to his heart!

As the express train rushed out of the darkness and drew up at the Mount Hermon School station, hundreds of torches flashed in the darkness, a brass band sounded its welcome, and cheers rang from three hundred students. Up to the car windows and along the platform streamed a crowd of young men.

" Where is he? " cried a score of voices, and quicker than it takes to tell it, came the answer:

" Here, back there."

On the lower step of the car platform stood the man they wanted, bare-headed, his face beaming with joy at such a welcome from his " boys " after a year's absence.

The cheers were still ringing when the train pulled out for South Vernon, where Mr. and Mrs. Moody left it for their drive across the river to Northfield. At Revell Hall, the first of the Seminary buildings, his " girls " had gathered for a welcome less noisy but no less hearty.

From his carriage Mr. Moody told them that God had answered their prayer for him in his hour of danger, and that his first word, now he was among his own again, must be one of testimony to God's faithfulness and mercy. It was characteristic of the man whose big-heartedness made him beloved by this great company of students that, before he entered his own home, he went first to the house near by to see his aged mother.

The next morning, a clear, crisp New England winter Sabbath, the Mount Hermon boys walked four miles to join in the morning worship in Northfield Church with the young ladies of the Seminary and the townspeople. In place of the usual sermon, Mr. Moody told in simple, heartfelt words the thrilling story of the voyage.

CHAPTER XXXVI

World's Fair Campaign

AMONG his other qualifications for the career of an evangelist Mr. Moody included a peculiar genius for recognizing opportunities. On no occasion was this gift better illustrated than in the evangelistic campaign conducted in Chicago during the World's Fair in 1893. The idea of making such a carnival the scene of a wide-spread evangelistic effort was as novel as it was daring. But the plan was under consideration for months, and was arranged while the Exposition buildings were still under construction. During the previous season, in his missions in Great Britain, he alluded frequently to this purpose of his, and sought to enlist the prayers of Christians everywhere for the effort.

Like his Master, Mr. Moody could not look upon the multitude and not be moved with compassion. The great cities always attracted him by the opportunities for work they presented, and Chicago, during the World's Fair, was, to use his own words, "the opportunity of a century." Its ordinary cosmopolitan population was swollen by the influx of thousands, many of whom belonged to the worst classes of society. At best, religious work is difficult there, and during the Fair the distractions and activities were multiplied enormously. Added to this, the fact that in summer there is always a lull in Christian activity made the outlook far from promising. The most experienced pastors and laymen of the city looked forward to the Fair with misgivings and apprehensions altogether reasonable.

"It was a question," said a leading pastor, "what was to become of us during the six months. We knew it would be a time of great excitement, and what should become of the spiritual life of the churches, we knew not."

As far back as his Palestine trip Mr. Moody had looked forward to this work. Sitting on Olivet, watching the city over which the Saviour wept, he thought of the city where he had begun his early Christian efforts, the city with its noble churches and earnest preachers, its faithful Sunday-school and Association workers, its devoted Christians and philanthropists. Side by side with the city of temples and saints he saw another one, inhabited by men who cared for none of these things; he saw the gilded gambling halls and the dingy barrooms, the parlors of shame and the miserable dives, the sacrilegious concert-rooms and the vulgar variety shows, alike desecrating the day of rest. He saw, as few men see it, the chasm which divided the classes, and he knew that even with a church on every block in Chicago there would still be a vast unchurched population, a city in a city going down to death, many of them crying piteously:

"No man cares for my soul!"

Into the city of wealth and culture and piety and the city of poverty and ignorance and crime he saw a multitude pouring from every State and Territory and town in this country and from every nation under heaven. Where would they turn when they reached their destination? The White City, their goal, would be visited, but so would the places of sin and sorrow. The closed church doors and the open saloons, the darkened house of God and the brilliantly lighted devil's den burdened his soul. The contrast was an inspiration, and during all the thirteen intervening months he worked with one great object in view.

"Just as I was preparing to leave London the last time," he said, "I called upon a celebrated physician, who told me that my heart was weakening and that I must let up on my work, that I must be more careful of myself; and I went home with the thought that I would not work quite so hard. I was on the steamer Spree, and when the an-

INTERIOR CHICAGO AVENUE CHURCH, CHICAGO.

Largely built from hymn-book royalties and contributions of Sunday-school children of the world.

LECTURE-ROOM, BIBLE INSTITUTE, CHICAGO.

Superintendent R. A. Torrey delivering Bible lecture.

Office, Ladies' Department, Bible Institute, Chicago.

Reception-room, Men's Department, Bible Institute, Chicago.

nouncement was made that the steamer was sinking, and we were there in a helpless condition in mid-ocean, no one on earth knows what I passed through as I thought that my work was finished, and that I should never again have the privilege of preaching the Gospel of the Son of God. And on that dark night, the first night of the accident, I made a vow that if God would spare my life and bring me back to America, I would come to Chicago, and at the World's Fair preach the Gospel with all the power that He would give me."

This was his one purpose, to preach the Gospel. Congresses for discussion of the relative merits of different religions had no attractions for him, and he felt no call to offer apologies for Christianity, but for six months he tried to give the Gospel an opportunity to speak for itself.

When the Fair managers decided to keep open on Sundays, some said, "Let us boycott the Fair"; others, "Let us appeal to the law, and compel them to close on Sundays." But Mr. Moody said, "Let us open so many preaching places and present the Gospel so attractively that the people will want to come and hear it."

His plan of campaign was simple. Chicago is naturally divided into three sections by the forking river: the north side, the west side, and the south side. In each section a church centre was selected: Chicago Avenue or "Moody's Church" on the north, the First Congregational Church on the west, and Immanuel Baptist on the south. Later many other churches were offered and occupied.

Mr. Moody was not able to carry on the work alone, but associated with him many prominent Christian workers from all parts of America and Europe. Buildings and tents sufficient to hold large audiences were secured, and, most important of all from a business man's point of view, money to pay the bills of speakers and singers, buildings and advertising. In this one detail of raising funds for the support of the work there was sufficient to tax the utmost strength of most men. At one time the daily expenditures in the rent of halls, cost of advertising, salaries and entertainment of speakers, clerks, and others amounted to $800. This sum had to be met by Mr. Moody's personal efforts. A large force of secretaries wrote appeals under his direction, and the coöperation of the religious press in giving full notice to the work aided greatly in securing the generous support of the Christian public.

But this was only an incident of the work to which Mr. Moody gave himself. Rising at six o'clock in the morning, he would begin the day's work by an hour of solitary communion with God. Then in quick succession would follow the day's routine. The regular work of the Bible Institute with its lectures and classes was continued as usual, and its three hundred students proved most helpful in the work. Under Mr. Moody's personal supervision meetings were extended in every direction. As there were great districts which it was desired to reach, where the residents would not enter a church even if one were accessible, he decided to hire theatres. He offered a large sum for the use of the Auditorium on Sundays, but could not secure it at any price. But soon a footing was obtained in the Haymarket Theatre, and here he preached every Sunday morning until the end of the campaign, with the exception of two Sundays, when he was absent from the city. As the movement grew, other theatres and halls were rented, until eight or nine were under his control, some on Sundays only, but others throughout the week.

Five tents were in constant use, pitched at strategic points in the midst of non-churchgoing communities. Two gospel wagons were in use, from which tracts were distributed, addresses given, and gospel hymns sung to the motley audience that would gather wherever a halt was made in the thickly populated tenement district. A shop in the heart of the city was rented and fitted up as a mission hall. A number of Institute students lodged overhead, and meetings were held not only every afternoon and evening, but a special squad came on at ten at night, in order to reach the drunkards and harlots who haunted the vicinity far into the morning hours.

Special efforts were made to influence the neighborhood of the

Fair grounds. Here, on the open prairie, hotels and other buildings had grown up like gourds, without any effort to keep corresponding pace in providing church accommodations. But Mr. Moody secured the use of half a dozen tents, tabernacles, and hotel parlors. The most notable meetings of the campaign, judged from the popular standpoint, were probably those held in Tattersall's Hall and Forepaugh's circus tents. When Mr. Moody announced the meeting in Tattersall's, with its seating capacity of ten to fifteen thousand, he said: "We've got something better than the Military Tournament, and we must get a bigger audience than they." The vast audience was all that could be desired.

Forepaugh's circus came to Chicago in June, and established itself on the lake front. The manager rented the tent to Mr. Moody for Sunday morning, but reserved it for his own shows in the afternoon and evening. When the circus advertisement appeared the manager had included the morning meeting in his announcement as follows:

"Ha! Ha! Ha!
"Three Big Shows!
"Moody in the Morning!
"Forepaugh in the Afternoon and Evening!"

The great canvas ellipse covered an immense area, having a seating capacity of ten thousand, with standing room in the arena for ten thousand more. While it was being prepared for the meeting, a circus man chaffingly asked Mr. Moody if he expected to get three thousand hearers. His curiosity was probably satisfied when on two successive Sundays the large area of the tent was crowded to overflowing with those who were eager to hear the "Old Gospel." In the centre of the arena a rude platform was erected for the speakers and a few of the singers, while the rest of the song corps were massed around them. An observer thus describes the scene:

"The surroundings were the usual circus furniture—ropes, trapezes, gaudy decorations, etc., while in an adjoining canvas building was a large menagerie, including eleven elephants. Clowns, grooms, circus-riders, men, women, and children, eighteen thousand of them, and on a Sunday morning, too! Whether the Gospel was ever before preached under such circumstances I know not, but it was wonderful to ear and eye alike."

When that mighty throng took up the hymn, "Nearer, my God, to Thee," a visible sense of awe fell upon the multitude. After an hour of singing and prayer Mr. Moody rose to preach, his text being, "*The Son of Man is come to seek and to save that which was lost.*" The Spirit of God was present. The hush of Heaven was over the meeting. Towards the close of the address there was a slight disturbance, and a "lost child" was passed up to the platform. Mr. Moody held her up so that her parents might see her; and when her anxious father reached the platform Mr. Moody placed the child in his arms and said:

"That is what Jesus Christ came to do: to seek and to save lost sinners, and restore them to their Heavenly Father's embrace."

Mr. Moody rented this circus tent for two Sundays. It was a revelation to the circus manager that so many people would come to listen to songs and sermons. His afternoon and evening shows were so thinly attended that he abandoned Sunday exhibitions, and asked Mr. Moody to keep him supplied with an evangelist to hold gospel meetings in the tent on Sundays in other cities, promising to bear all the travelling and other expenses of such an arrangement. While the opportunity in Chicago was exceptional, there were serious objections to complying with such a request.

Every variety of gospel meeting was held: men's, women's, children's meetings; temperance, soldiers', jail meetings; open-air and cottage meetings; meetings for Germans, Poles, Bohemians, French, Jews, and even for the Arabs in the Fair grounds; meetings for praise and for prayer; all-day and all-night meetings.

Chicago at all times is a cosmopolitan city, and this was, of course, especially apparent during that notable season. Strangers from all parts of the world came by thousands, and it was Mr. Moody's purpose, as far as possible, to reach all people and all nations. To do this he enlisted the aid of prominent European ministers and evangelists. Pindor, of Silesia, came to preach to the Poles; Rabinowitz, of Russia, to the Jews; Monod, of Paris, to the French; Stoecker, of Berlin, to the Germans. To mention Americans who ministered in German, Swedish, Bohemian, and other tongues, as well as in English, would be to name most of the prominent evangelical preachers, teachers, and singers of this country. Paton, of the New Hebrides; Thomas Spurgeon and Varley, of Australia, and hosts from England, Scotland, and Ireland took part. The coöperation of many Fair visitors, like Count Bernstorff, of Berlin, and Lord Kinnaird, of London, was also secured during their stay in Chicago. As the last weeks of the Fair approached, the work gathered momentum. A large hall in the centre of the city was secured, where daily a two hours' midday service was held.

Mr. Moody urged Christians everywhere to pray and labor with unremitting diligence. "It seems as if we had only been playing during the past weeks," he said; "now we are going to work. We have just been fishing along the shore; now we are going to launch out into the deep. Friends, help fill up the churches. Let us see whether we can't wake up this whole city. There is now before us the grandest opportunity for extending the Kingdom of God that this country has ever seen. Hundreds of thousands of people will come in during these last weeks of the World's Fair. It is possible to reach them with the gospel message. We want to get still more buildings for meetings near the Fair grounds. We'll hire all the theatres we can get. I'll use all the money you will give me to push the work. We are spending now about $800 a day in this work, and could spend $8,000 a day if we had it. We are getting new places for meetings as fast as we can. We want to press these closing days of the World's Fair as never before."

On several of those last Sundays Mr. Moody controlled as many as one hundred and twenty-five different meetings—assuming, when it was necessary, the expenses of rent and incidentals, furnishing speakers and singers, and working up the attendance, which would aggregate upwards of one hundred thousand each Sunday. High-water mark on weekdays was reached on Chicago Day, October 8th. Chicago determined to celebrate, on a colossal scale, the twenty-second anniversary of the great fire of 1871. Mr. Moody also determined to make special efforts. The Fair arranged extra attractions, and over seven hundred thousand people passed through the gates that day. Mr. Moody held continuous meetings in three large central halls, and in one case the attendance was so large that the speakers had difficulty in pushing their way in.

In all the trying circumstances of the work Mr. Moody's generalship in marshalling his forces was second only to his faith in the work and his tact in avoiding internal difficulties. Only those who were familiar with the inside workings of the campaign realized how difficult his duties were at times, and what heroism, self-effacement, and skill it required to keep a large force of helpers engaged in so tremendous a work without friction.

Mr. Moody's own estimate of the results of the work, given in an interview at the close of the campaign, thus describes the six months' effort. In replying to various questions, he said:

"The principal result of our six months' work is that millions have heard the simple Gospel preached by some of the most gifted preachers in the world; thousands have apparently been genuinely converted to Christ, and Christians all over this land have been brought to a deeper spiritual life and aroused to more active Christian effort for the salvation of others."

"Have you learned any new lessons or suggestions about Christian work from your experience and observation during the six months' labor?"

"I have learned that the summer, so far from being the worst, is the best time to carry on Christian work in our cities. I have learned to appreciate more than ever the power that there is in concentrated and united Christian action. I have been impressed with the fact that it is the Christian people of the land that take an interest in and patronize such expositions as the World's Fair."

"Would such an extensive, long-continued series of gospel meetings be practicable and advisable at other times and places?"

"Certainly. A gospel campaign such as that in Chicago this summer would be practicable, I believe, in any other large city, even where there was no Fair."

"What do you consider to be the most effective agency, or agencies, in the prosecution of your campaign?"

"The preaching and singing of the old Gospel and the power of the Holy Ghost."

"Will you gratify a curious public by stating what has been the aggregate expense of your entire six months' labor?"

"The entire expense, exclusive of the ordinary expenses of the Institute, was $60,000; an additional large expenditure had to be made to enlarge the buildings before the beginning of the campaign."

"Do you mind telling how these enormous expenses have been met?"

"By the gifts of generous Christian individuals and societies all over the United States, Canada, and England. Some of this money was given in answer to personal appeals, and some without any suggestion from me."

"What assurance, if any, did you have at the beginning that the means would be provided for the prosecution of the work?"

"Only that I knew the work ought to be done, and that I knew we have a God who will always sustain us in doing what we ought to do."

Many people who went to Chicago to attend the Exposition became so interested in the gospel meetings that they divided their time between the Fair and the meetings. The Rev. Dr. Frederick Campbell, at that time a Chicago pastor, in writing of the campaign, said:

"A great feature of the entire period of the World's Fair has been a series of evangelistic meetings conducted by Mr. Moody. There is probably nothing to match it in the entire history of the Christian church; even the Apostles never saw things done after this fashion. Mr. Moody's true place is in Chicago, where everything is done on a mammoth scale and with mammoth energy. He has once more proved himself to be a most remarkable instrument in the hands of Providence for working out divine plans. As a Christian he is thoroughly permeated with the spirit of the Gospel and baptized by the Holy Ghost. As an organizer he is a general; massing, distributing, and controlling forces of men and women in the most remarkable manner. I do not discover that there has been a failure in any of his plans; the audacity with which he has undertaken unheard of things for Christ has been an assurance of success. If ordinary preachers had a little more of his audacity, with the faith and works which should accompany it, they would achieve greater things."

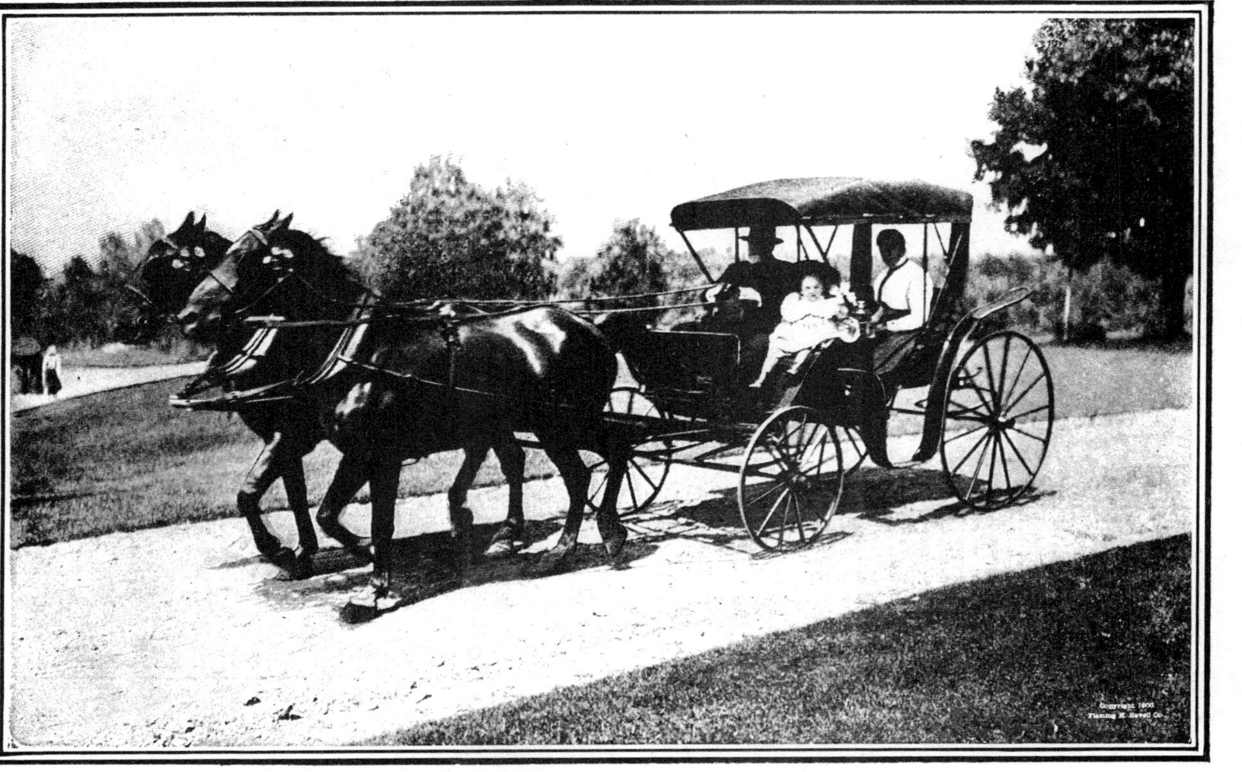

A Favorite Pastime : Mr. Moody Taking his Grandchild for a Drive.

Mr. Moody and Grandson, Dwight L., II.

A Brown Study.

CHAPTER XXXVII

The Use of the Press

IT has been said of Mr. Moody that his most prominent characteristic was his "consecrated common-sense." One of the best illustrations of this was his keen appreciation of the great evangelistic possibilities of the press. For some years the Chicago papers were not disposed to treat his missionary efforts with any seriousness, and "Crazy" Moody, or "Brother" Moody, as he was familiarly known, was the butt of many a good-natured jest. It may be that his aversion to the title of "brother" in later years may be attributed to this early experience, for we never heard him use the term.

As the growth and results of Mr. Moody's work made apparent the sound judgment that in every case accompanied his zeal, the secular press became more friendly. His success in raising money and securing teachers for his school, the confidence shown by wealthy people in his efforts to erect Christian Association buildings, his indefatigable activity in reaching and holding those who were not desired elsewhere or for whom no special efforts had been made, his practical work for the soldiers, his growing popularity in Sunday-school conventions—all these gradually won for him the respect of those who had been at first inclined to be amused by his zeal.

Mr. Moody seldom replied to misstatements in the newspapers, but when, in his early evangelistic career, it was stated in the press that he was making a good thing financially out of his religious work, he referred to the criticism. There were tears in his eyes, and his voice quivered as he said:

"As I know my heart, before God, I have never let the desire for money determine my conduct in any way. I know I am weak and come short in many ways, but the devil has not that hold upon me. I have never profited personally by a single dollar that has been raised through my work, and it hurts me to be charged with it, above all things. May God forgive those who say this of me."

More than $1,125,000 was received from royalties on the hymn-books, which was used for benevolent objects. Mr. Moody was a good financier; he appreciated the value of money, but he never used it to build a fortune; he desired it simply that he might use it in doing good.

On two other occasions Mr. Moody made a public denial of newspaper reports—not for the sake of personal gratification, but solely because of the injury to the work in which he was engaged. In 1877 the Boston papers accused him of having purchased a racing horse, for which it was claimed that he had paid $4,000. Finding that the statement was being credited by some, and that these were prejudiced by it, Mr. Moody made a plain statement of the facts of the case. He had bought a roadster whose special virtue was its gentleness as a family horse—not its speed as a racer. The price, he also stated, had been exaggerated, and there should be deducted from the amount claimed $3,750, as he had only given $250.

The second statement that brought forth a public denial from Mr. Moody was a newspaper report circulated in Richmond, Va., while he was conducting a mission in that city. One of the local papers printed a letter in which the writer stated that on a certain occasion he had heard Mr. Moody make most disparaging references to Generals Robert E. Lee and "Stonewall" Jackson. The rumor was at first ignored. Later it was found that the meetings were being seriously affected, and that a bitter opposition was rapidly growing. Mr. Moody's high regard for the men referred to, and his public tributes to their memory, were not sufficiently known to prove the falsity of the story to the public. Fortunately, his addresses had all been printed at the time when it was claimed he had made the offensive remarks. Absolutely denying the charge at one of his meetings, he brought out this fact, and challenged any one to find any reference to the disparagement of either of the two brave generals, for whom he had the highest personal regard. What was apparently a serious obstacle to the work was then turned to the good of the meetings, and a most successful mission followed.

Although an appreciative friend of the public press, Mr. Moody never compromised in his denunciation of its evils. He had no patience whatever with the Sunday newspaper, but did not spend his time in condemning the editors and reporters of the papers that published a Sunday edition. On the contrary, he felt that both editors and reporters were among his best allies. While he reached an audience limited by the walls of the building where he spoke, they were able to carry his message into places that no minister or city missionary could visit. With their assistance he could reach an audience a hundred times larger than could be accommodated in any church or hall. Thus, while he never flattered representatives of the press, he was extremely cordial to them, and was able to trace many a conversion to their agency.

In Great Britain, the press, at first suspicious of the Americans, finally took up the matter in earnest, and column after column was devoted to reports of Mr. Moody's sermons and accounts of the services. Later, on his return to America, one or two daily papers in each city where he held his great campaigns would report his sermons, either wholly or in part. Frequently the same paper would publish a stenographic report of everything said, sermon, prayers, and hymns, even though the series of meetings lasted for three or six months.

"It kept me busy," he once said, "in a city where, for six months, every word that I spoke was printed daily in one of the papers." But one of the most important conversions resulting from that series of meetings occurred, not in the crowded hall, but in a narrow cell in the city prison, where Valentine Burke, a criminal, was led to Christ

WANAMAKER LAKE IN SUMMER DRESS.

NORTHFIELD IN WINTER DRESS.

gestion, having for its purpose the report of evangelistic missions, missionary efforts, and plans of Bible study. For eighteen years this monthly has appeared regularly, its daily Bible notes being read by thousands, who have followed with great profit the consecutive course through the Bible, under Major Whittle's direction. During the last months of Mr. Moody's life he took a still deeper interest in this effort, and arranged to make this magazine a special organ of the various institutions he had founded.

Mr. Moody was always fearful lest his connection with some publication, either of the hymn-book or public sermons, should be considered as a money-making scheme on his part. For this reason, while it was imperative that he should have a hymn-book, he was loath to consent to any authorized edition of his sermons. These were published, sometimes quite fully and more frequently in part, in the daily press, and numerous publishers were very ready to adapt these to book form, so that " Moody's Sermons " appeared in every conceivable shape for a number of years before any authorized works were issued.

A volume of sermons resulted from each of his first series of meetings in this country. The meetings in New York, Philadelphia, Boston, Chicago, and other leading cities were reported verbatim by one or more papers, and at the close of the meetings the reports were collected in a large volume. Mr. Moody, however, had no part in their compilation, and no profits accrued to him or his work from their sale, which was exceedingly large.

His reluctance to sanction any volume was first overcome in connection with the unpretentious work entitled " Twelve Select Sermons." This was issued both in England and America, but for several years after its appearance he would not consent to give his approval to the publication of any additional compilation. Convinced at last of the large numbers who might be reached by this means, and annoyed by the fragmentary character of many of the sermons printed, he supplied other small volumes, which appeared at irregular intervals.

Altogether there have been issued twenty-five volumes, in addition to single sermons.

One of his early publications was entitled " Heaven." One day on the railroad train he heard the newsboy, with a bundle of books under his arm, shouting, " Here you are, ' Ingersoll on Hell ' ! " He caught the boy, and placed a copy of his own book in his hand, saying, " Here, my lad, here is another book; give them that at the same time." The boy went on through the car, shouting, " ' Ingersoll on Hell '; ' Moody on Heaven! ' ' Ingersoll on Hell '; ' Moody on Heaven ' ! "

It may not be inappropriate here to refer to Mr. Moody's attitude and thought regarding the late well-known and gifted agnostic.

When Colonel Ingersoll died, in the summer of 1899, and his family were overwhelmed with grief, the Young Women's Christian Conference was in session at Northfield. On this occasion Mr. Moody made his first public allusion to Mr. Ingersoll when he said:

" Mr. Ingersoll and I started out in life about the same time, and in the same State. Of course I have been interested in watching his career, but I have never mentioned his name in public until to-night, and I don't believe in talking about a man after his death. I am sorry for his wife and children, for it is said that he was a kind husband and father, and I don't want to tear open that wound. My feeling toward him has always been that of deepest pity, for a life like his seems so barren of everything that has made my life joyous and blessed.

" How dark must be the life of a man for whom, by his own confession, it was like ' a narrow vale between the peaks of two eternities; we cry aloud, and the only answer is the echo of our calling,' and for whom death seemed like ' a leap into the dark.' How different from that of a believer in Christ! For him not only is the present life filled with the peace of God, but the future is bright with hope. He knows that for him death is only the exchanging of a shifting tent for an enduring mansion. How much Colonel Ingersoll's sorrowing wife and daughters need our prayers, as they stand by the still body of their loved one, if they really believe the hopeless doctrine he taught!"

"Do you believe Mr. Ingersoll's influence was overrated?" asked a friend.

"I do not wish to talk about it," answered Mr. Moody. "I believe that Ingersoll was driven away from Christianity by the abuse of Christians. He was railed at by them, and he saw the dark side of Christianity. He got twisted when he was young."

"Do you believe he died without any hope of the future?"

"I don't know. I don't see how a man can *live* without such a hope. It must be terrible. We are not his judges. It is for God alone to judge him."

Like all the institutions and organizations that owe their birth to Mr. Moody, the Bible Institute Colportage Association grew out of a need that he observed as he travelled to and fro in his evangelistic work. He was holding meetings in a Western town in the fall of 1894, and wanted some books to give away. He called at a local bookstore, but, although the shelves were loaded with fiction of all kinds, not a single religious book could be had.

This caused him to make an investigation, and he discovered that, in one of the great States of the Middle West, there was not one bookstore that pretended to carry even a limited assortment of religious books. Determined to do something to fill the gap which he had discovered, he returned to Chicago and consulted prominent Christian workers, who said, "People won't buy religious books; they are too expensive."

"Then their price must come down," said Mr. Moody. The only way to reduce the price, without working on a charity basis, would be by printing large editions, and Mr. Moody organized a colportage department in connection with the Bible Institute, his Chicago school for the training of Christian workers.

At first, ordinary methods were adopted to bring about the sale of good books, the main thing being to lower the prices. In the spring

to bear on them by this channel and their whole destiny changed for good. What we propose is that Christians should be more active in carrying the Gospel to them while they are behind the bars. If it were not for atheism and infidelity, there would be no need of prisons. It is sin that is at the root of the matter; and the only sure cure is regeneration, a new heart, and a new life in Christ Jesus."

Mr. Moody's plan was to get people sufficiently interested to send one book, if they could not send more, and then follow it with their prayers. Hardly a day passed, after he began this work, without his hearing of definite cases of conversion and blessing through such agencies.

CHAPTER XXXVIII

Preparing Sermons

"WERE one asked what, on the human side, were the effective ingredients in Mr. Moody's sermons, one would find the answer difficult," said Henry Drummond in describing his friend as a preacher. "Probably the foremost is the tremendous conviction with which they are uttered. Next to that come their point and direction. Every blow is straight from the shoulder, and every stroke tells. Whatever canons they violate, whatever faults the critics may find with their art, with their rhetoric, or even with their theology, as appeals to the people they do their work with extraordinary power. If eloquence is measured by its effects upon an audience, and not by its balanced sentences and cumulative periods, then there is eloquence of the highest order in them. In sheer persuasiveness Mr. Moody has few equals, and, rugged as his preaching may seem to some, there are in it pathos of a quality which few orators have ever reached, and an appealing tenderness which not only redeems but raises it, not unseldom, almost to sublimity. No report can do the faintest justice to this or to the other most characteristic qualities of his public speech. Take this extract:

"'I can imagine that when Christ said to the little band around Him, "Go ye into all the world and preach the Gospel," Peter said, "Lord, do You really mean that we are to go back to Jerusalem and preach the Gospel to those men that murdered You?" "Yes," said Christ, "go hunt up that man that spat in My face; tell him that he may have a seat in My Kingdom yet. Yes, Peter, go find that man that made that

New Birth

Most Solemn Question
that will ever
Come before us in
this life

The foundation of
All our Hopes in the
life to Come

It is the A. B. C
Of our Blessed
Hope

Nothing will up
set false religion
like it

It will change
our thoughts about
God & the Bible sooner
than any thing else

I Believe it is the
Greatest Blessing
that will ever come
to us in this life

cruel crown of thorns and placed it on My brow, and tell him I will have a crown ready for him when he comes into My Kingdom, and there will be no thorns in it. Hunt up that man that took a reed and brought it down over the cruel thorns, driving them into My brow, and tell him I will put a scepter in his hand, and he shall rule over the nations of the earth, if he will accept salvation. Search for the man that drove the spear into My side, and tell him there is a nearer way to My heart than that. Tell him I forgive him freely, and that he can be saved if he will accept salvation as a gift." '

" Prepared or impromptu, what dramatist could surpass that touch: ' Tell him there is a nearer way to My heart than that ' ? "

For years Mr. Moody never expected to do any more in the way of preaching than to give five- or ten-minute addresses to his Sabbath-school children. By and by he procured a copy of the " Topical Text-book " as a help in Bible study, and began to prepare an address on the Bible. This was the subject of the first attempt at a Bible reading. His method was simple, and suited to the needs of the case. He would call upon some one in the audience to read a certain text. This would give him time to collect his thoughts, and he would then say a few words or relate an anecdote to light up the text. When he found himself running dry, he would call for another text to be read, and on this he would offer a few comments in a similar fashion. When his audiences became larger, so that he had to read the text himself, he had to make better preparation beforehand as there was less opportunity for impromptu comment.

These " Bible readings " were given in the home circle of his friend, D. W. McWilliams, of Brooklyn. Conducting, as he was at the time, a series of evangelistic meetings in the Cumberland Street chapel of the Lafayette Avenue Presbyterian Church, a lady of the congregation asked him to help them to understand better the leading doctrines of the Bible. For this purpose Mr. Moody met, quite informally, a few interested friends. Mr. McWilliams' drawing-room was the place of gathering. The method of study was quite new to all, even to the leader. A theme was taken, or a single word, such as *grace, hope, adoption, assurance, love,* etc. The Bible was searched by means of concordance and topical text-book for all passages bearing on the theme. These were emphasized and illustrated. None were more impressed with the wonderful interpretation of the Scriptures by the Scriptures than Mr. Moody. This plan gave a new direction to his study and his preaching.

"At this time" (February, 1872), says Dr. Cuyler, "he had not become much known in Brooklyn. The weather was severely cold; the attendance was very small, but my wife and daughter reported to me that Mr. Moody's quickening addresses made them a spiritual feast. One evening I attended the meeting (there were not over thirty or forty present), and after it was over I said to him:

"'Brother Moody, this seems rather slow work.'

"'Very true,' replied my sagacious brother; 'it is slow, but if you want to kindle a fire you collect a handful of pine whittlings, light them with a match, and keep blowing until they blaze. Then you may pile on the wood. So I am working here, with a handful of Christians, endeavoring to warm them up with love for Christ, and if they get well warmed, a revival will come and sinners will be converted.' He was right; the revival did come; it spread through the Lafayette Avenue congregation, and a large number of converts made their public confession of Christ before our communion table.

"That happy experience in that little chapel found mention in several religious papers, and taught many ministers the secret of kindling a flame by the breath of the Holy Spirit."

The acquaintance formed at this time with Rev. Dr. Theodore L. Cuyler ripened into a warm and lifelong friendship. When Mr. Moody decided to go to Scotland, he suggested that a note of introduction might be of service. Dr. Cuyler sent a hearty letter to Dr. Andrew A. Bonar, of Glasgow, which was published in the newspapers of the city.

"As I look back now to that incident," says Dr. Cuyler, "it seems about as amusing as if Paul had asked for a note of introduction from some brother at Jerusalem, in order to gain a fair hearing at Corinth òr Athens. Nowhere did Moody and Sankey do a more glorious work than in dear old Scotland."

During the brief visit to England in 1872, following this experience in Brooklyn, these Bible readings were repeated in a few modest public gatherings. Returning to Chicago, Mr. Moody was anxious to repeat these "readings" in his own city. How this came about is interestingly told by Mrs. E. P. Goodwin, wife of the pastor of the First Congregational Church, who says:

"Mr. Moody began his Bible readings in our church in Chicago. The circumstances were these: We had heard of his Bible readings given with success in England and New York. Therefore, commissioned by Mr. Goodwin, I went to ask Mr. Moody if he would give a series in our church. He met me at the door, hat in hand, and invited me into the parlor. I made known my errand. He was much agitated, and, with tears streaming down his face, he replied, 'Mrs. Goodwin, I had taken my hat to go over to Dr. Goodwin, and see if he would *let* me give some readings. I lived in Chicago many years, knowing but one truth, and thinking that the only necessary one, ignoring all related truths, till I built up a wall of prejudice all around me. I didn't know that there was a minister in Chicago who would let me into his church, but I thought I would try Dr. Goodwin.'"

A series of twelve lectures was given, with the following subjects:

Tues., Oct. 22—"Love."	Tues., Nov. 26—"What Christ Is to Us."
Tues., Oct. 29—"Blood."	Tues., Dec. 3—"Grace."
Wed., Oct. 30—"Prayer."	Tues., Dec. 10—"Believing."
Tues., Nov. 5—"Faith."	Tues., Dec. 17—"Walking with God."
Wed., Nov. 6—"Promise."	Wed., Dec. 18—"Heaven."
Tues., Nov. 12—"Assurance."	
Tues., Nov. 19—"Holy Ghost."	

The lectures were in large part new, and Mr. Moody had worked assiduously on them. He was at white heat. The effect was electric. It seemed that he must have surpassed himself at each lecture, and that he could not again be lifted to equal fervor. While preparing the lecture upon " Grace " he became so excited that he seized his hat, went out into the street, and accosted the first man he met with the abrupt question, " Do you know what *grace* is? "

At the close of this series another course was arranged to be held in the Third Presbyterian Chapel, Dr. A. E. Kittredge pastor; and subsequently another series, enlisting a union of the churches of the West Side, at the Union Park Church, Dr. F. A. Noble's.

Mr. Moody was an untiring Bible student. He usually rose about daybreak in summer, in order to have a quiet season alone with his Bible and his God, while his mind was fresh, and before the activities of the day divided his attention. The walls of his library are filled from floor to ceiling with well-filled shelves. He used to say it was worth going a thousand miles to get a good thought. With what keenness he listened to other preachers for good thoughts and illustrations, and how his face lit up as he took out the notebook which he kept in his hip-pocket! He urged this habit of making notes of all the good things one read and heard, believing that it would make the Bible more deeply interesting day by day. He never really changed his method of making sermons, which was as follows:

Having decided to prepare an address on any text or topic—he preferred to use subjects mostly—he first took a large envelope, and on the outside wrote the title or reference: " Heaven," " Psalm xxiii.," " Backsliders," " Let the wicked forsake," " How to deal with inquirers," etc.

Many people wished to learn the secret of his sermon-making. " I have no secret," he said to a body of young men. " I study more by subjects than I do by texts. If, when I am reading, I meet a good thing on any of these subjects, I slip it into the right envelope and let it lie there. I always carry a notebook, and if I hear anything in a sermon that will throw light on that subject, I put it down, and slip it into the envelope. Perhaps I let it lie for a year or more. When I want a new sermon, I take everything that has been accumulating. Between what I find there and the results of my own study I have material enough.

" Then I am all the time going over my sermons, taking out a little here and adding a little there. In that way they never get very old. I am never ashamed to repeat a sermon. A great many people are afraid to repeat. I heard of a man who preached a sermon that he had given a good many times before, and when he had finished another preacher said to him:

" 'I have heard you preach that sermon at least five times in the last five years, and I know it by heart.' Said the other:

" 'I heard *you* preach five years ago, and I can't remember anything you said.'

" If you have got a sermon that is really good for anything, pass it round. If the Lord blesses it here to-night, why can't He bless it ten miles away, or ten years hence? Study by subjects, and get so full of your subject that all you need to do is to stand up and say as much as you can within the time. On some subjects I think I could speak without any difficulty for eight, or nine, or ten nights. When I began I couldn't speak more than five minutes. Then I would speak for five minutes and sit down. By and by I got so that I could speak for fifteen minutes.

" If any one were to ask me when I began to preach I couldn't tell him. I began with the children. By and by they brought their parents. Then I noticed that about half the audience were adults.

" I like to work up a Bible character. When I get hold of a man who is versed in the Word of God, I just pump him. It is a great privilege to have the thoughts that these men have been digging for all their lives."

Hundreds of his sermon envelopes are in his study—many of them showing signs of frequent use, many representing sermons in embryo.

When he wished to preach on a certain subject, he ran through the envelope of clippings, and selected such points and anecdotes as he wished to use on that occasion. Weaving these into an outline, he wrote out catchwords, and fastened the sheets into his Bible by means of elastic bands.

This method of making sermons he found to possess many advantages. It gave him full opportunity for impromptu speaking, since he was not bound hard and fast to a written manuscript. Many of Mr. Moody's best and most often-quoted sayings were impromptu. He always insisted that what the church needs is "men who can think on their heels."

He must have repeated some of his sermons hundreds of times, but they always sounded fresh to the hearer. Undoubtedly the secret lay partly in the nature of his subject, partly in the freshness of his delivery; but credit must also be given to his method of sermon-making, which permitted a flexibility of outline that meant continual change in the substance of his address, and to the order in which his points and anecdotes were marshalled.

There are three books which Mr. Moody advised every Christian to procure: (1) A good substantial copy of the Bible, with large, clear print; (2) Cruden's "Concordance," and (3) the "Topical Text-book."

We have already seen how he turned to this last when preparing for Bible readings. He always kept one at hand in his study, with a concordance, though he had been a Christian five years before he heard of the latter. Shortly after his conversion a sceptic in Boston was arguing with him, and Moody tried to defend the Bible and Christianity. The sceptic made a misquotation; Moody said it was not in the Bible, and he hunted for days and days to prove the sceptic wrong. He realized then that if he had a concordance he could have found the passage in question in a few moments.

Mr. Moody's Bibles are among the most precious treasures that he has left behind. He had a large number—upward of a score—in constant use. In his study are to be seen several that have been almost worn out; leaves loose and ragged-edged, but invaluable because of the notes and suggestions written on the margins and blank spaces. He had a dozen "interleaved" Bibles—that is, Bibles in which every other page is left blank for inserting notes and comments upon the Scriptures. Mr. Moody found that notebooks and clippings accumulate quickly, and are likely to be laid aside and never referred to again. He therefore adopted these interleaved Bibles, where notes are always at hand. From these he used to give out "nuggets" at his meetings, and when his friends borrowed a Bible in order to copy the notes, they were expected to write some "nuggets" of their own before returning them.

"Don't be afraid to borrow or lend Bibles," he used to say. "Some time ago a man wanted to take my Bible home to get a few things out of it, and when it came back I found these notes in it:

"'Justification, a change of state, a new standing before God.
'Repentance, a change of mind, a new mind about God.
'Regeneration, a change of nature, a new heart from God.
'Conversion, a change of life, a new life for God.
'Adoption, a change of family, a new relationship toward God.
'Sanctification, a change of service, separation unto God.
'Glorification, a change of condition, at home with God.'

"In the same handwriting I found these lines:

"'Jesus only:
'The light of Heaven is the face of Jesus.
'The joy of Heaven is the presence of Jesus.
'The melody of Heaven is the name of Jesus.
'The harmony of Heaven is the praise of Jesus.
'The theme of Heaven is the work of Jesus.
'The employment of Heaven is the service of Jesus.
'The fulness of Heaven is Jesus Himself.
'The duration of Heaven is the eternity of Jesus.'"

Of all the volumes he possessed he prized most highly a large pulpit Bible that contains the following inscription:

BETSY MOODY COTTAGE, NORTHFIELD SEMINARY.

THE "REVELL": FIRST PERMANENT BUILDING ERECTED FOR SEMINARY PURPOSES.

THE NORTHFIELD CHURCH.

"THE NORTHFIELD" HOTEL.

"MR. D. L. MOODY, from MRS. C. H. SPURGEON.

"In tender memory of the beloved one gone home to God. This Bible has been used by my beloved husband, and is now given with unfeigned pleasure to one in whose hands its service will be continued and extended.

"S. SPURGEON.

"*Westwood, London, Nov.* 20, 1892."

This is the original Bible in which Mr. Spurgeon kept track of his sermons as they were printed. By means of red-ink entries in the margin, he knew at once in what volume or magazine any sermon might be found. It was not the Bible Mr. Spurgeon used daily, but Mrs. Spurgeon transcribed the inscription from that one and pasted it in the fly-leaf of the copy she gave Mr. Moody. It reads as follows:

"C. H. SPURGEON.

"The lamp of my study. 1858.

"The light is as bright as ever. 1861.

"Oh that mine eyes were more opened! 1864.

"Being worn to pieces, rebound 1870. The lantern mended and the light as joyous to mine eyes as ever."

After Spurgeon's Bible came into Mr. Moody's possession, together with a complete set of his sermons, he was in the habit of turning to it first to see if Spurgeon had preached on any part he was then studying.

CHAPTER XXXIX

Asking and Answering Questions

MR. MOODY was a born teacher. He was also a great learner. His capacity for drawing out information from people with whom he came in contact was marvellous. If driving about a new place, he never rested till he had found out all he could about the country and the people, especially their spiritual condition. If with a minister, he would have the best that that man could give him regarding the passages of Scripture which were especially in his mind at the time. Early in his public speaking he would gather around him Bible teachers, evangelists, and pastors, secure their best thoughts on some subject upon which he was to speak, and then go directly from such a conference to a meeting to deliver a heart-searching sermon, the actual material for which he had secured from his friends, absorbed, and made his own. In answer to an inquiry how far a young man was at liberty to use other men's thoughts, he replied: " Always give due credit if you can, and if you can't, or if you don't want to mention the man's name, say, 'Some one has said.' Don't be afraid of using other men's thoughts. The chances are that the man you get it from read it in some other form. There is practically very little that is original, and it's better to give the best of others' thoughts than what is poor, even if it is original."

In Sunday-school conventions, in Christian work, in revival meetings, in conferences, and in his schools he set apart times for answering questions. Sometimes he would sit on the platform and put a leading clergyman in the witness-box and question him steadily for an hour, to the great edification and spiritual refreshment of the audience. Again, he would himself be the witness and let the audience try their hand at questioning. In order that the time might not be consumed with foolish questions, or with those which were asked for the sake of discussion rather than profit, he insisted that they should be submitted in writing. Frequently conferences were held at the close of each revival meeting, where Christian workers could find out how to carry on evangelistic work in their own churches.

The following practical questions and helpful answers illustrate this phase of his teaching:

Q. " What more can be done against intemperance? "

A. " It would take all day to answer that. There are two sides in this matter, and I want to give a rap at both. I think every Christian church ought to be a temperance society. Look at the men who are stumbling over this great evil, going down to a drunkard's grave! I am a total abstainer; have never touched liquor, and never intend to do so. I am able to do a day's work without it.

"Now for the other side. I think the temperance man makes a great mistake who always harps on that one question. Everything in its own place. If I go to prayer-meeting I don't want to hear incessantly about temperance or the higher Christian life. We have a man in our city who comes to our prayer-meetings every day, and it doesn't matter what our subject is, he always gets up and talks on the higher life. And so with temperance. Only when you get a chance for a word slip it in; give strong drink a rap."

Q. "How about temperance meetings Sunday evenings?"

A. " I wouldn't have a temperance meeting on Sunday night. I would hold Sunday evening sacred to preaching the Gospel of the Son of God. In the Bible you have any quantity of subjects, but if you undertake to preach temperance sermons once a week the people will get tired of it. The Gospel covers temperance and everything else. A great many will not come to a temperance meeting, but they will come to a gospel meeting, and may get temperance thrown in.

Q. "Would you have a stated after-meeting every Sunday night?"

A. "Yes; every time I preached the Gospel I would look for results. There are three or four kinds of meetings. When we come around the Lord's table, that is worship. When we expound the Bible, that is to feed the Church of God. But when we invite men to come to God, then we ought to expect that they will come right then and there."

Q. "How would you conduct an after-meeting?"

A. "I never would conduct it fifty-two Sundays alike. There are very few men who could do that successfully. If the sermon is over at half-past eight, when the audience expected to stay until nine, they are in good mood to stay a half hour longer. There are two ways of inviting people to stay to an after-meeting. One is, to send them all home. The benediction is a polite invitation for people to go. I wouldn't pronounce any benediction at the first meeting, and I wouldn't say, '*If* any are concerned about their soul they are invited to stay.' You stick an 'if' four feet high before them, and it will take an earthquake to move them into an inquiry-room. When I was converted it took three months to screw up my courage to be examined by a committee to be taken into the church. You might as well try to get a man to go before a justice of the peace. I would say, 'Now, we are going to have a second meeting, and if any one must go, won't you just slip out while we are singing?' I would put it as though I expected no one to go."

Q. "Do you believe it is a good thing to use a stereopticon on Sunday night?"

A. "I wouldn't do it, because every Sunday night I would hold an after-meeting for inquirers, and I couldn't do that very well after a stereopticon lecture. Those lectures may do very well on a week-day night, but Sunday evening I hold sacred to proclaiming the Gospel in all its simplicity and following it with an after-meeting."

Q. "How can a minister have special meetings when he has failed to get an evangelist?"

A. "There is a plan that is working very well in England and in some parts of this country. Let a minister who has special evangelistic gifts give two weeks to a brother minister, and let that brother minister preach for him the Sunday between. Then that minister has two weeks in which he can go all through his parish and invite people out that perhaps he wouldn't like to ask to come to hear himself. He can get his whole church to work in the same way. Then, if people are converted, the church members will be more likely to look after them than if there had been some great union meeting. That plan helps the minister who has been preaching, too. He goes back to his own church all on fire, and preaches to his people with new interest.

"A series of meetings is a good thing, because if a man is awakened on Sunday, and there is to be a meeting on Monday, he is likely to come; and the impression is deepened; on Tuesday it grows deeper, and Wednesday or Thursday he will attend the after-meeting. I think if that could be done, many a church would double its membership right off. It is perfectly feasible. Let a minister go away for ten days and preach the best sermons he has. He has nothing to do but to pray and meditate and study, while the other minister with his members is out gathering the people."

Q. "Would you advise a young man to go into the ministry?"

A. "Never. If God calls a man, all right; but I have seen too many man-made ministers. If a man is called by God, he will succeed; but if he is sent by man, he will fail. I should advise every man to engage in Christian work, but not to give up all other occupations and live by the pulpit. All are called to be disciples and witnesses, but there needs to be a special call to be an apostle."

Q. "Is it a good thing for a minister to study elocution?"

A. "Yes and no. It is a good thing to learn to read well. But when it comes to modern elocution, these studied gestures in the pulpit—my word, I am tired and sick of them! Some men remind me of a windmill, with their practised gestures. How would Moses have succeeded if he had gone down into Egypt and tried elocution on Pharaoh? I like the oratory that moves men, but I have no use for the elocution where a man is showing off."

Q. "What would you do if you were a pastor in a town where there are five churches and only room for one?"

A. "Get out mighty quick. No power on earth can make me believe it is God's will that a Methodist and a Baptist and a Congregational and a Presbyterian and an Episcopal church should be in one town where there is not room for more than one or two. There is scarcely any difference in their creeds, and it is waste of time to be preaching in such a town. I believe that sort of thing is the work of the devil."

Q. "What would you do in a neighborhood of about one hundred families and no church, where there are no Christians except one godly family?"

A. "One godly family can evangelize one hundred families very easily. Let any man or woman who can read well get a good sermon by some prominent man, and let it be announced that this sermon is to be read on Sunday morning or evening. Then get the people together and read that sermon and pray that God may bless it. It may be just as effective as an original sermon. That has been done all through the mining districts. It is a sight in Colorado on Sunday to see the miners come out of the bowels of the hills and gather in the schoolhouses or under the trees while some old English miner stands up and reads one of Charles Spurgeon's sermons. They have conversions right along."

Q. "How can we get hold of strangers in these great cities?"

A. "I believe that if you would have in the pews a blank card with a place for name and residence, and if the minister would say when strangers are present that he or his wife would be glad to visit them if they would write their name and address on the card, and leave it in the pew—I believe that if a minister would do that constantly, he would reach a great many people and bring them into the church. In all the cities a great many people are lonesome or homesick, and want sympathy, but they don't know how to get it. I heard of a man who went to a church for six months without a single person speaking to him. Of course he was as much to blame as the church, but one morning the minister preached on recognizing friends in Heaven, and as the man went out he asked the sexton to ask the minister if he wouldn't preach on recognizing friends on earth, for he had been attending his church a half year and no one had spoken to him. It would be a good thing to have a committee at the door, and let no stranger get out without a word of welcome."

Q. "If you are advertised to preach, and there is a small audience on account of the bad weather, is it best to turn it into a prayer-meeting?"

A. "No, sir, I don't think so at all. If I expected five thousand people there and found only five, I would give them the best I could. Another thing—don't abuse the people who come for those that don't come. A rainy, stormy night is the time I expect the greatest blessing, because people have made a sacrifice to come. I was advertised to speak in Boston, and three thousand tickets had been given out. There came up the biggest blizzard they had had in Boston for eight or nine years. I had hard work to get to the city, and there I had to plough my way through deep snow-drifts. Less than one hundred people were in that big hall, and the leaders wanted to know if it would not be best to close the meeting and wait until the storm was over. 'No,' I said, 'not by a good deal.' I never preached so hard in my life as I did to that one hundred people. I put half a dozen sermons together, and threw them right at them. If a man ploughed through that snow to hear me I ought to do my best to pay him for coming. What we want is to turn defeat into victory. If a man can't do that he is a failure."

Q. "Ought a man to be admitted into the church if he has not been regenerated?"

A. "No, you hurt the church and hurt the man. A great many churches think that by admitting a man you bring him under good influences that may lead to his conversion; but they find it leads to just the reverse. He gets settled in his self-righteousness, and it grows harder and harder to reach him. The moment you begin to talk to him he runs up his lightning rod. 'Oh, I am saved! I am a member of the church!' There he sticks."

Q. "Is it right for any man or woman who has not been converted to have anything to do in an evangelical church?"

A. "I never set an unconverted man or woman to work, but Christian men need to be warmed up and then set to work to convert those who are not Christians."

Q. "Would you tell a man whose speaking injures a meeting not to take part in a prayer-meeting?"

A. "Yes, mighty quick. I would rather hurt the man's feelings than hurt the whole meeting. Some time ago I said to a man, 'You ought not to have said what you did to-night, and, besides, your record is all bad, and you ought not to take part at all.'

"'Sir,' he said, 'you hurt my feelings.'

"'Well,' I said, 'you hurt mine. I have feelings as well as you, and you hurt the feelings of five hundred other people besides.'"

Q. "What would you do if members in your congregation are at swords' points with others and won't make up?"

A. "I should keep at them until they did make up or left the church. No blessing can be expected to come to a church as long as the members go to the Lord's Supper and have an open quarrel. I believe the reason that there are so few conversions in many churches is because of these church feuds. God isn't going to bless a church in that condition."

Q. "What can be done to influence young men in the church and Sunday-school who are not Christians?"

A. " It depends altogether on what class of young men they are. It may be wise to begin by gathering them together for a social time. Ask them to your house to tea, and get acquainted with them. Find out something that they can do, something they would like to do. Another good way is to visit them personally. Men like to be treated as men. They like to have a man take an interest in them. If a minister calls on men in their office or store or on the farm, they will usually manage to go to hear him preach."

Q. " How can a man who wants to preach overcome nervousness? "

A. " That is a practical question, my friend. Do you remember the first time you got up to preach, and how your knees went thump, thump? I'll tell you what to do. Get so full of your subject that you forget yourself. Be occupied with the subject, and you are all right. This opens the question of preaching. Let me say right here that I like to say ' to speak ' better than ' to preach,' because if I can only get people to think I am talking with them, and not preaching, it is so much easier to hold their attention. The other night I was walking home in the dark, and two people right behind me were talking about the meeting. One of them said, ' Did Moody preach to-night? ' The other said, ' No, he didn't preach, he only talked.'

" ' Did you ever hear him before? '

" ' Yes.'

" ' How do you like him? '

" ' Well, we don't like him. He never has the church service, and he doesn't have on any robes; and then his preaching—why, he doesn't preach at all, he just talks.' I thought that was quite a compliment. I am glad if I can make people think I am talking with them. I think sometimes we almost preach the people to death—it is preach, preach, preach. If you can get the idea out of their minds that you are going to preach, and just let them think that you are going to talk, you are more likely to reach them.

Four Generations of the Moody Family

man asleep will publish to the whole audience that you are a dry preacher."

Q. "How long should a sermon be?"

A. "It is very much better to get a reputation for being brief than to have people say that you preach long sermons. Say what you have got to say in just as few words as you can. Then stop when you get through. Some men go on and feel around for a good stopping place. I'd rather stop abruptly than do that. Don't waste any time. Remember, we are living in an intense age. Men think quicker than they used to. The time was when if a man wanted to do a little business in Boston, he would write half a dozen sheets of foolscap and send them by mail. Now he puts it all in a telegram of ten words. What we want in our preaching is to condense. Get a reputation for being short, and people will want to hear you."

Q. "What would you do if the choir disturbed you?"

A. "I remember preaching once at Limerick when our hymn-books were new. A young man came in and joined the choir. There were three or four hundred people on the stage, and he took a front seat. He took up a hymn-book just as I began to preach, and turned over the leaves. Beginning with the first hymn, he went on as if he were going to examine every page in the book. I thought to myself, 'Have I got to preach until he gets all through that book before I can get the attention of the people?' What to do I didn't know. Finally I used him as an illustration. Speaking of a young man in America, I said, 'He was about the age of this young man reading a hymn-book.' The result was that when I asked all those in the house who wanted us to pray for them to rise, he rose. That young man was the first soul God gave me in Limerick. If he had gone on reading the hymn-book, it would have been almost impossible for me to get hold of him or the people. Get the attention of your audience somehow. If you are going to be a public speaker, train yourself for that."

Q. "What should be done after the attention is gained?"

A. "Aim at the heart. Just keep thundering away at the man's heart and you will get it, and if you get his heart, you will get his head and his feet and everything—you get the whole man. The story of the Prodigal Son will melt any man's heart. So will the story of the Good Samaritan. Or take any of the miracles of healing—how Christ saw a man blind or paralyzed and came to him and had compassion on him. Just open the heart of Christ to the people and draw the multitude around Him. If you want to get hold of an audience, aim at the heart; and there is nothing that will warm up the heart like the Gospel of Jesus Christ."

CHAPTER XL

Later Experiences with the Young Men's Christian Associations

REFERENCES have frequently been made to Mr. Moody's early work in behalf of the Young Men's Christian Association. His loyalty to that organization was never lessened in later years, notwithstanding the growth of the institutions directly dependent upon him for support. It is true he emphasized the directly religious features of the work above every other branch of effort, recognizing in the Christian life of the organization the vital force which could make it most useful in the truest sense. Educational privileges and opportunities for athletic prowess he recognized as secondary to the original plan and purpose. The Association, to his mind, was a means to an end, and he had little sympathy with the spirit that willingly sacrificed the preaching of the Gospel to what are called " Association methods." He was strongly opposed to the exclusion of women from the Sunday gospel meetings of the Association, believing that in many instances mothers, sisters, or friends might be counted on as efficient helpers in bringing to the meetings the very men whom the Association should reach. Instead of poorly attended gospel meetings supported by a few elderly Christian men, he believed the Association meetings would be well attended by the very class they should reach if they were but thrown open to mixed audiences.

These views he often expressed, and in consequence it was felt by some that Mr. Moody was disloyal to the organization. But if he

"I am satisfied that we owe our Association in Richmond largely to Mr. Moody, for which the city owes him a lasting debt of gratitude, and I am positive that his memory is warmly cherished by all our people."

It could almost be said that Mr. Moody's evangelistic tours could be traced by his influence upon these organizations. Mr. H. J. McCoy, of San Francisco, writes of his efforts in that city:

"The work of the Young Men's Christian Association for the moral and spiritual protection of young men owes a debt of gratitude to Mr. Moody; for its growth and development throughout California, and particularly in this city, are largely the result of his effort and timely help in 1881, when he came to San Francisco, and, by the blessing of God, rescued the Association and raised the debt of $84,000 on the Sutter Street property. Through his wisdom and forethought the work was reorganized, placed on a firm basis, and started on legitimate lines of effort for young men, Mr. Moody contributing liberally of his own private funds toward the indebtedness. Mr. Moody came to this coast at the request of the International Committee of the Young Men's Christian Association, which committee heartily coöperated and ably assisted him in the work at that time, a work that meant so much to the young men of the Pacific Coast.

"Through his efforts I came to the secretaryship of the San Francisco Association in August, 1881. For more than twenty-five years he was a close personal friend, and to him, more than to any other man, living or dead, I owe the fact of my being in Christian work."

From Mr. W. M. Danner, secretary of the Denver Young Men's Christian Association, comes a similar testimony as to interest taken in Association work during Mr. Moody's last year of evangelistic effort:

"Mr. D. L. Moody's work in Denver in 1899 resulted in the raising of $3,600 for the current expenses of the Association. This was only incidental to the great meetings held, but was sufficient to save the Association from the miserable deficit that had been embarrassing the organization for years."

Frequently Mr. Moody's indirect influence in behalf of the Associations was no less strikingly helpful in a material way. A former secretary of the Albany Association writes:

"In 1886 Mr. Moody held a service or services in Albany, N. Y., in the management of which the Young Men's Christian Association took a prominent part. Mr. Moody, as was his custom, at the closing service of the convention made an earnest appeal to the people of Albany to provide better facilities for the work among young men, and earnestly advocated the need of a building for the Association, stating at this service that the organization had, under God, done more in developing him for service than any other agency. The suggestion bore fruit. Mr. Charles F. Waterman was led to make a generous subscription and to advocate earnestly the need of such a building. Through Mr. Waterman and the earnest advocacy of the movement by Mr. Moody, Mr. James B. Jermain became interested and made the Association a gift of its present building, and later largely increased this gift, so that his entire benefactions to the Association exceeded $100,000. I fully believe that credit for the suggestion of the erection of this building belongs to Mr. Moody."

The Rev. S. A. Taggart, of Pittsburg, Penn., for many years State secretary of the Young Men's Christian Association, writes at length regarding Mr. Moody's efforts in behalf of young men in Pennsylvania:

"Mr. Moody was one of the pioneers of the Young Men's Christian Association on the continent of America. Previous to the Civil War (1861-65) the Associations in this country were few in number and had gained little more than a foothold. The oldest of them had been formed scarcely ten years. Many were disbanded during the years of strife, and the existence of those that were left was for the most part little more than nominal. It was only after peace had been declared that they began to take on an aggressive spiritual life. In these initiatory aggressive movements Mr. Moody very early appeared upon the scene. The Christian soldiers, on their return home, called to mind the impressive meetings of the Christian Commission in the various camps, and the next question was, Why not have a Young Men's Christian Association in our town or city? Soon Mr. Moody was in demand for the promotion of Associations in all sections of the Northwest. It was about this time, too, that he was chosen the executive officer of the Chicago Association.

"He told me of his first visit to Pittsburg in the interest of the Association. He had been to Philadelphia in 1866, and on his way stopped, between trains, in Pittsburg. He said, 'My time was limited. I rushed down the street and stopped at a store, and said to the first man I saw, "Give me the names of some of your most earnest ministers." He said, "My pastor is one." "Who is he?" "Herrick Johnson," he replied. "Where does he live?" He pointed me to his house. I rang the door-bell, and was shown into the house, and found myself in the midst of what seemed to be a dinner party. I saw that they were astonished at my abrupt entrance. I was overflowing with zeal. I told Dr. Johnson that Pittsburg ought to have a Young Men's Christian Association, and urged it upon him at length. He agreed with me at once, and said that a movement was then on foot in the interest of such an organization.'

"In less than two months Mr. Moody was back (January, 1867) in Pittsburg, attending a Christian convention. His efforts in behalf of the young organization at that time were exceedingly useful and greatly appreciated. Before the winter was over a deep religious interest prevailed throughout the city, and a large number of young men were led to enter upon a Christian life. Soon his services were in great demand among Associations, not simply in the region of Chicago, but as far east as Boston and Philadelphia.

"He attended the Indianapolis convention in 1870. It was at this convention that he uttered those pithy sayings: 'The law says do, grace says done; the law says do and live, grace says live and do; the Gospel says to the sinner, "Come," it says to the Christian, "Go."' These sayings soon found an echo in every Association hall in the land. They could readily be expanded into volumes, and they formed a large part of the basis of what in after years was Mr. Moody's working theology.

"Over thirty years ago, while I was stopping in Chicago for a day or two, I got my first impression of Mr. Moody by personal observation. Passing along Madison Street, my attention was called to a bulletin board at the Association building, on which was the announcement: 'Meeting to-morrow night in Farwell Hall at 7.30. D. L. Moody, speaker. Subject, Jesus.' A few minutes later I attended the noon-day meeting at which Mr. Moody spoke. He did not seem to be afraid that he would exhaust his subject of the next evening, although his theme was 'Jesus.' There was an urgency about him far beyond the ordinary. He had seemingly such a vivid and large conception of Christ that he was bound to tell it out. If I could make a composite of all that he has ever preached or said in religious meetings since that time and blend it into one word, it would be 'Jesus.'

"In less than two years from that time I was elected State secretary of the Young Men's Christian Associations of Pennsylvania, a position entirely new and without precedent in any State in the Union. However attractive it seemed, I soon found that it involved peculiar problems and difficulties. I turned for counsel and help to those who were older and had larger experience. I thought of Mr. Moody among others, and in the fall of 1871 visited him in Chicago. I found him in the office of the employment department of the Chicago Association, dealing with young men who were out of work. I told him I had come for his help. He said, 'I can't promise to help any one; I am too busy. If I were able to divide myself into two or three men I would have no spare time.' The outcome of our conference was that he agreed to come the following winter to help in conventions in Philadelphia, Pittsburg, Scranton, Harrisburg, Erie, and other places, if he could find the time. It was scarcely a week after this that tidings came of the Chicago fire. Mr. Moody's mission and the Young Men's Christian Association buildings, as well as his home, were in ashes. Thousands of people were homeless and destitute, and a multitude of new cares were thrust upon him. I felt that his agreement to come to Pennsylvania must be postponed indefinitely. Early in 1873 I was in Philadelphia and had occasion to visit Mr. John Wanamaker, of our State committee. Mrs. Wanamaker, being present, said, 'Get Mr. Moody to come to Pennsylvania by all means; he has been in our church, and in Dr. Cuyler's in Brooklyn, holding meetings. He is the greatest man in America to get men to think of their sins and of another world. Dr. Cuyler agrees with me.'

"The Association at Pittsburg had been conducting special meetings during the last week of May, 1873, and Mr. Moody gave a single Bible address May 27th, the last service he held in this country before his departure on what afterwards proved to be a wonderful mission. I have never forgotten that address. I took no notes of it, and yet for nearly twenty-seven years I have carried the theme and its four divisions in my memory. His subject was the love of God. The four points were, first, the love of God in the gift of His Son; second, the love of God shed abroad in our hearts as a preparation for His service; third, the love of God in the afflictions that come to His people; fourth, the love of God in death.

"Upon the last point his words seemed almost prophetic of his dying moments. 'People say to me, have you grace to die? I say no; I have only grace now to hold this meeting. The Lord promises to give grace when we need it and not before, and when death comes, and not before, will He give us dying grace. They say to me, "How do you know He will be with us in death?" I say because He tells us in His own Word, "*Precious in the sight of the Lord is the death of His saints.*" His Spirit inspired one of His servants to write for our comfort, " For I am persuaded that neither death, nor life, nor angels, nor principalities, nor powers, nor things present, nor things to come, nor height, nor depth, nor any other creature shall be able to separate us from the love of God which is in Christ Jesus our Lord." As if some one might be doubting it, the first thing he says is, "For I am persuaded that death cannot separate us from the love of God." My friends, when we are called upon to die, if we love God we will know in a moment that God will take care of our loved ones.' may be sorry to part from our loved ones, but He will give us light. It might please Him, in the hour of death, to give us a little sight of the glory of the future before we pass out of the body. If so, this world will be spoiled forever; we will not even want to look back; we will know in a moment that God will take care of our loved ones.'

" I cannot help comparing these words with the utterances of Mr. Moody more than twenty-six years afterwards, when he came to the close of life:

" ' Earth recedes; Heaven opens before me. I have been beyond the gates. God is calling. Don't call me back.' I cannot but think he must have caught a sight of the future glory.

" In closing the meeting he said: ' I am going over to the manufacturing towns in England for three months to preach the Gospel while our church in Chicago is being completed. I want you to pray that I may be so full of the love of God that I can speak of nothing but Jesus Christ and Him crucified.' We who heard him little imagined that in less than six months audiences of from five to ten thousand people would be listening to the story of the cross from his lips in the city of Edinburgh, Scotland, or that such a widespread awakening would follow his labors that he would spend twenty-six months, instead of three, in his mission abroad.

"The great spiritual awakening attending Mr. Moody's labors abroad was felt by the Associations in this country long before his return. This was evident in the State and international conventions and by the increased evangelistic spirit shown among many of the organizations. This spirit grew in intensity upon his return.

"For over twenty-five years during the latter part of his life Mr. Moody had no official relation with any local Association, and yet during all that time his spiritual power, attested in his multiplied labors, served as a kind of dynamic force, communicating itself through the network of conventions to the greater number of Associations all over the continent. So all-pervading was his influence in the life of the Associations in this country that it would be hard to tell what might have been their course had no such relation ever existed. This is true not alone in the spiritual life of the Associations, but to a great extent also in their temporal equipment. Many Association buildings owe their origin, in whole or in part, to the unselfish efforts of Mr. Moody. Notably is this the case in Pennsylvania, at Philadelphia, Scranton, Reading, and Williamsport.

"It was during the year 1885, through the joint invitation and cooperation of pastors and Associations, that he held several days' services in each of the following places and in the order named:

"Harrisburg, Scranton, Germantown (Philadelphia), New Castle, Pittsburg, Reading, Williamsport, Bellefonte, Altoona, York, and Chester.

"These gatherings partook of the character of conventions, three sessions a day being held. The evening services were evangelistic. The various cities were not visited consecutively, but at such periods as he could best give the time. The first was visited as early as January, and the last as late as December of that year.

"At most of these places the local committees of arrangements had the advantage of using the large skating-rinks that had been erected a little while before. They had been seated and comfortably heated, and accommodated very large numbers of people. I think I make a conservative estimate when I say that in the aggregate at least five hundred thousand people heard him, and one hundred and fifty thousand different persons were in attendance during these gatherings. They were attended by a wonderful interest. At one place I was told that nearly two hundred ministers outside of the city were present. The same was true, to a great extent, elsewhere. The after-meetings were attended by many inquirers, and the reports of pastors bore witness of much substantial fruit.

"At a convention in Scranton Mr. Moody called upon me to speak upon the subject, 'What more can be done for the young men of this city?' He followed this by announcing that a collection would be taken that night for a building for the Young Men's Christian Association of Scranton, and that he would like to raise $75,000. This practical part of the subject was new to the people. I could see many of them shaking their heads in doubt. In the meantime the alert board of managers of the Association had taken advantage of the occasion to invite a special company to dine with Mr. Moody at the hotel that evening. Around the table $25,000 was subscribed for the new building. One who had been specially invited to be present, and from whom, by reason of his wealth, they had hoped for help, was not there. Mr. Moody proposed to go and see him at once before the meeting of the evening. Some shook their heads and said they feared it would be of no use. Mr. Moody said to Colonel Boies, 'Get your sleigh and drive around with me to see this man before the meeting; I like to talk to rich men, particularly if they don't want to give. They are a neglected class and need a missionary. No one ever thinks of speaking to them about their souls or their stewardship.' He called to see this man and said to him, 'We need a Moses to lead the way for the young men of Scranton. The Association is out on the street nearly all the time begging for its living, when it ought to be trying to save the ten thousand young men of the city. We want you to give $20,000 to lead the way for a building.' This request staggered the old gentleman for a time, and he could make no reply, but finally said that he could not give. Mr. Moody then talked to him about $10,000, but with no satisfactory understanding. He said to him, 'You will be at the meeting to-night?' 'Yes,' was the reply. 'Well, I want you to take a seat on the platform.' When the time for the meeting came we had worked our way with difficulty to the platform. Mr. Moody said to me, 'Do you see Mr. X—— anywhere?' Before I could reply he caught sight of him on the edge of the platform and worked over as near as he could get, and in a shouting whisper said, 'How much is it—ten, ten?' 'Oh, no,' was the reply, 'just the half, just the half.' When the name of this man, among others, was announced that night as giving $5,000, it produced a deep impression. He was known as slow in giving, and yet for that very reason it seemed to inspire the whole city with confidence that the project must go through to success. From that hour this man took the deepest interest in the building project, and was greatly blessed in his gift. The result of the subscriptions and collection that night was less than $35,000, but the sequel showed that Mr. Moody understood the situation. He had been informed that many who were interested in the business enterprises of Scranton lived in New York City and elsewhere, and he assured the people of Scranton that the building would soon be erected.

"That night we took the train for the next place of meeting, Germantown, Philadelphia. I was anxious about the situation at Scranton, and was wondering where the rest of the money would come from for the building. Mr. Moody said to me, 'Write to your friends in New York and find out if Mr. Samuel Sloan, the president of the Delaware, Lackawanna, and Western Railroad, will be in his office on Saturday, and at what hour, and tell them to telegraph you in Philadelphia.' After the Germantown meeting we were invited to take breakfast at Mr. John Wanamaker's on Saturday, where a large company were present. While we were in the midst of the meal, I received a telegram stating that Mr. Sloan would be in his office in New York that day at a certain hour. I handed it to Mr. Moody; he read it, and immediately arose from the table and said, 'Friends, I am sorry to leave you, but the King's business requires haste,' and in a few minutes he was on the train for New York. Calling upon Mr. Sloan, he soon secured his hearty coöperation in the proposed Scranton building. While thus engaged in conversation an old gentleman came in, to whom Mr. Sloan introduced Mr. Moody, saying, 'This is just the man you want to see to help you at Scranton.' Before Mr. Moody could say a word, the old man said, 'Is this the man who has been creating the great stir at Scranton? I am afraid he is getting the people to give more than they are able; I will not give anything; I have given away over $700,000 to various things within a short time. Why don't you go to the people who don't give anything instead of coming to us who give?' Mr. Moody said, 'I would like to tell you a short story.' 'No,' said the old gentleman, 'I don't want to hear any story.' 'You must sit down and hear this story,' interposed Mr. Sloan. 'Mr. Moody, you must not be discouraged; this is the way he always does when he is making up his mind to give.' Finally the disturbed old gentleman listened as Mr. Moody went on. 'There was a man once who went to solicit money and came to one who made your objection, "Why don't you go to the people who never give, instead of to us who do give?" To this the solicitor replied, "If you wanted a good pail of milk, would you go to a cow that was milked regularly or to one that was only milked once in a long time?" The story had the desired result, and Mr. Sloan assured Mr. Moody that, 'although our friend doesn't laugh now, you will not be away from here ten minutes before he will be in all the offices of this building, telling what a good story Moody told.'

"Mr. Moody said nothing more, but in a few days a subscription came from the old gentleman for $5,000. The result of Mr. Moody's efforts on his rest day in New York for the Scranton fund was an assured increase of nearly $30,000 more, making a total of over $60,000 in less than four days; the whole amount needed, $75,000, was secured in less than six weeks. He often related this experience, and called it a 'red letter week.'

"I had tried for some time to think of some one with whom Mr.

Moody was not acquainted, to assist him with more than an ordinary contribution in his educational work at Northfield. After considerable thought I said, 'I have a friend in the oil regions whom I have known for a long time. I knew him when he was poor, and he is now prosperous, and his prosperity has not hurt his Christian character. I wish you would write to him explaining your work and its needs.' A short time after this I received a letter from Mr. Moody, in which he said, 'The Lord answers prayer, and I must testify to His goodness. I wrote to your friend, and, after finishing the letter, I prayed that God might incline him to give the sum I had named, if he was able to give it. He has sent me his check for $5,000.' Some days afterwards I was in the place where this man resided and called upon him. He said to me, 'I think you must have set Mr. Moody after me, as I have never met him. I received a letter asking me for $5,000 for his schools in Northfield. When I read the letter I thought I could not give anything, then I thought I would send $500 anyhow. In a little while I raised it to $1,000. On my way home to luncheon I thought of the hundreds of poor young men and women getting an education for $100 a year and the large extra expense resting on Mr. Moody, for which he must make provision, and the thought came to me, "Make it $2,500." Before I reached home I thought, if my wife agreed with me, I would make it $5,000. When I showed her the letter she said, "Give him the sum he asks for." This all occurred within an hour, and that afternoon I sent him my check for the full amount.'"

The Rev. George A. Hall, at present one of the State secretaries of the Young Men's Christian Association of New York, was one of Mr. Moody's warmest friends for twenty-five years. He prizes greatly two letters, the first received at the beginning and the other at the end of that close friendship. When Mr. Moody left Brooklyn for Philadelphia, in November, 1875, and put Mr. Hall in charge of the young men's meeting there, he wrote:

"My dear Hall: I wish you would drop me a line and let me

know how the work goes. I do hope you can arrange to stay in Brooklyn this winter. If you can, I will try and help you some time this winter or spring. The work there has stirred up the young men in this city, and there is a great work started, although I have not said one word to the unconverted yet. I am just sure God is going to do a great work this winter, and I do hope you will stand by me. The eyes of the world are on Brooklyn now, and it is quite important that the work be kept up there. Much love to all the young men."

While on his way to Kansas City, November 8, 1899, Mr. Moody stopped in Philadelphia, and then wrote the following letter, which serves as a valedictory:

"DEAR HALL: It will be a treat to be in a convention with you once more, and, God willing, I will be with you. It must be hard on to thirty years since we were at Pontiac, Ill., with our friend, Culver, who has gone home. What an army has gone since then! What a grand time we will all have when we get home! I am on my way to Kansas City."

Nor were Mr. Moody's labors for American Associations only. At his suggestion and by his efforts Lord Overtoun undertook the Glasgow Bible Training Institute, which is equipping trained workers for Christian service. In Aberdeen Mr. Moody raised $25,000 for the erection of a building for the local Young Men's Christian Association, and in Dundee succeeded in raising $27,000 for a similar purpose. In other cities he aided indirectly in the work, laying a memorial stone in the Liverpool Association in 1876, and the cornerstone of the Cork Association in 1892.

Owing to his efforts several missions have been erected as living testimonies of the permanency of the evangelistic missions conducted, and, with many of these, local Associations are affiliated and in active coöperation.

At a memorial service held by the Chicago Association after Mr. Moody's death the following resolution, combining a brief history of his relations with that organization as well as a tribute to his memory, was adopted:

MEMORIAL TRIBUTE TO DWIGHT L. MOODY

The Young Men's Christian Association of Chicago holds this memorial meeting to pay tribute to the memory and character of Dwight L. Moody. The great work of Mr. Moody's life was not local or limited. His name has long ceased to be a Chicago possession. Yet while the voices of two continents recount his services in every strain of affectionate appreciation we may here recall the days and deeds which prepared him for his larger career.

The services of Mr. Moody to this Association in its early days were of inestimable value. From 1861 to 1870 he was the most active and persistent leader in the work of the Association. During part of this time he was the librarian, a position which afterward grew into the general secretaryship. From 1865 to 1869 he was the acting president of the Association. He gave to it the first years in which he wholly devoted himself to Christian work. Before this a well-known business man, in whose store he was employed, said of him, "Mr. Moody would make quite a good clerk if he had not so many other things on his hands." Those "other things" were the eternal interests of his fellowmen; and such a spirit as his could not long be confined even by the bonds that hold most men to the appointed tasks by which they earn their daily bread. With an enthusiasm that could not be dampened and an energy that continued to the end, Mr. Moody entered upon the ministry to which he was called of God. It will ever remain a precious memory of this Association that he began here this larger ministry, and obtained here the preparation so needful for his subsequent career. What he did for communities and for nations in later years he did for this Association in its earlier days.

This Association has claimed him as its greatest single champion. For years he was its leading delegate to Association conventions, where he stood for the supremacy, even to exclusiveness, of evangelistic work in the Associations. During the dark days of the Civil War he was the leading spirit in making the Association a power for good in the armies

College Students' Conference.

A Corner in the College Camp.

MR. MOODY AND HIS GRANDDAUGHTER IRENE.

of the Union as well as at home. He was active in securing its first, second, and third buildings. The first, Farwell Hall, which was also the first Association building in the world, was opened in 1867, while Mr. Moody was president of the Association. Four months later it was burned to the ground. "When the flames were fiercest the call for prayer was sounded, and the daily prayer-meeting gathered in the lecture-room of the Methodist Church at the usual hour for prayer and praise." After the great fire of 1871, in which the second building was burned, Mr. Moody served on a strong committee of the Association for general relief work. He also, for some time afterward, rendered various and important services to the Association. Only last year, in connection with the fortieth anniversary services, he expressed the hope "that the greatest work and greatest successes of the Association are yet before it."

The Chicago Association honors and cherishes the memory of Dwight L. Moody for what he wrought here, and for the greater work which he has since pursued with such success for the world's evangelization. It rejoices that one whose training in Christian work was in part obtained in its service should be so manifestly used of God to advance His Kingdom among men. It extends its sincere sympathy to the members of the family in this hour of bereavement.

CHAPTER XLI

The Inquiry-room

IT will be remembered that just before Chicago was destroyed by flames in 1871 Mr. Moody had dismissed an audience, telling them to go home and think what they would do with Christ. He never met them again. This dismissal he regarded as one of the greatest mistakes of his life, and he determined never to repeat it. From that time on he laid great stress on the after-meeting, which took place at the close of an evangelistic address, in which he tried to bring individual souls to an immediate decision as to the great issues he had just brought before them. These meetings were probably the most characteristic and original feature of his work.

"Personal dealing is of the most vital importance," said Mr. Moody in discussing the inquiry-room and its uses. "No one can tell how many souls have been lost through lack of following up the preaching of the Gospel by personal work. It is deplorable how few church members are qualified to deal with inquirers. And yet that is the very work in which they ought to aid the pastor most efficiently. People are not usually converted under the preaching of the minister. It is in the inquiry meeting that they are most likely to be brought to Christ.

"Some people can't see the use of the inquiry meetings; they think they are something new, and that we haven't any authority for them. But they are no innovation. We read about them all through the Bible. When John the Baptist was preaching he was interrupted. It would be a good thing if people would interrupt the minister now and then in the middle of some metaphysical sermon and ask what he means. The only way to make sure that people understand what he is talking about is to let them ask questions. I don't know what some men who have got the whole thing written out would do if some one should get up and ask, 'What must I do to be saved?' Yet such questions would do more good than anything else you could have. They would wake up a spirit of inquiry.

"Some people say, 'All you want to do is to make the preaching so plain that plain people will understand it.' Well, Christ was a plain preacher, and yet he asked, '*Have ye understood all these things?*' (Matt. xiii. 51.) He encouraged them to inquire. I think sometimes, when the minister is preaching over their heads, people would be greatly relieved if he would stop and ask whether they understood it. His very object is to make the Word of God clear. Christ was a plain preacher; but when He preached to Saul the man was only awakened. Christ could have convicted and converted him, but He honored a human agency, and sent Ananias to tell the word whereby he was to be saved. Philip was sent away into the desert to talk to one man in the chariot. We must have personal work—hand-to-hand work—if we are going to have results.

"I admit you can't lay down rules in dealing with inquirers. There are no two persons exactly alike. Matthew and Paul were a good way apart, and the people we deal with may be widely different. What would be medicine for one might be rank poison for another. In the fifteenth of Luke the elder son and the younger son were exactly opposite. What would have been good counsel for one might have been ruin for the other. God never made two persons to look alike. If we had made men, probably we would have made them all alike, even if we had to crush some bones to get them into the mould. But that is not God's way. In the universe there is infinite variety. The Philippian jailer required peculiar treatment; Christ dealt with Nicodemus one way and with the woman at the well another way. It is difficult to say just how people are to be saved, yet there are certain portions of Scripture that can be brought to bear on certain classes of inquirers.

"I think it is a great mistake, in dealing with inquirers, to tell your own experience. Experience may have its place, but I don't think it has its place when you are talking with them. For the first thing the man you are talking to will do will be to look for your experience in his case. He doesn't want your experience; he wants one of his own. No two persons are converted alike. Suppose Bartimæus had gone to Jerusalem to the man that was born blind and said, 'Now, just tell us how the Lord cured you.' The Jerusalem man might have said, 'He just spat on the ground and anointed my eyes with the clay.' 'Ho!' says Bartimæus, 'I don't believe you ever got your sight at all. Who ever heard of such a way as that? Why, to fill a man's eyes with clay is enough to put them out!' Both men were blind, but they were not cured alike. A great many men are kept out of the Kingdom of God because they are looking for somebody else's experience—the experience their grandmother had, or their aunt, or some one in the family.

"Always use your Bible in personal dealing. Do not trust to memory, but make the person read the verse for himself. Do not use printed slips or books. Hence, if convenient, always carry a Bible or New Testament with you.

"It is a good thing to get a man on his knees, but don't get him there before he is ready. You may have to talk with him two hours before you can get him that far along. But when you think he is about ready, say, 'Shall we not ask God to give us light on this point?'

"Sometimes a few minutes in prayer have done more for a man than two hours in talk. When the Spirit of God has led him so far that he is willing to have you pray with him, he is not very far from the Kingdom. Ask him to pray for himself. If he doesn't want to pray, let him use a Bible prayer; get him to repeat, for example, 'Lord help me!' Tell the man, 'If the Lord helped that poor woman, He will help you if you make the same prayer. He will give you a new heart if you pray from the heart.' Don't send a man home to pray. Of course he should pray at home, but I would rather get his lips open at once. It is a good thing for a man to hear his own voice in prayer. It is a good thing for him to cry out, 'God be merciful to me, a sinner!'

"Urge an immediate decision, but never tell a man he is converted. Never tell him he is saved. Let the Holy Spirit reveal that to him. You can shoot a man and see that he is dead, but you cannot see when a man receives eternal life. You can't afford to deceive any one about this great question. But you can help his faith and trust, and lead him aright.

"Always be prepared to do personal work. When war was declared between France and Germany, Count von Moltke, the German general, was prepared for it. Word was brought to him late at night, after he had gone to bed. 'Very well,' he said to the messenger, 'the third portfolio on the left!' and he went to sleep again.

"Do the work boldly. Don't take those in a position in life above your own, but, as a rule, take those on the same footing. Don't deal with a person of opposite sex if it can be otherwise arranged. Bend all your endeavors to answer for poor, struggling souls that question of such importance to them, 'What must I do to be saved?'"

Mr. Moody summarized his suggestions on this important subject thus:

"(1) Have for constant use a portable reference Bible, a Cruden's Concordance, and a Topical Text-book.

"(2) Always carry a Bible or Testament in your pocket, and do not be ashamed of people seeing you read it on trains, etc.

"(3) Do not be afraid of marking it or making marginal notes. Mark texts that contain promises, exhortations, warnings to sinners and to Christians, gospel invitations to the unconverted, and so on.

"(4) Set apart at least fifteen minutes a day for study and meditation. This little time will have great results and will never be regretted.

"(5) '*Prepare your heart to know the way of the Lord, and to do it.*' (Ezra, vii. 10.)

"(6) Always ask God to open the eyes of your understanding that you may see the truth, and expect that He will answer your prayer.

"(7) Cast every burden of doubt upon the Lord. '*He will never suffer the righteous to be moved.*' Do not be afraid to look for a reason for the hope that is in you.

"(8) Believe in the Bible as God's revelation to you, and act accordingly. Do not reject any portion because it contains the supernatural or because you cannot understand it. Reverence all Scripture. Remember God's own estimate of it: '*Thou hast magnified Thy Word above all Thy Name.*'

"(9) Learn at least one verse of the Scripture each day. Verses committed to memory will be wonderfully useful in your daily life and walk. '*Thy Word have I hid in mine heart, that I might not sin against Thee.*' Some Christians can quote Shakespeare and Longfellow better than the Bible.

"(10) If you are a preacher or a Sunday-school teacher try at any cost to master your Bible. You ought to know it better than any one in your congregation or class.

"(11) Strive to be exact in quoting Scripture.

"(12) Adopt some systematic plan of Bible study: either topical, or by subjects, like 'The Blood,' 'Prayer,' 'Hope,' etc., or by books, or by some other plan outlined in the preceding pages.

"(13) Study to know for what and to whom each book of the Bible was written. Combine the Old Testament with the New. Study Hebrews and Leviticus together, the Acts of the Apostles and the Epistles, the Prophets and the historical books of the Old Testament.

"(14) Study how to use the Bible so as to 'walk with God' in closer communion, also so as to gain a working knowledge of Scripture for leading others to Christ. An old minister used to say that the cries of neglected texts were always sounding in his ears, asking why he did not show how important they were.

"(15) Do not be satisfied with simply reading a chapter daily. *Study* the meaning of at least one verse."

CHAPTER XLII

His Belief and Practice

IN the beginning of Mr. Moody's public efforts his work, being independent of and outside the established churches, was often misunderstood by clergymen. He felt that there were scores of men in every denomination who could reach the people far better than he, if they would but lay aside a little clerical dignity and make the outsiders feel that the church was as desirous for their salvation as was the Master. In his later years he worked more in harmony with the ministers, and won the confidence of the great majority, hundreds availing themselves every year of his invitation to Northfield.

He did not mince words when he felt that criticism was a duty. His picture of a man following his minister's sermons carefully and cutting out of a Bible whatever the minister said was not authentic, was amusing, though sad. One day this man carried to his pastor a badly mutilated Bible, from which numerous leaves and parts of leaves had been cut, saying:

" Here, Pastor, is your Bible."

" My Bible? " said the clergyman impatiently.

" Yes; I have cut out all that you say is fable and allegory and folk-lore and also the mythical and so-called unauthentic parts, and here is what is left."

" Give it to me," said the preacher.

" No, you don't," the man replied. " You haven't touched the covers yet, and I am going to cling to them at least."

"I believe," said Mr. Moody, "that there are a good many scholars in these days, as there were when Paul lived, 'who, professing themselves to be wise, have become fools'; but I don't think they are those who hold to the inspiration of the Bible. I have said that ministers of the Gospel who are cutting up the Bible in this way, denying Moses to-day and Isaiah to-morrow, and Daniel the next day and Jonah the next, are doing great injury to the church; and I stand by what I have said. I don't say that they are bad men. They may be good men, but that makes the results of their work all the worse. Do they think they will recommend the Bible to the finite and fallen reason of men by taking the supernatural out of it? They are doing just the opposite. They are emptying the churches and driving the young men of this generation into infidelity.

"My mind is made up," he said at another time, "on the question proposed; namely, the relative merits of Christianity and infidelity, under whatever name it appears. Somebody once asked Charles Sumner to hear the other side of slavery. 'Hear the other side?' he replied, 'there is no other side.' I would as soon discuss the merits of Christianity and infidelity as the common laws of morality."

For honest doubt he had the utmost sympathy, and he spared neither time nor effort to lead a man to make a right decision, but he had no patience with a man who asked him hard questions simply for the sake of argument. No man could distinguish between the real and the false more readily. He often told this experience:

"A man came to me with a difficult passage in the Bible and said:

"'Mr. Moody, what do you do with that?'

"'I do not do anything with it.'

"'How do you understand it?'

"'I do not understand it.'

"'How do you explain it?'

"'I do not explain it.'

"'What do you do with it?'

"'I do not do anything with it.'

"'You do not believe it, do you?'

"'Oh, yes, I believe it.'

"'Well, you don't accept anything you can't understand, do you?'

"'Yes, I certainly do. There are lots of things I do not understand, but I believe them. I do not know anything about higher mathematics, but I believe in them. I do not understand astronomy, but I believe in astronomy. Can you tell me why the same kind of food turns into flesh, fish, hair, feathers, or hoofs, according as it is eaten by one animal or another? A man told me a while ago he would not believe a thing he had never seen, and I asked him if he had ever seen his own brain? Did you ever notice that the things at which men cavil most are the very things on which Christ has set His seal?'"

When a liberal preacher declared that the story of Jonah and the whale was a myth, reporters asked Mr. Moody his opinion of the question. His reply, contained in four words, was telegraphed far and wide:

"I stand by Jonah."

While holding tenaciously to the Bible as the inspired Word of God, and preaching the doctrines with Calvinistic fervor, he had sympathy with men who looked at truth from a different view-point, if the difference was merely intellectual. When Lord Overtoun invited him in the name of many Scotch Christians to return to Scotland and hold evangelistic services there in 1899, Mr. Moody was obliged to decline, and in doing so said:

"The work in my own country has never been so promising as it is now. Destructive theology on the one side and the no less evil spirit of extreme intolerance on the other side have wrought wide dissensions in many communities in America. Instead of fighting error by the emphasis of truth, there has been too much 'splitting of hairs,' and too often an unchristian spirit of bitterness. This has frequently resulted in depleted churches, and has opened the way for the entrance of still greater errors. Under these conditions the question of the authorship of the individual books of the Bible has become of less immediate importance than the knowledge of the Bible itself; the question of the two Isaiahs less urgent than a familiarity with the prophecy itself."

In this connection it is interesting to see how firmly he clung to the Word of God:

"Why should I get a new remedy for sin when I have found one that has never failed?" he said. "The Gospel has stood the test for eighteen centuries. I know what it will do for sin-sick souls. I have tried its power for forty years. It is a singular fact that few men, otherwise well educated, are acquainted with the English Bible. I can secure a hundred men who can teach Greek and Latin well where I can find only one that can teach the Bible well.

"Take the Bible; study it; leave criticism to the theologians; feed on the Word; then go out to work. Combine the two—study and work—if you would be a full-orbed Christian. The Bible is assailed as never before. Infidels cast it overboard, but it will always swim to the shore. The doctrines, the promises, the messages of love are as fresh to-day as when first spoken. Pass on the message; be obedient to commands; waste no time in discussion; let speculation and theorizing pass into the hands of those who like that kind of study. Be willing to do little things for the Master."

In the last summer of his life Mr. Moody thus defined the Northfield platform:

"The central idea of the Northfield Conference is Christian unity, and the invitation is to all denominations and to all wings of denominations; but it is understood that along with the idea of Christian unity goes the Bible as it stands. We seek at these meetings to find points of common belief. Too frequently when Christians get together they seek for the points upon which they differ, and then go at it. The Christian denominations too often present a spectacle of a political party split into factions and unable to make an effective fight. Do you know that every twenty-four hours three hundred persons die a drunkard's death in this country? In the last four years there were thirty-eight thousand five hundred and twelve murders in this country. Here are things to unite on and combat."

Mr. Moody was kindly inclined to all men whom he felt were endeavoring to do a work for the betterment of man, and although there may have been many so-called churches with which he could by no means agree, he was never heard to speak an unkindly word regarding them. His theory evidently was that it was far better to spend his time in building up than endeavoring to tear down.

Mr. Moody was, until his death, a member of the "Chicago Avenue Church" in Chicago, an independent organization, although formed on Congregational lines. Started as a home for the converts resulting from Mr. Moody's mission work in North Market Hall, its purpose has been stated thus:

"Our church: Unsectarian, and in fellowship with all who love the Lord Jesus Christ.

"Our theme: Jesus Christ and Him crucified, Who is over all, God blessed forever.

"Our object: The perfecting of the saints; the salvation of the lost.

"Our hope: The coming of our Lord Jesus Christ."

The present membership is about a thousand. The average attendance of children in the Sunday-school is close on two thousand. In the congregation the rich and the poor meet together; the learned and the ignorant sit side by side, and listen with pleasure and profit to the earnest sermons of Dr. Torrey. After-meetings are frequently held, and conversions are constantly occurring.

The Northfield Church, of which Mr. Moody's children are members and which Mr. Moody heartily supported, is attended by the students from the Seminary and the Training-school. Before the Mount Hermon chapel was built the students from that school walked over every Sunday to the morning service.

Dr. C. I. Scofield, writing of Mr. Moody as an evangelist, calls attention to his strength and faithfulness under the trial of temptation:

"Three supreme testings await strong men in this life," he says—"the testing of poverty and obscurity, of prosperity and applause, and of suffering. Many who enter life conscious, even though dimly, of great latent capacities turn sour and bitter under neglect, narrow circumstances, and lack of appreciation. Others who pass that first trial successfully are corrupted or enfeebled by success and adulation. Many who stand erect alike in obscurity and success fail utterly under the testing of suffering. By God's grace Mr. Moody passed unscathed through them all. Perhaps it has happened to few men, suddenly lifted into the fellowship of the noble and famous of the earth, to be so little moved from the serenity of their minds, the even tenor of their ways.

"Doubtless this self-poise was in part an inheritance—the hill-town New Englander's habitual self-respect. But doubtless, too, Mr. Moody had so great a sense of the essential dignity of even the least of the sons of God, that he was little affected by earthly titles or personal fame.

"On one occasion it was whispered to him, with some agitation, that a certain exalted personage had entered the hall.

"Mr. Moody quietly replied:

"'I hope she may be much blessed.'

"This independence, springing as it did from elevation and simplicity of character, and not at all from self-assertiveness, commended Mr. Moody to all.

"In the superficial view it was always Mr. Moody's generalship, his mastery of vast numbers of men gathered in meetings, which first impressed the observer; and for the following reason: Mr. Moody's grip of his audience was not due in the first instance to his power as a preacher. Other men, as Whitefield and Wesley, and the great Welsh field-preachers, have drawn vast audiences, and have in the end powerfully swayed them, however turbulent or tumultuous they may have been when these great masters of the 'royal art of preaching' rose to address them. But D. L. Moody never began to preach until he had gathered his audience into almost perfect *rapport* with himself. This was his unique distinction among other equally great preachers.

"To accomplish this result he devised a method perfectly adapted to himself, but which in the hands of his imitators is by no means sure of success. Briefly, it was the conduct of a remarkably intense and spiritual preliminary service of song and prayer, interspersed with brief, pungent, characteristic sayings of his own. From the time he came before his great audiences to the moment when he rose to preach he kept the entire body absorbingly occupied with something interesting. Singing by the great massed choir, by quartettes, duetists, soloists, and by the whole assembly, never ceased, except for prayer. But it would be an utter misapprehension to suppose that either Mr. Moody's purpose or the actual result achieved was the entertainment of the people. His own manner showed at once his tremendous earnestness, his profound concern for souls.

"As a preacher D. L. Moody was much criticised from the standpoint of academic homiletics. Nor would any think of defending his preaching method on that ground. But the fact that for thirty-five continuous years, in the centres of culture and of active practical thought in the English-speaking world, this self-taught preacher drew the greatest audiences which have faced any modern speaker on any theme—this fact, one would say, should suggest to teachers of homiletics that possibly they might learn something from him.

"His method was devoid of mystery. Drawing his matter from the Scriptures, he utterly eschewed formal introduction, and plunged at once into the subject itself. He came early into the possession of a strong Saxon vocabulary, and his sense taught him the value of the short sentence and of aphoristic forms.

"Of all this, the man himself, as he stood before his audience, was utterly unconscious. He was tremendously in earnest, absolutely sincere, perfectly incapable of phrase-making. It was his supreme possession by the Spirit, united with his powerful understanding, which were his safeguards against bathos, turgid rhetoric, pose, and artifice. Like all natural orators, he made great and effective use of illustration. And yet it is doubtful if he ever used even the most telling illustration purely for effect. He told an anecdote, or referred to a Bible story or incident, because it made his point clear.

"Among his natural gifts were humor, always refined, pathos, and a descriptive power which was due to his imagination. Few men ever equalled him in ability to summon before an audience the whole setting of a Bible incident. And he had the sovereign grace of brevity. He knew when to stop, and he never weakened his sermon at the close by recapitulation."

CHAPTER XLIII

Traits and Characteristics

OF some prominent preachers it has been said that when you see them in the pulpit you wish they might never leave it, and when you see them out of it you wish they might never enter it. This could never be said of D. L. Moody. His character could bear a rigid examination; as one of his closest friends said, " Doubtless he had faults, but I never saw them." If his preaching was persuasive in the pulpit while addressing thousands, it was in the quiet seclusion of his home life, or in the companionship of a few warm friends, that he was most truly eloquent. Impulsive, energetic, and resolute by nature, he yet possessed in a great degree the quiet strength of patience, sympathy, and unselfishness.

To the stranger his most prominent characteristic was enthusiasm. Like the Apostle Paul, he could say, "*For me to live is Christ,*" and as a result of that life his gain came at the end of earth's career. "*This one thing I do*" was the key to his life of service. Writing to Major Whittle in 1874, from Scotland, he said: " I have done one thing on this trip, and the work is wonderful. *One thing* is my motto." Nothing could swerve him from this deep-rooted purpose of his life, and in all the various educational and publishing projects to which he gave his energy there was but one motive—the proclamation of the Gospel through multiplied agencies.

But all this enthusiasm was perfectly controlled by what was perhaps his most remarkable quality, quoted before as " his consecrated common sense." While his enthusiasm prompted him to seize every avail-

MR. MOODY AS A GRANDFATHER.

Mr. Moody Inspecting Northfield Buildings.

Northfield Seminary Buildings.

able opportunity for work, it was his keen insight into the conditions of any occasion that enabled him to judge of its fitness for his special effort. For this reason he frequently stood out against the advice of his friends, not that he did not welcome advice and appreciate it, but its value to him was chiefly suggestive, and if no new view of the matter was offered it was not likely to be followed. To such an extent is this true that it may be safely said that in the beginning of all his greatest and most successful efforts he stood alone, acting against the advice of those best able, apparently, to judge of the matter, with the one exception of his most valued human adviser, the companion of his life, his wife. He entered upon his first campaign in Great Britain against the counsel of all his friends; against the advice of everybody, he guaranteed the financial liability of the first publication of the "Moody and Sankey Hymns"; the Northfield schools and Chicago Bible Institute were established in the face of great opposition, and were the subject of much criticism until they demonstrated their success; and as to the founding of the Colportage Association, it was generally felt that in this work, at least, Mr. Moody had exceeded the limits of his strength. But in all these cases, as in many others, the results have not only surprised his advisers, but have far surpassed even the founder's expectations.

To many men of less simplicity of heart such evident superiority of judgment would have resulted in an intolerable conceit. But, although Mr. Moody was self-reliant—or, more truthfully, God-reliant—he was humble to a degree. It never ceased to be a wonder to him that people wanted to hear him preach, and at the Northfield conferences it was only after repeated and most urgent requests that he could be induced to include himself among the speakers. "I haven't the cheek to get up and speak when all these great preachers are here," he would say in reply to the urgent invitations.

The well-known head of a prominent lecture bureau relates that, being in Chicago with Henry Ward Beecher at the time Mr. Moody was president of the Association, he requested him to introduce Mr.

Beecher on the evening of the lecture for which he was engaged. "What," responded Mr. Moody, "introduce Beecher? Not I. Ask me to black his boots and I'll gladly do it." It is well known that Mr. Moody was much impressed by Mr. Beecher's great power as a preacher, and believed he might very largely extend his influence, especially over young men. With this in view he visited Brooklyn and urged with great persistence that Mr. Beecher should give himself to evangelistic effort. It is asserted that the suggestion was actually considered by Mr. Beecher, and that for a time he seriously contemplated such work.

Toward the close of the early mission in Brooklyn Mr. Moody was interviewed by a representative of the secular press, to whose inquiry regarding his training for evangelistic work he made this characteristic response:

"I am the most overestimated man in this country. For some reason the people look upon me as a great man, but I am only a lay preacher, and have little learning. I don't know what will become of me if the newspapers continue to print all of my sermons. My stock will be exhausted by and by, and I must repeat old ideas and teachings. Brooklyn hears, every Sunday, a score of better sermons than I can preach. I cannot get up such sermons as Drs. Storrs and Budington and Cuyler and Talmage, and many others, who preach here week after week."

Mr. Moody's abhorrence of any appearance of obsequiousness was frequently in evidence. So pronounced was this aversion that at times he would take special precautions against being introduced to a person of special note who might have attended his meeting. Speaking on one occasion in Washington, a person of particular distinction was seated on the platform behind Mr. Moody. After the service, he specially avoided an introduction, explaining afterward that "there were a lot of people scraping and bowing around, and I'm not much on that line."

On one of his earlier trips abroad it is related that he received a most impressive introduction to some lord as he was beginning a service in a crowded hall. "Glad to meet you, Lord ———," was the brusque acknowledgment; "won't you please give those two old ladies a seat down there in the middle aisle?" pointing to two women who had just entered.

But with all this strong aversion to an approach of servility Mr. Moody was an ardent hero-worshipper. Seldom could he speak of Abraham Lincoln without tears, and he had a great and favorite fund of anecdotes illustrating the nobility of his character. In much the same spirit he would speak of Robert E. Lee, U. S. Grant, "Stonewall" Jackson, and William E. Gladstone. Nor did he limit his admiration to those who had passed beyond public criticism, but ardently expressed his regard for the statesmen then making the nation's history. President McKinley he considered to be the peer of Lincoln and Grant; and during the dark days of weighty responsibility attending the Spanish-American War, the chief executive had no sympathizer who remembered him more earnestly in prayer or more enthusiastically praised the wisdom which distinguished his policy.

It has been noted that Moody frequently determined upon a course that did not appear wise to his friends. This meant that their perspective was confused by what appeared to be insurmountable obstacles. Such obstructions never obscured Mr. Moody's vision, for if once he thought an object worth attaining, he undertook its achievement with an enthusiasm and vigor equalled only by his determined perseverance. It was this last trait that contributed very largely to his success. Many of his enterprises would have been abandoned by a less courageous and persistent character. For him obstacles were only an incentive to greater effort. "I hate the word 'can't,'" he would say. "When a man says 'you can't,' it always makes me want to prove that I can."

The beauty of nature was an unending source of delight to him. Northfield is famous for its natural scenery, and mountain drives through the surrounding country reveal new beauties with every changing season. It was on these lovely excursions that Mr. Moody would confide to his most intimate friends his deep secrets and most cherished purposes. The surroundings seemed to influence him powerfully, and often on these drives he would suddenly break off his conversation, and, reining in his horse, pour out his heart in praise to God for His mercies, or unburden his soul in a simple prayer for guidance or relief.

The very spontaneity of such prayers revealed the atmosphere of his life, which was one of constant communion with God. It was not surprising, then, that he should seldom have long seasons of agonizing prayer such as some have experienced, for his closeness to God was not limited to special seasons, but was a continuous and uninterrupted experience.

Intense conviction and determined concentration upon the "*one thing*" he did absorbed him, and he often gained a reputation for brusqueness. After a service conducted in a spirit of deep earnestness he was not the man to enter into a conversation over trifling things with one who claimed an acquaintance of a dozen years back. Or if, on such an occasion, some dapper young theological student should hinder him in dealing with an anxious inquirer by accosting him with an inquiry as to "the secret of his power," it was more than probable that a very apparent brusqueness would appear in his manner.

He had little sympathy with controversy of any sort, or with habitual disturbers of Christian unity, and he never allowed himself to be hindered by cranks of either sex. "From long-haired men and short-haired women, good Lord, deliver us," was a part of his litany.

On one occasion, after a morning session of the August Conference, a man upbraided him for not teaching the doctrines of holiness. "Why, I have not sinned for years," claimed the stranger. "Haven't you?" said Mr. Moody; "well, before I accept your word for it I should like the testimony of your wife." The perfectionist thereupon gave such an exhibition of temper as to warrant the spectators' sympathy for his wife and Moody's scepticism.

It was often remarked that Moody had a wonderful gift of intuition, by which he would readily make a wise decision. This would at first seem to be so, but such an impression was in reality the result of a superficial knowledge of the man. His conclusions were really made by a rapid deduction. Experience had crystallized into a few clearly defined laws and established certain criteria. This was illustrated perhaps as well by his quick and precise estimate of the capacity of a hall or church as by any other means. Such an estimate is very hard to make offhand, and it is extraordinary how difficult it is to secure reliable data on the subject, even those best able to judge being inclined to greatly overestimate the figures. "The old Illinois Street Church was just one hundred by fifty, and I always measure everything in my mind by that," was the explanation of his unerring accuracy in this line, and, even when examining the largest audience-rooms, he always referred to the church where he first had an experience in building. On much the same principle he judged character at first sight, and it was an exceptional case where his first impression was wrong. "When you shake hands with a man, look out for him if his hand is as limp as a dead fish," was his frequent warning. At another time he warned against those who "tell all they know at first acquaintance."

In public speaking his method of judging his audience was of the same nature. "I always select a few people in the audience here and there, to whom I speak. If I can interest them and hold their attention, I have the entire audience. If any one of these goes to sleep or loses interest, I work to secure the attention of that one."

Mr. Moody was rich in friends, whom he had found in all parts of America and Great Britain. Of their confidence and regard for him there is no need to speak, as the work which they enabled him to establish and maintain at Northfield and Chicago most clearly indicates their appreciation of his aims and judgment. For twenty years he raised an average of over $100,000 annually for the support of his several enterprises. In addition, over $1,000,000 was invested in the permanent equipment of the schools, and many hundreds of thousands were secured by him during his public life for incidental undertakings in behalf of Young Men's Christian Associations and other organizations.

Any real friendship he counted a special blessing, not to be held lightly. It has been said, however, that few of his friends enjoyed any very great degree of intimacy. This is partially true, and few men ever entered into that close inner circle of fellowship in which he would lay bare the inmost secrets of his soul. There were a few of those, however, whose friendship he knew to be true, and among these was Henry Drummond, for whom Moody had a love, as he himself expressed it, like that which David felt for Jonathan. The mutual regard of these two men, so different both in nature and in training, was most significant of the breadth of charity in both. Moody, who loved Drummond as a brother, and appreciated his deep spirituality, would say of him, "He was the most Christlike man I ever knew." Drummond, who knew and thoroughly appreciated Mr. Moody as few have done, testified to his friend's character in equally vivid terms. In the course of a short biographical sketch of Moody, in "McClure's Magazine," he gave the following appreciation:

"Simple as this man is, and homely as are his surroundings, probably America possesses at this moment no more extraordinary personage; not even among the most brilliant of her sons has any one rendered more stupendous or more enduring service to his country or his time. No public man is less understood, especially by the thinking world, than D. L. Moody. It is not that it is unaware of his existence, or even that it does not respect him. But his line is so special, his work has lain so apart from what it conceives to be the rational channels of progress, that it has never felt called upon to take him seriously. So little, indeed, is the true stature of this man known to the mass of his generation, that the preliminary estimate recorded here must seem both extravagant and ill-considered. It will surprise many to know that Mr. Moody is as different from the supposed type of his class as light is from darkness; that while he would be the last to repudiate the name; indeed, while glorying more and more each day he lives in the work of an evangelist, he sees the weaknesses, the narrownesses, and the limitations of that order with as clear an eye as the most unsparing of its critics. But especially will it surprise many to know that, while preaching to the masses has been the main outward work of Mr. Moody's life, he has, perhaps, more and more varied irons in the fire—educational, philanthropic, religious—than almost any living man; and that vast as has been his public work as a preacher to the masses, it is probably true that his personal influence and private character have done as much as his preaching to affect his day and generation. Whether estimated by the moral qualities which go to the making up of his personal character or the extent to which he has impressed these on whole communities of men on both sides of the Atlantic, there is, perhaps, no more truly great man living than D. L. Moody. I have met multitudes and personally know, in large numbers, men and women of all churches and creeds, of many countries and ranks, from the poorest to the richest, and from the most ignorant to the wisest, upon whom he has placed an ineffaceable moral mark. There is no large town in Great Britain, and I find that there are few in America, where this man has not gone, where he has not lived, for days, weeks, or months, and where he has not left behind him personal inspirations which live to this day; inspirations that from the moment of their birth have not ceased to evidence themselves in furthering domestic happiness and peace; in charities and philanthropies; in social, religious, and even municipal and national service."

From those who had opportunity of knowing him best through close and constant companionship, come the most unreserved and spontaneous testimony to Mr. Moody's simple, open, and unselfish character. Mr. Sankey's experience would be largely the record of this entire work, but in the following he has epitomized his impressions:

"One of the greatest compliments to his preaching was that the sermon that would hold the rapt attention of the most intelligent of his congregation would also be listened to with the same eagerness by the children present. Any one—every one—understood what he said. His meaning was clear to every child. It was also convincing to the old. No other preacher ever mastered this art—if anything connected with Mr. Moody may be called an art—of reaching the understanding of old and young at the same time. His simplicity of language was remarkable. The strong individuality of the man spoke out in every sentence. The beauty of his powerful nature shone in his works.

"One of the reasons of his phenomenal success in bringing souls to God was that he believed absolutely, implicitly in the message he gave to men. His faith was the faith of a little child. No doubts ever dimmed his faith in the Word of God. To him it was the truth, and the whole truth.

"He never sat down and folded his hands and waited for the Lord to bring about what he wanted. He did not believe in passive Christianity.

"Mr. Moody never tried to exalt himself—never thought of himself. He made no attempt at fine speeches or rhetorical phrasing. He once said:

"'Christ talked in parables. Oh, how I wish I could talk in parables! I would if I knew enough!' His simple, direct manner of work has often been described. His tremendous earnestness, his indomitable energy, his lovable personality, and, above all and through all, his thorough goodness, won him the hearts of millions. No one could meet him without admiring him. No one could know him without loving him. The rich, the learned, the poor, the happy, and the miserable—convicts shut in by iron bars and the great ones of earth—alike found that he had a message for each.

" Now the world grieves that one of the noblest souls of earth has passed beyond our ken. Our comfort lies in the fact that one day—' when the mists have rolled away '—we will meet him again."

One of Mr. Moody's most efficient helpers in later years was Prof. D. B. Towner, who was associated with him for the last fourteen years of his life, beginning with the Cincinnati meetings in the fall of 1885. After that time, Professor Towner had charge of the music at all the college conferences; he also attended several of the August Conferences, assisting Sankey and Stebbins in the singing. Since 1893 he has been connected with the Bible Institute. In speaking of Mr. Moody he said:

" During all these years there has never been the slightest misunderstanding between us, and I have never met a man who came so nearly to Christ's standard as he. He was absolutely unselfish, always sharing everything with his helpers and looking after their comfort with the care and tenderness of a father. Never in the fourteen years that I have been associated with him has he said an unkind word or given me an unkind look. My own father could not have been more kind or solicitous for my comfort and welfare. My love for him was stronger than for any man in the world, and his influence on my life for good has been greater than that of any ten men that I have ever known. I never knew such a friend, and shall never cease to thank God that I was privileged to know him and labor with him.

" After his meetings in Oakland, Cal., in the spring of 1899, when I accompanied him as his singer, we took the train for Santa Cruz. We were hardly seated when in came a party of young men, one of whom was considerably under the influence of liquor and very badly bruised, with one eye completely closed and terribly discolored. He at once recognized Mr. Moody, and began to sing hymns and talk very loudly for his benefit. Mr. Moody caught up his bag and said, ' Towner, let us get out of this.' When I reminded him that the other car was full, he settled down, protesting that the company should not allow a drunken man to insult the whole car in such a manner. Presently the conductor came, and Mr. Moody called his attention to the poor fellow in the rear of the car. The conductor attended to his duty, and when he reached the young man he said a few words to him in a low voice, and the fellow followed him into the baggage car, where he bathed his eye and bound it up with his handkerchief, after which the young man soon fell asleep.

"Mr. Moody sat musing for a time, and then said, 'Towner, that is an awful rebuke to me. I preached against Pharisaism last night to a crowd, and exhorted them to imitate the Good Samaritan, and now this morning God has given me an opportunity to practise what I preached, and I find I have both feet in the shoes of the priest and Levite.' He was reticent all the way to Santa Cruz, but he told the incident that night to the audience, confessing his humiliation.

"During the Columbian campaign in Chicago Mr. Moody used to preach in the Haymarket Theatre on the West Side. One night the crowd came early, and he closed the meeting before the cab came to take him to his rooms in the Bible Institute. Starting down Madison Street on foot, knowing he would meet the cab, he had not gone far when he was accosted by a rough-looking fellow, who asked for money. Mr. Moody told him that he did not have a cent with him. The stranger seemed rather cross, began to complain about the way he was treated, and said he was starving and must have some money. Mr. Moody did not care to proceed any farther for fear he might follow and give him trouble, so he entered into conversation with him, and presently the cab drove up.

"'Lend me a dollar?' said Moody to the driver.

"'Certainly, Mr. Moody,' was the reply.

"At this remark the tramp said, 'Is this Moody, the evangelist?'

"Mr. Moody said it was, and that he had just been preaching at the Haymarket, at the same time handing him a dollar that the driver had put into his hands. But the poor fellow drew back, saying:

"'No, no; my father is a poor Methodist preacher, and I will starve before I will take a penny from you, Mr. Moody.'

" On another occasion he came upon a crowd of rough fellows. He did not want to seem to shun them, and yet he did not care to go through the crowd, so, stepping boldly up to a big, burly fellow who seemed to be the leader, he said:

" ' Won't you please hold my coat for me? ' and to another, ' Would you just hold my Bible? ' After the coat was on he said, ' Thank you, gentlemen; when you get old and stiff I hope some one will be as kind to you.' It is needless to say that he could pass through safely then."

But while Mr. Moody was a devoted friend he was not the man to condone a fault in any one he loved. On occasion he has severed relations with one whom he believed to be wrong, though this often cost him such suffering as only a true and loyal heart can feel. On the other hand, he would make any personal sacrifice to help a friend, and occasions have not been wanting where he has stood by a friend in difficulty at the expense of great personal loss, necessitating more than temporary inconvenience.

The home, above all other places, is where a man most truly reveals himself, and here Mr. Moody was at his best. Home was the sweetest place upon earth to him, and had he chosen only his own comfort and pleasure, he would have devoted his last years to work at Northfield, in connection with his schools, without heeding the calls to service in the outer world. Entering into all the plans and interested in everything which demanded the attention of the members of his family, he made their life his own. A child's pleasures afforded him keen enjoyment, the student's school or college experience enlisted his hearty sympathy, and his advice in business affairs or even domestic problems was most highly valued. Nothing was too trifling for his notice, and in the home and community he became the great burden-bearer.

Of later years it was his custom to spend the months from October to April (inclusive) in evangelistic work, returning to Northfield about the first of May. There was no place he loved more than this, and he always regretted to have to leave it even for short absences during the summer months.

His correspondence was always large, and he made it a point to open every letter himself. Inquiries connected with the different schools were separated and given to subordinates, and general letters were usually handed to his secretary. In special cases he would indicate by brief notes what reply should be made. Letters received prompt attention; even those from disagreeable people were usually courteously acknowledged.

" In nothing, perhaps, is Mr. Moody's generalship more manifest than in his capacity for detail," wrote a friend. " Nothing is too minute for his best thought, for he knows how much results depend on little things. Along with this genius for details goes remarkable quickness of insight and decision."

" The old proverb, ' A prophet is not without honor save in his own country,' cannot be said of D. L. Moody, for surely no person could be more sincerely loved and honored by his townsmen than was he," wrote a correspondent of the county paper in describing him as a citizen and neighbor. " Expressions of sorrow are heard from all classes of people in the town, and could each tribute be represented by a blossom on his grave, it would be piled high with flowers. His townsmen have been proud of him as a citizen, as a man, and as a religious worker. Although not all of them have indorsed his religious belief, they have thoroughly believed in his honesty of purpose and sincerity, and are convinced that the results of his life-work will be lasting and of inestimable value to future generations. They know that Northfield has been changed from a quiet farming town, with corresponding disadvantages, to a thrifty village with a steady growth; and that there and at Mount Hermon have been established two of the best fitting-schools in the State, all through the energy and perseverance of this man. Every effort has been made by him to bring these schools within the reach of the boys and girls of the town, and many an ambitious father and mother have been able to educate their children through his efforts.

" Last summer he was told of a woman who was supporting her

family by taking in washing. Her daughter was ready for the Seminary, but she almost despaired of her ability to send her. Mr. Moody instantly replied:

" 'Tell the principal to put her on the free list, and find her a room in the buildings. The town girls must be helped first.'

" This is only one instance of many. Under certain provisions, a few years ago, he offered every Northfield and Gill boy free tuition for the first year at Mount Hermon, and several boys have availed themselves of this opportunity each year since.

" He was instantly alert and ready with money and work to forward any plans to benefit the town. At the time the Village Improvement Society was formed he subscribed $100 to improve the street, knowing that it would be expended in a part of the village remote from the school and his residence. Every year since its formation he has given generously of money, and has also offered valuable advice and wise suggestions.

" He was very proud of the magnificent trees of the village, and nothing irritated him more than any attempt to injure them. He had a large number of trees and shrubs set about his place and on the Seminary grounds. It must have been very gratifying to him to see Seminary Hill in all its June splendor, knowing that in his childhood it was considered one of the most barren places in town. One old man once said that that side-hill wouldn't bear white beans when he was a boy.

" He was a kind neighbor, sickness and trouble finding him ready with sympathy and material help. The delicacies of his garden and fruit orchard found their way into many a humble home. He encouraged his wife and daughter to interest themselves in helping the sick and needy in all parts of the town.

" During the autumn, when fruit was abundant, the Seminary girls were given free access to his orchard and grapery, to eat and carry baskets full to their rooms. Each fall all the surplus apples from his own orchard and from the Seminary campus, and all he could solicit from neighboring farmers, to the extent of hundreds of bushels, were distributed among the poor in Boston and New York.

"He had a strong aversion to committees. A few months ago an organization was being effected in the Town Hall, and a motion was made to appoint certain committees. Mr. Moody rose and said, 'We don't want committees. When you want anything done, tell Mr. So-and-so to do it, and you will accomplish something. One is enough to constitute any committee. If there had been a committee appointed, Noah's ark would never have been built.'"

Mr. Moody was accused of lowering the pulpit by some people in Boston because he declared that the churches should seek those who did not seek the churches. His reply was: "If lowering the pulpit means bringing it to the people, I would to God I could. If I wanted to hit Boston, you don't think I would mount my guns on Bunker Hill Monument and fire into the air, do you?"

On Sunday evening, April 21, 1895, Mr. Moody was holding a meeting in a specially constructed building in the city of Fort Worth, Tex. The roof was flat, and, as it turned out, insufficiently supported. During one of the meetings, when the audience present numbered about four thousand, a heavy rain fell, and the water collected on the flat roof. In the very midst of Mr. Moody's sermon a loud crash was heard, and a large section of the roof over the middle of the vast auditorium fell in.

"I was sitting a little distance from the front, in company with a distinguished general of the Confederacy," says Dr. C. I. Scofield, at that time a pastor in Dallas, Tex. "I was struck, as all present were, with the perfect presence of mind of Mr. Moody, and the manner in which he held control of the audience, preventing a stampede, which would inevitably have resulted in great injury to limb and possible loss of life. When quiet was restored, and the people had gotten safely out of the building, this general turned to me and said:

"'Dr. Scofield, I have seen many brave men in my life put into positions of great personal danger, and I believe I know a brave man when I see him tested. I want to say to you that I have never seen a braver man than D. L. Moody.' "

Mr. Moody was quick to take in a situation, and prompt in giving an answer to what would require a good deal of thought and consideration on the part of many. Referring to an incident where this characteristic was marked, a friend says:

"I was very anxious to learn Mr. Moody's opinion of a certain minister, Dr. X., who had been spoken of as a desirable man for a pulpit then vacant. I ventured to say:

" 'Mr. Moody, confidentially, what is your opinion of the Rev. Dr. X. for such a pulpit?'

"Mr. Moody rose from his seat, went to the window, and looked out for several minutes, without saying a word. I feared that I had offended him. He then turned and said, 'There is too much tomahawk about him.' We resumed our pleasant conversation about other matters, and the subsequent history of that clergyman proved the correctness of Mr. Moody's judgment."

Quite as interesting was the answer which a clergyman received who had gone to Northfield to interview Mr. Moody concerning a man whom he wished to procure for Christian work. When asked for the interview, the subject having been mentioned, Mr. Moody, without naming a time or making further explanation, said:

"Get his boots, if you can; they are better than most men's whole bodies."

Mr. Moody had little regard for red tape, and could not always be held to the requirements of parliamentary procedure. One afternoon, while the trustees of the Seminary were considering ways and means, a member of the board was obliged to withdraw before the end of the meeting. He was about to enter his carriage, when Mr. Moody raised a window and said:

"Will you give a thousand dollars if I will do the same?"

"All right," came the answer. Mr. Moody, as he closed the window, remarked that he did not have a thousand dollars himself, but he would raise it some way or other. In response, one of the trustees smilingly remarked that that was a somewhat irregular proceeding, but Mr. Moody answered:

"Oh, well, we do everything up here differently from other people."

Once, while driving in the woods, he found a plank broken in the flooring of a small bridge. Returning, he called to one of the farm hands working on the hotel grounds, and said:

"A plank is broken in the bridge," describing the location; "take a new one and go over and put it in." The man hesitated, then said:

"That bridge does not belong in our district!"

"I know," said Mr. Moody, "and my horse doesn't belong in that district, either, but it might have broken its leg just the same."

Mr. Moody was as careful of details as he was of great plans. While preaching he would stop in the middle of his discourse, if necessary, and say:

"Will the ushers please open the windows, and let in a little fresh air? It is getting close in here." At another time he would rouse the audience by saying:

"You are getting sleepy while I am talking to you about Assurance. I don't want you to think I am a dull preacher; you need some fresh air." Then, after a few minutes' interval:

"Shut the windows. I see they are putting on their wraps."

Mr. Moody was averse to having his photograph taken, and only twice did he sit for a picture alone after he began his evangelistic work. When his grandchildren were born, however, he was induced to reconsider his objections, and some of the best pictures are those in which he figures with one or another of the little ones.

Bishop Huntington, of the diocese of Central New York, came to Northfield in the early part of Mr. Moody's evangelistic ministry, as he said, "to seek an interview."

"When I reached there I found him pitching off a load of oats in the barn. In a serious and candid talk, under a tree in the yard, he said some words which I have recalled and repeated many times.

Ashuelot River and Road.

One of the many charming scenes in the vicinity of Mr. Moody's house.

EAST HALL, NORTHFIELD SEMINARY.

A QUIET SPOT—WANAMAKER LAKE—SEMINARY GROUNDS.

They were these: 'I know perfectly well that, wherever I go and preach, there are many better preachers known and heard than I am; all that I can say about it is that the Lord uses me.' That, I take it, was the faith of the spirit of his whole extraordinary career, and the sacred secret of his power. He was strong because he was simple. He prevailed and succeeded because he was genuine; because he was a willing instrument of the will of God."

One morning he arose somewhat earlier than was his custom, in order to study and prepare his address for the morning session of the students' conference. He went to the window and looked out to see if the indications were for a pleasant day. As he did so, he saw a student carrying a heavy valise. It was evident that the young man was on his way to the station to catch the early morning train.

"I had started to read my Bible," said Mr. Moody, in speaking of the matter afterward, "but somehow I couldn't fasten my attention to the Book. I could see before me as I read that young man trudging along with that heavy valise. Perhaps he had given the quarter that it would cost him to ride to the station in the collection taken up at my request the day previous. Yes; and he had nearly two miles to walk. Surely that box must be heavy! I couldn't stand it any longer. I went to the barn and hurriedly had my horse hitched up, overtook the young man, and carried him and his baggage to the station. When I returned to the house I had no further difficulty in fixing my attention on the subject I was studying."

He had the largest confidence in the medical profession, for, to use his own words:

"Never yet, in all my years of work, have I called on an able doctor, telling him of the sickness and need of some poor and friendless person, that he did not at once go to the rescue without money and without price. These are the men who are called devils by the faith healers. God heals through doctors and medicine. Do you ask what I would do if I were ill? Get the best doctor in town, trust in him, and trust in the Lord to work through him."

When special services were being held in the Congregational church, he told the people they were not making effort enough to get their neighbors to come to church.

"Why don't you bring somebody in your big wagon?" he said, addressing one well-to-do farmer by name.

"Because my wagon is always filled from my own house," was the reply.

Mr. Moody at once said he must have a wagon, one way or another, adding that he wanted to invest $25 in one himself, and called for contributions. People in the audience added $100 more, and later $80 additional was subscribed. This was the beginning of the church wagons which, in the summer season, are seen driving from the hotel and through the streets, carrying people to and from the services free of charge.

One of the most trying positions into which Mr. Moody was frequently brought was that of a father confessor. It was quite impossible —even if it were desirable—to prevent persons with great burdens on conscience and heart making known their peculiar condition. One case of special interest occurred during the mission in St. Louis. A very gentlemanly man called and confessed that he was a transgressor of the civil law. His crime was ever before him. If he confessed before the authorities, a commitment to the penitentiary for a long term would undoubtedly be the result. "Mr. Moody," the man said, with deep emotion, "I want your advice. I am willing to suffer for my sin—but I have a beautiful home, a devoted wife, several lovely children. A public confession means to these disgrace and poverty. What is my duty before God? I have been forgiven by Him; I only desire to know what is the right course to pursue, and I believe I am willing to take it, regardless of the consequences."

Mr. Moody's heart was touched. He felt obliged to reply, "My friend, I cannot undertake to advise you. You must go to God and ask Him." The next day the man again called and said, "Mr. Moody, I do not think I need your advice now. I have fully determined what is right. I purpose giving myself up." He spent one week more with his wife and children, then placed himself in the hands of the law, and was sentenced for a long term. The wife was obliged to support herself and children, and this she did for some time. Mr. Moody endeavored, without success, to obtain a pardon for the penitent. A few years later he renewed his efforts; he was very hopeful, and made a special trip to the State capital to interview the governor. Mr. Moody was very cordially received, but when the object of his call was stated, the request was positively denied, and Mr. Moody returned home, greatly saddened. Later, under another administration, a pardon was obtained, and the family are now happily reunited.

The Rev. Dr. Henry Clay Trumbull says that one element of Mr. Moody's power was his fearless independence in speech and manner. He dared to be himself, and he would never risk trying to be anybody else. When holding meetings in Baltimore in 1878, he telegraphed Dr. Trumbull, asking if he would come down and aid in the work. The following incident, connected with that visit, is related by Dr. Trumbull:

"I went down, joined him in his meeting, and then passed the night in his temporary home. In the morning he asked me to conduct worship in his family group. I said I would read the passage for next Sunday's lesson, 'Zaccheus the Publican.' Noticing my pronunciation of the proper name, he said, 'Is that the way to call it?' 'Yes,' I said, 'the proper pronunciation is "Zach-che'us," but we Yankees most always start the emphasis a little too soon—"Zach'-che-us!"'

"'Zach-*che'*us,' 'Zach-*che'*us,' said Moody, trying the word to his ear; and then added, 'I guess I'd better stick to the old way.' He measured himself aright, as he did many others.

"Moody knew his power, and knew his lack, and he had due regard for both. He never attempted what was outside of his limitations, but he was fearless in the use of what he had.

"Moody was no Oriental scholar, nor did he assume to give a

Bible picture in its Eastern setting. But he did give the idea of the Bible scene as he had it in his mind, and as he wanted his hearers to have it in theirs. I once heard him, in telling the story of Daniel, picture Daniel as taking out his watch to note the time as noon approached, when he would pray as usual, lions or no lions. In his earnest, graphic, vivid way he made that scene so real that no one thought of any anachronism on his part.

" So, again, as he told the story of Noah's warnings before the Flood, he pictured the scoffers of that day while the Deluge was delayed.

" 'They'd say to one another, " Not much sign of old Noah's rain-storm yet." They'd talk it over in the corner groceries evenings.'

" Then, as if in explanation, he added:

" 'I tell you, my friends, before the world got as bad as it was in Noah's day, they must have had corner groceries.'

" Everybody could understand that kind of talk.

" Yet, Moody was a hard student, and he gained and grew steadily in intellect and knowledge as years went on. He told me of the surprise expressed by one man who found him in his study with his books open before him.

" 'You don't mean, Moody, that you use commentaries, do you?'

" 'Of course I do.'

" 'Then I shan't enjoy your sermons as I have, now that I know that.'

" 'Have you ever liked my sermons?'

" 'Of course I have.'

" 'Then you've liked Moody's commentaries, have you?' "

The Rev. S. A. Taggart, State secretary of the Young Men's Christian Association of Pennsylvania, accompanied Mr. Moody during a number of meetings in that State, and relates several characteristic incidents. He says:

" Mr. Moody had a fine sense of the fitness of things. In one of the cities where meetings were being held a prominent representative of Christian work called upon him. He was a very dignified man, with a seeming air of wisdom, and carried a fine gold-headed cane. I saw Mr. Moody looking at the cane, and it seemed to act as a sort of non-conductor of freedom of intercourse. After the man had gone he said to me, 'Why don't you carry a gold-headed cane?' I told him I did not have enough dignity. 'Why don't you carry one?' I said. He replied: 'I would cut a nice figure coming into an inquiry meeting to-night with one. I think the inquirers would be looking more at the cane than listening to me. A good while ago I was down in the South, and a delegation waited on me and presented me with such a cane. I soon found myself being charged extra at the hotels, and the porters, newsboys, and bootblacks were charging about double. I asked a newsboy why he did it. "Oh," he said, looking at my cane, "you men can afford it, and you don't come around very often." I hurried to Chicago for fear I would run out of money, put the cane in the closet, and have never carried it since.'

"In another city Mr. Moody said to me: 'There seems to be something here out of the ordinary, obstructing the work and hindering a great blessing.' I found out the next day that the town had a considerable number of freethinkers, or theoretical infidels, and they were out at the meetings to see Mr. Moody, as they said, hypnotize the converts. I told him of the state of things. Always very earnest in his seasons of prayer in his room before the meetings, that night he was even more so than ordinary. His burden of heart seemed to be very great. He preached with great earnestness, and then called for all who desired to stay for the after-meeting. Nearly the whole congregation remained. He came down from the platform to get nearer to the inquirers. He began to instruct them, and in a little while got upon a chair, to get a better view of his audience, and launched out in a most wonderful discourse. His invectives against sin, and lashings of the conscience, were awful. All his resources of apt Scripture quotation and illustration were at perfect command. He seemed to be wrestling with an unseen power, and might have made a good picture of Elijah on Carmel. I saw men whose faces grew pale under conviction of conscience. Then he began with the wooings of the Gospel, in a strain of tender and heart-breaking entreaty, and before he was through the whole audience seemed to be completely broken. One man arose and said, 'Mr. Moody, I want to be a Christian.' It seemed but a moment after that when forty or fifty men were on their feet making a similar declaration. The only time I ever heard Mr. Moody make a comment on any of his sermons was that night, when he said 'Thank God for that victory.'

"When Mr. Moody came to know William Thaw, of Pittsburg, and his broad generosity in giving to all kinds of good work, he was greatly impressed. He once went to him to ask for $10,000 for his schools. Mr. Thaw told him that he had changed his method of giving; in place of large amounts he preferred to give more frequently, and in lesser sums, and to a greater number of objects; that his usual gifts ranged from fifty to five hundred dollars in each case. 'But I will make an exception of you and give you $5,000,' he said. Mr. Moody replied: 'I am a very busy man, Mr. Thaw, and I hardly see how I can find the time to come and see you once a month or so to get the other $5,000 in the smaller installments.' Mr. Thaw was so greatly amused at this idea of Mr. Moody's that he gave him the whole amount at once.

"Elijah was one of Mr. Moody's ideal characters, but Elijah under the juniper tree was to him the very reverse. But once did I see him when he seemed to be cast down. In the place where he was holding meetings some one had insidiously circulated the false report that he was making a great amount of money out of his work. He heard about it, and it greatly disturbed him. He said: 'I have a notion to take the train and go home. I think I can suffer almost anything but this.' I told him that I felt confident that not a single Christian man in the place gave credence to such a report for a moment. He said to me: 'If the committee or any one else asks you how much I charge, tell them not one cent, and if they offer anything for me, refuse to take it.' The false report, however, only served to acquaint the people of the place with the fact that great financial burdens were resting on Mr. Moody in the education of hundreds of young men and women, and the offerings in that place were very generous, and when they were presented to him it was with the distinct understanding that the people knew of his burden and wanted to help him bear it."

Mr. Moody frequently showed his high appreciation of music, especially vocal music, and the prominence given to praise in all his services was an evidence of this. Few people knew, however, that he had absolutely no musical ear, being unable to distinguish one tune from another. Paradoxical as it may appear, no one more readily detected any difficulty in the singing or appreciated more highly a well-trained chorus. His use of music in his services was most effective.

The singing had a great and at times overpowering religious value. Before the evangelist arose the throngs were often touched and persuaded. A great number of cases came to be known in which the momentous decision for Christ was actually made during the singing. Never was a more thoughtless criticism uttered than that Moody used music merely to attract.

In an attempt to present the man's characteristics from all sides and points of view—as an evangelist, an American, a citizen, a director, a friend and father—it has been impossible to do more than touch upon what was most apparent to his friends. But the keynote of the whole is struck in the following anecdote, which appeared in "The Youth's Companion":

"A young missionary far in the interior of China received for baptism a little child. The name given was Moo Dee, so unusual a combination that the minister asked its origin. 'I have heard of your man of God, Moo Dee,' was the reply. 'In our dialect Moo means love, and Dee, God. I would have my child, too, love God.' Mr. Moody knew no Chinese, but his name alone told in that language the secret of his life."

CHAPTER XLIV

In the Home Circle

"THE city is no place for me. If it was not for the work I am called to do, I would never show my head in this city or any other again. It is a rush all the time, and a drive. The quiet days at Northfield, how I long for them!"

Mr. Moody frequently expressed his simple taste and love of nature, as in the foregoing extract from a letter written in 1896 while at work in New York.

When in St. Louis, in April, 1897, he wrote:

"I am thinking next Wednesday morning I will look out on dear old Northfield and will take a walk about and see things. I am just longing to see you all and to sniff the fresh morning air. It is a great joy to think that in so short a time I am to be free once again.

"The papers push the meeting, and the news goes far and near, and God is using the press greatly. This year it has been a great joy to be used after working forty years and not be laid aside, and then I have great reason to thank God for my health; not a cold, not a headache, but joy and strength and pleasure in the work."

But it was his devotion to his work that was the ruling passion. It was ever the aim of his life to be used in preaching the Gospel, and in this he found his greatest joy.

"I do hope the Lord will help me in England as He has here," he wrote from Ireland in 1892. "It is a privilege to live if I can be used as I have been of late."

Mr. Moody's hobby was his garden and his chickens. He must have *life;* and he loved to see things grow. " Send me a good farm letter," he would frequently write home. Feeding his chickens furnished him with an excuse for exercise. He would spend hours " puttering around " his hen-houses and garden, as he expressed it, but all the time his mind was ready to deal with more important things, and some associate was frequently at his side seeking advice or discussing plans. His garden was hardly conducted on a profitable basis.

He usually devoted the early hours to Bible study, rising about five o'clock. While undoubtedly a hard worker when engaged in an evangelistic mission, Mr. Moody probably accomplished more in the four months at home than during the rest of the year. A friend thus described one day's programme:

" Rising early, he rode about his farm, visiting the hotel and the barns connected with the Seminary grounds, giving an order here, making a suggestion there, and greeting the men pleasantly as he passed them. After breakfast he was seen driving to the Seminary, where, at nine o'clock, he spoke to the girls on the Holy Spirit, giving them as many helpful thoughts as in an ordinary sermon. On his way to deliver an address at eleven o'clock, at the annual meeting of the Franklin Conference of Congregational Churches held in the village church, he stopped to give an interview to a correspondent regarding his plans for the winter and his views upon the preaching of the day. Following the address, whose good points were doubtless emphasized by a large basket of provisions prepared by Mrs. Moody for the conference delegates, he drove four miles to Mount Hermon to speak at noon to the young men."

In his thoughtful and delicate attention to his aged mother he was an example to many a less busy man. Seldom a day passed when absent from home that he did not send her some message, either a short note or a newspaper report of his work, and when at home he was never so busy but that he found time to visit her to whom he owed so much.

Her birthday fell on the same day as his own (February 5th), and his letters to her on successive anniversaries were peculiarly tender.

"You and I have now passed one more milestone on our way from earth to Heaven," he wrote at one time. "We have both reason to thank God for all His goodness to us."

"By the time you get this letter," he wrote from Perth, Scotland, in 1892, "you will be passing another milestone that will bring you nearer the Eternal City. I want to send you my best wishes for the new year you will be starting out on. I hope it will be full of joy and sunshine and peace."

The last birthday letter he wrote her was from San Antonio, Texas, on February 2, 1895:

"By the time this letter gets to you, you will have entered your ninety-first year. Only think, when you entered this world, Napoleon was fighting his great battles! It seems a long time as you look at the history that has been made. Nations have risen and fallen. Some have come and gone. Yet you live and have all your faculties and good health. You have much to praise God for, and all your children rejoice to think you have been spared to us so long."

An incident that occurred an hour or two before the death of his mother shows the true unselfishness and self-forgetfulness of this great heart at a time of personal sorrow. When it was known that she was passing away his daughter had a great longing that her grandmother, before going, should see her baby, then only six weeks old. Knowing this, and also that the end was near, Mr. Moody hurried down to his daughter's house and told her to come at once.

Directly they entered the room he took little Emma in his arms and, going up to his mother, said, "Mother, this is Emma's baby; she is here." Getting no answer, he walked to the other side of the bed to try and attract her notice. Again unsuccessful, he walked several times around the bed, holding the child in different positions, now high, now low, but all of no avail. Finally kneeling by the bed and holding the baby on his left arm, he took his mother's hand, and, laying it on the child's head, said, "With a great-grandmother's blessing." Even this did not seem to satisfy him, and, longing for some sign that she was conscious of what had taken place, said, " Mother, if you know what has taken place let us know in some way." It was only when, in response to this, the lips moved faintly that he seemed satisfied, and, turning to his daughter, said, " Mother knows now; she has seen your child."

At the funeral services he offered the most affectionate tribute to that mother's wisdom and loving devotion.

Holding in his hands the old family Bible and the worn book of devotions, he stood by the form of the departed one, and said:

" It is not the custom, perhaps, for a son to take part in such an occasion, but, if I can control myself, I should like to say a few words. It is a great honor to be the son of such a mother. I do not know where to begin; I could not praise her enough. In the first place, my mother was a very wise woman. In one sense she was wiser than Solomon; she knew how to bring up her children. She had nine children, and they all loved their home. She won their hearts and their affections; she could do anything with them.

" Whenever I wanted real, sound counsel, I used to go to my mother. I have travelled a good deal, and have seen a good many mothers, but I never saw one who had such tact as she had. She so bound her children to her that it was a great calamity for them to have to leave home. I had two brothers that lived in Kansas and died there. Their great longing was to get back to their mother. My brother, who died in Kansas a short time ago, had been looking over the Greenfield papers for some time to see if he could not buy a farm in this locality. He had a good farm where he was, but he was never satisfied; he wanted to get back to mother. That is the way she won her family, she won them to herself.

" I have heard something within the last forty-eight hours that nearly broke my heart. My eldest sister has told me that the first year after my father died mother wept herself to sleep every night. Yet she was always bright and cheerful in the presence of her children. Her sorrows drove her to the Lord. I would frequently wake up and hear her praying. She used to make sure her children were all asleep before she poured out her tears.

"There was another remarkable thing about my mother. If she loved one child more than another, no one ever found it out. Isaiah, he was her first boy; she could not get along without Isaiah. And Cornelia, she was her first girl; she could not get along without Cornelia, for she had to take care of the twins. And George, she couldn't live without George. What could she ever have done without George? He stayed right by her, through thick and thin. She couldn't live without George. And Edwin, he bore the name of her husband. And Dwight, I don't know what she thought of him. And Luther, he was the dearest of all, because he had to go away to live. He was always homesick to get back to mother. And Warren, he was the youngest when father died; it seemed as if he was dearer than all the rest. And Sam and Lizzie, the twins, they were the light of her great sorrow.

"She never complained of her children. It is a great thing to have such a mother, and I feel like standing up here to-day to praise her. And just here I want to say, before I forget it, you don't know how she appreciated the kindness which was shown her in those early days of struggle. Sometimes I would come home and say, 'Such a man did so and so,' and she would answer, 'Don't say that, Dwight; he was kind to me.'

"Friends, it is not a time of mourning. I want you to understand we do not mourn. We are proud that we had such a mother. We have a wonderful legacy left us. What more can I say? You have lived with her, and you know about her. I want to give you one verse, her creed. It was very short. Do you know what it was? I will tell you. When everything went against her, this was her stay: 'My trust is in God.'"

Many of his earlier sermons contained effective illustrations suggested by the daily life of his children, and his influence upon the lives of the children in other homes was great.

No work was so important as to make him neglect his family duties and privileges. He took keen interest in the experiences of his sons at school and college, and shared their joys and entered into the excitement of their sports with the zest of a fellow-student. The slightest matter that caused sorrow or pain to any member of his family, even the youngest, engaged at once his personal concern, and no drudgery of house or farm was beneath his notice or sympathetic interest. He had learned the secret of being a confidant of all, sharing others' burdens, weeping with the sorrowing and rejoicing with those glad of heart.

As a grandfather he seemed to experience a special joy, and entered into sweetest and happiest relations with the little ones who laid hold of his heart. Irene Moody, born on August 20, 1895, and Emma Moody Fitt, born on December 16th of the same year, were the oldest grandchildren who claimed his love.

"Do you know I have a granddaughter? I am taking a present over to her," he shouted from his buggy to a friend on the natal day of his oldest grandchild as he pointed to a basket of doughnuts. He was happy as a schoolboy on a holiday, and told the news to everybody he met. Later, that day, he made a second trip to Mount Hermon to see the baby, this time bringing over an immense cauliflower, the best his garden had produced.

This same playful nature was shown in his first letter to little Emma Fitt on January 7, 1896, when she was three weeks old:

"This is my first letter to my dear little grandchild. I wanted to get a letter to you before you got your first tooth. Hurry up and get them all before the hot weather comes on, for I will get you some candy and you will want teeth to eat it. I want you to hurry up and grow so I can come early mornings and take you out riding when your mother and father are fast asleep. We will slip over the river to see Irene, and have some good times. Your mother is so proud of you, and your nurse is so fussy. Only think, Emma, what your mother said the other day—I, your grandfather, could not kiss you on your lips! Did you ever hear anything like that? But I got a kiss on your lips all the same, and I will get a good many more when I get home."

"I have just heard," he wrote a few months later, "that the milk you get at my house does not agree with you. But I think the fault is not with the milk but with the cooks. You know, or you should be old enough to know, that when you cook milk and put it in a bottle and put a black rubber nipple on it—well, you will be disgusted when you get a little older and know how your parents have treated you! You must not blame my old cow, for she is as good as she can be. I do not want to turn you against your parents, but if they do not treat you right, slip down to my house and get some doughnuts and ice-cream."

In another letter to the same grandchild he wrote:

"In six days you will be one year old, and your grandmother will make you a cake and have it all frosted over with white sugar, and they will put one tiny little candle in it. . . .

"I am going to steal up to your house next summer and take you out riding before your parents get up. Only think, some fine June morning we can go up Lovers' Retreat. The birds will sing you a beautiful song. What times we will have together! I get real home-sick thinking about it. . . .

"And now, my dear Emma, I am praying for you that the Lord will watch over you day and night and keep you from all harm. You will never know how much your grandfather loves you. I shall be glad to get you into my arms again."

And so his loving heart went out to his grandchildren, and they in return loved none better than him. When boasting one day that his grandchildren always gave him instant obedience, a member of the family asked the secret of his power.

"I am very careful never to ask them to do a thing which I am not sure they want to do," he replied laughingly. He studied men, and so far as possible he led instead of driving. In the summer months he would usually be seen with one or more of the little ones seated beside him as he drove around the town.

"I saw him one morning driving with his little four-year-old granddaughter into the yard of his house," writes a friend. "The child had gone to sleep in the buggy, leaning against him. Rather than disturb her, Mr. Moody had the horse gently unharnessed and taken away, while they sat on. Presently he, too, was overcome with sleep."

God had ordained something other than unbroken joy for the happy grandfather. His only grandson and namesake, who was born on November 7, 1897, was taken home on November 30, 1898, while Mr. Moody was absent in Colorado. In a letter to the parents, written from Colorado Springs, he said:

". . . I know Dwight is having a good time, and we should rejoice with him. What would the mansions be without children? He was the last to come into our circle, and he is the first to go up there! So safe, so free from all the sorrow that we are passing through! I do thank God for such a life. It was nearly all smiles and sunshine, and what a glorified body he will have, and with what joy he will await your coming! God does not give us such strong love for each other for a few days or years, but it is going to last forever, and you will have the dear little man with you for ages and ages, and love will keep increasing. The Master had need of him, or He would not have called him; and you should feel highly honored that you had anything in your home that He wanted.

"I cannot think of him as belonging to earth. The more I think of him the more I think he was only sent to us to draw us all closer to each other and up to the world of light and joy. I could not wish him back, if he could have all earth could give him. And then the thought that the Saviour will take such good care of him! No going astray, no sickness, no death. Dear, dear little fellow! I love to think of him, so sweet, so safe, and so lovely! His life was not only blameless, but faultless; and if his life here was so sweet, what will it be up there? I believe the only thing he took away from earth was that sweet smile, and I have no doubt that when he saw the Saviour he smiled as he did when he saw you, and the word that keeps coming to my mind is this: 'It is well with the child.' Only think of his translation! Thank God, Dwight is safe at home, and we will all of us see him soon.

"Your loving father,

"D. L. Moody."

The next few months were filled with anxiety as his oldest grandchild, little Irene, was slowly recovering from a protracted and unusually persistent attack of pneumonia. Later it was found that the germs of consumption had become implanted in the weakened system, and after a few weeks' wasting illness she joined her little brother, just four months before their grandfather followed them.

Mr. Moody's own deep affliction in the bereavement was hidden from the parents in his unselfish efforts to cheer and comfort them. At the funeral service of little Irene, unannounced and unexpectedly, he arose and paid the following tribute to the little life he loved so dearly:

"I have been thinking this morning about the aged prophet waiting in the valley of the Jordan, so many years ago, for the chariot of God to take him home. Again the chariot of God came down to the Connecticut Valley yesterday morning about half-past six and took our little Irene home. The one was taken at the end of years of active service; the other at the early dawn of youth. But the service of the prophet was no more complete than that of the little handmaid of the Lord, for God called both, and He never interrupts the service of His own.

"Irene has finished her course; her work was well wrought on earth. She had accomplished more than many in their threescore years and ten. We would not have her back, although her voice was

MRS. D. L. MOODY WITH GRANDCHILDREN.

Interior Great Hall in Kansas City, Where Mr. Moody's Last Meetings were Held.

the sweetest voice I ever heard on earth. She never met me once, since she was three months old, until the last few days of pain, without a smile. But Christ had some service for her above. My life has been made much better by her ministry here on earth. She has made us all better. She has been a blessing to all the conferences here this year. She has brought a wealth of sympathy into the meetings such as we have never had before. During the young men's conference I tried to keep it secret, but while I was on the platform my heart was over at the home. On the day after the conference closed she left for the Adirondacks, and we feared we might never see her again. During the women's conference my heart was yonder in the mountains at Saranac. The last night of that conference, while I was trying to speak to the young women words of cheer and encouragement, I was constantly thinking of the little girl, and within twelve hours I was by her side.

"The last few days have been blessed days to me. I have learned many new and precious lessons. She was very fond of riding with me, and on Monday morning, twenty-four hours before she fell asleep, she asked me to take her driving, and at 6.30 we were out together. She never looked more beautiful. She was just ripening for Heaven. She was too fair for this earth. I thank God this morning for the hope of immortality. I know I shall see her in the morning, more beautiful in her resurrection glory than she was here."

On November 13, 1899, a fourth grandchild was born—Mary Whittle Moody—and early the next day the following telegram and letter were sent to her parents. The grandfather's cup of joy had been filled once more.

"Thankful for good news. May she become famous in the Kingdom of Heaven is the prayer of her grandfather,

"D. L. MOODY."

"MY DEAR WILL: I am full of praise and thanksgiving to-day and am delighted to think of May and yourself with a daughter. Dear little child, I already feel my heart going out towards her. Kiss the dear baby for me. I do feel as if our prayers have been answered. Thank God for another grandchild."

These messages were sent from Kansas City only two days before he was obliged to lay down his active labors. At the same time he wrote his only other surviving grandchild, Emma Fitt, then nearly four years old, one of those simple, loving letters that bound his grandchildren to him with undying love. It was as follows:

"MY DEAR EMMA: I am glad that you have a little cousin. Will you kiss her for me, and will you show her your grandfather's picture? (referring to a newspaper clipping he enclosed). I do not think she will know me, but you can tell her all about me, so she will know me when she gets older, and we will play together with her. I am going to send her a little kiss, just one little one.

"Your grandfather,

"D. L. MOODY.

"I will put the kiss in a little box and you can take it to her."

Little Mary, the new-born babe, was carried to her grandfather's house ten days later, but she will have to learn of his loving, playful, tender heart from the precious letters and photographs for whose possession the family are now so thankful.

"Has grandpa gone to Jesus' house?"

"Yes."

"Where Dwight and Irene are?"

"Yes."

"Well, I want to go there, too, and I'll just hug grandpa when I see him, and we'll all play together."

These questions were asked by the remaining four-year-old grandchild when told that she would never again see her grandfather down here.

With advancing years there had been no irascibility, so common in many elderly men, but the spirit had grown more sweet and tender in its ripening for Heaven. The little ones were drawn to him, as they were drawn to his Master, and in their company he seemed to have a foretaste of that society which he now enjoys, for has it not been said that of such is the Kingdom of Heaven?

CHAPTER XLV

Within the Gates

"HAWLEY, were you ever homesick for Heaven?" Mr. Moody asked once, at the close of a long, tiring day's work. "Do you know, I've just been reading something from Rutherford, and I think I understand sometimes how he felt. See this," and then he handed the book with this passage marked:

"His absence is like a mountain upon my heavy heart; O, when shall we meet?

"O, how long it is to the dawning of the marriage day: O, sweet Lord Jesus, take long steps.

"O, my beloved, flee like a roe or a young hart upon the mountains of separation.

"O, that He would fold the Heaven together like an old cloak and shovel time and days away and make ready the Lamb's Wife for her Husband.

"Since He looked upon me, my heart is not my own; He hath run away to Heaven with it.

"How sweet the wind that bloweth out of the quarter where Christ is!"

This conversation took place in the early sixties. During the last year of his earthly career, the same longing was at times greatly intensified. Mr. Moody had been spared from bereavement to an unusual degree, and when called upon to lay away the form of his aged mother, in her ninety-first year, there was only a sense of joyful victory that God had so long granted to her a mind and body unimpaired.

It was his solicitude for others that made him conceal from those nearest him his first symptoms of a break-down, although doubtless he himself little realized their serious nature. An illness in the home of one of his family seemed to him an imperative call for Mrs. Moody to remain at Northfield; at the same time he reassured her as to his own health.

An invitation had been accepted to conduct a series of meetings in the large Convention Hall of Kansas City, and Mr. Moody started for the West early in November. Here he was joined by Mr. C. C. Case, who conducted the choir during the mission, and thus describes the few days of sickness preceding his return on November 17th:

" Tuesday morning at breakfast I saw that he looked pale and ate little. I asked how he rested, and he said, 'I slept in my chair all night.' Of course I knew if he could not lie down he was a sick man. I asked him what was the matter; he said he had had a pain in his chest for a couple of weeks, and added, 'I did not let my family know it, for they would not have let me come on here.' I had to urge him for an hour or two before he would consent to call a doctor, but finally he gave in. The doctor put a mustard plaster on his chest, which at once relieved the pain. He preached six sermons after that, but I could see that he was all the time growing weaker, and the last two days he had to be taken to the hall in a carriage, although it was only two blocks away. When he began speaking he did not show his weakness, but preached with his old-time fire and spirit; but when he got back to his room I could see that he was very much exhausted. I tried to make him advise his family of his condition, but he would not until the day he started for home.

" I think he enjoyed his work in Kansas City as well as any he ever did, from what he said to me. The crowds were greater than any that I had ever experienced with him. The singing pleased him very much, for I had nearly a thousand voices in the choir. We had an 'Old Men's Quartet' that he particularly enjoyed. Their ages varied from sixty-seven to eighty-two, and he would announce their selections by saying, 'I want my *boys* to sing so and so.'"

The following letter was written at this time to a very dear friend in Scotland:

"KANSAS CITY, November 12, 1899.

"MY DEAR MRS. MCKINNON:

"I am off here all alone, thinking of the past, and you and your good husband have come into my mind, and I just long to see you both once more. It would do my eyes good to see you all, and ride down that western coast [of Scotland] once more. I wonder if I should like your new house as well as your old one?

"I cannot tell you how much I miss dear Drummond. It does not seem possible I shall not see him again on earth. What a grand time we shall all have when we get to Heaven! Only think what a lot have gone home since 1873, when we first met. I get homesick for them sometimes, and yet I would not be off until the work that the Lord has given me to do is finished. The work is sweeter now than ever, and I think I have some streams started that will flow on forever. What a joy to be in the harvest field and have a hand in God's work!

"Will you give my warmest love to all old friends, and take much for yourself?

"Your loving friend,

"D. L. MOODY."

In conversation with Mr. Vining, a warm friend and former student of Mount Vernon School, he talked of the institutions which he had founded, and said that the work in Kansas City was, he believed, as great as any God had given him to do. He spoke of the bereavements that had occurred in his family during the past year, and, picking up a copy of his book, "Thoughts from My Library," he read a selection that has a peculiar interest now. It was a comment on the text (Psalm xxx. 5), "*Weeping may endure for a night, but joy cometh in the morning.*" The extract ends with the words:

"I have heard it in the Land of Light from which I come. There is a time approaching, steadily if not quickly, when 'the Lord will wipe away tears from all faces.' This weary world shall obtain joy and gladness at last, and sorrow and sighing shall flee away. 'Wherefore comfort one another with these words.'"

In view of the approaching end, the following paragraphs from one of the last sermons in Kansas City are significant:

"I have no sympathy with the idea that our best days are behind us," and he smiled as he related the impression that he had a year before when he saw in the papers that "Old Moody is in town." "Why," he said, "I am only sixty-two; I am only a baby in comparison with the great eternity which is to come.

"We say this is the land of the living! It is not. It is the land of the dying. What is our life here but a vapor? A hearse is the most common sight. Families broken into. Over there is one who has lost a father, there a mother, there is a place vacant, there a sister's name is no more heard, there a brother's love is missed. Death stalks triumphant through our midst, in this world. Only yesterday I met a mother who had lost her babe. Death in front of us, death behind us, death to the right of us, death to the left of us. See the hospitals in our land, and the asylums for the insane, and the blind, and the aged.

"See the great number of jails in our land. Seventy thousand criminals in our country. But look at the other world. No death, no pain, no sorrow, no old age, no sickness, no bending forms, no dimmed eyes, no tears. But joy, peace, love, happiness. No gray hair. People all young. River of life for the healing of the nations, and everlasting life. Think of it! Life! Life! Life without end! And yet so many men choose this life on earth, instead of the life in Heaven. Don't close your heart against eternal life. Only take the gift, only take it. Will you do it?"

Near the close of one service, Mr. Moody leaned on the organ and asked the ministers:

"Will you ministers allow me to say a word to you?"

"Yes, yes; say what you want," they answered.

"Well, I'm not a prophet, but I have a guess to make that I think will prove a true prophecy. You hear so much nowadays about the preacher of the twentieth century. Do you know what sort of a man he will be? He will be the sort of a preacher who opens his Bible and preaches out of that. Oh, I'm sick and tired of this essay preaching! I'm nauseated with this 'silver-tongued orator' preaching! I like to hear preachers, and not windmills."

Had he known that this was to be his last sermon, could he have made a more urgent and characteristic appeal in closing than the following?

"Suppose we should write out to-night this excuse? How would it sound? 'To the King of Heaven: While sitting in Convention Hall, Kansas City, Mo., November 16, 1899, I received a very pressing invitation from one of your servants to be present at the marriage supper of Your only-begotten Son. I pray Thee have me excused.'

"Would you sign that, young man? Would you, mother? Would you come up to the reporters' table, take a pen, and put your name down to such an excuse? You would say, 'Let my right hand forget its cunning, and my tongue cleave to the roof of my mouth, before I sign that.' I doubt if there is one here who would sign it. Will you then pay no attention to God's invitation? I beg of you, do not make light of it. It is a loving God inviting you to a feast, and God is not to be mocked. Go play with forked lightning, go trifle with pestilence and disease, but trifle not with God.

"Just let me write out another answer: 'To the King of Heaven: While sitting in Convention Hall, Kansas City, Mo., November 16, 1899, I received a pressing invitation from one of Your messengers to be present at the marriage supper of Your only-begotten Son. I hasten to reply. By the grace of God I will be present.'"

Under the imperative order of his physician Mr. Moody reluctantly consented to cease work, and, leaving Kansas City by the evening train, travelled directly home without breaking the journey, which required a day and two nights on the road. On the way an incident occurred that cheered and encouraged him greatly. From St. Louis to Detroit the train was delayed by the burning out of the locomotive fire grate, and it was feared that connections would be missed at a later point. The new engineer, who was to take the train from Detroit to St. Thomas, learning that Mr. Moody was on the train, returning home sick, sent word to him that he would do his best to make up the lost time. "Tell him," he said, "that I was converted under him fifteen years ago, and I owe everything to him." The division from Detroit to St. Thomas was covered in the darkness of that night at a speed averaging a mile a minute, including stops, and the connection for the East was secured.

The first intimation that Mr. Moody's family had of his illness was a telegram:

"Doctor thinks I need rest. Am on my way home." This was followed at short intervals by other telegrams:

"Improving rapidly. Have not felt so well for a week."

"Have had a splendid day. No fever. Heart growing better all the time. No pain. Am taking good care of myself, not only for the loved ones, but for the work I think God still has for me to do on earth."

Arriving at Greenfield, Mr. Moody was met and driven twelve miles to his home. He went upstairs with little difficulty to prepare for tea, but never descended again.

On reaching Northfield, he telegraphed Kansas City friends:

"Have reached home safely. Have travelled backward and forward for forty years, and never stood trip better. Regret exceedingly being forced to leave. Had I been with you to-night I would have preached on 'Thou art not far from the Kingdom.' My prayer is that many may be led into the Kingdom under Mr. Torrey's preaching. I want to thank the good people of Kansas City for their kindness and prayers."

It was hoped that a complete rest would restore the weakened heart, and specialists were consulted who gave encouragement for an ultimate restoration of health, even if the old-time vigor could never again return. But day by day his weakness increased. At first it was almost imperceptible, but it grew steadily more noticeable, until the least effort seemed to tax his strength.

Until within a few days of the end he took the keenest interest in everything, and insisted on being told all the latest news of the war in South Africa, over which he was greatly exercised. A few days before the final summons he was resting quietly with closed eyes, when suddenly he remarked:

"I know what I would do if I were old Krüger."

Thinking that he had been dreaming, his son inquired if he had had a good rest.

"I wasn't asleep," he replied; "I was thinking of that horrible war."

"Well, what would you do if you were Krüger, father?"

"Oh, I would just send a message to Lord Salisbury, and state that there had been so many hundreds killed on the Boer side, and so many on the English side. And I would say that, as an old man, I should soon have to stand before God, and that I didn't want to go before Him with all this blood on my conscience, and I would tell England to make her own terms of peace."

It was suggested that possibly England herself was not entirely innocent.

"That's quite so; but if Krüger placed himself in that position, after showing the fight he has, England would have to make the best of terms, or answer for it to the best element in her own land, as well as the entire civilized world."

God had tried His servant in many ways, but it is doubtful if he ever experienced a severer trial than that of the last few weeks. After sixty-two years of an unusually active life, with the remembrance of not more than one or two days of slight illness, to be suddenly laid aside to wait patiently and in extreme weakness for God's will, was indeed a severe test. But in this he was found "not wanting," and it was with a sense of exultant and victorious joy that he entered the presence of his Lord and heard the words, "Well done, good and faithful servant."

As time wore slowly away—slowly to a man of such tremendous activity—he would say that every night he longed for the morning. As he grew weaker, he said he knew now what that verse meant: "The grasshopper shall be a burden." On Thursday, December 21st, he had seemed rather more nervous than usual, but nevertheless spoke cheerfully about himself. Asked if he was comfortable, he said: "Oh, yes! God is very good to me—and so is my family."

No man loved his family and lifework more devotedly, and he had often said: "Life is very sweet to me, and there is no position of power or wealth that could tempt me from the throne God has given me."

To the world, Friday, December 22d, was the shortest day of all the year, but for Dwight L. Moody its dawn ushered in that day that knows no night. For forty-six years he had been a partaker of the divine life, and the transition from the seen world to the unseen, from the sphere of the temporal to that of the eternal, was no interruption in the life with which his friends were familiar. For nearly half a century his one aim in life had been to do the will of God, and he responded with a characteristic readiness to God's summons. Only a few days before his going, in conversation about some future plans, he referred to the possibility of his lifework being nearly completed. In reply to a remonstrance and an attempt to encourage him, he said:

"I'm not discouraged. There's lots of hard work left in me yet, I believe. I want to live as long as I'm useful, but when my work is done I want to be up and off."

A few days before the end, came an illustration of his characteristic combination of faith and works. While the best medical advice had been secured, he observed the injunction of St. James to call in the elders and to anoint with oil, praying for the restoration of the sick.

To within a few hours of the end Mr. Moody shared with his family the conviction that he was improving. One of his last undertakings was to assume the publication of a monthly periodical, to be the organ of the new Northfield Extension work. The first number under the new management was received Thursday morning. At once he asked to see a copy, but was advised to wait and not to tax his strength. But he insisted on being allowed at least to examine it, "just to see how it looks," and for several minutes went through it carefully.

After a rather restless night he fell into a quiet sleep for over an hour, from which he awoke in a sinking condition. During the earlier hours of the night, Mr. Fitt, his son-in-law, had been by his bedside, and he had seemed to rest and sleep a greater part of the time. At three in the morning the elder son took the place as watcher in the sick-chamber, and for several hours Mr. Moody was very restless and unable to sleep. About six o'clock he quieted down, and soon fell into a natural sleep, from which he awoke in about an hour. Suddenly he was heard speaking in slow and measured words. He was saying:

"Earth recedes; Heaven opens before me." The first impulse was to try to arouse him from what appeared to be a dream. "No, this is no dream, Will," he replied. "It is beautiful. It is like a trance. If this is death, it is sweet. There is no valley here. God is calling me, and I must go."

Meanwhile the nurse was summoning the family and the physician, who had spent the night in the house. Mr. Moody continued to talk quietly, and seemed to speak from another world his last message to the loved ones he was leaving.

"I have always been an ambitious man," he said; "ambitious to leave no wealth or possessions, but to leave lots of work for you to do. Will, you will carry on Mount Hermon. Paul will take up the Seminary, when he is older; Fitt will look after the Institute, and Ambert (his nephew) will help you in the business details." Then it seemed as though he saw beyond the veil, for he exclaimed: "This is my triumph; this is my coronation day! I have been looking forward to it for years." Then his face lit up, and he said, in a voice of joyful rapture: "Dwight! Irene!—I see the children's faces," referring to the two little grandchildren God had taken from his life in the past year. Then, as he thought he was losing consciousness, he said, "Give my love to them all." Turning to his wife, he exclaimed, "Mamma, you have been a good wife to me!" and with that he became unconscious.

For a time it seemed that he had passed on into the unseen world, but slowly he revived, under the effect of heart stimulants, and, suddenly raising himself on his elbow, exclaimed: "What does all this mean? What are you all doing here?" He was told that he had not been well, and immediately it all seemed to be clear to him, and he said:

"This is a strange thing. I have been beyond the gates of death and to the very portals of Heaven, and here I am back again. It is very strange." Again he talked about the work to be done, assigning to the sons the Northfield schools, and to his daughter and her husband the Chicago Bible Institute.

Then, in answer to the query of the daughter, "But, father, what about mother?" he replied, "Oh, she's like Eve, the mother of us all," evidently meaning to imply that she was to mother the whole, and to be to all the interests as well as to the children the same helpful adviser and balance that she had been to him for so many years.

To the plea of his daughter that he should not leave them, he said: "I'm not going to throw my life away. I'll stay as long as I can, but if my time is come, I'm ready."

Then a new thought seemed to possess him, and he exclaimed: "I'm not at all sure but that God may perform a miracle and raise me up. I'm going to get up. If God wants to heal me by a miracle that way, all right; and if not, I can meet death in my chair as well as here." Then, turning to one of the attendants who was applying warm cloths, he said, "Here, take those away. If God is going to perform a miracle we don't want them, and the first thing I suppose we should do would be to discharge the doctor." He did not insist on this, however, but was determined to get up and could not be dissuaded. He then walked across the room to an easy-chair, where he sat down for a few moments. A second sinking turn left him exhausted, and he was willing to return to bed, where he remained, quietly awaiting the end, for an hour. To the very last he was thinking of those about him and considering them. Turning to his wife, only a little while before he passed away, he said: "This is hard on you, Mother, and I'm sorry to distress you in this way. It is hard to be kept in such anxiety." The last time the doctor approached to administer the hypodermic injection of nitro-glycerin he looked at him in a questioning and undecided way and said in a perfectly natural voice, "Doctor, I don't know about this. Do you think it best? It is only keeping the family in anxiety."

In a few moments more another sinking turn came, and from it he awoke in the presence of Him whom he loved and served so long and devotedly. It was not like death, for he "fell on sleep" quietly and peacefully.

Of his awaking consciousness beyond the thin veil which separates the seen from the unseen we may not know just now, but of the welcome in that City for which at times he felt such a strange homesickness we may be sure. Did he not himself testify to having been "within the gates" and "beyond the portals," where he had caught a glimpse of child faces "loved long since and lost awhile"? During his earthly pilgrimage it had not been given him to sing the sweet and joyful melodies that filled his soul, but at that Christmastide he joined in Heaven's glorious anthems of praise to Him whose love had been a consuming fire and whom he had served with such devotion when on earth.

Of that larger life he had spoken in no uncertain way.

"Some day you will read in the papers that D. L. Moody, of East Northfield, is dead," he had said. "Don't you believe a word of it!

At that moment I shall be more alive than I am now. I shall have gone up higher, that is all—out of this old clay tenement into a house that is immortal; a body that death cannot touch, that sin cannot taint, a body fashioned like unto His glorious body. I was born of the flesh in 1837. I was born of the Spirit in 1856. That which is born of the flesh may die. That which is born of the Spirit will live forever."

CHAPTER XLVI

AT REST ON ROUND TOP

IN seeming accord with Mr. Moody's feelings that "everything before a true believer is glorious," even Nature assumed no sign of mourning on the day that his earthly tabernacle was laid to rest on Round Top. December 26th was the date fixed for the funeral services, and, as some one expressed it, it was "one of the Lord's own days." The winter's first snow rested on the distant hills of southern Vermont and New Hampshire, while a clear sky and a frosty atmosphere combined to make it a day of unusual brightness. During the morning friends arrived from all directions, representing every phase of society and every shade of theological belief.

Mr. Moody's wishes were studiously observed with respect to any outward appearance of emblems of mourning. About the home everything was, apparently, as usual. No crape was seen on the door, and the window blinds were all open. In the chamber where he lay "asleep in Jesus" there was only a sense of quiet repose in the loved form, and looking upon him as he lay upon the couch one would have thought that he was taking one of those short naps with which he was accustomed to refresh himself before conducting a service.

After a brief service at the house, conducted by Dr. C. I. Scofield, pastor of the Northfield Church, and the Rev. R. A. Torrey, pastor of the Chicago Avenue Church, Chicago, the casket was placed upon a bier, and carried by thirty-two Mount Hermon students to the Congregational Church, half a mile away.

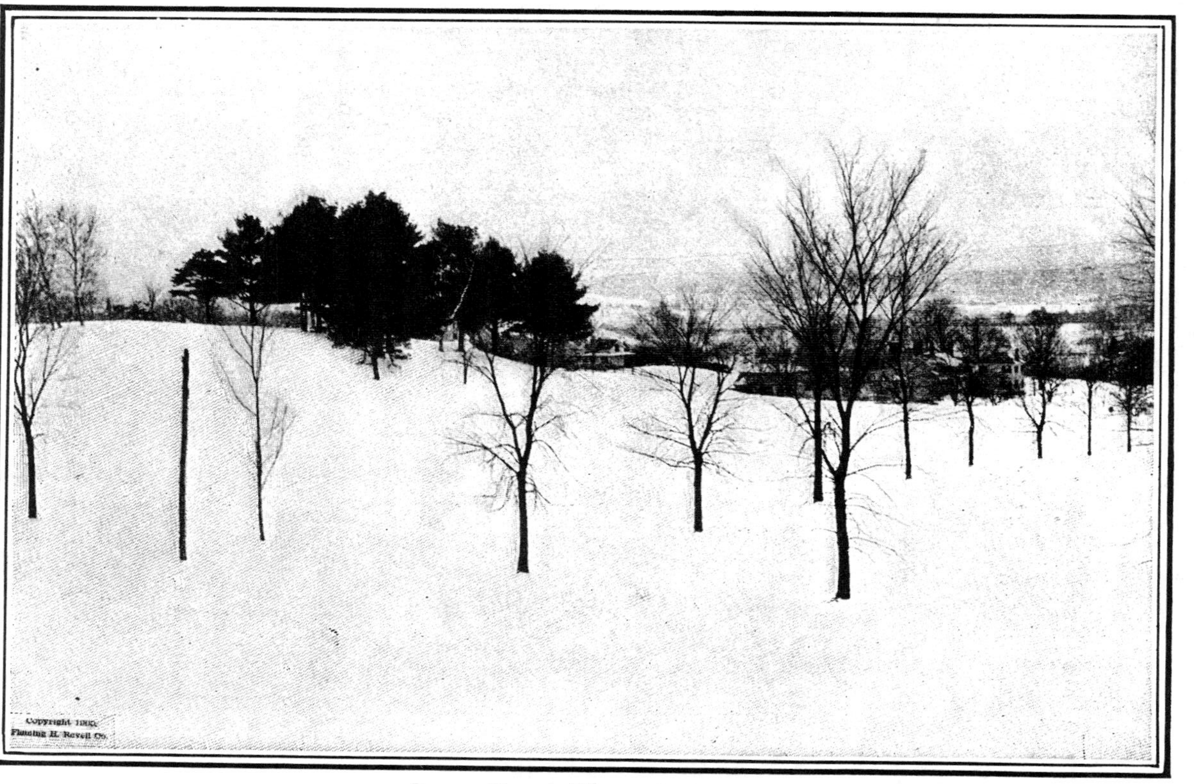

Round Top in White Apparel.

At Rest on Round Top.

Four months before, Mr. Moody had planned the funeral services of his grandchild Irene. "Just this once let me have my own way," he had pleaded, and every one had gladly fallen in with his simple arrangements. As the family and friends followed the white casket borne on a bier by twelve Mount Hermon students, the special friends of the little one, Mr. Moody had remarked to his son, "That is just as I would want it. No hearse and no mourning, but just let Mount Hermon boys bear me to my resting-place." Little was it thought that in so short a time that wish would need to be fulfilled.

At the church an opportunity was given to look for the last time upon the one whom so many had loved. Among all the saddened faces his alone looked untroubled. The form lay quietly at rest waiting the moment when Christ should change it into one "like unto His own glorious body," while he himself, the soul so dearly loved, was "absent from the body and at home with the Lord."

The public service was held at 2.30 P.M. Old associates, neighbors, and relatives had come from far and near. Simple tributes of love and joyous notes of praise were offered by several of his friends and fellow-laborers.

Dr. Scofield had charge of the services, which began with the singing of "Immanuel's Land," one of Mr. Moody's favorite hymns. At the close of the service the Mount Hermon Quartet, always a great favorite with him, sang the following lines by Major Whittle, set to music by his daughter, Mr. Moody's daughter-in-law:

"A lamp in the night, a song in time of sorrow,
A great glad hope which faith can ever borrow;
To gild the passing day with the glory of the morrow
Is the hope of the coming of the Lord.

"Blessed hope, blessed hope,
Blessed hope of the coming of the Lord!
How the aching heart it cheers,
How it glistens thro' our tears,
Blessed hope of the coming of the Lord!

"A star in the sky, a beacon bright to guide us,
An anchor sure to hold when storms betide us,
A refuge for the soul, where in quiet we may hide us,
Is the hope of the coming of the Lord.

"A word from the One to all our hearts the dearest,
A parting word to make Him, aye, the nearest;
Of all His precious words the sweetest, brightest, clearest,
Is the hope of the coming of the Lord!"

The keynote of the service was one of exultant victory. Personal bereavement and selfish sorrow seemed drowned in the consciousness of his glad triumph and joyous welcome by the One he had served so devotedly. There were in all the messages a word of inspiration and a call to greater service, so that even in his death he still published the message of his life: Service for the Master.

Toward the close of the exercises a striking scene occurred. Up to this moment no sunshine had entered the church, the afternoon being slightly clouded. Suddenly a single ray shone through the upper window at the extreme end, opposite the platform. It fell upon the side and close to the head of the casket. Then moving slowly as the sun descended, as though searching for its object, it fell full upon the exposed face—a halo of light from Heaven—suffusing the familiar and natural features with a brightness in keeping with the glad heart that had throbbed in life. The sunshine touched no other object; the face only was illumined, and then, as though its mission had been accomplished, its token from the upper world assured, the sun set behind the distant hill.

Dr. Scofield gave a short address, saying: "'We know: we are always confident.' That is the Christian's attitude toward the mystery of death. In this triumphant assurance Dwight L. Moody lived, and at high noon last Friday he died. We are not met, dear friends, to mourn a defeat, but to celebrate a triumph. He '*walked with God and he was not, for God took him.*' Here was no anti-climax. This strenuous soul was not appointed to the slow decay of his powers. There in the West, in the presence of great audiences of twelve thousand of his fellowmen, God spoke to him to lay down all that work and come home. He would have planned it so. So much strength was given as sufficed for his journey back to his beloved Northfield. So much additional strength as kept him hovering between two worlds, until our hearts could be braced for his home-going, and then he fell on sleep.

"This is not the place, nor am I the man, to present a study of the life and character of Dwight L. Moody. No one will ever question that we are laying to-day in the kindly bosom of earth the mortal body of a great man. Whether we measure greatness by quality of character or by qualities of intellect or by things accomplished, Dwight L. Moody must be accounted great.

"The basis of Mr. Moody's character was sincerity. He had an inveterate aversion to all forms of sham, unreality, and pretence. Most of all did he detest religious pretence or cant. Along with the fundamental quality he cherished a great love of righteousness. His first question concerning any proposed action was: 'Is it right?' But these two qualities, necessarily at the bottom of all noble character, were in him suffused and transfigured by divine grace. Besides all this, he was, in a wonderful degree, brave, magnanimous, and unselfish.

"Doubtless this unlettered New England country boy became what he was by the grace of God. The secrets of Dwight L. Moody's power were: First, in a definite experience of Christ's saving grace. He had passed out of death into life, and he knew it. Secondly, he believed in the divine authority of the Scriptures. The Bible was to him the voice of God, and he made it resound as such in the consciences of men. Thirdly, he was baptized with the Holy Spirit, and he knew it. It was to him as definite an experience as his conversion. Fourthly, he was a man of prayer. He believed in a mighty and unfettered God. Fifthly, he believed in works, in ceaseless effort, in wise provision, in the power of organization, of publicity. He expected the supernatural to work, but through the natural. He hitched his wagon to a star, but he always kept the wheels on the ground and the axles well oiled.

"I like to think of Dwight L. Moody in Heaven. I like to think of him with his Lord and with Elijah, Daniel, Paul, Augustine, Luther, Wesley, and Finney. Farewell for a little time, great heart. May a double portion of the Spirit be vouchsafed to us who remain."

President H. G. Weston, of the Crozer Theological Seminary, followed Dr. Scofield. In closing a beautiful tribute to his friend he said:

"I count as one of the greatest blessings of my life my acquaintance with Mr. Moody, the influence he has had on me, and the privilege of studying God's methods in his life and work. He was the greatest religious character of this century. We instinctively attribute the success of every man who is eminent in attracting and influencing others to some special natural endowment, to education and training, or to a peculiar magnetic personality. Mr. Moody had none of these, yet no man has surpassed him in his power of attraction and influence, both over masses of men and over individuals of strong character, of executive ability, of great resources, whom he fastened to himself with hooks of steel, making them not only his lifelong friends, but his constant partners in all his good works. This marvellous power, wielded for so many years, undiminished to the end, we cannot explain by any one peculiar natural gift. He had none of them.

"What had he? He had life. I do not mean the manner of living, but what the Bible means by this word—what Christ means when He declares the purpose of His coming: '*I am come that they might have life, and that they might have it more abundantly.*' God gave him life, made him a partaker of the divine nature; and from the moment he received it the development, growth, and manifestation of that life became the whole object of his existence. To it he devoted every power of his being, and that devotion kindled into intensest activity every latent energy of his nature, making him the complete, rounded, many-sided man that he was, of instinctive judgment and tact, and gave him his wonderful mastery of man.

"Then he nourished and strengthened that life by devotion to God's Word. He prized it as the treasure by which his life could be enriched. He realized to the full Christ's words: '*Man shall not live by bread alone, but by every word that proceedeth out of the mouth of God.*' That Word he hid in his heart, as the seed is hidden in the earth that it may swell and grow. He hid it there, ready for use on every occasion and in every emergency. It was sweeter to him than honey and the honeycomb. His mind and heart were given to the Word of God.

"But his life, like that of Christ's, was for others. He did not search the Bible to add to his knowledge, but to save men from sin. His first and dominant purpose was to have every man receive that life of which he had been made a partaker; to this his sermons were devoted; he counted everything but loss unless this were attained, and he coveted for all the means of developing and utilizing that life. The sight of poor boys and girls deprived of the means of education would not let him rest until he had provided some method by which their lives should be enriched and made more in accordance with Heaven's designs for them. He dotted this fair plain with houses that young men and young women should have the means of so enlarging their lives that they might be useful to their fellows. His work was in the line of Christ's miracles, which never enriched the object with bounties of land or money or resources, but always gave power to life, making the dead eye to see, touching the dead tongue, the dead ear, the dead limb, and in His highest miracles bringing the dead to life.

"This likeness to Christ, this knowing the power of His resurrection, this conformity to His death, was the reason for every man's giving him credit for the utmost sincerity. It was the reason men listened to him and believed him, and were influenced by him in the mass and as individuals. They saw not the man, but the truth he spoke. He had that wonderful egotism by which he could constantly speak of himself and yet never draw attention to himself. Men saw in all that he was and did the truth as it was in Jesus.

"And so because Mr. Moody could in his measure use those great words of Christ, '*I am come that they might have life, and that they might have it more abundantly*,' because these words expressed his whole being, I loved and honored and valued him, and because of what he was, and, therefore, of what he did, I had rather be Dwight Moody dead, lying there in his coffin, than any living man on earth."

Bishop W. F. Mallalieu, of the Methodist Episcopal Church, succeeded Dr. Weston, and spoke as follows:

"'Servant of God, well done;
Thy glorious warfare's past;
The battle's fought, the race is won,
And thou art crowned at last.'

"I first met and became acquainted with him whose death we mourn, in London, in the summer of 1875. From that day when he moved the masses of the world's metropolis to the hour when he answered the call of God to come up higher I have known him, esteemed him, and loved him. Surely we may say, and the world will indorse the affirmation, that in his death one of the truest, bravest, purest, and most influential men of this wonderful nineteenth century has passed to his rest and his reward. With feelings of unspeakable loss and desolation we gather about the casket that contains all that was mortal of Dwight L. Moody. And yet a mighty uplift and inspiration must come to each one of us as we think of his character and his achievements, for he was

"'One who never turned his back, but marched breast forward;
Never doubted clouds would break,
Never dreamed, though right were worsted, wrong would triumph.'

"In bone and brawn and brain he was a typical New Englander. He was descended from the choicest New England stock; he was born of a New England mother, and from his earliest life he breathed the free air of his native hills, and was carefully nurtured in the knowledge of God and of the holy traditions and histories of the glorious past. It was to be expected of him that he would become a Christian of pronounced characteristics, for he consecrated himself thoroughly, completely, and irrevocably to the service of God and humanity. The heart of no disciple of the Master ever beat with more genuine, sympathetic, and utterly unselfish loyalty than did the great, generous, loving heart of our friend.

"Because he held fast to the absolute truth of the Bible, and unequivocally and intensely believed it to be the unerring Word of God; because he preached the Gospel rather than talked about the Gospel; because he used his mother-tongue, the terse, clear, ringing, straightforward Saxon; because he had the profoundest sense of brotherhood with all poor, unfortunate, and even outcast people; because he was unaffectedly tender and patient with the weak and the sinful; because he hated evil as thoroughly as he loved goodness; because he knew right well how to lead penitent souls to the Saviour; because he had the happy art of arousing Christian people to a vivid sense of their obligations and inciting them to the performance of their duties; because he had in his own soul a conscious, joyous experience of personal salvation, the people flocked to his services, they heard him gladly, they were led to Christ; and he came to be prized and honored by all denominations, so that to-day all Protestantism recognizes the fact that he was God's servant, an ambassador of Christ, and indeed a chosen vessel to bear the name of Jesus to the nations. We shall not again behold his manly and vigorous form, hear his thrilling voice, or be moved by his consecrated personality, but if we are true and faithful to our Lord, we shall see him in glory; for already he walks the streets of the Heavenly City, he mingles in the songs of the innumerable company of white-robed saints, sees the King in His beauty, and waits our coming. May God grant that in due time we may meet him over yonder."

The Rev. R. A. Torrey said in his address:

"God has laid two thoughts upon my heart for this hour. The first is found in the words of Paul in I Corinthians, xv. 10: '*By the grace of God I am what I am.*' God has wonderfully magnified His love and grace in D. L. Moody. God was magnified in his birth. The babe that was born sixty-two years ago on yonder hill, with all the possibilities that were wrapped up in him, was God's gift to the world. How much that gift meant to the world! How the world has been blessed and benefited by it we shall never know this side the coming of our Lord. God's grace was magnified in his conversion. He was born in sin, as we all are, but God, by His providence, and by the power of His Word, by the regenerating power of His Holy Spirit, made him the mighty man of God that he became. How much the conversion of that boy in Boston forty-four years ago meant to the world no man can tell, but it was all God's grace that did it. God's love and grace were magnified again in the development of that character that has made him so loved and honored in all lands to-day. He had a strength and beauty of character possessed by few sons of men; but it was all from God. To God alone it was due that he differed from other men.

"The other thought is found in Joshua, i. 2: '*Moses My servant is dead; now therefore arise, go over this Jordan, thou, and all this people, unto the land which I do give to them.*' The death of Mr. Moody is a call to go forward—a call to his children, to his associates, to ministers of the Word everywhere, to the whole Church. 'Our leader has fallen; let us give up the work,' some would say. Not for a minute. Listen to what God says: 'Your leader is fallen; move forward. Moses My servant is dead; therefore arise, go in and possess the land. Be strong and of good courage, be not afraid. As I was with Moody, so I will be with thee. I will not fail thee nor forsake thee.'

"The unanimity upon this point of all those who have been associated with him is remarkable. The great institutions he has established at Northfield, at Mount Hermon, at Chicago, and the work they represent, must be pushed to the front as never before.

"Mr. Moody himself said, when he felt the call of death at Kansas City, 'I know how much better it would be for me to go; but we are on the verge of a great revival like that of 1857, and I want to have a hand in it.' He will have a mighty hand in it. His death, with the triumphal scenes that surround it, are part of God's way of answering the prayers for a revival that have been so long ascending in our land."

The Rev. Dr. A. T. Pierson spoke next, saying:

"When a great tree falls you know its greatness not only by its branches, but by its roots, by how much soil it tore up as it fell. I know of no other man who, falling in this century, has uprooted a wider tract than this man who has just left us.

"I have been thinking of the four deaths during the last quarter of a century—of Charles H. Spurgeon, of London; A. J. Gordon, of Boston; Catherine Booth, mother of the Salvation Army, and George Müller, of Bristol, England, not one of whom stirred the world more widely than Dwight L. Moody.

"Now, I think we ought to be very careful of what we say here. There is a temptation to say more than ought to be said, and we should be careful to speak as in the presence of God. This is a time to glorify God.

"Dwight L. Moody was a great man, but his greatness was the genius of goodness. That man, when he entered the church in 1856 in Boston, after ten months of probation, had been held at arm's length all that time because it was feared that he was not a sound believer. The man the church held out at arm's length has become the preacher of preachers, the teacher of teachers, the evangelist of evangelists.

"When, in 1858, he decided to give God all his time, he gave out the key to his future. I say everything D. L. Moody has touched has been a success, whether as an evangelist or as an educator and organizer. Do you know that, with careful reckoning, it has been estimated that he has reached one hundred million people in the aggregate, by his voice and pen, since he first became a Christian? Take into consideration all the people his books have reached and the languages into which they have been translated; look beyond his evangelistic work to the work of education—the schools, the Chicago Bible Institute, and the Training School here. Scores of people in the world owe their spiritual life and power to Dwight L. Moody as the means of their consecration.

"I want to say a word of Mr. Moody's entrance into Heaven. When he entered into Heaven there must have been an unusual rejoicing. I ask you whether you can think of any other man of the last half century whose coming so many souls would have welcomed at the gates of Heaven? It was a triumphal entrance into glory.

"No man who has been associated with him in Christian work has not seen that there is but one way to live, and that way, to live wholly for God. The thing that D. L. Moody stood for, and will stand for, through centuries to come, was his living only for God. He made mistakes, no doubt, and if any of us is without sin in this respect, we may cast a stone at him, but I am satisfied that his mistakes were the mistakes of a stream that overflowed its banks. It is a great deal better to be full and overflowing than to be empty and have nothing to overflow with."

John Wanamaker, of Philadelphia, said:

"On the call of the moment the first thought I would express is that Mr. Moody's life has given to us a better idea of what the man Christ Jesus was. By this man's living among men we have had given to us a splendid commentary on the Holy Scriptures. His life sketches for us speaking likenesses of Paul and Nehemiah. There was much in Mr. Moody like Oliver Cromwell. Very surely we may call Mr. Moody the Stonewall Jackson of this century of the Church of God.

"Sturdy and strong and aggressive he was, but was there anything more beautiful in his character than his gentleness and kindness?

Each of us who knew him was taken into his family and treated as his kin.

"Not only is it that one hundred millions have heard the Gospel from his lips, but with the Northfield buildings, with buildings for Church and Christian Associations, and schools erected through his revival work, the whole nation has been blessed. The great things that have grown out of his energy and untiring efforts make many of our lives look small to-day in comparison with his.

"Reviewing his life from the time I knew him first, about 1859, I can call to mind many who, during these forty years, have been distinguished in the business world, in railroad enterprises, and in public life, but I do not know of one who has made so much of his life or who would not say, if he were to speak, that he would be glad if he had chosen the course that Mr. Moody took to make his life potential for good. He has done the best business of us all. God's work looms up larger than ever to us to-day.

"It is like a vision to me to recall my last interview with Mr. Moody, about the 10th of November last, when, in answer to his telegram, I met him in the Philadelphia railroad station on his way to Kansas City. He could only stop over a train, and his purpose was to ascertain the exact situation of his prospective winter work at Philadelphia. We talked for nearly an hour upon the outlook, and I went to my home to tell my family that Mr. Moody looked to me that night as the prophets Elijah and Hosea must have looked, and I told them, as I now tell you, that his eyes were full of tears and that he sighed again and again, saying, 'If only it would please God to let me get hold of this city by a winter of meetings! I should like to do it before I die, and possibly from Philadelphia the influence would go out to other large cities.' Somehow my heart grew heavier as he talked. I witnessed what seemed to me like agony of soul in his care for the Church at large and his anxiety for a revival. It was with this burden that he undertook a railway journey for a thousand miles of fatiguing travel, and under this burden he has staggered to the grave.

To us of like years, let me say the sixties are fast quitting work, and we may well hasten to finish what we have yet to do."

After the public service the loved form was carried again by the Mount Hermon students to Round Top, the Olivet of Northfield, just at the crown of the little hill, where many of the best meetings are held every year.

Those who were gathered at the grave sang, "Jesus, Lover of my soul." Dr. Torrey offered prayer, and Dr. Scofield pronounced the benediction, and the loved form was laid away till the day break and death and sorrow shall be no more.

Mr. Moody hoped that the Lord would return while he was living. As he was walking one evening towards the Auditorium with a friend, he sat down on the grass of Round Top to rest. Looking out over the beautiful summer landscape spread before them, gilded with the glory of the westering sun, he said:

"I should like to be here when Christ comes back!"

His longing was not gratified during his life, but his body rests there, awaiting the voice of the archangel and the trump of God.

From the crest of the hill where the grave was made one may see Mr. Moody's birthplace; a little more to the west, his own home for the last quarter of a century; about as far to the north the Seminary buildings, some of them only a two-minute walk; the Colportage building not far away, while the last two buildings erected at Mount Hermon, the chapel and Overtoun Hall, four miles distant, appear across the beautiful Connecticut Valley.

Surely he "started some streams that will flow on forever"! He lies in the very midst of them, a constant inspiration to those he left behind to carry on his work.

CHAPTER XLVII

Memorial Services

MR. MOODY'S departure from this earthly life brought expressions of personal sorrow from all parts of the world. For days and weeks telegrams, cables, letters, and copies of resolutions from Christian organizations were received from every part of America and from distant lands. All united, without regard for any social distinction, in testifying to their love and admiration for this humble servant of God.

In many of the leading cities in America and Great Britain memorial services were held, in which his former associates spoke of the result of the missions which he had conducted. In New York City two large meetings were held, while Brooklyn, Boston, Philadelphia, Baltimore, Washington, and San Francisco showed their appreciation of his life-long devotion to the cause of the church by gatherings representing all denominations. Then came the news of similar gatherings in London—one at Exeter Hall, another at St. James' Hall. Others were held in Liverpool, Edinburgh, and Glasgow; and after these came the echoes of meetings in Japan and other foreign lands.

Perhaps nothing so displayed the catholic nature of Mr. Moody's work as these assemblages. At the services in London tributes were paid to his memory by the Revs. F. B. Meyer, Guinness Rogers, Munro Gibson, Hugh Price Hughes, H. W. Webb-Peploe, and by Lord Kinnaird, and in America equally representative speakers took part.

In Boston Tremont Temple was filled. Clergymen of all denominations crowded the platform, and when the choir that had so often assisted Mr. Moody in his meetings in that hall sang " Eye hath not seen " it did not require much imagination to think of it as one of Moody's meetings of former years. Henry M. Moore, for thirty years one of Mr. Moody's most intimate friends and most valued helpers, presided, and addresses were made by Bishop W. F. Mallalieu, the Rev. Drs. L. B. Bates, A. H. Plumb, George C. Lorimer, and H. I. White and John Willis Baer. Dr. Joseph Cook addressed another memorial meeting in Park Street Church, Boston, about the same time, and spoke with his old-time force.

In Brooklyn, where Mr. Moody had preached just before going to Kansas City, other services were held, in which Drs. J. F. Carson, Theodore Cuyler, David Gregg, A. C. Dixon, A. T. Pierson, and Messrs. Edgar W. Hawley and Ira D. Sankey were among the speakers. On the evening of the day of his death, at the Plymouth Church prayer-meeting, the pastor, Dr. N. D. Hillis, and the former pastor, Dr. Lyman Abbott, reviewed his life-work. On the following Sunday Dr. Hillis delivered a sermon in which he spoke of him as " the last of the great group "—Spurgeon, Brooks, Beecher, and Moody.

Of the memorial services held at colleges and universities, the one at Yale University, at which Prof. George P. Fisher, of the Yale Divinity School, several local clergymen, and Mr. Ira D. Sankey took part, was of special interest.

In New York City one of the meetings was presided over by Mr. William E. Dodge. In speaking of his friend, whom he had known and loved for forty years, Mr. Dodge said:

" In the whole history of the Church of Christ very few have touched so many hearts and influenced so many lives as the dear friend whom we come to thank God for to-day. I am sure it is not exaggeration to say that if all those whom he led to a better life were to be gathered together, a half dozen halls of this size would not hold them. We are now met to thank God with all our hearts for so glorious and fruitful a life and to pray that that influence may be continued. He is not dead; he has gone to the better life above; he lives with us to-day, and will live on by his example and by the inspiration that came from his words and life.

"When Mr. Moody became a Christian it was like the conversion of St. Paul—clear, decided, and for all his life. From the beginning his theology was very simple. His creed was, '*God so loved the world that He gave His only begotten Son, that whosoever believeth in Him should not perish, but have everlasting life.*' This message he repeated with all his courage and manliness and strength through all his life, and so earnestly that it told wherever he carried it.

"Mr. Moody's early work, too, was very simple. I remember, more than forty years ago, going with him one Sunday morning to that poor little school there in Chicago, and I then got sight of the peculiarity of the man, his directness, his simplicity, his kindliness, his humor, and the manliness of his character that won those children and won their parents.

"There were two early influences that directly affected his life more than any others. One was the companionship and help that came to him from the brotherhood of the Young Men's Christian Association. All his life he acknowledged that as having formed part of his character, and all through his life he was the warm friend of those associations, helping and aiding them in every possible way. But a stronger and greater influence was his beginning in the study of the English Bible.

"He devoted himself to an intense study of it, and from it got two things: In the first place, he gained that clear-cut, plain, simple Anglo-Saxon of the King James version, that gave him such an immense power over people everywhere. In the second place, he gained an arsenal and armament of promise and warning, which he used through all his life with such magnificent power. There was something wonderful about his simple directness. I could give by the hour instances of the clear way in which he went directly to a point.

"When I first met him in Chicago, while he was very little known, he went to call on a leading merchant and one of the most influential men in that city, and as he went out he turned and said: 'If you were only a Christian man, what an influence you would have in this growing city!' That man had been a communicant of a church for years, and it had never been known. It was the turning point in his life, and he was Moody's best friend and helper for many years. There was a manliness about him, an earnestness, a hatred of cant and mere religious form. He had the most intense and superb enthusiasm of any man I ever knew, but it was tempered by a strong, clear, common sense. And then he had, in addition to that, a wonderful intuitive knowledge of men. We know very much of his wonderful success as a preacher; but those who knew him best and were nearest to him know that the great power of his life was in personal conversation with men.

"The greatest sermon that I ever heard from Mr. Moody, far away the strongest, was one night on Madison Avenue, at half-past twelve, coming up from one of those great meetings at Madison Square. Three or four of us were together. We had been kept at the hall by those who insisted upon talking and getting advice and help from Mr. Moody, and he was tired by a long day's work. Suddenly a gentleman came up from behind and said, 'Mr. Moody, how shall I accept Christ and change my life?' He turned, and, standing there in the moonlight, on the corner of the street, in a few short, cleanly cut, kindly, earnest words put the whole truth so clearly to that man that there was no getting away from it and he became a changed man from that day.

"I was privileged to be with him at that wonderful series of services in the Haymarket Theatre, London, the most wonderful meetings that I have ever known; and what struck me and surprised me was the number of educated and cultivated people who came there.

There were a large number of literary men, who did not at all believe in religion, who came for the very purpose of hearing his simple, clear-cut English phraseology, which is so little used nowadays. His work in the universities was simply wonderful. When he went to Oxford and Cambridge, they determined to run him out of town. They did not want that kind of talk there. But his manliness and straightforwardness and courage conquered them, and the number of young men whose lives were changed, and who are now a power for good all over the world, wherever England has a place, would astonish us.

"The schools he established after all this great work are models of organization and executive ability. I hope with all my heart they will be carried on as a memorial. What touched me more than anything else in Mr. Moody was his extreme modesty about himself. He was the most masterly man I ever knew. He would direct and control and suggest to others like a general. We all know how that showed at his great gatherings. But when it came to himself, he was the most modest of men. I was privileged to be in the house with him during all the time of those great meetings at Madison Square. I never heard him speak of himself. You would not know he had anything to do with those great gatherings. On one occasion he said to his friends, 'My only wonder is that God can use such an instrument as I am to do such work.'"

Dr. Theodore L. Cuyler paid a notable tribute at this meeting, in which he said:

"The most extraordinary gospel preacher that America has produced in this century has gone up to his resplendent crown. More than to any other man was the privilege accorded to Brother Moody of having poured the Gospel of redeeming love into more human ears and more human hearts than any man in modern times. Spurgeon, in his peerless way, preached one day in the week; Moody preached six days, and in one week reached forty to fifty thousand souls.

"Our dear brother was more endeared to us because he was such a thoroughly typical American. He tasted of the soil, and on his garments was the smell of the New England fields that the Lord had blessed. If I were called upon to name the two most thoroughly typical Americans of the nineteenth century, men who had fought their way up from obscurity to wide influence, the men whom our American boys should be taught to study as the model patriot and the preacher of righteousness, I should not hesitate to name Abraham Lincoln and Dwight L. Moody. When the nation's life was to be preserved and its liberties secured, Almighty God called a poor boy from the log cabin in Kentucky, cradled him on the rocks of hardship, gave him the great West for his university, and then anointed him to be our Moses to lead us through a sea of blood to a Canaan of freedom. In like manner Almighty God called the farmer boy on the banks of the Connecticut, gave him for his education only one Book, filled him with the Spirit of Christ Jesus, then sent him out as the herald of salvation until Great Britain hung on his lips.

" Lincoln and Moody possessed alike the gift of an infallible common sense. Neither of them ever committed a serious mistake. They were alike in being masters of the simple, strong Saxon speech, the language of the people and of Bunyan, the language that is equal to the loftiest forensic or pulpit eloquence. Lincoln's huge, loving heart gushed out in sympathy for all sorts and conditions of men, and made him the best loved man in America's history. And Moody's big, loving heart, fired with the love of Jesus, made him a master of pathos that touched the fount of tears in thousands of hearts, and often brought weeping multitudes before his pulpit.

" Finally, Lincoln, the liberator, went up to his martyr crown carrying four millions of shattered manacles in his hands. Moody, the liberator of immortal souls from the fetters of sin, fell the other day a martyr to overwhelming work, and went up to be greeted at the gates of glory by thousands whom he had led from the cross to the crown.

" And now, for a moment, let me say—it may not be known to all of you—that on a Sabbath, shortly before our brother started for Kansas City, he delivered his last sermon in New York, in yonder Fifth Avenue Presbyterian Church. In that discourse I think the premonitory shadow was already falling. He uttered this wonderful sentence. Said he: 'You may read in the papers that Moody is dead. It will not be so. God has given me the gift of the life everlasting.' Aye, aye, thanks be to God, Moody is living. Moody lives; his spirit is in this hall to-day. Methinks I hear that trumpet voice calling on the pastors and churches of New York to seek through this Week of Prayer a baptism of fire that shall kindle this city and perhaps set the nation aflame."

The Rev. David J. Burrell, pastor of the Marble Collegiate Reformed Church, said:

"I met Mr. Moody when I was a theological student, thirty-one years ago, in Chicago. I was a boy, rooming up above old Farwell Hall, where Mr. Moody preached, and his apartments were just below mine. The old hall burned up. The fire caught in the early morning and burned slowly through the forenoon. We tried to remove our personal effects and to help out some sick people, and at last I found my way out into the street, coatless and hatless; the cordon was round about in front, and there was Mr. Moody.

"It was now near noon. He had under his arm a bundle of handbills, and he beckoned to me and said: 'Take these and distribute them in this great company. Help me out.' I looked at the bill: 'Our beautiful house is burned up. The noon-day meetings will be held, as usual, in the Clark Street Methodist Episcopal Church.' 'We must get these out,' he said.

"'And where is your wife, and where is your little girl?'

"'I saw them safe.'

"'Where are your personal effects?'

"'Oh, never mind them; our noon-day meeting must go on.'

"It was always thus. 'One thing I do.' He has left that thought with me. We are talking about his memorial. I am going to build him a monument, please God, in my own ministerial life. I am going to honor his memory by a more consuming earnestness in doing this one thing."

The last address was delivered by the Rev. Dr. J. M. Buckley, who said:

"Our friend died when he was most desired—desired to maintain those wondrous Bible conferences; desired as a nucleus of undenominational activity; desired to sustain those educational institutions which he had founded; desired to raise up more workers filled with his spirit; desired to go to and fro through the country to awaken communities, to snap the chains of conventionalism, to elicit and evoke the tremendous latent forces of the church, and to unite Christians in the only way in which they can ever be united—by a firm and unswerving belief in the fundamental principles of the Gospel and in active, soul-saving, consecrated labor. At this hour, a young man, D. L. Moody was called away.

"By nature God endowed Mr. Moody physically in an astonishing manner. There was a man in Connecticut who adored Mr. Moody, and he invariably amused himself when sitting in the cars in this way: When Mr. Moody came in he would say, 'Do you know him? That is Huntington, the greatest railroad man in this country.' Never did he hear one word of question from the men who had never seen Huntington. At other times he would suggest he was a Western judge. In every case every man seemed to think it exactly right. They saw that tremendous head, monster chest, prompt, intense, direct action, a man obviously born to command. This man invariably told people afterwards, before they left him, 'No, that's not Mr. Huntington; it is Mr. Moody,' and their curiosity was greatly excited.

"Physically, many men reminded other men of Mr. Moody, but D. L. Moody never reminded men of another man, in the ordinary sense of the term. That indefinable personality that will not show in a photograph, and cannot be painted in oil, was in Mr. Moody.

"He could improve, and that was one of his glories. Two hundred years from now the higher critics will be trying to prove that there were two Moodys, and they will do it by getting up, word by word and sentence by sentence, the language that Mr. Moody used when he began in Chicago. They will make a parallel of these with the highly improved style of his later years. Some persons say Mr. Moody was not a cultivated orator. Note that passage quoted by Drummond; observe that when in London he described the ascension of Elijah several Parliamentary orators rose to their feet and actually looked in the air, after the ascending prophet. Take his sublime eulogy of Joseph of Arimathea, delivered in this house less than a year ago. Not far from yonder box sat a bishop noted for sound judgment, who said: 'That is a piece of work any man might be proud of.'

"Nearly twenty-five years ago the gentleman who presides to-day sat on the platform in the Hippodrome. At that time New York beheld an emperor—an emperor of a great territory, which is to be in the future one of the greatest empires of the world, unless it becomes permanently republican. I refer to Dom Pedro, the Emperor of Brazil. He went on the platform and took the seat vacated by Mr. Dodge.

"Two-thirds of the audience knew who he was, but the man of the occasion was Mr. Moody, and he was preaching at the time. What did he do? Did he exhibit the fawning and obsequious bow that many persons make when the President appears, or even the Secretary of State? Mr. Moody never referred to Dom Pedro, but introduced in the midst of his discourse these words: 'What will you do with Jesus? What will you do with Jesus? An emperor cannot buy Heaven, but he can have it as a free gift.' After he said that he paused, and Dom Pedro bowed his assent, and afterwards remarked to the gentleman who wrote the account: 'That is a man to be heard and believed.'

"Mr. Moody had his prejudices, for I once heard him declare that he would own fellowship with everybody that believed himself to be a sinner and trusted in Christ; but, said he, 'God being my helper, I will never own fellowship with a man who denies the deity of my God and Saviour Jesus Christ, or sneers at His atonement.'

"Moody was told that he must die. What then? Oh, the blessing to the church of the manner of his death! God showed, I believe, in a peculiar way for the church and for Him, that '*Precious in the sight of the Lord is the death of His saints.*' There is something worse in this world than agnosticism, something worse than blank infidelity. It is the practical effects of a belief that we cannot be sure of the future.

"There were those in the time of Paul who said, '*Let us eat, drink, and be merry, for to-morrow we die.*' Ah, if there were no life afterwards, I, too, would drink anything that would make me oblivious to my doom. But listen!

"'*I heard a voice from Heaven saying unto me, Write: Blessed are the dead which die in the Lord from henceforth: Yea, saith the Spirit, that they may rest from their labors, and their works do follow them.*'"

Among those who spoke briefly of their friendship for Mr. Moody, or took part in the devotional services, were the Rev. Drs. Arthur T. Pierson, John Balcom Shaw, Wilton Merle Smith, A. C. Dixon, and Messrs. R. Fulton Cutting, Ira D. Sankey and John R. Mott.

It was fitting that the Seminary's special memorial of Mr. Moody should be at the first chapel service held after the funeral. On other opening days he himself had been the welcome speaker, bringing some stirring message for the new term. This day perhaps the silence that replaced the living voice proved as powerful an appeal as had the actual words. Brief tributes were paid by the Rev. C. I. Scofield, John Willis Baer, and trustees of the school. The closing moments were spent in a consecration service led by Mr. Baer, who, after a warm personal tribute to Mr. Moody, invited the young women to enter into a covenant to live higher lives. Many rose in response to this appeal, and later fully twenty-five expressed, by rising, their desire to become Christians. It was keenly felt that Mr. Moody's interest was still with the work he had loved, and that his presence was not far away.

At a later date a meeting for personal testimony was held by the students. One who was closely associated with Mr. Moody in this work gave the following testimony:

"I should like to speak especially of the place that prayer had in his life. I have been looking through some of his letters lately, letters which I received from him during these years that I have been at Northfield, and there is scarcely one of them in which there is not some mention of prayer. Sometimes he wrote asking me to pray for the work in a certain city, that the ground might be ready for the seed; again he would write that he was to speak upon the Atonement or upon the Holy Spirit, and would ask me to pray that God would make it real to the people; then there would come a letter saying that the work was deepening, that he believed it was in answer to prayer, and that he hoped to see the good work extend over the land from sea to sea.

"We all remember how he used to come up to chapel the morning before he started on one of his evangelistic tours, and ask us to pray for him. We saw then his humility and how completely he depended upon God. God was very real to him. He walked with God, and so did not have to turn out of his way to speak to Him. I have been driving with him off on some retired road about Northfield. We would be talking together, when, suddenly, he would pause for a moment and speak to God just as naturally as he would speak to his friend.

"When we teachers have been invited to his home of an evening we have begun by telling amusing stories; and, as you know, no one enjoyed hearing or telling a good story more than Mr. Moody. The conversation might drift into a talk about the needs of the country town or of the outlying districts of our own town, and our evening would end with prayer.

"Last summer, during the August Conference, I was at his home one afternoon, and he said to me: 'The sweetest thing has come to me to-day. I was feeling somewhat troubled this morning because the Seminary accounts were behind, and we needed a good deal of money to pay up the bills. I didn't see how I could do anything about raising the money, now, with this conference upon my hands, so I just committed the matter to the Lord. This afternoon, while I was driving a lady over to Mount Hermon, she said to me, "Mr. Moody, I have decided to give you $10,000 to use for your school, just as you like," and, instead of waiting till some future time to give me the money, as I thought she might, she has already given me the check for this sum, which is just what I had in mind as necessary to meet the present needs of the Seminary. It brings the Lord so near.'

"Certainly all of Mr. Moody's work was begun and continued and ended in prayer, and as I have thought of this work which he has left us to do, I realize how much we need to learn this lesson of prayer, and I pray that God may pour upon us '*the spirit of grace and of supplication.*'"

The keynote of the memorial service at Mount Hermon, held in the new chapel that was presented to the school on the sixtieth anniversary of Mr. Moody's birth by Christian friends in Great Britain and America, was "The Power of an Endless Life." In response to the invitation to let this power rule forever in their lives, nearly the whole school arose. This was but one instance of the work he directly accomplished after his death in the body. And who can doubt that, indirectly, that work has never stopped?

CHAPTER XLVIII

Tributes from English Friends

VOLUMES, many and large, would be required to reproduce the tributes that have been received from sympathetic friends. Two only are here presented; and these from close associates of later years who were peculiarly near to Mr. Moody.

BY REV. F. B. MEYER

" D. L. Moody always reminded me of a mountain, whose abrupt bold front, scarred and furrowed with storm, forbids the tourist. Yet soft valleys nestle in its mighty embrace, and verdant pastures are watered by the waters that furrow the summit. He was preëminently a strong man. His chosen friends were men. He was happiest when giving his famous address on 'Sowing and Reaping' to an audience of men only. Strong natures were strongly influenced by him. If a number of his friends were together, their conversation would almost inevitably turn on Moody; and if he entered any group, he would at once become its centre, to whom all thoughts and words would turn. All who knew him intimately gave him reverence as an uncrowned king, though his crown, like that of the Huns, was of iron.

" Nothing short of an indomitable resolution and will-power could have conducted the uncultured, uneducated lad from the old shanty in Chicago to the Opera House in London, where royalty waited on his words—rugged, terse, full of mother wit, direct and sharp as a two-edged sword. For as the man was, so he spoke. Alone, except for the help of God; unlearned, except for what he gained from his incessant study of Scripture and ceaseless observation of character; unassisted by those adventitious circumstances of prepossessing appearance, musical speech, and college education, on which others have climbed to prominence and power, he made his way forward to the front rank of his time, and became one of the strongest religious factors of the world.

"The charm of his character was his thorough naturalness. Perhaps it was this that carried him so triumphantly through his career. That a matter had always been dealt with in a certain way was no reason why he should follow the beaten track. On the contrary, it was a reason for striking out in some novel and unconventional method. He was perfectly unmoved by the quotation of established precedent, utterly indifferent to the question as to whether the course he proposed would bring praise or blame. When he had mastered all the difficulties of a problem, he would set himself to its solution by the exercise of his own sanctified tact and common sense. There was no limit to his inventiveness, to his rapid appreciation of the difficulties of a situation, or to his naïve solutions. I have often compared his method of handling a perplexity with his driving, for he always went straight before him, over hedges and mounds, up hillsides, through streams, down dikes, over ploughed fields. The last day I was with him at Northfield he drove me from the Conference Hall over ground so irregular and uneven that every moment I expected we should be overturned. But we came out all right at the gate we wanted, and it was certainly the shortest cut. So it was always with him. If he could not untie knots, he would cut them.

"At the same time he was absolutely simple and humble. In all the numberless hours I have spent with him he never once manifested the least sign of affectation, never drew attention to himself, never alluded to the vast numbers that had attended his meetings, the distinguished persons who had confided their secrets to him, or the enterprises which had originated in his suggestion or been cradled under his care. It seemed as though he had never heard of D. L.

Moody, and knew less of his doings than the most ordinary reader of the daily press. Not unfrequently I said to myself, when in his company, Is this the man who can gather, and hold, ten thousand people, by the month, in any of the great cities of the world?

"There was an appearance of abruptness in his manner, which was undoubtedly assumed as a protection of a very tender and sensitive spirit, much as oysters will form for themselves strong shells against the fret of the waves and rocks. He had seen others carried away by the adulation of their admirers and weakened by the soft caress of the world; he knew that the personal element is apt to intrude between the speaker and the interests of those whom he would fain save for Christ's sake; he was absolutely determined that people should not rest on him, but on the Word of God, to which he was ever pointing them, and he therefore incased himself in the hard shell of an apparently rugged and uncouth manner. It was only when the crowds had gone, and he was able to reveal himself without risk of being misunderstood, that he cast away his reserve and revealed his true and tender self.

"If it be asked what was the secret of that power which, in England and his own country, would hold in rapt attention, for months, ten or fifteen thousand people, the answer must certainly be found in the tenderness and compassion of his nature. That he could tell a good story, call forth ripples of laughter by the touch of quaint humor, narrate Bible stories as though he were personally acquainted with the actors or had witnessed the occurrence in his travels, were as the small dust of the balance, compared to the pathos which trembled in his voice and moved vast audiences to tears. His power was that of the heart rather than of the head. Whilst he was speaking his hand was on the pulse, he was counting heart-throbs, and touching those deep elemental emotions of the heart which cluster about mother, father, home bereavement, Heaven.

"He was more thoughtful for others than any man I have ever known. How often have the meetings in Northfield been interrupted because some shabbily dressed person hadn't a seat! How many times all the comforts of his home have been freely offered to some sick or friendless student! Whatever trouble befell any one in the town of Northfield seemed to be Mr. Moody's; and his well-known buggy would be seen making its way to the home of bereavement or affliction with some kindly inquiry or alleviation. It was because of acts of this kind that, when his mother died some five years ago, the Roman Catholic element in the community asked that one of their number might lead the horses that bore the bier, a request which, of course, was readily granted.

"The most pathetic revelation of D. L. Moody was made last August, at Northfield, when all through the long summer days his little grandchild, whom he loved passionately, was dying. Again and again he asked me to beg the people not to express their sympathy when they met him, lest it should break him down altogether. And how the strong frame would shake with convulsive sobs as we prayed that her life might be spared! God, however, knew better, and took the little one home that she might be there in time to greet the strong, true nature that loved her so sincerely, when in turn His servant was called to enter his reward.

"I never guessed the intensity of his tenderness till I saw him with his grandchildren. He used to drive them about in his carriage or carry them in his arms. One of the most striking incidents in my memory was when he stood with them beside his mother's grave in a summer sunset, and asked us to pray that they might be in the coming century what she had been in this. And when little Irene was dying he used to be on the watch below her window to keep all quiet, would steal down from the meetings to hear the latest news, would be the nurse and playmate of her little cousin, that all might devote themselves to the chamber of sickness. So touched because a little child had sent the invalid a pet lamb! How moved he was as we saw it together!

"He was a great Christian strategist, and never so happy as when organizing some great campaign, like that during the World's Fair at Chicago, when he occupied the largest halls in that city, with evangelists gathered from all parts of the world; or when, in later years, he promoted the distribution of Bibles and the holding of evangelistic meetings among the American soldiers in Cuba. He was the Von Moltke of the religious world in the United States. He would lay plans for a winter's campaign in such a city as New York or Boston, would engage some large central building, and hold two or three meetings a day, interesting reporters and gaining the attention of the press, working out presently into new quarters of the city, until the whole community had felt the impact of the religious momentum communicated through him. Ministers would open their churches and respond to his appeals for help; lists of converts would be furnished to the several churches; and the whole campaign would be so contrived as to increase the zeal and activity of the churches that had ranged themselves under his leadership.

"He was absolutely fearless. I remember one occasion when he felt it laid on his heart to speak some unpalatable truths to a number of ministers and others. Before me, as I write, is the large circle that sat around his spacious dining-room in the summer evening, the monument of ice-cream which he carved with such precision, and then the direct, unvarnished words, which wounded deeply, that a better condition of soul-life might be induced. Whether in a crowd or with an individual, he never, to win a smile, or avoid a frown, swerved a hair's breadth from what he thought right.

"As a conversationalist he was charming. He would sit on the porch of his unpretending but comfortable house overlooking the lovely landscape, telling story after story of marvellous conversions. One day, for instance, a gentleman drove up as we were talking, and he told me that he had won him to Christ when quite a lad by a conversation on the roof of a Chicago hotel, that being the only quiet spot he could find for his purpose. Or he would recall reminiscences of men whom he had known. He had a great fund of information about agriculture, had travelled widely and observed shrewdly, was in keen and close touch with the great religious movements of the time, and was specially fond of asking questions of any one who seemed likely to communicate reliable information.

"His was a triumphant home-going, and as the story of it has spread from land to land it has stirred thousands of hearts to a deeper and more entire consecration to the service of Jesus Christ. His voice is hushed, his heart has ceased to beat, he has left a great void behind him; but he has already entered on higher service, and in the foremost ranks of the sons of light his strong and noble spirit is still abounding in the work of the Lord, where neither weariness nor pain can fetter or slacken its celestial ardor. I count it almost the greatest privilege of my life to have known him so well."

BY REV. G. CAMPBELL MORGAN

"My personal acquaintance with Dwight Lyman Moody was not of long duration according to the measure of the calendar," he says. "If, however, 'we should count time by heart-throbs,' then I may claim to have known him; for it has been one of the greatest privileges of my life to have come very near to him in the ripest years of his life.

"I first saw him in 1883 during his second visit to Birmingham. Bingley Hall was being crowded daily with eager crowds who had come by train from the whole surrounding district. Once only I spoke to him. The impression of those days, therefore, is that of the man in the midst of the rush of work. No detail of arrangement escaped his notice. A vacant seat, the opening and closing of doors, a tendency to drag the singing, all these he noted and rectified. Yet he was by no means a man who cared for detail for detail's sake. The supreme passion of his life was the winning of men for Christ, and no detail was insignificant that would hinder or help.

"Two pictures of those old days are deeply engraved on the tablets of my memory. The first picture is that of Moody as a prophet, and the vast audience, numbering at least twenty thousand, were hushed, subdued, overawed. Knowing the terror of the Lord, he persuaded men. I dare affirm that thousands of people stood face to face that evening with the awfulness of their own sin, startled and smitten. The other picture is that of Moody coming to the close of an address on the King's invitation to the Marriage Supper of the Lamb. The graciousness of that invitation had possessed him that night with new force, the deepest fountains of his nature were touched, and he stood before the great crowd, moved with his Master's compassion, pleading with tender urgency and fine pathos, a strong man moved to tears. At last he cried, 'Let those who will accept the invitation say "I will,"' and from every part of the hall instantly, immediately the cry of a multitude went up, 'I will.' I did not see him again for thirteen years, but through them all the force of his character had an influence on my life that I should find it hard to measure.

"In 1896 I visited the United States for the first time. The Northfield Conference was in session, and I managed to spend a few hours there. Arriving late at night, I found my quarters and retired. The next day was a field day for me, as well as a revelation. Everywhere Mr. Moody was the moving spirit. Bright, cheery, and yet in dead earnest, he seemed to make everything go before him. In the interval of the meetings he gave me a drive round the campus in his buggy. Every point of interest was pointed out, and in a few brief words the story of how the different buildings were erected was told. Passing a certain house, he said, 'People sometimes ask me how I found Northfield. I tell them it found me. I was born there.' Suddenly he pulled up his horse to speak to a group of children. 'Have you had any apples to-day?' said he. 'No, Mr. Moody,' they replied. 'Then go down to my house and tell them to give you all you want.' Away they went, and so did he, both happier. Down a narrow lane he drove next, and through a gate to where a man was at work in a field. 'Biglow,' said Mr. Moody, 'it's too hot for you to work much; half a day's work for a day's pay, you know, while this heat lasts.' I sat by his side and watched and began to understand the greatness of the man whose life was so broad that it touched sympathetically all other phases of life.

"After the evening meeting, at his invitation I gathered with the speakers at his house. Then for the first time I saw him in a new role, that of the host. He sat in his chair at the head of the table, directed the conversation, and listened with the patience and simplicity of a child to every word that others spoke. That night the talk turned on the most serious subjects, the inner life of the people of God and its bearing on the work of the churches among the people. As we departed I went to bid him good-bye, as I was to leave by an early train on the morrow. 'Oh,' said he, 'I shall see you in the morning; you are to preach at ten o'clock.' That was my first notice. What did I do? I preached as he bid me, as other and better men have ever been glad to do. That was his way. After speaking next morning I hurried away, but in that brief stay Moody had become more to me. Strong, tender, considerate, from that day I more than revered him—I loved him.

"I look upon him as one of God's choicest gifts to the church and the world during this century now drawing to a close. His value will never be rightly appreciated here, where the view is partial and transient. Yonder in the perfect light we shall know. To some of us Heaven is more to be desired to-day for his presence there, and earth is more to be loved for the great love he lavished upon it. Oh, the gap! Yet he would not have us dwell upon his removal, but upon the abiding Presence of the Lord he loved and served. He has entered on the higher service. It is for those of us who remain to tighten the girdle and take hold afresh on the work of God's to-day. Presently we shall meet him again in the light of the glory of the Lamb, and then certainly we shall love him more than ever.

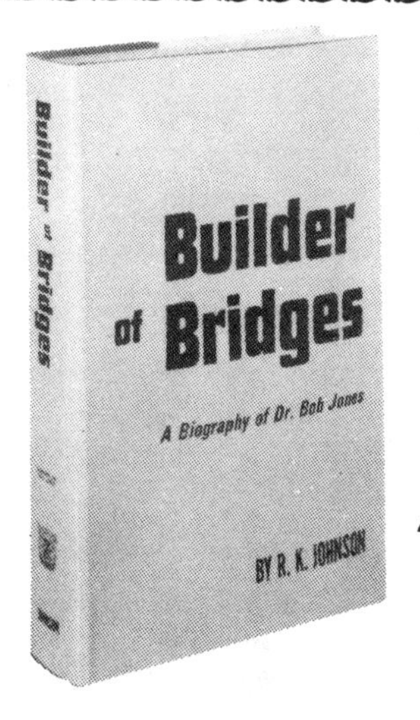

Builder of Bridges

A Biography of Dr. Bob Jones

BY R. K. JOHNSON

The Sword of the Lord is proud to be the publishers of this attractive volume on the life of one of God's choicest servants of our day, the late Dr. Bob Jones, Sr., evangelist, founder and first president of Bob Jones University. This authorized biography is written by a man who maintained closest associations with Dr. Jones for the past 35 years or more, and was most intimate in relations with other members of the family, and therefore gives to us an accurate, carefully documented and stirring account of the life and ministry and accomplishments of this truly great servant of the Lord.

Dr. Johnson traces the life of Dr. Bob Jones from his early Welsh ancestry, his birth in Alabama; his boyhood, schooling, his conversion; his early start in preaching, his rapid rise to fame and notoriety; his romance and marriage; his numerous spectacular evangelistic campaigns; his vision and its fulfillment of "the World's Most Unusual University," Bob Jones University; his courageous and noble fight for the faith against the rising spectre of the sinister, deceptive new evangelicalism movement, epitomized in ecumenical evangelism; his prolonged illness and his victorious Home-going.

Every young ministerial student should read and ponder this volume; every pastor and Christian worker will be inspired and challenged to live a more useful and fruitful Christian life as a result of reading this great biography of a truly great man of God. It is a big book, page size 6" x 9" cloth binding—many, many pictures, 361 pages, **$6.95**

Postage and handling rates: up to $2.00, 70¢; up to $5.00, 90¢; over $5.00, 15%. Tennessee residents please add 6% sales tax.

SWORD OF THE LORD Murfreesboro, Tennessee 37130